FROM THE MYSTERIES

Genesis
Zarathustra

Hermann Beckh

Translated by Alan and Maren Stott and Hannes Kaiser
Edited with Introductions by Neil Franklin

TEMPLE LODGE

Temple Lodge Publishing Ltd.
Hillside House, The Square
Forest Row, RH18 5ES

www.templelodge.com

Published in English by Temple Lodge 2020

Originally published in German as three separate titles: *Der Ursprung im Lichte, Bilder der Genesis*, Munich 1924; *Zarathustra*, Stuttgart 1927; and *Aus der Welt der Mysterien*, Basel 1927

A CIP catalogue record for this book is available from the British Library

ISBN 978 1 912230 44 0

Cover by Morgan Creative featuring image of Isis nursing Horus, Seventh Century BCE
Typeset by Symbiosys Technologies, Visakhapatnam, India
Printed and bound by 4Edge Ltd., Essex

Contents

IV.
APPENDICES

Foreword

Hermann Beckh throughout his life was a man intensely impressed by aesthetic perceptions, which for him were self-evident spiritual realities. Whether it was the music of Wagner, the course of the visible night sky during the year or the structure of the Act of Consecration of Man, Beckh perceived the world around him as an expression of the cosmic order, divinely conducted in harmonious relationships.

In Bavaria as a judge in his early twenties, Beckh upheld the law while coming to realize that Natural Law was often ignored in the face of the power of the privileged classes. As a scholar of Oriental languages, he found the divine harmonious law expressed in Sanskrit as *rta*, in Avestan as *asha*, in ancient Egyptian as *maat*. A pre-eminent Old Testament interpreter today, Margaret Barker, has spent some 40 years insisting upon the sovereignty of the 'everlasting covenant' in the earliest Jewish texts, the fundamental order of the cosmos and of subsequent ritual. When Beckh studied Rudolf Steiner's *Knowledge of the Higher Worlds: How is it Attained?* and *Occult Science: an Outline*, he likewise found that human life and cosmic history were well ordered in lawful, harmonious stages: he became a member of the Anthroposophical Society.

What validity can be found for Beckh's perceptions? There is no answer to be found in waking consciousness and acute scholarship can only point to tracks in the snow. If we remain in the belief that human knowledge is limited to sense-perception and logic then we can only confront entropy in association with material or quantum laws. Nevertheless, the world of dreams has a certain lawfulness; with training, consciousness can remain alert in profound sleep; many people even have an access to pre-natal consciousness. To even a casual reader of Rudolf Steiner's work, it must be clear that the three deeper domains of consciousness can be realized; Hermann Beckh in his role as Professor of Oriental Studies recognized the same fact in Buddhist texts. Is it not possible that Beckh, working with anthroposophy in meditation and with Sanskrit, Pali and Avestan texts for decades, experienced something of the same? Not only experienced this but meticulously cultivated more profound levels of consciousness?

A text by Rudolf Steiner, a mantra from the Rig-Veda or a Gatha from the Zend Avesta can easily be reduced to reasoned concepts according to today's philology and its consensus 'reality'. We live in a world of cheap paperback translations. Yet words and sounds are not simply vehicles for our own presumptive notions. For our contemporaries, the seas or oceans are primarily the blue areas in an atlas, the dangerous world for the real trawlers or the focus of materialist environmentalists. Yet for millennia Latin *mare*, Hebrew *mayyim* have been connected to the sound *mā*: mother, silence, death. Logical positivists will argue that consensual dialogue can only be reliable when dealing with waking sense-perceptions. Is this not a severe limitation in which the first casualty is imaginative cognition?

In the short books published here, written between 1924 and 1927, Hermann Beckh, more than anyone else after the death of Rudolf Steiner, begins to prise up the heavy stone which conceals what Isaiah called 'the treasures of darkness, the hidden riches of secret places'. Everyone is faced by the choice: sense-perception and logic is the foundation stone of our identity, or, beneath the stone there lies in dreams, sleep and pre-natal consciousness a far greater reality which has left its mark—how could it not?—in the sacred records of earlier civilizations. This legacy can now be received in waking clarity.

N.F.

I.

OUR ORIGIN IN THE LIGHT, PICTURES FROM GENESIS

(Translated from the German by Hannes Kaiser, revised by Alan Stott, with added editorial notes)

Introduction to *Our Origin in the Light: Pictures from Genesis*
(Genesis 1–9)

By 1924 Hermann Beckh, now in his fiftieth year, had been teaching in the Stuttgart Seminar of The Christian Community for some 18 months. Here and elsewhere he celebrated The Act of Consecration of Man, and presumably the other sacraments—certainly that of marriage. In this period, 1922-24, he had already displayed his incomparable talents, erudition and spiritual wisdom in a range of formats: lecturing, scholarly articles, a large number of periodical pieces and the historically important booklet *Vom Geistigen Wesen der Tonarten* (published 1923, but with a Foreword composed a year earlier). As early as 1921-22, while still finding his way to the priesthood, he had found that his investigations, which united scholarship and meditative insight into the origins of Indo-European languages, produced a perhaps surprising result. There were clear connections between the older languages—especially Tibetan and Sanskrit—and classical Hebrew. During these years Professor Beckh began not only to publish his findings on Hebrew in the midst of the learned essays, but also to express the discovery that this language revealed features of lexis, grammar and pronunciation, which suggested:

> if it is... true that the early sacred languages, in the first place Hebrew, stand still closer to the origin of language, then such a document of humanity as Genesis, especially its first chapter, not only from the viewpoint of its content, but also that of its language has to be of highest significance...

The next step appears to have been a journey to Zürich to present a lecture to the university people on June 21: an in-depth analysis of the six words of divine creation in Genesis 1:3 as found in the Masoretic text. Out of this there appeared the published article *Yehi 'or. Es werde Licht* (Let there be Light). Here there were striking developments. Obviously the new focus is on Hebrew, but now more especially on the nature of the verb as an expression of will. At the same time, Professor Beckh strongly highlights the contribution made by Fabre d'Olivet's *La Langue Hebraique Restituée* (1815), to what may be termed the fruits of *Natursprache* research or, following Novalis, 'genetic etymology'. However it is also remarkable that the article (and presumably the original lecture) is also deeply concerned with drawing attention to Eve, 'the mother of all living'. Beckh can now emphatically come to the conclusion, that:

> ...we still have to acknowledge according to the facts that no text of the world allows us to feel *the direct activity of the Creator-word* so powerfully as that early Hebrew account in Genesis: precisely from the linguistic viewpoint, no other account of creation can compare with the beginning of Genesis.

It was as if Professor Beckh had made a promise, but one that was put on hold for some 18 months while his attention was occupied in Stuttgart with teaching, sacramental work and periodical publications. He was nevertheless prompted at Christmas 1923, standing before a Christmas tree with candles, to craft a very short but fine article for *Tatchristentum* (the original periodical of The Christian Community) entitled 'The Dream of Eden in the Light of Christmas', which may originally have been an address during The Act of Consecration of Man. The heavenly light of Paradise is restored to mankind at Christmas, but for The Christian Community and the celebrating priest this is no vague image or symbol. Even Jakob Böhme's vast study of Genesis, *Mysterium Magnum* (1623) already firmly placed itself within the long tradition of Christian insight which observes that the 'substance' of Paradise is consubstantial with the 'substance' of the resurrected, spiritual body.

By 1924 the time had come to produce a miniature masterpiece. Hermann Beckh had long ago shown his professorial mastery of Oriental languages and sacred texts for the University of Berlin; he had placed this at the service of anthroposophy, and had gone on in 1922-23 to frame the text which is now recognized as the forerunner of later twentieth century anthroposophical studies on the spiritual powers that underlie classical music in the West.

At precisely this time Friedrich Doldinger (1897-1973), another founding priest of The Christian Community, was inspired to create a new publishing company in Munich, *Michael-Verlag*. The first fruit of this service was to begin a series of most artistically presented small hardback books under the heading *Christus aller Erde*. Volumes 1 and 2 were issued in 1923 with offerings from Friedrich Rittelmeyer and Christian Morgenstern. Numbers 3 and 4 presented Johannes Werner Klein on Baldur and Christ; then an introduction to the Christian festivals through the year co-authored by Rudolf Meyer and the young Emil Bock. By 1924 The Christian Community was in a position to form its own *Verlag der Christengemeinchaft*, taking on *Christus aller Erde* and retaining Doldinger as editor of the series. Amid the changes the projected Volumes 5 (on the priesthood of women) and 6 (on bread and wine) were delayed until 1926. Yet somehow the editor managed to produce a Volume 7 in 1924: Hermann Beckh's work on Genesis. It only remained to paste a narrow slip of paper bearing the name of the new publishing company over the top of *Michael-Verlag* on the title-page.

Hermann Beckh had set himself to address Genesis 1-9 (from the Creation to Noah) out of a careful study of Steiner's lectures on Genesis, his own knowledge of the ancient languages and sacred texts, and an appreciation of what Fabre d'Olivet had achieved. All of these studies are informed by disciplined meditative work within the *Natursprache* tradition. Among other things, Beckh's text shows that he had adapted to the format of *Christus aller Erde*. The erudite scholarship is restrained and the overall composition becomes a work of art.

Der Ursprung im Lichte, presented here for the first time in English, consists of seven sections. With these the author tactfully sets up a signpost to their structure resembling a lemniscate. Part 1 introduces the activity of the seven Elohim, whereas Part 7 concludes with the seven colours of the rainbow, the new covenant to mankind. Part 2, the Yahve-creation of Adam from 'dust' relates to Part 6 on Cain—the son who could work within a hardening earthly substance. Part 3 addresses the nature of Paradise, including the Tree of Knowledge leading to Part 5 on the Fall. The centre, or fulcrum, of the whole account is found to be Hermann Beckh's consideration of Eve. At the same time, the first nine chapters of Genesis as a whole are examined as an ongoing process: the progressive introduction of the Divine Will into the Earth and the foundations of human independence.

There can be little doubt that when Hermann Beckh accepted the request from Friedrich Doldinger his own encounter with the sevenfold lemniscate had become more profound through the Act of Consecration of Man. Yet we should not imagine that such a chiasmic structure—or rather a form in movement—is something that is uniquely or distinctly rooted only in Goethe, Jakob Böhme, or anthroposophy. The older Jewish world celebrated the form. A simple example can be found in Isaiah 6: 9-10, moreover sevenfold lists constantly reappear, for example, in Deuteronomy.

In the earlier articles on speech and language Beckh had striven, with considerable success, to convey the philological understanding that the verb is primary in the evolution of language:

> These facts of historical linguistics show especially how speech developed everywhere out of the spirit of the verb…

At the same time, *Yehi 'or* also carefully formulated the insight that the archetype of the verb representing an act of free will is precisely manifested in Rudolf Steiner's *The Philosophy of Freedom*:

> We lay hold of the activity of spiritual life where this activity is experience of concentration on to the essence of words, then we find in this experienced inner activity that which we have called the *inner life of the verb.*

One can fairly say that the entirety of Hermann Beckh's earlier articles on speech and language were dedicated to a crystal clear *apprehension and experience* of 'the inner life of the verb' as a supersensible fact that was also the essential foundation for Böhme's approach to Genesis, and the further research of Fabre d'Olivet. Here, though, we cannot avoid the encounter with the Divine Will (as verb) entering into life through seven forms. In other words Hermann Beckh, who was later to produce the extensive books on Mark's Gospel and John's Gospel, had already a firm approach to the sevenfold structures of John's Gospel and the Book of Revelation. The first nine chapters of Genesis can thus be seen as an Old Testament foreshadowing of Christian Wisdom.

All the same, Beckh was not a man of abstract ideas. Wisdom, whether Tibetan, Sanskrit, Avestan or Hebrew is concretely embedded *in language*, lying as a 'Lost Word' waiting for a different consciousness to awaken it as a Snow White in her crystal coffin. While it was necessary for this account of Genesis to conclude with the Covenant of the Rainbow, the issue of the fragmentation of languages had only to wait a short time. Beckh's next step was to write the essay on The Tower of Babel for an issue of *Die Christengemeinschaft* in its first year (1924), edited by Friedrich Rittelmeyer.

If Genesis 1-9 embraces the descent of the Word as divine archetype into seven metamorphosing conditions, it may be expected that a residue of this might be found in language. It is a striking fact, then, that grammars of classical Hebrew, well known to Professor Beckh, are concerned to indicate that this language rests on Verb Roots—also explored by Fabre d'Olivet at the end of his extremely substantial study. The root itself, usually trilateral, remains outside or hovering over the spoken language as a concealed source, and then enters speech in seven modes of the verb: four are basic modes, active and passive, and three are causative, they have become, in a sense, creative. It is also a fact of Indo-European languages that one can speak of a 'descent' of the verb through participles, and then the gerund, to form the noun. Beckh must have understood—although he does not seem to have been explicit—that this process has left traces for the philologist to uncover and for everyone to experience within themselves.

N.F.

Preface

For this little book, the author did not intend to approach the questions of Genesis from the viewpoint of current theology.[4] A manner of observation, wanting to remain within the confines of our given current consciousness, is incapable of reaching towards visions drawn from an entirely different consciousness. It would require the realization that Genesis—especially in its first nine chapters—contains visions coming from such a higher consciousness, visions received in the form of *pictures*. To make these pictures accessible to contemporary consciousness is a task which could be felt as fulfilling a general human need. This cannot be achieved by theological means alone.

To gain access to depths of consciousness of the kind which inspired Genesis—and the Bible in general—is a task that has already been attempted in the past. Take for example Philo the Gnostic, Jakob Böhme, Saint Martin and Fabre d'Olivet, who each tried to approach Genesis by their individual, non-theological spiritual paths.[5] None of them, however, would be able to give us today what our contemporary consciousness needs. Rudolf Steiner's anthroposophical, spiritual-scientific approach has been of decisive and epoch-making importance for the questions addressed here.

Tremendously enlightening—and at the same time answering the needs and questions of the present age—is everything said from a spiritual-scientific perspective with regard to the questions of the primordial past in Steiner's book *Occult/ Esoteric Science* [GA 13], and, with regard to Genesis, especially in his lecture-cycle *Genesis: Secrets of the Bible Story of Creation*, Munich 17-26 Aug. 1910 [GA 122, hereafter cited as *Genesis*]. For a contemplation of these issues intending to be contemporary, it is no longer possible today, no longer even thinkable, to ignore Rudolf Steiner's discoveries and walk past them.

The writer of this book acknowledges his deep gratitude and indebtedness to anthroposophy and its founder, although he did not use or exploit the results of spiritual science in an external way. He strove towards his own Imaginative vision of what Steiner describes, and as a result of that which revealed itself to him, this little book came about as initiating an approach of some years of inner meditation. For example, what the author wrote about the butterfly with regard to the picture of the Fifth Day of Creation is something he experienced independently as a vision before Rudolf Steiner's deeply inspiring Dornach lectures[6] on the being of the butterfly came to his knowledge. Hence for everything that is claimed here, the author takes sole responsibility. And he needs strongly to object to anyone putting the blame on anthroposophy for any shortcomings, dislike or criticism of his work. The author hopes that the sensible reader of this first attempt to present such difficult problems in a new way, may judge it mildly.

The relationship between the author's presentation and anthroposophy can especially be seen in the footnotes, where all relevant references pertaining to anthroposophical literature can be found,[7] especially references to Steiner's lecture-cycles, which since Christmas 1923 (the Dornach Christmas Foundation Assembly of the General Anthroposophical Society) have received official permission to be circulated in written form. Anthroposophy is also mentioned in relevant places in the body of the text itself. Besides a general anthroposophical outlook, one might also be able to feel the influence of the sacramental life as a spiritual foundation for this work and how it is presented. In particular, The Act of the Consecration of Man, the Eucharist of The Christian Community, and the Baptism ceremony speak of the mysteries of creation, and its marriage ritual speaks of the mysteries of the Paradise story.

The Dream of Eden in the Consciousness of Humanity

Primordial memories lie over the childhood of the race like deeply meaningful dream pictures—the tremendous biblical pictures of our human origin in the light and descent into the earthly realm; of Paradise and the Fall; of the strife between brothers; of the Great Flood; and of the forefather of the new human race who survived the Flood. Later generations take as a fable what sounds across to us from an unbelievably distant past. Darkness of intellect has spread a veil of oblivion over the memories of our childhood, into which a glimpse of the lost light of Paradise was still alighting. Icy-cold intelligence has hardened what was once flowing life in the streams of the primordial waters. And everything academic knowledge has accumulated to interpret the early dream of humanity weaves only more strongly the veil of oblivion, making the hardening of our souls only frostier. With the loss of Paradise came humanity's gradual loss of any memory of it. Memory, by its nature itself something supernatural, today mainly feeds on our sense impressions. It touches no more on that from which all sensory life originates. Only inside our heads is memory still alive; in our hearts it has died. In the earthly light, the celestial light shining from the primordial beginning has been extinguished. Thus for a heart incapable of remembering, the Dream of Eden has turned into a mirage. Despite the wakeful alertness of our external senses, the human soul lies in a deep sleep.

But through this deep sleep of humanity runs something like an experience of inner light, in which—sometimes more clearly, sometimes more obscurely—the Dream of Eden lights up. Solemnly it used to stand before the opened eye of the soul of the early Chaldean when he looked up to the star-lit sky and read in it the glowing script of the universe, in that light-filled primal home of the patriarchs whence Abraham journeyed into the land of Canaan. Something like a memory of primordial light still sounds today in the biblical name of that homeland.[1] In subdued form, this dream then lived on in the soul of the patriarch. And it was again under a star-lit sky that it shone strongly once more during a prophetic night before the eye of Jacob's soul. In purest light, illuminating tremendous connections between Earth-evolution and human evolution, that Dream then took form in the spirit of Moses—the one to whom we owe the inspiration of

Genesis. In him the earlier light-experience and that 'I'-force met, by which the later rational consciousness of humanity was carried. That earthly light slowly came to outshine the earlier celestial light. *'Forthwith, no prophet in Israel stood up like Moses whom the Lord (the I am) knew face to face'* [Deut. 34:10]. Out of the spiritual darkness of the ages, only once more did the inner experience of light rise high enough for a realization of the connections between cosmos and humanity, in the dream wisdom of Solomon. In this the Dream of Eden turns into the blueprint for the Temple, which the hand of the skilful master-builder[2] raises out of earthly material. In the mysterious Temple imagery, the human past and the human future unite.

Thereafter, humanity's earlier experience of light progressively faded. Eden's world of light became ever less substantial. And the Earth would have been forever alienated from the cosmic heights had not the cosmic heights lovingly bowed down to her. Into the Earth's darkest night the most radiant cosmic light shines forth—the revelation of the most sublime cosmic love. In that child, whose earthly sheaths are to become the vessel for the cosmic light, the blueprint for the Temple, the dream of Eden itself, becomes man. All this lives in the Christmas story of the Gospels; it lives in the picture of the Grail carried down from starry heights by hosts of angels. In the Holy Grail, the rays of forgotten primordial light are collected in order to become the new Sun of Life for the future of the Earth.[3]

Since days of yore, a deep inspiration of the folk-soul has given the day before Christmas the name 'Adam and Eve'. A memory of Paradise—an image of the human being in his original innocence, the way he was in his primordial childhood in the light—used to become alive in the Christmas light. In this light, the human soul looks up to the Christmas star and once more reads the mysteries of the cosmos. Man's faded primordial memories can become alive again in this light.

In the same light the attempt will be made here to read the pictorial script of the first chapter of Genesis. This is not possible for modern day-consciousness, but only by allowing the soul access to the kind of consciousness which created these pictures. It will be attempted to show how in each individual case such an access can be found. The most important aspect is the fact that the pictures speak for themselves, that through their warmth the heart can be kindled and the soul can open itself.

1. Primordial Creation[8]

Genesis 1:1

We approach the first chapter of creation in Genesis with a feeling of awe,[9] as if we were approaching an altar, an exalted altar dedicated to the great cosmic sacrifice—for all cosmic evolution, all forming of Being, all creative outpouring of divine-spiritual Being with a gesture of giving, is sacrifice. Seven[10] radiant flames ray towards us, living flames from which light-filled countenances of divine beings—the Creators of world and of man—behold us. The Bible calls them the *Elohim,* (cf. Steiner. *Genesis.* Lecture 2); they are creative forces and the emanations of the One who works through them: the Divine Father Whom we sense out of the consciousness of our humanity. Looking up to them in awe, we see in them our own origin in the light, the divine origin of our human existence, which at this stage is still contained as a seed for the future within the divine thoughts of the Elohim. For in the primordial beginning, all divine activity manifests as the power of thought, the power of contemplation.[11] For at that stage, the Spirit can only find within Himself the material with which He can create. For outside Himself, any outer material sensory or supersensory element that He could mould, is not yet present.

But this divine thinking is different from human thinking that can merely depict. Only by moving from mere pale thought towards *reverence*, towards contemplation, and taking into it something of the picture-forming spiritual power of the artist, only then can we feel this reverence-inspired contemplation, this contemplative reverence. We feel our way towards that which is working in the primal beginning as a divine thought. This is not only a thinking that depicts, but one that forms and fashions, weaving the world, creating being in the primal beginning. Divine thinking cannot be comprehended by human thinking. But human thinking can feel it is immersed in and sheltered by divine thinking, when it raises itself in devotion above itself. It can find a sense for what the word means that the Bible uses for the cosmic pondering,[12] the creative weaving of the Elohim[13] at the beginning of the creation of Heaven and Earth.

Genesis 1:2

Earthly thinking differentiates concepts; divine thought differenti-ates within essential reality an upper, Sun-radiant, creative masculine pole—the heavenly realm—and a below Moon-like, dark, feminine receiving pole—the earthly realm.

Thought thus raised to consciousness by reverence and devotion is formed into a picture, the same picture that the Hebrew seer beholds as the becoming of Earth-evolution. This picture of contemplative thought is the bird that spreads its wings and brooding hovers over the egg. The eagle or dove spreads its wings above the egg; in the primal beginning the spirit of the Elohim, the Spirit of God, the Holy Spirit, broods[14] over the primordial waters[15] of the first etheric, earthly substantiality that is rhythmically moved by the pulse of the blowing cosmic breath.[16] In the brooding causing cosmic warmth, the physical primal seed of the becoming human entity is formed.

Genesis 1:3-5

The image of the First Day of Creation ends with the creation of light. The darkness of the depths, permeated by the brooding warmth of cosmic primordial fire, is illumined by a radiance streaming from the centre of the primordial light of the creative powers. 'And the God-head of the Elohim spoke: Let there be light. And[17] there was light.' Still this is no light which earthly eyes would have been able to see, just as there were no earthly eyes either to perceive the light, or an earthly consciousness to feel the light. But for the consciousness of the Elohim, through the deed of their divine speech, the light, which until then they had carried within themselves as an inner light, becomes outer light.[18]

In the primordial differentiation of above and below, of heavenly and earthly, there is the power of divine *thought*; in the calling forth of light out of darkness the power of the divine *word* is at work. No earthly ear could have heard, no earthly consciousness comprehend, this word. But within earthly thinking the mystery of the divine thought is contained; in earthly speaking the mystery of the divine word is also contained. Hence earthly speaking, if we devotedly enter into the spirit and the life of the Word, holds the key to that which as Divine Word, as Cosmic Word, sounds in the primordial beginning calling forth light out of darkness: *'The hidden is made known, the inner made outer, the enclosed radiates light and warms its surrounding by the power of love working and creating in the heart.'* And so we can try to grasp this Mystery of the Word within our speech. If we enter into the primordial formative forces of the sounds, we will be able to recognize this meaning in the sounds of that Hebrew word, which here, before ever being applied to human speech anywhere, at first stands for the speaking of the Godhead.[19] Genesis itself points to this primordial meaning of sounds when it speaks of the mystery of divine naming. All earthly naming, however far it has strayed from the primal word, leads back to this mystery of divine naming.[20]

In all these pictures, the coming-into-being of the cosmos and the coming-into-being of man are still so closely interlinked that we can say: it is in fact man's being, initially of his heavenly—or the heavenly–earthly part—which, stage by stage in these pictures, we progressively follow into existence.[21]

- The thinking head of this 'Adam Kadmon'[22]—'Primordial Man'— in radiant heights we find again in divine contemplation;
- the rhythmical system of our breathing and feelings—we find [this] in the cosmic rhythms of the waving primordial waters (which are something entirely different from today's physical oceans);
- the will living in the limbs—we find in the darkness of the depths, into which the light from the heights radiates (just as today the originally 'dark' human will receives its light from thinking).

The primordial trinity of thinking, the feelings and the will—mirrored in the human physiognomy—already lies resting as a seed in the first image of creation; and therein the divine Trinity of Father, Son and Spirit of:

- primordial Cosmic Existence,
- primordial Cosmic Word,
- primordial Cosmic Light.

Between the Unity of the primordial Divinity and the Seven creating Powers lies the Mystery of the Divine Trinity.

Genesis 1:6-8

In the picture of the Second Day of Creation, through the power of the sounding Cosmic Word, the primordial trinity is mirrored once more in the Earth and causes a separation of elements there: a light-filled in-between space[23] separates the waters above from the waters below. We will only understand this picture in the right way, if we take earthly water and earthly air as pointers to the primordial Mysteries of the elements of water and air. In a tremendous picture Genesis puts before us the primordial supernatural seed for all we experience today as chemical reactions relating to the separation of matter into its elements.

With the coming-into-being of the physical elements, physical corporeality is created in the primordial picture of heavenly man. This primordial physical entity lives, yet still almost lifeless in the primordial darkness, which is first permeated by primordial warmth, then by primordial light. The first stage of human evolution is taking place within it.[24] In four such stages, the evolution of heavenly man is brought to completion.

Genesis 1: 9-13

The great impact of the introduction of life brings the second stage of cosmic becoming and human becoming on the Third Day of Creation. Genesis gives us the picture of a germinating plant world. A shooting, sprouting and blossoming begins; life radiates from the lap of the godhead where it had lain dormant; it enters the earthly realm which had hitherto seemed lifeless. In order for this to happen, preparation was made; the differentiation of elements had to reach the point where the dry element was separated from the moist. This 'firm' Earth is a picture in which we glimpse something higher. It is not yet today's Earth upon which feet could have rested. It is the mystery of the Earth germinating in the spirit, the ether of the earthly realm, the mirror[25] of the divine life, into which the light of the godhead radiates, the Earth of Light.

In this Earth of Light, divided from earthly water and fructified by the dews of heavenly waters, out of the primordial lap of light, the divine life radiates, which becomes the living, paradisal Earth.[26] The *maya* of the material-earthly element itself becomes spirit and life. At the altar of the great sacrifice of cosmic consecration, the mystery of transformation, of transubstantiation, is carried out which we re-create in memory at the earthly altar.[27]

Here, too, world evolution and human evolution are still one. With and within the burgeoning, etheric life of the Earth, the human being's living-etheric part at the same time evolves, or rather the primordial heavenly blueprint of this part of his being.

None of today's plant species, not even their first tender, seed-like beginnings, had then evolved. The mystery of the plant species and their evolution still rested within primordial space, which at the same time was the primordial space of evolving man. In his artistic intuition, Goethe could see this primordial plant-being that still contained within its bosom the mystery of all the species of plants, their evolution and differentiation. He called it '*Urpflanze*'—'primordial, or archetypal, plant'. The picture of the Third Day of Creation speaks of this light-filled primordial plant, not that of today's vegetable world.

Here again one can ask, what possibility, what path is there for the seeking human soul to penetrate the depths and undercurrents of consciousness of this picture? Such a path exists: Rudolf Steiner describes it in his book *Knowledge of the Higher Worlds: How is it Attained?*[28] It is the quite concrete path of entering into the primordial etheric of the plant, and through this into the etheric world as such. Only when we inwardly devote ourselves to the life of plants will we be able properly to understand what is given here: the several mysterious-seeming meditations on the seed, the growing and the fully grown plant, etc. When we fully engage our souls in the observation from the seed of the lily-of-the-valley, from the tuber of the hyacinth, and so on, how the first tender green shoot rises, how out of the shoot the leaf develops, how to the leaf the bud is added, and how the bud turns into a blossom. The blossom in wilting turns into a fruit, which fruit then again contains the new seed within, in which the whole process of becoming takes a new beginning. In letting all this work sympathetically on our souls, we grow beyond the mere external, spatial view of the plant's existence towards viewing the plant in its becoming and existence in time. Before the beholding soul, the light-filled primordial plant appears, the etheric primordial picture of the plant, and with it the primordial image of the etheric human being, the primordial picture of the etheric body.

Genesis 1:14-19

In the same way that the second phase of world-evolution leads from the lifeless to the living, the third phase leads from the living to sentient being. Out of the primordial light-filled lap of divine life there streams the life of conscious feeling into that which hitherto had been non-sentient life. Here again, world-evolution contains human evolution. Into the primordial picture of the evolving heavenly human being the starry life of the feelings now shines, which hitherto were hidden in the lap of the deity.

But before that starry life of conscious feelings can be kindled in the creature on the Fifth Day of Creation, there shines forth the lighting up of the stars in the picture of the Fourth Picture of Creation. In order fully to comprehend this Picture, we need to outgrow our current imagination, which in order to understand the starry heavens uses earthly concepts and viewpoints. These are applied to the cosmos. We ourselves, however, have to develop a 'starry consciousness' that no longer measures cosmic dimensions against earthly standards, but integrates cosmic standards back into life on Earth. Then we can sense how from the stars there streams towards us not a reflection of this physical earthly life, but cosmic Life, cosmic Love, and cosmic Being.

This cosmic nature is what the Hebrew seer sees streaming from starry spaces in the picture of the heavenly lights, of the Sun and Moon, the planets and the fixed stars, as similarly we see them today with our physical eyes. Such physical eyes, or an earthly consciousness similar to those which could have seen stars out there, had not evolved then. Neither does Genesis mention stars that would have been there for an earthly consciousness to see; they were there only for the consciousness of the Elohim, *'and the Godhead saw that it was beautiful'*.

Genesis 1:20-23

The dialogue between the soul and the cosmic spaces lights up in the stars. Inner starlight shines forth in the feelings of the soul. Man shares this starry life of the feelings with the animal world; distinguished from this is the conscious life of the 'I'. And so, in the picture of thriving animal life, the seer depicts this flaring up of the feelings in the world of Creation. Before the inner eye, first the picture of caterpillar and butterfly arises.

In the mystery of caterpillar and butterfly, the soul first recognizes the mystery of its life of feelings.[29] To the primordial plant and the primordial blossoming of the Third Day of Creation depicting etheric life, on the Fifth Day, when the starry life of the Fourth Day is reflected within and illumines creation, the primordial butterfly is added as that which frees itself spiritually from the earthly realm. Spiritually it escapes from the spirit-form of the caterpillar. This is a picture for all that binds spirit to the earthly realm. The great primordial contrast from the beginning of Genesis between Heaven above and Earth below now reappears as that of butterfly and caterpillar. The same cosmic thought that devised the primordial plant, also thinks the primordial butterfly fluttering around the primordial blossom. When we manage to experience before our soul the butterfly neither as a merely outward appearance before our physical eye, nor as a mere memory drawn from outer sense-impressions, but when we spiritually experience it, we can find the path to a true inner experience of the Fifth

Picture of Creation, as many have experienced it in the deeper recesses of their consciousness.

Corresponding to all the differentiation of this feeling-life, the picture, too, begins to move. Before our spiritual eye the pictures acquire something of an independent life. The form of the butterfly metamorphoses into that of the bird;[30] those of caterpillar and worm into the form of the dragon.[31] Just as the primordial plant holds the mystery of all the different species of plants, these primordial animal-forms hold the mystery of all the animal species, their evolution, differentiation and interconnection with the starry regions of the cosmos. The outer physical animal-forms, however, only appear later during the creation of the Earth in Genesis 2.[32] Again what takes place is at the same time a stage in human evolution. The feeling-soul streams into the human being, or rather the heavenly archetype of this feeling-soul, or sentient soul. And this primordial picture is still kept completely within the divine thinking which, carried like a seed, now 'expresses' it, manifests it. For an Imaginative consciousness, however, from this moment onwards the picture of the winged animal-form appears, above all in the form of the butterfly.

Genesis 1:24, 25

On the Sixth Day of Creation the human 'I', or ego—the reflection and the image of the Creator Godhead Himself—is added to the sentient soul. The primordial image of Man's being now finds its completion, and with it the archetype of the human form. It signifies the fourth stage of human becoming, the crowning finale of the creative work of the Elohim. Before this, the primordial image of the earthly animal has to be added to that which lives in water and air, as it rays out of the cosmos into the evolving earth. That which appears as the Lion is not the earthly lion of today, but the cosmic Lion as the sum total of powerful forces raying down from a certain region of the cosmos. It is perceived by the becoming human being as forces of the heart. To the eye of the seer this process appears in the form of the picture of the Lion. Divine thinking, by moving through a whole evolutionary sequence of animal forms, out of them finally creates the human form.[33]

Genesis 1:26-31

The human 'I' is to govern the separate forces of sentient life. The command outwardly to rule is but a picture given in Genesis of this inner constellation of forces. Heavenly Man, the man of primordial beginnings, *Adam Kadmon*, still unites in his being all those entities which later earthly man gradually excluded. He, the reflection and image of the Creator God, is himself still the world; he unites within himself all the world's polarities: 'And the deity of the Elohim in their creative thinking wove the human being in their own image, as an image of the divine they created him. And they created him male-female.'[34] The primal contrast between male and female—which already gently appears in the primal creative polarity of above and below, of Heaven and Earth—is a contrast which heavenly Man, as thought and very image of the gods, still carries within himself. What Man thus still carries united within himself appears before the eye of the seer in the double image of the male-female form. In this image is seen the primordial unity of what later separated in the earthly realm, the primordial union of male and female in the lap of the divine life. Of this, all earthly union is an imperfect image.

'And the deity created man in their image, in the image of the divine they created him. And they created him male-female.' With this, perhaps the most powerful sentence of the Bible, we are presented with a mystery, which in the truest meaning of the word is still a mystery of the future. For that reflection and image of the creating gods has not yet become a reality on the Earth. Through the Fall, the human being lost this heavenly image. He is no longer able to sense what the gods had ordained for him. They wanted to create beyond themselves, wanting to establish that being which would unite within himself the whole radiating splendour of the seven lights, which in the very beginning illumined the cosmic altar of creation. This being was to carry this spiritual-creative force into earthly existence, to continue working and building at this earthly existence with divine-creative forces. Out of himself man was supposed to find the means to take into his own being the divine creating will. This will lead the world further, according to the divine intention.

However, in order to do this, man also had to be given the possibility of straying from the divine, of turning away, of sinning. Hence in addition to the primordial creation, another creation had to be added, of which Genesis 2 narrates. Therein the human being succumbed to the forces of temptation. Through the Fall he became the earthly man of today. He lost the heavenly primordial image from his consciousness. And only through the fact that this primordial image stepped down from the heavenly heights and became an earthly human being, could he find it again. Only then for the first time was there a heavenly

Man on Earth, in the way the Elohim had intended him. Yet only in a far distant future will this lost heavenly primordial image be able to live again amongst humanity itself. In this respect, for us today the Man of Genesis 1 is actually still a Man of the future. We need to regard the work of creation as something that only in the future will be completed. The most mysterious of all pictures of the biblical creation story remains for man today the one in which this creation will find its crowning completion—his own image, his heavenly primordial image.

With regard to this picture, too, we would like to pose the question that already came to us regarding the other images of the biblical story of creation: 'What can we do, what paths can a searching human soul take, in order also to work through for itself the living composition of this last and greatest picture of the Elohim creation? What experiences, what inner soul-work or meditative work is deemed necessary to clear the pathways for ourselves towards this last and greatest picture of primordial creation, the image of heavenly Man himself?'

No mere outward or particular path or means can we find that will lead us to an Imaginative vision of this last and highest. Here only one thing will help the seeking soul—to gain an ever greater, deeper and fuller understanding of our own being. The soul is to learn to explore ever more thoroughly the heights and depths of the word 'human being'. In self-awareness, the human being must learn to look at what has become earthly in him, what within has succumbed to the forces of temptation, to the forces of death, to the condition of sin. We first need to be fully aware of our *lower nature* before we can rise towards a vision of the heavenly aspect of our being. Only then will we understand the true and full meaning of the phrase the 'image of God', only then will the picture of the Sixth Day of Creation truly come alive for us. Not through this or that particular meditation or exercise, but only through an ever fuller and deeper understanding of our whole human nature. *Through a knowledge of the human being, through anthroposophy* in the highest sense of the word, can we really come to terms with the final and highest of the biblical Pictures of Creation. True knowledge ['wisdom'] of man, 'anthroposophy' [= anthropos-sophia], has to kindle in us its light and become our soul-guide on the dark path leading up to those light-filled heights from which the primordial image of heavenly Man, the light-filled creation of the Elohim, shines down to us.

2. The Second Creation

Adam Kadmon lived breathing in the light of the divine, still as a member of the Godhead. He is the heavenly Man of the primordial beginning, the creation of the Elohim who created him in their supernatural realm, who fashioned his being out of their own members. If the human being was really meant to unite all the forces of the divine Creator within himself, if he was meant to take into himself out of his freedom the divine Creating Will, with the objective to continue to build the earthly existence self-creatively, then he first had to be given the possibility to awaken towards this freedom. If he had been created solely out of the members of the divine being, he would never have managed to become independent of those in whose lap he still lived. Consequently, the Godhead had to transform what was fashioned out of His own members by giving man an element foreign to his divine origin, an element which the Bible calls 'dust of the earth'. Not without reason does the Bible here use a different word for earth than when it speaks of the primordial creation.[35]

This dust of the earth, or earth of death, is something entirely different from the light-Earth of the primordial creation, that living, fruit-bearing paradisal Earth which brings [allows] the Tree of Life to spring forth. With the light-Earth, the divine light came shining from the heavens, permeating the earthly realm, transforming, transubstantiating it. The dust of the earth—although it also still needs to be imagined as completely supersensible—the death-earth of Genesis 2, stands in pure contrast to the heavenly sphere; though a manifestation of the spiritual, it fell away most strongly from the spiritual life.

Genesis 2: 1-4
In order for it to acquire this form at the moment in time when man was to awaken to his earthly 'I', when the earth should be added to him, who is the descendant of the heavenly Man,[36] for this a transition period was necessary. This is presented at the beginning of Genesis 2 in the image of the great day celebrating rest. This has been adapted from our earthly-human conditions in a naive, but pointed and meaningful, way. We can experience this day celebrating rest in an inward and spiritual way. A feeling develops that rest is more than just an outward resting; we work in a higher sense on that which transcends our everyday experience, working on our inner higher man that inwardly

celebrates. And we can especially develop an awareness of how new forces for everyday life and work come flowing towards us, when for the duration of the day of celebration we are able to immerse ourselves in a higher spiritual life. If we manage to raise and expand all this on to the cosmic level, we can gain an experience of the great cosmic celebration of the day of rest that follows the Six Days of Creation. We can understand what the Bible means by connecting the blessing and healing of the earthly day of celebration with those cosmic events. Then we will take this cosmic day of celebration, this great cosmic rest of the Seventh Day, knowing that the term 'day' is but an image. We look through the picture to those vast expanses of time during cosmic becoming known to the Indian as *'Days and Nights of Brahman'*. And it will dawn on us how this great cosmic rest is not merely a time of idleness for the Creator-beings; during that time, turning away from their work on earthly conditions, they devote themselves to their own higher spiritual entity, to that which is above the Earth. This is precisely how the strong divine forces mature which are necessary to further the earthly realm, and into heavenly Man to implant that earthly seed, the creation of the Elohim, from which as earthly man he can awaken to independence and the experience of his earthly 'I'.

Genesis 2:5-6

In Genesis, the mystery of the creation of earthly man out of heavenly Man (or as we might say, how heavenly Man was transformed into earthly man), is significantly bound to a name appearing here for the very first time as the name of the divine. That is the name 'YHVH' ('Yewe', 'Yahwe', 'Jehovah', or however the unutterable Y-H-V-H is rendered by adding vowels to make a word). 'Yahve-Elohim'—as Genesis says—'formed man as dust out of Earth and blew the breath of life into him through his nostrils, and so man became a living soul'. In this Being, now called 'Yahveh-Elohim', the creative power of the Elohim works on. It has been leading man up to this point where to him, who so far had only been a Spirit-man, a heavenly Man, the element of Earth, and with it the earth-bound 'I', could be added. Yahveh-Elohim is the Creator-being who unites in Himself the forces of the others when it comes to leading over the spiritual primordial creation into the second creation.[37] He is the one with the special relationship to everything earthly; the one in whom man's earthly being is mirrored as in a divine looking-glass.

With this earthly potential added to him, man is meant to awaken to his earthly 'I'. Flowing divine cosmic breath turns into earthly air for breathing; divine cosmic 'I'-force turns into an earthly human 'I'.[38] The heavenly Man hitherto did not yet breathe on the Earth. Only now, though still entirely in the supernatural realm, there stirs within him the mysterious rhythm of inhalation and exhalation. This begins at our birth; when it ceases it signifies our earthly death. Birth and death as we know them today, and which paradisal Man did not yet know, are closely connected with the mystery of the breathing rhythm, in which cosmic realities are reflected on Earth. In man, the earthly-human 'I' connects with earthly breathing, just as in the divine, the forces of the cosmic 'I' connect with the flowing cosmic breath. And in a mysterious way, it is the name 'Y-H-V-E' itself that expresses this link between divine cosmic 'I'-forces and the essence of flowing breath. For the ancient Indian that connection gave expression to the word *atman*, which originally means the same as German *atmen* 'to breathe'; it also means the 'I', or self. And if we pose the question, 'How can the searching human soul find a living understanding, a living experience of the tremendous Genesis Imagination of the Creation of Man and Earth?' (Gen. 2:7), one possible answer—though not the only one—might point to those mysteries of the breath which the early Indian called Yoga.

Another path, one closer to us today, is the immediate artistic behold-ing of what appears as a pictorial element in the name YHVH itself. As though mysteriously interwoven within this name, everything living as the mystery of the creation in the tremendous picture in Genesis of the creation of earthly man is contained in the pictorial quality of the name of YHVH itself, and how it relates to the creation of Man and Earth. We find all this expressed in an extraordinarily artistic way in Michelangelo's 'Creation of Adam'. Here we can strongly experience how the divine spark of life, the spark of earthly life, jumps over from the outstretched hand of the Creator to his creature, earthly man.

- In this outstretched hand of the Creator there lives the same active and will-imbued, affirming, actively creating, mascu-line creative, imparting force that as primordial forming force is expressed in the sound *y*, the initial sound of the name 'Y-H-V-H'. (The Hebrew word for 'hand', *yad*, is related to the name of this first letter.)
- The original meaning and forming force of *h* is similarly living in the German word *Hauch* 'breath'. In 'HVH' as a verb in Hebrew means 'to be', spiritual primordial being; in it there lies the mys-tery of breathing existence. This is the female primordial force,[39]

which then in its linguistic development became 'EVA'. The ego-imbued male principle connects with what lives as breathing existence, with the female primordial force of the universe.

Thus the name of Eve herself is mysteriously interwoven with the divine name of YHVH. Mankind beholds in this name its own divine primordial mystery, as it says of the primordial creation: 'And he created them, a male, a female.' A mysterious female figure in Michelangelo's painting also hints at the fact that the human being's female half, as the primordial Female of the world, Eve, still remains in spirit-heights with the divine Creator.

The whole mystery of the heavenly Man of primordial beginnings, Adam Kadmon, and how he was transformed into earthly man, is thus reflected in the name of YHVH. Whereas all other names of the divine are words used by mankind to name or signify the divine, the unspeakable name 'YHVH' is felt as the one which man cannot and may not pronounce. It is the one name which the Divine, not man, gave to Itself. Every human being can only say 'I' about themselves; this 'I' is the name of that which sounds towards us out of the veiled most inner sacred temple of our soul. Likewise 'YHVH' is the name in which the Divine says something like 'I' to itself.

The word 'Elohim' in Chapter 1 and at the outset of Chapter 2 still stood alone to signify the divine. Now for the first time it combines with the name 'YHVH' in the creation of earthly man of Genesis 2. This we can feel with a shudder of awe: it is a word in which a heart in devotion opens up towards the lofty heights of the human primordial beginnings, to the spiritual creator-forces. From there, shining back into itself, it receives the Light.

3. Paradise

Even after he had received the seed of earth from Yahveh, Man was still living in innocence in the light of the divine. His consciousness was still that of heavenly man, not yet that of the earthly man he had become. He still lived completely on forces from the Tree of Life. He was completely unaware of the forces from the Tree of Knowledge, which was to become the Tree of Death to him; in this unawareness lay his innocence.

Genesis 2:8-10

The Bible paints this picture in mighty strokes. It speaks of Eden as the higher realm of light, which includes the home of man, which, despite its having shrunk in size is still as big as the world. This homeland, this dwelling place itself, the Bible calls the 'Garden of Eden'. It speaks of the trees Yahveh-Elohim himself planted in this Garden, with the central Tree of Life and the Tree of Knowledge of good and evil. And finally it speaks of the headwaters of four rivers, which have their common source in *one* river originating in Eden and from there watering the Garden.

We can recognize that everything the Bible speaks about in these light-filled pictures of Paradise lies still high above in the supersensory realm, on mountain tops of the supersensory. Nowhere on Earth is it the way things have become today, but still high above,[40] meaning more than just spatial dimensions. And one very revealing picture that might bring us a step closer towards visualizing the great Paradise picture of Genesis, is the one we have just set forth: the picture of the earthly mountain top. Not without deeper meaning do those to whom we are indebted for inspiring Genesis—and the rest of the Bible—speak of holy, sacred mountains; not without meaning does Christ lead us to the mountain top to gain the highest view, the most intimate dialogue with the Spirit.

Those who can understand the holiness and inspiration of a mountain top do not just breathe physically, but they breathe, see and hear the Spirit. They can experience in the mountain air something of the divine breath, in the light of the heights something of the light of the higher worlds, and in a mountain flower something of the colours of the higher worlds. On a mountain-top, we may not only feel closer to the boundary of the physical world, but also to the worlds of Spirit.

A mountain spring, a mountain stream—water still close to its divine origins—hint at freedom and purity, at happiness and content, qualities we will no longer be able to find in a river in the lowlands. The former reminds us of our youth, the latter of old age and death.

Living with and spiritualizing such ideas might bring us a step closer to the great picture of Paradise and the mystery of its Garden and rivers, and we might find in the headwaters of the rivers of Paradise a picture of the youth of the human race still surrounded by flowing, rushing water. But despite all our efforts, we will still not penetrate the supernatural reality behind the picture. And so the questions arise:

- How does the darkened consciousness of today find access to the most light-filled Imagination of the Bible, the Imagination of Paradise?
- Is the light we once used to live in, is the Garden we once used to walk in, gone dark for us forever?
- Will the cherub with the flaming sword forever keep guard over the gate to the fields of light?

Answers will only come if we enter more deeply into the riddle of human consciousness. For although for our normal waking consciousness, the realms of light of our human origins are far removed, yet in the regions of deep sleep, which we enter every night, they have not ceased to exist.[41] Gradually we enter the realms of light, yet we no longer know we do. For the human soul, our nightly sleep has become mere oblivion and stupor, since the times when the forces of death laid hold of human consciousness. And the Guardian at the Threshold of Paradise, whom the human soul must pass each night on her inward path, erases the soul's memory because of the way the soul is constituted today—with our waking consciousness, our day-time interests, our personal preoccupations and all the other effects of our fallen human condition.

Even today, each night during sleep the human being still receives a part of the rejuvenating forces flowing into his whole being from the realms of light; those realms themselves remain darkened and veiled for his consciousness. He can only gain a victory over this darkening by strengthening his inner soul-life, through those rejuvenating forces which from the heights of the forgotten light gave themselves to us and entered human evolution with a new impulse. In them, the forces of the Tree of Life come alive again, which through his Fall man had to renounce. By connecting in our soul with those forces of purity and innocence, we can also transform our sleep in such a way that during sleep we do not completely surrender to the consciousness-erasing forces of death, but carry some remaining awareness into the realms of light.

An ancient and profound legend[42] speaks of three seeds from the Tree of Life which Adam took with him when he was driven out of Paradise.[43] After Adam's death, his [third] son Seth took the three seeds and placed them in Adam's grave. From his grave a tree arose, from whose wood wonderful things were made: the powerful magic rod of Moses, a pillar in the temple of Solomon, and finally the cross on Golgotha. These simple pictures are profoundly linked to human evolution, especially to the turning point [of time] which can bring us the re-transformation of decaying forces of awareness into up-building ones, and the transformation of the Tree of Death itself into the Tree of Life. In a certain stream of spiritual life, those forces leading to a revival of Paradise were seen in the vision of the Holy Grail.[44] The Paradise Imagination and the Holy Grail Imagination are inwardly connected. Within the Holy Grail, the light of Paradise is metamorphosed into the Sun of Life for the future.

Hence the experience of deep sleep, of wakefulness during deep sleep, can lead towards an experience of the distant primordial past of mankind in Paradise, an experience which the pictures of Genesis portrayed. The burgeoning plant life of which the Third Day of Creation speaks will then start spreading around us. We then realize: 'We ourselves, with our whole physical organization and bodily being, which we, together with our sentient soul, left during sleep—we ourselves are this sprouting Garden!'

The starry life, kindled when our feeling life began on the Fourth Day of Creation, and which we have now integrated into ourselves, allows us to look down on to the sprouting Garden. We recognize how everything born on the Fifth Day of Creation from the different starry regions of the cosmos, everything moving about as sentient life forms in water, air and earth—and appearing to clairvoyant vision in pictures of animal beings—how all this is linked with the life of our own inner organs. Sentient life, beheld in such Imaginations, starts to spread within the burgeoning Paradise Garden. Gradually we realize, 'This sentient life—we ourselves are this, or rather we *were* this in a very distant primordial past when still living within our super-sensible being.'

We seek for that which drove us out of Paradise and into our life of the senses, and before us there appears the serpent-form of the Tempter in the Garden, with the whole picture of the story of the biblical Fall.[45] Now we know the force which darkened for us the light in which we once used to live. We recognize the path leading us back to a vision of the realms of light and towards a new awareness of our origins in the light.

The same path which the Bible describes for us as the descent of humanity from the heights of light into the dark depths of our current earthly existence and earthly consciousness—we must find it again in the opposite direction, to get back to the heights of light.

The path through the depths of self-knowledge allows us to revisit within ourselves the forces of temptation, the forces of the Fall, and its consequences for us. The path leads past the Guardian at the Threshold, who guards the gate of Paradise denying entry into the realms of light to the unbidden. All the steps of descent, in the order the Bible describes them, must one after the other turn into steps to climb for the soul searching to reascend. The descent was a path into ever deeper states of sleep and unawareness; the ascent is a path of ever clearer awakening.

Gilgamesh, the great son of the ancient Assyrian culture, failed on this path. He could no longer find the forces within himself to illuminate his consciousness during sleep. He could not manage to stay awake during his stay in the realms of light into which he had forced entry by striding courageously through darkness and dangers of death. He could no longer manage this, because already in his epoch the human soul had succumbed too much to the forces of death. What Gilgamesh was no longer able to do, became only possible again when on the cross of Golgotha, Christ won his victory over the forces of death.

The great biblical Imagination of the two Trees of Paradise—the Tree of Life and the Tree of Knowledge of good and evil, embraces us on many levels. Right into the details of human physiology, into the secrets of our brain and of the marrow of our spine, we can detect the essence of these two Trees. At least to a certain degree we can grasp the pictures in thinking before we gain the Imaginations themselves and realize the profound reality speaking through them.

These two Trees stand before us like great benchmarks in the life of each individual as well as in human evolution in general. The way the life of each individual, figuratively speaking, takes its beginning in childhood from the forces of the Tree of Life. Later, especially from puberty onwards, it becomes increasingly a servant of the forces of the Tree of Knowledge. Similarly, something of the forces from the Tree of Life flows into general human evolution, right up to the prehistoric times of Ancient India and Ancient Persia, whereas the following cultures come to be increasingly under the rule of other forces [from the Tree of Knowledge].

The forces of the one place us into life, giving us the freshness of childhood and the blossom of youth, yet in the way we have become in physical life, they do not give awareness. Those other forces that give knowledge at the same time cause our physical organism to wilt, leading to our deaths. We can only gain awareness when we are within our physical body while disintegrating, wilting processes are at work within us, brought about by the forces of death. Between processes of blossoming and processes of wilting, between growth and decay, all life, all development proceeds.[46] The cycle of the year, the annual changing of the seasons, speaks most strongly and most immediately to us about these facts of all life. Nature speaks to us in pictures behind which we can divine the deeper mysteries of spiritual life. And we may inwardly connect these pictures from nature, appearing afresh before our senses every year, with those of the Scriptures.

Genesis 2:10-14

With regard to the mystery of the four rivers of Paradise, a few indications have to suffice. It should by now be clear that we have to go beyond mere outer geographical descriptions. What looks like reminiscences of certain locations on Earth are but pictures for a higher reality. During the time to which the image refers, this reality was still lying in higher regions of existence. When it speaks of the headwaters of the four rivers, Genesis leads us on to the highest mountain tops of the supersensory world. Man will have to find these headwaters within his own being; at that time they still encompassed the whole wide world. We meet again in the four sacred rivers the secret of the fourfold structure leading man in four stages up to his lofty spiritual existence through the creation of the Elohim. They all originate in Eden, in the all-encompassing realm of light in the middle of which lies the Garden of Paradise, the inner human sanctuary. Today the human being with all his members is connected with the whole world and its streams of etheric life; this was even more the case during his time in Paradise.[47]

In a particular way we find the first of the four rivers linked with mysteries of the physical world: 'The name of the first river is Phišon, which flows around the whole land of Havilah, where gold is found. And the gold of the land is superb; also there is the noble substance Bedolāh and the gem Soham' [Gen. 2:11-12]. The secret of gold, the secret of precious stones, and other secrets of a higher alchemy are interwoven with the secrets of Paradise and those of its rivers.[48] Looking beyond physical gold and physical gems and breaking through to the origins of all things physical in the light and forces of the supersensible spiritual world, we come to understand at last the mysterious link between human nature and incarnation and all the physical substances and elements. We know how carbon is present in the Earth as diamond and in man as the chemical base for everything organic. We can divine something of the higher alchemy indicated in the Book of Genesis. From an entirely new angle, an approach opens to the biblical picture of Paradise and its rivers that is full of riddles.

Just a few indications will be given from an anthroposophical perspective regarding the secret of gold. In this perspective, the material world is transformed again into spirit; matter, too, becomes a spiritual phenomenon. From this angle, we acknowledge light as a spiritual element, as *the* primordial element of the spiritual realm, and all matter (so-called) as an intensification and darkening of light. Then the secret of gold would be, that therein—even within concentrated matter, within the realm of the mineral world, within that dark antagonist of light—a primordial shining of the Sun coming to meet us, as if enchanted into the physical substance itself. In gold, the mystery of the light within all physical matter gleams for us. And in gemstones, the mineral world reaches a point where it becomes translucent again for the light; it meets us again as related to the light. The black colour of coal, the dark antagonist of light, turns to light again in the diamond in which the secret of colour shines for us.

Before it turns into higher reality within us, all this can become a symbol for man's task to transform his own substance by purification and spiritualization, leading everything that has gone dark within us back into the light. The Rosicrucians used to call this process 'working with the Stone of the Wise'.[49] In such inner work, the human soul finds a secure way back into the mountain heights of the supersensory realm, where with the great pictures of Genesis our origins in the light began; a way back into the realm of light, back to the source of the eternal rivers.[50]

As a glance into the future, such an image stood before the spiritual eye of Novalis, when, in *Christianity in Europe* [often referred to as *Christianity or Europe*], he wrote:

> Just as the human soul rises towards heaven of its own accord once she is freed of her fetters, the higher organs too of their own accord separate out first—from the overall uniform mixture and complete dissolution of all human potentials and forces—as the primordial nucleus of earthly creativity. The Spirit of God hovers above the waters, and as the waves are retreating, at first a heavenly island as a dwelling place for the new Man, as a river-homeland of eternal life, will emerge.[51]

4. Eve

Genesis 2:15-20

Yahveh breathed earthly air into the human being. He planted in him the element of Earth-dust, which he still carried within himself in an innocent and unconscious way. The human being, at first, is still living in the light of Paradise; he does not yet feel separated from his divine Creator. Yahveh is still the spiritual-heavenly aspect of the human being and the sole content of his consciousness. The mystery of primordial Man, the creation of the Elohim, is the unity between the male and the cosmic female. This was still alive in the human being. It is expressed in the name that reflects his spiritual essence, the name of Yahveh Himself, 'YHVH'. In his innocent closeness to God, in a state of harmonious balance of all the innocent, divine forces of his full humanity, the human being is still 'building' on his own earthly being, working creatively on his earthly surroundings.

This closeness to God, in which human beings in their innocence are still living, and which in the human paradisal consciousness is still beyond the polarity of the sexes, is expressed in the power of the divine-creative Word that still passes through the human being without hindrance. Language, still supersensory, had not yet become earthly. Paradisal Man was himself still a carrier of the Cosmic Word. He experienced himself and his surroundings through the Cosmic Word, for there was as yet no separation between man and world as is apparent today. For whatever he subsequently extracts out of his being in terms of lower organisms, he gives names out of the essence of the divine Cosmic Word. The Word, the secret of name-giving, which in the primordial beginning was with God, is now with man, because man himself is still with God. The divine power of the Word lives in the secret of breathing itself; the human being has not yet placed this power out of himself, it has not yet become his outward assistant.

It is one of the mysteries of the name 'YHVH', that the primordial feminine principle of the world, Eve, before becoming outwardly united with Adam, in the light of the divine was still directly connected with the hand of the Creator God, with the Will aspect of the Divine itself. As already mentioned, Michelangelo with his painting 'The Creation of Adam' expressed this mystery. Then, the primordial Cosmic Female was not yet 'HVH' (the Hebrew form of the name

'Eva' or 'Eve'), but 'ḤVH', divine primordial essence, divine-*feminine* primordial force. Only after the biblical Fall did the spiritual actually become earthly, which finds its linguistic expression in the transition from the spiritual 'H' to the earthly 'Ḥ' (– *ch*). Only then does the primordial Cosmic Female receive the name 'HVH' ('Eve'), primordial Mother of all Living: '*And Adam gave his wife the name Eve, for she is the mother of all living,* (Gen. 3:20).

Genesis 2:21-25

The preliminary stage of Eve's becoming earthly takes place in the pre-earthly supersensory realm; still in Paradise the feminine part of the human being takes on an outward existence. This event, which marks a decisive turning point in the evolution of human consciousness—the descent of the human being into earthly conditions—is what Genesis narrates in the picture of *Adam's sleep.* We found how it helps our ascent from current earthly consciousness back to the forgotten heights of light, when we illuminate our sleep, when we wake up while still sleeping. So when, rather than an ascent, a descent into earthly consciousness and earthly darkness is narrated, it gives rise of itself to the reverse image, the image of falling ever more deeply asleep and the dimming down of the primordial consciousness.

It is true that from the perspective of the spiritual world, our current waking consciousness is seen as a deep sleep of the human soul. So we can easily comprehend the following first part of the picture Genesis gives us: 'And Yahveh-Elohim let a deep sleep descend upon man, and he fell asleep.' In his earlier, higher consciousness of Paradise, the human being had as yet no need for sleep. Now the first sleep comes upon him, and what people today experience as the necessity for sleep, takes here its historical evolutionary beginning. With regard to this 'sleep', we must of course keep in mind that the human being was not then what we are now; his sleep, too, was different from our modern sleep. We find processes described here which still lie high above all current earthly existence and earthly consciousness.

The twilight of an originally higher consciousness, a darkening of consciousness, a sinking down of the human being into regions of spirit are still of a very light-filled nature. But in comparison with the primordial regions of light they have already become murkier, more dreamlike, more dimmed down—this is what the picture of Adam's sleep reveals to us. This is not solely an Imagination we find in the Bible, in Genesis, but it is a common human image, you might say a picture, which we encounter frequently where earlier states of clair-voyance at one time inspired literature, as in fairy tales and old leg-ends. Think of *Mary's Child* in the Grimms' collection, of the poor girl who is allowed to stay with the Virgin Mary in heaven, but who is then banished from heaven by Mary for telling an untruth. 'Then the girl sank into a deep sleep, and when she awoke she lay down on the earth in a wilderness.'

Or take the Grimms' fairy tale *Briar Rose*, where the princess after pricking herself on the spindle, falls into a deep, one-hundred-year sleep until the prince comes and awakens her with a kiss. In this beautiful fairy-tale picture we can see reflections of real events that took place within human consciousness. At a certain moment in time human consciousness loses the remains of ancient clairvoyant forces and crosses over in sleep into the age of understanding, into a state of 'waking' consciousness. This, from a higher spiritual perspective, is nothing but a sleep. Humanity will continue to slumber until out of regions from where the Christ once descended, a higher consciousness will approach once again. This is in order to free the human soul from its narrow earthly confines and reconnect it to the cosmic regions and the cosmic light.

A similar motif to that of *Briar Rose* can be found in Norse mythol-ogy. The Valkyrie whom Wotan sent into a deep sleep falls in love with the earthly man who awakens her.[52] From a state of divine con-sciousness, the Valkyrie sleeps into an earthly-human consciousness. Likewise Adam, the man of Genesis, crosses in sleeping from a still completely divine consciousness into another, already much more earthly and more human state of consciousness. This nevertheless is yet a much higher, lighter and more spiritual consciousness than that of today.

What actually is this damping down, this confining of the conscious-ness of the paradisal human being? What does Adam actually lose in his sleep? What had made his earlier consciousness more divine? Here we have to remember that the divine image and nature of man in his primordial origin, Adam-Kadmon, meant that his consciousness still encompassed the wide cosmic regions. He had not yet become frag-mented; in his consciousness, he had not yet fallen out of the ring of eternity. The two primordial opposites of creation, the unfolding of which lies at the heart of all cosmic evolution, were still united within Adam-Kadmon forming the ring of eternity. Because Man and Woman were still united within him in the Divine, his consciousness was still a pure mirror of Yahveh's consciousness. This male-and-female unity within his own being is what the human being loses by developing an earthly consciousness through the force that pulls down, the earthly element implanted into him.

In this way the circle of his consciousness becomes narrower, no longer encompassing the wide cosmic spaces. The Beings who previously had been but integral parts of his own physical and etheric organization, these the human being now experiences as outside, distanced from himself, forming parts of his surroundings as outer entities. And as he pushes out the female aspect of his being, he pushes out what until then, while still within him, conditioned in particular the all-encompassing cosmic richness of his consciousness. Previously he was but a human being; now he becomes Man and Woman. For the male aspect in him, the female counterpart has become his outer surroundings. That part of his surroundings, which awakens his consciousness in a particularly earthly way, gradually turns his consciousness into a sensory consciousness. With his female counter-image, the life of his senses awakens. And this counter-image also awakens in the human being the memory of his earlier divinity. The human being's consciousness, inwardly narrowed to a smaller focus, outwardly becomes richer.

All this, the Bible presents to us in way the picture of Adam's sleep develops. 'And Yahveh-Elohim fashioned the rib he had taken from the human being into the Woman, and he brought her to the Man' (Gen. 2:22). It says prior to that, how He takes out one of Man's ribs and covers the wound again. In the image of the rib, Genesis shows us that which used to be a part within the human being, out of which subsequently Woman was formed.[53] Like other aspects we have already mentioned, the rib too is a picture for something supersensory. Paradisal Man did not yet have a hardened skeleton as we do today, not for a long time, and his physical aspect, too, was still completely etheric. Wonderfully mirrored in the words of surprise that Genesis allows the man to speak after the event, we see the fact of consciousness, how the human being through Eve experiences his outer surroundings. His consciousness in a different way becomes a consciousness of the world around him.

And there is also deep meaning in the picture of the final sentence, 'And they were both naked, the man and his wife, and were not ashamed'. The picture of nakedness does not refer to our current physical human form (which was not his form then) but to the earthly aspect implanted by Yahveh into him. He had this within himself, but he did not know this yet; for still in his consciousness there only lived the divine consciousness of paradisal Man. To possess an earthly essence and to experience it, means in the picture language of the Bible, to experience yourself as naked, to be naked and to know it.

Now for a spiritual consciousness such a knowledge of nakedness should turn into a feeling of shame. Paradisal Man was not ashamed of his nakedness because he was not aware of it, for he knew nothing yet about that earthly element of dust which he carried within himself. Still living in innocence from the forces of the Tree of Life, he had not yet eaten from the Tree of Knowledge. Man was only aware of the etheric of the Light Earth, not yet of that element of earthly dust and of death which he was carrying within himself. By focusing his consciousness still entirely on the radiant light of Paradise, also the earthly-physical aspect of his being was still clothed in the etheric body of the Light Earth as in a radiant garment.[54]

5. The Fall

The story of Paradise finds its dramatic turning point in the great picture of the Fall of Man, the picture of the Serpent tempting the first primordial human couple. Only a depth of self-knowledge can open an approach to this profound, universal document of primordial human self-knowledge.

Man's becoming an earthly being—long prepared by the impress of the element of earthly dust by Yahveh, by Adam's sleep, and by the evolution of the outwardly opposite sexes—is brought to a conclusion by the Fall. Only by falling into sin does the human being sink from primordial heights of light into depths of Earth. The Bible itself (Genesis, Chapters 3-11) shows that here, if we look closely enough, it has to do with long epochs of human development. The events in Paradise, still entirely taking place high above the earthly realm, are later mirrored in events taking place in more earthly spheres: in the story of Cain and Abel, and in the story of the Great Flood. Only after the Great Flood, during the events Genesis alludes to in the story of the Tower of Babel (Genesis 11), does the Earth reach a density that we would currently associate with the term 'earth'. And what is narrated about the confusion of tongues during the building of the Tower of Babel is the final direct consequence of this Fall into sin. The Word, which in primordial Man still lived as divine primordial Word, succumbs to earthly forces and is splintered.

The story of the Fall has its central earthly event in Cain's fratricide. The story of the Temptation in Paradise is a prelude to this on a higher level. The element of earth, according to the divine Creator Will was meant to awaken the earthly 'I' in Man. But it becomes for him the tempting earthly fruit which the forces standing in opposition to those of the Divine Creator, especially those in opposition to Yahveh, seek to use to attain their own purpose for mankind. An account of the events leading to that rebellion against the gods would lead us into even higher regions of the spirit. In Genesis only a faint reflection of those distant events can be felt in the story of Cain and Abel.[55] In the myths of the early Indians we find that the battle between gods and demons (cf. Rev. 12) is indicated in a series of pictures alluding to those events.[56]

When Yahveh implanted the element of earthly dust with the seed of death into the image of the gods, He gave the human being free choice to lead back to the Divine that which had become separated from it. Prior to that the human being was but an unconscious part in the life of the Divine. Now the human being in freedom and autonomy, by the power of his 'I', could have brought the earthly element into the Divine Will, and by continuing to create on Earth could have attuned it to the harmony of the Heavens. This newly awoken earthly 'I', the gift of Yahveh, could have united itself with the Divine 'I', the gift of the Elohim. Death could have been transformed into life.

This outcome, however, was initially thwarted, due to the work of another force standing in opposition to Yahveh. The Bible introduces it in the image of the Serpent, or Snake, that most earthly of all creatures on Earth. The Snake slithering on the ground is the living image of that element which leaves the unity of the ring of eternity, now worming itself into the earthly element. It strives apart, until the time will come when the Snake, in biting its own tail, will become again the symbol of the ring of eternity. Already in very ancient times, the snake was felt to be a symbol of the highest cosmic Mysteries.

So there is something two-edged about the human being's original gift from the gods. This two-edged element is the same that made man the crown of creation: Man is made in the image of God. This image is expressed by the 'I' now being added to the human being, to the merely sentient life shared in common with animals. When the 'I' becomes the earthly 'I', the image of the gods receives the possibility for stepping outside this image and, in opposition to the Divine Creator Will, experiencing itself as a creator within its own separate sphere, separate from the Divine, thus falling out of the Divine harmony. 'Lo, Man has become as one of us, and knows what is good and evil' (Genesis 3:22).

The picture for this two-edged quality of the gift of the Earth is found in the fruit given to Man by the Tempter through the hand of Eve. The Hebrew word expresses this double, two-edged quality also into the sounds of the word 'fruit'.[57] In translations, the fruit later turned into an apple. And still in Grimm's fairy tale [Snow White], we find the picture of an apple with a poisoned half, which points to the mystery of the human 'I'. Alienated from the divine, the originally divine-'I' forces become selfish cravings of the lower 'I'. The poison of selfishness the Tempter injects into earthly man. In this selfishness, man separates himself from the divine life, and in this separation lies his sin.[58] His separation from the divine causes his entanglement with what is earthly. Man succumbs to the death-forces governing in the seed of earth, which he could have overcome had he only stayed in harmony with the Divine Will. Those same death-forces also affect the human being's newly gained knowledge. The innocence of Paradise knew no distinction between good and evil, and in consequence the human being had still been entirely carried by the etheric forces from the Tree of Life. A distinction between good and evil was meaningless then, because human innocence was still beyond good and evil. The fruit from the Tree of Knowledge, now consumed by the human couple seduced by the Tempter, turns for them into the fruit of death. This knowledge unites the human being with the forces which bring death to earthly life.

Man's female counter-image formed from his rib had given the human being his first knowledge of an earthly world outside himself. This outward impression, however, gave him a sense of re-connection with the Divine from whence he came, but only as long as he remained in a state of paradisal innocence (Genesis 2:23). He recognized through the 'very image of his own soul in the reflection of female grace'[59] that element outside himself that raised his earthly incompleteness back to divine completeness. Only after Man tasted from the Tree of Knowledge did Woman, his experience of the Earth, turn for him into a temptress towards the earthly realm.

The great biblical picture of the Woman and the Fruit, the Tree and the Serpent, is one which is still repeatedly revisited even today. This is probably because modern consciousness with its downward outlook, otherwise no friend of pictures, believes that it has easy access to that particular picture. Yet in reality it could be the most difficult and cosmically most profound of all the great biblical pictures. There is a great danger of getting lost within the structure of this particular picture. Consequently, we have to be careful with an interpretation such as the following, to which even a cultivated and highly regarded artist of recent times has succumbed, an interpretation that confuses certain *effects* of the Fall with their *causes* and original character.

The interpretation runs like this: in Adam and Eve, after living long together in innocence, one day supposedly the snake of desire awoke, so that they were supposedly seized by the fire of a mad passion for each other, which passion supposedly led to their union, which, however, supposedly was not in the divine Creator's plan. We recall a recent painting depicting Adam kneeling in feverish desire before Eve who hands him the apple, while behind them the horrible Serpent raises its head... Today there are certainly many things like this as a consequence of the 'Fall'.[60] But to paint an image of the Fall itself along those lines misses the point, for the Fall still takes place in entirely different heights of consciousness, and—even though most modern artists possibly cannot portray it—things much more attractive would have had to appear before the still divine consciousness of primordial, paradisal Man in order to bring about his Fall.

In their myth of Prometheus, the ancient Greeks actually got much closer than this particular modern depiction to the *real* nature of that fire which was kindled in the human being by that force which, opposed to the divine, progressively replaced and suffocated the divine spark. Through the earthly nature of this fire, the human being increasingly succumbed to the forces of death working in the earthly element. Instead, the forces of his sensations, which he was meant to control, governed him.

Consequently, that emotional state came about which, in opposition to love, forces the human being to succumb to his lower nature. Every disorder between the sexes today, as Genesis 3:16 expresses very clearly, is a consequence of the biblical Fall. Only a kind of self-knowledge not stuck in such superficiality, but one that enters much deeper layers of consciousness, can really unlock the riddling picture of the biblical Fall.[61]

Genesis 3:7

We have already mentioned the image of nakedness and shame in another context. Only by eating from the Fruit of Knowledge does the human being awaken to the earthly element he carries inside himself. That is what Genesis wants to say with the image of nakedness and shame. The radiant Light which veiled and covered Man until then, now falls back from him.[62] The earthly world appears unveiled before him.

Genesis 3:8-14

The Temptation scene in the chapter on the Fall is followed by a climax of its pictorial language, when Man hears the voice of God again, Yahveh's voice 'walking in the Garden when the day had grown cool'—an evening wind was blowing. Then Man hears the Voice of the Divine in the same place where he can still hear it today if he goes deeply enough below day-consciousness, below those regions where he encounters the Tempter of mankind. In harsh daylight, the voices of the earthly realm so easily overwhelm those of the Divine within us. But when the day has gone to rest, the sounds of daily bustle have died down and a cool breath from above streams towards us, then when all has gone quiet the voices of the higher world can become audible again inside us. This episode in Genesis clearly shows us the depths of consciousness out of which the pictures of Genesis evolved, and it points to the necessary inner work with which we can find our way into them.

And then also the following becomes comprehensible. Man, shy and full of fear in his shame, hides from the Divine Voice within, accusing him. Man through whom the cosmic Word used to speak when he was still in harmony with and close to the Divine, calling all things and beings by their true divine Name, now misuses the word to devise and make excuses. In place of a sacred use of the Word (which is the exclusive usage in the Mind of the Divine Creator), the first unholy usage, the first *ab*-use of the word occurs.[63] Man in his alienation from his inner divinity, commits his first sin against the Word and its divine Essence. And together with the descent of Man himself, also the Word sinks more deeply into the earthly realm, until it fully arrives on Earth in the biblical story of the Tower of Babel and the ensuing confusion of languages.

This chapter, so rich in dramatic moments, concludes with the heart-rending picture of the Expulsion from Paradise by the cherub with the flaming sword, who then guards the future access to the Tree of Life. Man is protected from having his life in a way that might bind him for eternity to an Earth alienated from the higher worlds. That is the reason why death can still set man free from that same earthly element. In his book *Knowledge of the Higher Worlds; How is it Achieved?* Rudolf Steiner describes the path of the soul back into the light, out of her current state of restricted consciousness back to the light-filled heights from which it once descended. He describes the soul on its path encountering a spiritual being that denies anyone entry to the world of light who has not yet balanced out the effects of the Fall and who has yet to re-establish the lost equilibrium. Steiner calls this being the 'Guardian of the Threshold'—a term already used in earlier eso-teric literature[64]—the same being that each night during sleep denies the unprepared soul conscious entry into the world of Light, when it is gradually led towards its threshold. When the soul, however, in its nightly ascent manages a conscious encounter with this 'Guardian of the Threshold', it can gain most directly for itself the possibility to confirm everything that Genesis describes in pictures concerning the real stages of our descent. The soul will then find that these are real facts of consciousness, and that in these pictures an understanding appropriate for today can again open up.

6. Cain

Genesis 3:16

In a magnificent way the pictures in the chapter on the Fall also shed light on the riddle of womanhood. It concludes with a harrowing reference to the curse on woman, the curse of the sexes, which seems to run like a thread throughout human history. Whoever drew these pictures in such an impressive way for us in simple lapidary language, must surely have possessed a good knowledge of human history and was a master artist. But this is only one side of far-reaching questions. We should view the biblical pictures against a background so vast that above and beyond the curse, our ears can already discern again a higher and more encompassing blessing. From Eve succumbing to temptation and becoming the seductress of Man, the view swings back to Eve in Paradise before the Fall, where she still enjoyed a higher spiritual existence as the primordial cosmic female principle, still one with the divine in Yahveh. And our eyes turn from the primordial past to the future, alluded to in the blessed biblical words when Yahveh speaks to the Serpent, 'And I shall put enmity between you and the woman, and between your seed and her seed. He will bruise your head, and you will strike his heel' (Gen. 3:15).

The image of Eve before the Fall appears each time we look into the primordial past; an image of Mary, blessed among women, appears when we look into the future. It is not without profound significance for the future of mankind that it is again a woman, another Mary, Mary Magdalene, who reaches the grave first, 'early, when it was still dark', and sees the Risen One. Woman, who became earthly later than Man, goes before him on his way to the spiritual world. Here, too, the appearance of Christ on Earth signifies a turning point for human evolution. Early ecclesiastical hymns already point to the fact that in 'Ave Maria' we find the inversion of 'Eva', Eve. With all this we can learn to think of Eve not just in connection with the Serpent, the seduction and the Fall, but to realize again the original nobility and majesty of her name.[65]

With regard to Eve and her nature before the Fall, Genesis narrates little, apart from the allusion in the name YHVH, and apart from one dark and mysterious passage at the beginning of Chapter 4 that mentions Cain's birth. Eve speaks the mysterious words,[66] 'I gained

Yahweh as my husband'.[67] According to this, Cain would in fact not be the son of Adam, but of much higher descent, super-humanly begotten by the power of the Divine Creator even before the Fall. Only Abel could then be called a true child of Man, a son of Adam and Eve. Abel, descendant of the first human couple that committed sin, inherited the Fall, containing it so to speak within his heredity (as far as one can apply this expression taken from the modern physical world to the then much more spiritual conditions), whereas Cain, sinless and divine, commits the Fall out of himself. Indeed, we can even feel that Cain's deed *is* the real Fall into sin, the actualization in an already more earthly sphere of that which had its prelude in higher regions.

The key to the picture of sheep and crops, of Abel the shepherd and Cain the arable farmer, can be found in what is said about the characteristics of animal and plant in the primordial creation. Abel is more inclined to feelings for what is above the earth, Cain more to the life of the Earth; his own life-forces are very strong. Abel is the weaker from the very beginning, Cain the strong, super-powerful one whose forces remain unbroken even after his fall. This meaning already lies in their names: Abel, Heb. *hebel*, actually means a 'breath of wind'—that which is blown away into nothingness; Cain however—from the Hebrew root $\sqrt{q\text{-}n\text{-}h}$ expressing 'creative potential' or 'creative capability'— means 'strong expert', 'creative artist', one who carries strong creative qualities within himself.[68] Abel, perhaps: the one who is blown into nothingness; Cain: the one who creates out of nothing. Cain acts solely out of the impulses of his earthly 'I' (in which, even when in error, a higher Divine 'I' is reflected); Abel has not even brought such an 'I' to its initial unfolding. He is beyond sin, because the 'I', the prerequisite for sinning, for setting oneself apart, still does not exist in him. Cain is too strongly in his earthly 'I' to be able to remain within the Divine. Abel longs too strongly for the Divine, airy element to be able to prevail in the earthly realm.

Genesis 4:3-5

How one-sided each of the two is, finds its expression in the image of the sacrificial smoke: the smoke of Abel's sacrifice rises straight up to Heaven, whereas that of Cain remains below on the Earth. In Cain lives an innate, strong power which he draws from his closeness to—and direct descent from—the Divine. But by applying it within the earthly realm, by turning his divine 'I' into an earthly 'I', he loads guilt on himself.

Genesis 4:6-9

He who guarded and kept the Divine within himself now turns away from it, slaying his step-brother in whom he still perceives the Divine, though in such a way that he, Cain, no longer strongly feels it.

We do not gain a point of entry into this picture if we regard the event as a merely physical one (which, of course, it is not; here everything still has to be thought of as happening in higher realms), but only if we step down into depths of our consciousness where we can see the whole relationship between Cain and Abel in our own inner life; down into depths of self-knowledge where we encounter within our own 'I' the inner Cain who is still prepared to slay his brother, to slay that aspect in our soul that strives for the Divine. All human conflict, as history records it, leads us back to this deeply ingrained conflict within human nature, back to the Cain-nature within man.[69] Not as two individual personalities, similar to two modern physical people, but as two archetypes of humanity, two beings, Cain and Abel appear before our inner vision, archetypes which people still carry within themselves, though some of us might lean more towards the one, others more towards the other archetype. In the Abel-personality lives our non-personal aspect, which has not yet really attained the personal 'I'; in the Cain personality lives the power of the personal 'I'. Through the Cain-nature the way leads up to the super-personal, where the human 'I' reconnects with the divine Creative Will. In Christ is achieved this super-personal level, though only having going through the personal stage.

Genesis 4:10-16

Restless and cursed, Cain errs from life to life (which is the deeper meaning of the biblical image), until he who didn't know how to die, died in the Crucified One. The 'I' that cannot be lost, the part of us that cannot die, the part that man has to carry from life to life—that is the mark which Yahveh stamps on Cain's forehead. The death on Golgotha is the redemption of Cain and of the Cain-nature in man. The soil of the Earth spoiled with the blood of fratricide is washed clean of all sin by the holy drops of blood.

By the Christ's redeeming Deed—provided the human 'I' unites itself with it—our inner Cain-nature can be overcome and transformed. The Crucified-Risen One leads us back to the Cain before the Fall, the strong human-divine ancestor of our race. Adam was but the human ancestor, in whom universal humanity lived but not yet

the fully developed human 'I'. The Hebrew word *adam* is hardly anywhere in the Bible a particular name. Usually it simply means the
'human being'. Cain, however, is the strong ancestor of an 'I'-bearing
human race, the first fully conscious carrier of a human 'I'. For a deeper
contemplation, Cain almost blends with Adam, as the 'I'-bearing male
aspect of Adam the human being, whereas Abel carries female traces,
traces of Eve. The strong, solar force of the 'I' lives in Cain's nature,
whereas in Abel a lunar-like, female nature is developed. Out of the
strong powers of his Sun-'I', Cain can still hear the divine Voice even
after the terrible, heinous deed he fearlessly takes upon himself.

Genesis 4:17-24

Cain, who carries within himself these strong forces of personality, becomes the ancestor of a strong human race. Carriers of artistic impulses, people who were the first to work with artistic skill the
resisting earthly matter, keepers of secret wisdom, stem from the race
of Cain. Genesis names them, and right into the sounds of those names
we can recognize the greatness and uniqueness that lives in the race
of Cain: Jubal the musician and master of musical instruments; Tubal-Cain the craftsman with ores and metals. Already in their sounds
they tells us of the secret of their beings and their polar-opposite activities. Into all areas of spiritual and physical creativity, the artistry of the
sons of Cain diverges. Those descendants of Cain are strong, artistic,
creative people, great personalities who can work the spiritual right
into earthly matter.[70]

Not without a certain hidden allusion is it said later about the master-builder of Solomon's temple (1Kings 7:14), similar to Tubal-Cain in
Genesis, that he was a 'master in ore', 'gifted to forge all kinds of bronze
work'. Particularly because they work so strongly into earthly matter,
the forces living in the descendants of Cain are of the highest nature.

When we look back to earlier human cultures, we find in Ancient
India a predominance of those other forces that have not yet reached
that point, keeping themselves more to spiritual concerns. They are the
other forces, the lunar forces of the race of Abel-Seth that are at work
in Ancient India. Only in Iran [Ancient Persia], Zarathustra brings a
solar impulse giving rise to a Sun-culture, and here for the first time,
again in Asia, we find a transformation of the Earth out of the spiritual
inspiration.

Today's contemporary Western culture would not be possible
without the forces of the race of Cain. The future definitely belongs

to Cain-people, but first the curse of the race of Cain needs to be expunged by the deed of Christ. Human Cain-nature has to first die in Christ. Here lie the great spiritual tasks of the present and the future. And for the very reason that the power of the race of Cain lies in the personality, the 'I'-forces, the will-forces, this race cannot simply be passively redeemed by the deed of Christ. It needs consciously to take in that Christ-impulse with the forces of this personality, this will, this 'I'. Only then will Cain-people be able to find their way out of the land of Nod (= 'need'),[71] out of the harsh earthly necessities into which he has banished himself from the countenance of Yahveh; only then will he be able in future to find his way back into the realms of Light from whence he came, and meet his great ancestor there as he was before the Fall.

Genesis 4:25

The race of Cain is in the most eminent sense the race of the future, whereas Abel is the representative of that substance of humanity that was incapable of living. He is replaced by the same Seth who, according to the legend, took the three seeds from the Tree of Life and put them in Adam's grave. So there was not a race of Abel that would have formed within mankind an opposite to the race of Cain. Instead the race of Seth stepped in, which we can call the race of Abel-Seth as far as Abel-forces live within it—for still today, the Cain personality and the Abel personality are both spiritually present among mankind.

Genesis 4:26

For the evolution of human consciousness, the last sentence of the chapter on Cain is still relevant, 'At that time they started to proclaim the name of Yahveh in religious rites.'[72] This sentence leads us right into the beginnings of religion, the beginnings of religious cult in humanity. For an earlier humanity, for paradisal Man, such religion, such ritual was unnecessary, because he was still directly close to the Divine. This existed for him in a similar way as all the objects of the sense world exist for us today. So Man before the Fall was still aware of living among the Beings of the spiritual world. It would not have made any sense to 'preach' to him about what he saw and among whom he lived. Only gradually did the Fall bring about a change, and man sank from realms of light ever more deeply to Earth, increasingly losing his ability to see essential things concerning the spiritual world and to communicate with it. Cain could still cultivate a dialogue even after his fall.

Deep in his heart man longs to reunite with what he lost in gaining consciousness. This longing brought about a religious striving that in the human being's primordial time was expressed in the ritual element. It is in the religious rites where man seeks to carry cosmic rhythms back into earthly life, rhythms from which he had alienated himself after the Fall, the alienation of the earthly from the cosmic. Of course, we must not associate the Genesis story too closely with current earthly conditions. Everything was still completely different and pre-earthly. These expressions are only pictures which, borrowed from today's earthly conditions, always refer to events happening in yet much higher regions.

7. The Rainbow

In the beginning of evolution, man and cosmos, the human being and the Earth, were not separated as today, but still much more closely interwoven and still mutually affecting one another much more strongly than today. A final resonance of this primordial fact is contained in the story of the Deluge [Germ. *Sündflut*, literally 'flood of sin']. This term is well chosen and should not be replaced by alternative expressions or variations in spelling that might obscure its meaning. This catastrophe of the Great Flood brings the effects of the Fall to completion, for only now, after the Flood, does the human being arrive into the solid earthly conditions as we know them today. Only Noah's rainbow finally bridges the gap between the events of Genesis still lying in higher regions and those happening on the dense earth.

The account of the biblical Flood—like the many flood tales worldwide—certainly reflects human memories of certain primordial catastrophes that changed the surface of the Earth until it slowly gained its current form. Yet we should not think of those waters of the Great Flood only in terms of what finally really became earthly water. The picture of those waters also represents what in the wake of the Fall affected the human being's astral nature, stirring and whirling around his entire soul life (just as the primordial waters at the beginning of the first creation were connected to the soul-life of what becomes primordial Man). Fire catastrophes and water catastrophes accompany outwardly what inner vision reveals as uncontrollable fires of passion, uncontrollable floods of passion. Man still living in the supersensory can only escape the overpowering rising tide of his passions by increasingly hardening his bodily nature. He rescues himself into that solid body made of earthly matter which he carries today. It is this solid body—at first still carried by primordial waters, finally swimming on the supersensory ocean of passion—which we behold in Genesis in the picture of the Ark.[73]

Only in rough sketches is it intended to look at the different pictures in the story of the Flood. It can be understood that on entering a more solid bodily form, the human being takes the animals with him; out of himself he progressively excludes the animal qualities he used to carry inside himself. The earthly mountain top is significant for the transition from the super-earthly heights into the depths of Earth.

On Mount Ararat, the Ark first descends. The mountain-tops are the first to look out over the retreating waters of the Flood. In a similar way, in the Indian account of the Flood, it is the mountains of the Himalayas where Manu's ship first lands.[74] The earthly mountain with its springs and brooks was a picture helping us connect with the supersensory world, paradisal realms of Light and the source of its rivers. The image of the mountain appears where we finally reach firm land after the Flood. The Ark lands on the top of the mountain. On the mountain man's acquaintance with the solid earth begins.

With regard to this earth, more than just something material we have to learn to see through to the spirit. In the waters of the Flood we can see the 'Waters of Death', just as in the source of the rivers of Paradise we recognized the 'Waters of Life'. To the biblical history of creation we beheld a number of the evolutionary stages of the Earth element. Out of the first earthly element (*erets*) as the primordial opposite of that which is above, heavenly and Sun-like (*shamayim*) through the streaming in of light and of cosmic life, the Light-Earth, the Living Earth, the growing Paradise Earth is created. Its opposite is the 'dust of the Earth' which Yahveh then impresses into the human being. All this is still supersensory. We only come into contact with the really dense Earth after the Flood. What afterwards exists as dense Earth, forms a kind of balance between the opposites, between which evolution had progressed. On this Earth that balance is to be realized, of which Genesis 8:21f. speaks: 'I will not again curse the ground any more for man's sake... While the earth remains, seedtime and harvest, cold and heat, summer and winter, day and night shall not cease.' On and within the Earth, the Divine Itself shall become earthly. God Himself shall bind Himself with the earthly element, and by dwelling for three days in the depths of Earth and Death, He will call forth what is dying to new life. Through the Christ, earthly matter itself will be transformed again into spirit.

Genesis 8:7-12
In passing, we see in our imagination two characteristic, striking pictures in Genesis, the raven and the dove, who flutter to and fro as messengers between the past Earth and the future Earth, between Death overcome and Life newly-sprouting. The olive leaf, in itself a picture of the circulating life-juices permeating earthly existence and earthly growth, is a symbol of all that heals and blesses earthly existence. It gives new strength to that which is dying. As messenger and giver of

life we recognize the dove with the olive leaf. As resounding echoes of early Mystery images, the raven and the dove appear in fairy tales and legends. To Snow White [of the Grimms' fairy-tale of that name], slumbering in her glass coffin between death and re-awakening, the raven and dove appear, as well as the owl. Like Snow White's coffin, the Ark, too, preserves the seeds of life outlasting death and destruction. Like the Ark, the coffin is seen as a picture from a spiritual perspective, as the connection to the human physical body. The Gk. word σαρξ, *sarx* which lies behind the Germ. word *Sarg* ('coffin'), signifies the physical-bodily substance.

Genesis 9:8-17

The eloquent imagination of the Flood culminates in the profound image of the rainbow of the new covenant. Like a bridge Noah's gleaming rainbow arches between the still super-earthly and the entirely earthly part of Genesis, it closes one chapter of the Bible, and a new one begins.

Only after the Flood, after the separation of water, air and dense earth as we know them today, the physical conditions for the appearance of a rainbow were provided. Hence Noah's rainbow has a concrete, physically real meaning. It coincides with the solidification of the earthly realm and with the beginning of the current atmospheric conditions on Earth. But that only touches on the outward aspect of the rainbow. It does not say anything yet about what the rainbow can say to us as a meaningful symbol of the spiritual script of the cosmos. The rainbow is connected to the solidifying process of earthly existence, but only to the extent to which this earthly denseness itself is at once overcome again, changed into a mere phenomenon of the spirit. Goethe's *Theory of Colours* shows us how the spiritual trinity, light, opaqueness, darkness, prepares the conditions for the appearance of colours. The ancient Indian still knew how this trinity like a spiritual prism brings about all the material phenomena of the world.[75] By experiencing in a rainbow, how light, opaque and dark create the shimmering colour scale, we discover the innermost Mystery of all material existence. We recognize how out of that spiritual trinity the whole colourful veil of the sensory world is woven. Matter is transformed for us into spirit again when we begin to understand the language of the rainbow.

We are looking here at the great Being Who, by taking all earthly existence on his shoulders, transforms all matter into spirit, and death itself into life. Hence Noah's rainbow contains a promise of Christ, and at the very moment the conditions for our current, densely-material earth-existence first evolve, the Christ-force is announced. This spiritually balances out and transcends all solidified earth existence, raising the whole material world to the spirit, transforming it into spirit. And so, at the moment when one cycle of the Earth comes to an end and a new one begins, the rainbow appears as a promise of the future. In this symbol of the future, once more the primordial past is contained, for in the colours live deeds of light. In the light the flowing wisdom of the world, in its wisdom the essence of the creative cosmic forces. The moment the Earth, as we currently see it today, becomes dense, the creative Mystery of all earthly existence speaks to human beings in the rainbow from the arching heavens above.

After the cycle of creation has been leading us down from the primordial light into earthly opaqueness and darkness, now in the picture of the seven colours of the rainbow, once more the formative forces of the World-Creator appear to us, which in the beginning of the primordial creation, at the great altar of cosmic sacrifice, stood before the spirit eye in the picture of the Seven Lights.[76]

II.

ZARATHUSTRA

(Translated by Maren & Alan Stott)

Introduction to Beckh's *Zarathustra*

Hermann Beckh's small book *Zarathustra* was published by the Verlag der Christengemeinschaft in 1927 as part of their series *Christus aller Erde*, Band 24. The subject had scarcely been broached in the previous five years of The Christian Community and the whole area was little known at large in comparison with Indian or Egyptian studies in Europe. Fortunately Beckh had acquired a mastery of Avestan while working as Professor of Oriental Languages in Berlin, a very rare skill indeed. Coupled with this was the fact that both Beckh and Friedrich Rittelmeyer had a knowledgeable interest in Nietzsche's *Zarathustra*, which for many lay readers constituted a point of access to the subject. Beckh had made profound studies, and was still ardently pursuing, the role of Zarathustra in the birth of Jesus and the story of the Magi in Matthew's Gospel. The result was a book in three sections: first on Nietzsche, then the encounter with the Christian Mystery as introduced by Rudolf Steiner and finally on the text of the Zend-Avesta itself.

With each of the three sections Beckh was faced with an increasingly difficult task. One can say that the first account represents an address to a broad readership, a kind of public lecture; the second is addressed more to those familiar with Rudolf Steiner's lectures, especially on the Gospels; the third is ground for the author to enter previously unknown realms of esoteric knowledge. That this latter area, the content of the Zend-Avesta itself, was particularly meaningful to Beckh is borne out by the fact that his substantial article, Zarathustra, for the monthly *Die Drei* (January 1926) largely put aside *Thus Spake Zarathustra* and what had become recognized, one might say, as orthodox anthroposophy. It is very evident that Beckh wanted to push hard against the conventional margins and to find an entirely independent vision that leads from the ancient text, through Christ, and on into the future.

Here the middle section acts as a staging ground for the new discoveries to be found in the original language. Beckh sets out the generally accepted wisdom regarding the Tree of Life and the Tree of Knowledge as the path to the Solomon Jesus child; the introduction of the Magi leads to the Star of Zarathustra and the Mystery traditions of Hermes and Moses. But the author is insistent that these traditions, going back to earliest Egyptian circumstances, represent the ongoing legacy of a wisdom of the stars leading to the future recorded in Rev. 22:16. It is only towards the end of the section that Beckh firmly turns to Sirius as the central Imagination for the Star of the Magi, the Star of Zarathustra (the 'Golden Star'), the Blazing Star that leads on to Initiation.

In the background here one can simply accept that the 1920s in Germany saw a vast expansion of interest in astrology, quickly catching up with the earlier British forerunning: a simple point of cultural history that has been well documented over the last 50 years. Equally, it is difficult to resist the view that Hermann Beckh aided by Günther Wachsmuth were hard at work laying the foundations of a new astrosophy during this period, to be developed by Elisabeth Vreede from 1927. It was precisely because Beckh had the closest relationship to the stars that he was asked in 1927 to write a full length study of The Gospel of St Mark in reply to the materialist Arthur Drews' *Das Markus Evangelium* (1920) subtitled 'as evidence against the historical Jesus'. Drews had argued that Mark's Gospel was led by a mythological Sun-god who travelled three times around the astrological zodiac during the period of Christ's ministry. Beckh was in the best position to reply.

This background, however, simply detracts from Hermann Beckh's growing vision in 1926-27. At this time the Anthroposophical Society and The Christian Community had inherited Rudolf Steiner's lectures, including those which spoke about Sirius. An analysis of these references shows that Steiner had made six clear points:

- Steiner pointed to the rising of Sirius in that period as a prime example of an era when people could still relate their daily activities to the course of the heavens.[77]
- During the winter series of lectures in Dornach, 1910-11, the rising of Sirius was depicted as being indicative of the annual Nile floods, bringing renewed fertility, but also as a marker of historical epochs—the Sothic periods of some 1,400 years.[78]
- A further public lecture in Berlin two years later made it clear that the old Egyptian observation of Sirius was illustrative of a relationship to 'the laws of heaven' and should be understood as a last vestige of clairvoyance in the evolution of consciousness.[79]
- In the second series of the lecture *Karmic Relationships*, Rudolf Steiner explained that what we perceive as Sirius and other stars is a representation of 'colonies of spiritual beings'.[80]
- When Sirius, the Dog Star, was visible in the Sign of Cancer, the ancient Egyptians knew that the Sun would shortly enter this

Sign and that its rays would charm forth all that the flooding of the Nile bestowed upon the soil. *They said: 'Sirius is the Watcher; it is he who tells us what is to come.'*[81]

- The [ancient Egyptian] initiation itself was undertaken by a particularly high initiate. Much else was still done there according to prescribed rules. Such a sleep was something other than an ordinary sleep. All that remained was the physical body in the so-called coffin, and the etheric body and astral body came out; so it was a kind of death. This was necessary in order to free the etheric body, for only then can the astral body be pressed into the etheric body. Three and a half days this condition lasted. When the novice was then redirected to the physical body by the initiator, he was imprinted with one last formula with which he woke up. These were the words: *'Eli, Eli, lama sabachthani!'*, that is, 'My God, my God, how have you glorified me!' At the same time, a certain star, in the Egyptian initiation of Sirius, appeared to him. Now he had become a new person.[82]

When Beckh composed Zarathustra for *Christus aller Erde* he had a good working relationship with both the publisher Rudolf Geering in Basel, who was shortly to issue Beckh's major studies on Mark's Gospel and John's Gospel and with Günther Wachsmuth, the editor of Gäa-Sophia, also publishing articles by Beckh. Thanks to the recent research of Thomas Meyer we now know that both leading personalities had been members of Steiner's ritual order Mystica Æterna between 1906 and 1914. It is not known at the time of writing whether Beckh was also a member, yet it is a reasonable inference from his work that he had joined a Masonic Lodge while in Friedrich-Wilhelms University, Berlin, as a senior member of staff and proceeded, after 1912, to join Mystica Æterna. However this might be, whether it was from first-hand experience or from conversations with Geering and Wachsmuth, in all probability Beckh knew that the 1° ritual of Mystica Æterna led the candidate to a meeting with the guiding star Sirius:

> I come from the Universe, from the Dog-Star. I met this soul on my way here from the north. It has freed itself from its body. It has arrived at the portal of death. Listen now, thou soul, to the spirit which will and can lead thee to thy true human dignity...[83]

Here Sirius, played by Marie von Sivers, takes up the role of the angelic guide Raphael as found in the traditional Rose-Croix 18° rituals.[84]

Sirius, the 'Blazing Star' of Freemasonry, leads the candidate forward to initiation, something that was done quite literally in the ritual.

When Beckh was invited by Friedrich Rittelmeyer on behalf of the *Verlag der Christengemeinschaft* and by the editors of *Die Drei* to write about Zarathustra, he found that there was a great moment of destiny. He was the only person who could quote from the *Zend-Avesta* (transliterated) and the only person who had an Imaginative grasp of Sirius. He did not hesitate to outline the compelling vision of Sirius in its relationship with Orion and Gemini, which can be read in the following pages, and thereby inaugurate an entirely new stage in the dramatic development of cosmic Christianity.

N.F.

Foreword

In the three chapters of this work is mirrored the destined relationship the author experienced towards the concept of Zarathustra during three phases of his life, at first inspired by Friedrich Nietzsche [1844-1900], later from the Avestan philology, and finally through the spiritual research of Rudolf Steiner [1861-1925]. In each of these three life-phases Zarathustra met him in a different form. Out of Steiner's spiritual research the relationship of Zarathustra to the Christ-event and Christ's earthly leadership of humanity first became decisively clear for him. Out of this there arose at the same time the higher synthesis of those three figures of Zarathustra, especially the bridge from the Zarathustra of primordial time of the Avesta, but also to Nietzsche's *Thus Spoke Zarathustra*.[85] The mystery of Nietzsche, so deeply connected to the spiritual development of our age, appeared through this in a new and surprising light. Several sayings of Nietzsche, like the one of 'eternal return', received a new meaning not yet clearly recognized even by Nietzsche himself, pointing towards the Christ-event. In individual sections of the presentation one can feel how Zarathustra's concept of the return and of the great cycles of time of humanity in the light of the future of the Earth through Christ lights up before us as the great concept of the cosmic New Year.

Stuttgart, Advent 1925
Hermann Beckh

1. Zarathustra in the Present Age

Thus Spoke Zarathustra is today already somewhat forgotten. From the end of the nineteenth century it has steered the thoughts of the age towards the high aims of humanity, towards the questions of humanity's development and future. But like no other writing of Friedrich Nietzsche, the book of the hermit of Sils-Maria has awoken on the one hand an uncritical enthusiasm, and on the other hand, off-hand and narrow-minded dismissal. The one thing most people, friends and opponents, agree is that the name *Zarathustra* as used here is really only used as a poetic idea or whim, as a poetic reflection of the author, who possessed no real relationship to the figure of the great teacher of humanity and lawgiver of ancient Persia.

Thus judges the 'day' thinking of the everyday, surface consciousness. And in a certain trivial sense, this view is also right. But 'the world is more profound than the day thinks' [Nietzsche]. This sentence especially applies to the depths of the human being. The human being also possesses nightly, starry depths, of which the 'day would never have thought'. These depths Nietzsche only divined. Into them from time to time in twilight conditions of the soul, in that through his illness a displacement of the threshold of consciousness took place, a broken ray of inspiration fell. For the path of research, which through methodical strengthening of the soul—as Rudolf Steiner has shown in his book *Knowledge of the Higher Worlds: How is it Attained?* [GA 10]—leads in a healthy manner into those depths, was still closed for Nietzsche, who for the age was born premature. He, the lonely thinker of Sils-Maria, broke down from a knowledge for which his soul-organs—and those of his physical body—could not withstand. His illness expresses that the nocturnal treasures of the depths of the soul could not safely be brought to the shore of day-consciousness.

In those hidden starry depths of his nature, the human being and his consciousness is connected to the 'widths of space and the depths of time'. There he is really united with everything great and all the great ones of the past, also with much that rests in the future. In particular the discrepancy between these pictures and much that fills the consciousness of the present, causes the many difficulties of the soul of our present age. In those depths of the soul *Zarathustra* is more than a name that is then taken up arbitrarily with some whim of the day-consciousness and is set up somewhere. In these depths of soul in which the highest of all beings, the cosmic-earthly being of *Christ* is found, there also exists all those personalities of the past and the future who in their collaboration with Christ enable the tangible recognition of the *tremendous fact of Christ as the meaning of world-history.* There the soul carries out quite real dialogues even with Krishna, Buddha, with Moses and Elijah, with Solomon, Hiram, with Plato and Aristotle.

At this level the soul also lives together with the spirit-personality of the great lawgiver of primordial times, the first one who spoke to human-ity in a still child-like primordial time of the *meaning of the Earth,* of the development in the struggle between light and darkness, of personality, the education of the will and the freedom of the will. *Zarathustra* is the first who teaches the recognition of good and evil. He is also the first one who points towards Christ and the Christened future of the Earth, the proclaimer of the great cosmic-year and the return of all things. Here the soul finds Zarathustra in his full living reality, of whom we possess in books and outer documents only such a questionable tradition.

It was certainly only a reflection of this reality that shone in Nietzsche's soul over which the shadows of the approaching night already hovered. Even in this reflection, this shadow-picture, however, there still lived a remnant of reality which is not perceived by those who in *Thus Spoke Zarathustra* see only arbitrariness and poetic whim, if not even a megalomanic, as prophet of mental disturbance. We know something of a late, decadent clairvoyance reaching into our days, experienced here and there by country people, appears as the phantom of the 'midday woman' with her painful questioning. This phenome-non relates to the ancient Egyptian sphinx and the grand figure of the *Guardian of the Threshold,* who in those long-past initiations placed the first questions to the neophyte. In this kind of way what entered shad-ow-like and ghostly into the consciousness of the hermit of Sils-Maria, wandering lonely in the mountains of the Oberengadin on a day when he was particularly susceptible relates to that which to a higher spiri-tual vision is revealed as the full living reality of Zarathustra. Nietzsche himself spoke of how the first lightning-flash of the Zarathustra-con-cept lit up in him during such an excursion in the Oberengadin at the Lake Silvaplana 'at a mighty towering rock, not far from Surlei'.*

Spiritual science, anthroposophy, teaches us to differentiate on the one hand such uncontrolled impressions, as it were, coming over the

---

*Nietzsche, *Ecco homo* (written 1888), ed. G. Colli and M. Montinari, *Studi-enkritische Ausgabe* Bd. 6, Munich 1988, p. 335. The narrative here relates to Nietzsche's experience not far from Surlei in the summer of 1881.

soul, from full, genuine spiritual vision. Yet on the other hand it points to the partly true content that can be contained in such chaotic soul-experience, and was undoubtedly contained in what Nietzsche in his loneliness experienced with the figure of Zarathustra. Such a modern spirit-vision can today still find the vision of Friedrich Nietzsche, walking lonely on the mountain path, behind whom the walking shadow of Zarathustra in uncertain outlines, phantom-like becomes, visible, and brings that spirit-vision to life in himself.

*

With all this, it is in no way clear and how far true Zarathustra contents and genuine Zarathustrian spirit are contained in Nietzsche's *Thus Spoke Zarathustra*. Nietzsche himself was conscious of writing his *Zarathustra* out of the need, the moods and longings of another, new time. And yet the nebulous description, but yet to a certain degree real, vision of Zarathustra has worked into the way he wrote. With the whole question there is still one circumstance of a very essential significance, which a merely philological view does not see, the differentiation of a later Zarathustra from the one of primordial time. For the philologists, Zarathustra exists only for the more or less distant inspirer of the *Avesta* (Zendavesta), the bible of the ancient Iranians. This has been preserved in excerpts,[86] or rather its earliest parts, what are called the *Gathas* (songs, mantric verses). This *Avesta*, one of the most beautiful and important religious documents of humanity, is certainly an old though not a really ancient document of the Aryans. Some researchers believe its oldest parts and thereby the age of Zarathustra himself should be placed around the first half of the first millennium before Christ. However, already the high antiquity of the language of the Gatha-Avesta, which is close to the Indian Rig-Veda, speaks for a higher age. It seems to point us at least to Vedic times, that is, into the second millennium before Christ. But even then, the author or inspirer of that oldest part of the Avesta is still not the first Zarathustra of which spiritual research tells, but a later carrier of the name, who in a much later age renewed ancient Zarathustra-impulses. In the memory of humanity still something continued to live of that primal Zarathustra (as in general in times of earlier human consciousness, especially the memory was something completely different than today. It preserved still clear connections with the primordial age of humanity and the Earth). In his writing 'From Isis and Osiris' (ed. Parthey, 81), the Greek historian Plutarch[87] mentions the 'magician Zoroaster' (Zoroaster is the later Greek name for the Zarathustra of the Avesta) who lived five thousand years before the Trojan War. This would transpose—and spiritual science confirms this statement—the primal Zarathustra to a time long before historical time, c. 6000 BC.

A philologist who questions 'How does Nietzsche's book stand to the true Zarathustra?' will simply stick to the Avesta. If he does not find any traces that make sense for him, then he will take *Thus Spoke Zarathustra* merely as a poetic work, or will possibly dismiss it as the expression of an overwrought brain. And indeed in the Avesta one will not in fact find any essential, direct meeting point with Nietzsche appearing on the surface. One will not find much more with such research than that the words 'Thus spoke Zarathustra', or 'So spoke Zarathustra' (*aat aokhta Zarathushtro*), really do appear here and there in the Avesta (for example, Yasna 10, 17, Yasht 1, 5), but nowhere so characteristically and emphatically as with Nietzsche, always at the beginning of a section and not as with Nietzsche at the end. And, of course, one would also find that certain virtues that lift Nietzsche's Zarathustra so high, especially truthfulness and a readiness to defend truth and goodness, are also valued in the Avesta. Yet character and moods are so different in the Avesta from Nietzsche's *Zarathustra* that one cannot feel anything in common.

But this only shows that as long as we remain standing merely on the philological ground of Avesta research we will not reach the essential nature of the whole question. We reach this decisive matter only by raising ourselves from the Zarathustra of the Avesta to the primal Zarathustra. That later Zarathustra who inspired the Gathas was not that being who so strangely entered the consciousness the hermit of Sils-Maria, but that tremendous human figure of the primal Zarathustra who, over-towering and overshadowing the later Zarathustra, cannot be approached by any philologist, but only through spiritual research. And only from him do we find access to the significant mystery of Friedrich Nietzsche, which is such a question of consciousness for all of humanity of the present age.

***

If in the prescribed way we return to the first Zarathustra, we will initially find something of the true spirit of Zarathustra in the greatness of the *concept of humanity*, as it is illuminated by Nietzsche. This concept of humanity does not light up in the dreaming Indian,[88] living completely in the primordial blossoming of his Mysteries, in the paradisal heights of humanity's primordial childhood. But in the primordial Persian Zarathustra this concept of humanity lights up for the first time and with it the fully mature *age of the human personality*. It is deeply founded in Nietzsche's whole being, that he feels much more drawn to this primordial Persian spirit, to the greatness of this fully human and masculine personality of Zarathustra than to the early Indian spirit. This Indian spirit in its later time, in the time of Buddha (who is much later than the first Zarathustra), allows everything human and of humanity generally to dissolve into the impersonal element.

The figure of the primal Zarathustra means for human history in actual fact the *birth of the will* and the *birth of personality*, of the strong masculine ego-imbued, earthly personality. Something of this echoes in Nietzsche's *Zarathustra*, although with different emphases of soul. And with Zarathustra this will is a *will for the future*, the future of humanity with the Christ. This is even mightily expressed in the Avesta, in the prophecy of Christ[89] that points towards this future as a future of *the free will*, of the *sovereignty* in the *will*, 'when the living Conqueror of Death comes and through the will advances the world *through the will*'. Already for language and its development, it means something tremendous that here a word exists for the word 'will' ([Avestan] *vasna*), for which one does not find a completely corresponding expression, for example, in Indian [Sanskrit], basically not even in Latin and Greek.

And thus in Nietzsche's *Thus Spoke Zarathustra* we find tremendous words, true words of the primal Zarathustra, referring to the will. One of the most tremendous (in the 'The Grave-Song'[90]) we also find with him the connection with the will and the overcoming of the grave, resurrection (although thereby he is still far removed from the Christ-reality of resurrection):

> Yes, something invulnerable, unburiable, is within me, something that explodes rock: that is *my will*. Silently it strides and unchanging through the years…
>
> In you that also lives on what is unredeemed from my youth; and as life and youth you sit here hopeful upon yellow grave-ruins.
>
> Yes, you are still for me the demolisher of every grave: hail to thee, my will! And only where there are graves are there resurrections—

Some things here can even remind us of the prophecy concerning Christ in the Avesta. And as we find in the latter, we also find in Nietzsche's *Zarathustra* the connection of will-impulse and [R. Steiner's] *The Philosophy of Freedom*.

Willing liberates: that is the true teaching of will and freedom—thus does Zarathustra teach it to you.[91]

A piece of self-knowledge lies in the previous sentence:

All that is sentient suffers through me and is in prisons: but my willing always comes to me as my liberator and joy-bringer.[92]

To this the word of the Lion:

'Thou shalt' is the name of the great dragon. But the spirit of the lion says 'I will'.[93]
    To redeem what is past in human beings, and to re-create all 'It was' until the will speaks: 'But thus I willed it! Thus shall I will it—' —This I called redemption …[94]

And with all this the tragedy of Friedrich Nietzsche is only that he has this will of personality, this will for the future, which with Zarathustra is clearly a *future with Christ,* in such a way that he closes himself off from all this towards [recognizing] the *Christ*-impulse, that he turns *against* the Christ, where in the deepest ground of the soul *the Christ* would like to open his gaze towards the future of humanity. How closely words approach this Christ-impulse *subconsciously* is shown in the following extract from explanatory notes to *Thus Spoke Zarathustra* in the literary estate:

Each time the middle, when the *will for the future* arises: the greatest event is at hand! …
    Around the *middle of the track* there stands the *Übermensch**

How fitting it would be here, in place of what Nietzsche has given in the *Übermensch,* but in a distorted picture, an unclear concept not completely thought through, to put the right concept in the sense of Christ. Nietzsche was still unable in his day-consciousness to attain true Imagination in its purity; only broken rays shone into his consciousness, which itself eventually broke through the 'abundance of visions'.

***

And similarly there also appears broken and darkened with Nietzsche the other great thought, the thought of *eternal return,* or *recurrence,* the 'return of all things'.[95] We shall not enter into all the objections that already arise from the aspect of mathematics against Nietzsche's

---

*Friedrich Nietzsches Werke, Naumann, Leipzig 1904, 14. 263.

thought of the 'return of the same' in tremendous, inconceivable periods of time, a 'monster of a Great year'. And yet there stands behind
this non-thought of Nietzsche a genuine Zarathustra-thought, the great
Zarathustra vision of the future of humanity, but which in its reality is
much clearer and certain and does not know anything of a 'return of
the same', which speaks of periodical world-renewal in long periods
but which are precise and clearly surveyable. In all Zarathustra proc-
lamations there lies the great Zarathustra-concept of time, the concept
of the great human cycle of time and cosmic rhythms of time for which
the rhythmic cycle of the year is the small picture. In the section concerning the first Zarathustra, we shall get to know the great year, the
cosmic year of Zarathustra, which is something completely different
from Nietzsche's 'monster of a great year'.[96]

Nevertheless, with all this Nietzsche divined a true vision of
Zarathustra. And in many things what Nietzsche's Zarathustra says
so beautifully and in a concentrated mood about the return and eternal recurrence, concerning the 'nuptial/ wedding ring of rings', the
'ring of return', there lies a genuine Zarathustrian spirit. The concept
of eternity which nevertheless unites with *space* and *time* is the great
thing with Nietzsche *and Zarathustra* (the real Zarathustra). 'For I love
you, O eternity' (200; 245ff.), these are words inspired by this spirit of
Zarathustra, also the saying of the 'great hope' in Part 4, '—all those
who do not want to live, or they learn to *hope* again—or they learn
from you, O Zarathustra, the *great* hope'. For all this, there is above all
the unsurpassable, beautiful saying that already was been taken up
by the poet Christian Morgenstern [1871-1914] in a pure Christ-sense
in *Wir fanden einen Pfad* [1914]: '… do not throw the hero in your soul
away! Hold sacred your highest hope!'[97]

***

All that we find in *Thus Spoke Zarathustra* as the *Zarathustrian saying
of the 'great midday'*[98] is inwardly connected to the thinking of the age
and of Zarathustra's concept of the turning point, with his conception
of the great cosmic cycles and cycle of time. Here it really concerns a
most decisive Zarathustrian thought that still echoes and reverberates
in the Avesta, right to the passage that we will get to know in Part
3 of this book, where *morning, midday* and *midnight* are mentioned as
those which are 'female warning beings concerning the great decision
(world crisis) for him who rightly considers'. The daily turning points
for Zarathustra are pictures and parables of the great cosmic turning

points, female warning beings concerning the great world-crisis the world judgement, which at the same time is the beginning of a new cycle of time. And for us the world-crisis of Zarathustra that is connected to the great Christ-prophecy contains today the indication of that event which in religious terms we call the 're-appearance of Christ in the ether-body', the breaking in of the etheric and of the higher etheric consciousness into the world of the physical. In the Gospel 'lightnings' and other heavenly phenomena are frequently mentioned. And here we would also like to place the following words of Nietzsche, even if we know that Nietzsche himself does not connect their meaning with the Christ-event:

> O blessèd hour of lightning! O mystery before midday!—Raging fires will I yet make of them [my predecessors] one day and heralds with tongues of flame:—
> —they shall yet proclaim one day with tongues of flame: It is coming, it is near, *the Great Midday!*
> Thus spoke Zarathustra.[99]

The Zarathustra-thought of the 'great midday' sounds especially mighty, as the great judging hour of decision, in the following words which we—through omitting four words that speak of the 'blessedness of *Selbstsucht*, self-preoccupation'[100]—should mention here:

> But for all these the day is now at hand, the transformation the sword of judgement *the Great Midday*: then shall much be revealed!
> And whoever pronounces the I wholesome and sacred and selfishness blessèd, verily, he will also say what he knows, as a soothsayer, *'See, it is coming, it is night, the Great Midday!'*
> Thus spoke Zarathustra.[101]

***

If we clearly see how the great points of view of human development and cycles of time light up with Zarathustra, the looking out into the widths of space and overviewing the depths of time, the looking into the star-depths and looking up to the star-heights of the world and humanity, then we can also feel how this Zarathustra-spirit of the star-heights of humanity, of the 'widths of space and depths of time' also directly shines into Nietzsche's *Thus Spoke Zarathustra* when he wrote the words':

> The farthest in the human, the deepest, *star-highest*, its enormous strength: does that not all froth against itself in your pot?[102]

And like a tragic anticipation the closing words sound: 'No wonder that man a pot shatters!'

This prophetic spirit who sings in Nietzsche's *Zarathustra* 'The Seven Seals (or The Yea- and Amen-song)' [Part 3, 16], was the spirit of Zarathustra, in which the prophetic voice sounds so strongly, in particular in the prophecy of Christ.

> If I am a soothsayer and filled with that soothsaying spirit which wanders along a high ridge between two seas—
> wanders between past and future as a heavy cloud—[103]

In these words of Nietzsche there sounds the genuine spirit of Zarathustra. It is the characteristic thing with Zarathustra how here in the far *past* a personality stands before us who thinks so strongly and mightily the thoughts of the *future*, of the future of humanity. And these thoughts really do liken Zarathustra with Friedrich Nietzsche, when the latter is also in the tragic error of not recognizing the future of humanity as the future in Christ. Also not when he produces such words as these:

> But whoever discovered the land 'Human' also discovered the land 'Human Future'. Now you shall be seafarers for me, valiant ones, patient ones![104]

***

The new thing which Zarathustra, as the great teacher of the primal Mysteries of humanity has brought, especially as we look towards the completely different nature of India and the completely different nature of the Indian Mysteries, we can also call the teaching of the *meaning of the Earth*. Indeed, Zarathustra was the first to speak to humanity of the meaning of the Earth. For the early Indian, in the face of the reality of the divine-spiritual (Brahman), the Earth was *maya*, a mere magic illusion of the cosmic spirit. For the Persian it became the real battle ground on which the human spirit had to wrestle with the power of the adversary, the demon of darkness, *Ahriman*; it became for him the field of activity which he had to transform, to cultivate and to plough, in order from the world of dark matter to win the seeds of goodness, of light. Something of this noble spirit of combat, of this deeply religious feeling for the sanctity of the Earth and its task, also lived in Friedrich Nietzsche. Out of this religious feeling he too has coined the saying *of the meaning of the Earth*, although here again many things flow in that show how he does not grasp this meaning of the Earth in the full sense as a Christ-meaning. Often one feels how this Christ-meaning actually lives in the depths of souls, but is dismissed by the upper, surface consciousness.

How near to this *Christ-meaning of the Earth* does the saying stand *'The heart of the Earth is of gold'*.[105] Quite without knowing, unconsciously Nietzsche's spirit meets the Earth-Mysteries of the Christ (which for Zarathustra were still Christ Sun-Mysteries), the Mystery of the Sun-Spirit that has connected himself with the Earth, and the sunlight, which in the realm of darkness of the Earth, is transformed into gold.[106] How close to this Sun-Mystery of Christ penetrates in particular to that which Nietzsche's Zarathustra says concerning the *bestowing virtue:*

> Only as an allegory [*Abbild,* likeness, picture] of the highest virtue did gold assume the highest value. Gold-like shines the glance of the one who bestows. The gleam of gold makes peace between moon and sun.
> Uncommon is the highest virtue and of no use, luminous it is and mild in its lustre: *a bestowing virtue is the highest virtue.*[107]

These are probably the most beautiful, the most sublime words that Nietzsche ever produced, words in which he nearer than elsewhere arrived at the Christ-consciousness. These words were inspired by Him who governs cosmic development, yet not recognized as the Christ-Spirit. In Rudolf Steiner's description of cosmic evolution, where it concerns specific Mysteries 'Ancient Sun-existence' and the *sacrifice of higher beings,* for the substance of this sacrifice of the hierarchies, he purposely takes over the expression from Nietzsche of 'bestowing virtue'.[108] Our further exposition will show even more clearly how Zarathustra takes part in this great cosmic sacrifice. In ever higher stages, the last of which is connected to the tremendous sacrifice of life and sacrificial death of Christ on the Earth itself, his whole being was offered as a gift to the development of the Earth and of humanity.

In Nietzsche's consciousness there flashes in broken rays the tremendous sacrifice of Zarathustra, of the great gift of Zarathustra to humanity, in the way he speaks of the 'going-under' of Zarathustra. Already the first section, Zarathustra's Prologue, ends with the words: 'Thus began Zarathustra's going-under' [Parkes, p. 22]. And this descent, too, this gift of himself to humanity, unites him with the tremendous Sun-impulse, with all those sublime similitudes of Sun and gold, of gold and 'bestowing virtue'. This is possibly most beautifully expressed in Part 3:

> For I want to go to human beings one more time: *down among* them will I go under dying will I give them my richest gift!
> From the sun I learned this, when it goes down, so over-rich, gold it scatters then over the sea out of inexhaustible richness—
> —so that even the poorest fisherman rows with *golden oars!* For this I saw once and did not weary of my tears in watching.—
> Like the sun will Zarathustra too go down …[109]

***

The spirit of suppression, the spirit of darkness, with whom the spirit of Friedrich Nietzsche, as well as his whole time was heavily battling (and still is), Nietzsche in *Zarathustra* always calls 'the spirit of heaviness'. This 'spirit of heaviness', the spirit that really lives and works in the gravity of matter, in the darkness of materiality, that spirit that in the mineral element of the Earth is the rightful lord, but where penetrating into human thinking he fetters this thinking onto sensual matter becomes the enemy and adversary of humanity, is no other than the one who is called by Zarathustra *Ahriman* (Avestan, *Angromainyusch*). He is the cosmic adversary of the bright Sun-spirit *Ormuzd* (Ahura-Mazda), in that great teaching of duality of *light and darkness*, which is also impressively expressed in the Avesta, which contains only echoes of all this. And right into certain details of language in *Zarathustra*, we sometimes feel reminded of some expressions of words in the Avesta, when the spirit of weight, of Ahriman, is mentioned as 'my Devil and arch-enemy'.

Perhaps it serves the memory of Friedrich Nietzsche if we quote here a passage that comes into consideration here, from the chapter 'On the Vision and Riddle':

> A path that climbed defiantly through boulders, malicious, desolate, not graced by weed or shrub: a mountain-path crunched beneath my foot's defiance.
> Mutely striding over the mocking clatter of pebbles, trampling the stone that made it slide: thus my foot forced its way upward.
> Upward:—in defiance of the spirit that drew it downward, drew it abyssward, the spirit of Heaviness, my Devil and arch-enemy.[110]

In tangible and graphic details the picture of the lonely mountain wanderer of Sils-Maria can be conjured before us, and we can gather from this and many other passages how he loved the mountains, the heights and loneliness of the mountains. Also with the early Zarathustra, we find this splendour and sacredness of the mountain heights. As no other of the great initiates of humanity, Zarathustra has spoken of 'the sacred mountains'. We meet this in a powerful manner in the Avesta. For Zarathustra, and also for Friedrich Nietzsche, the mountain was not only an outer mountain but a picture of heightened consciousness, of elevation of soul and inspiration.

> I draw circles around myself and sacred boundaries; fewer and fewer climb with me upon ever higher mountains:—I build a mountain-range from ever more sacred mountains.—[111]

With all this we know that in the high mountains, in the loneliness of Sils-Maria, he did indeed receive his highest inspirations. From his letters we gather how much physical well-being was connected for him with his sojourn in the mountains. And when he makes his Zarathustra speak directly, 'With blissful nostrils I again breathe mountain freedom!',[112] this can also remind us of the Avesta, where the mountains are often called *aschahvathra*, that is, 'where in the great cosmic rhythm it is possible to breathe again in comfort'.

***

The word *ascha*, that is here translated as 'the great cosmic rhythm', and which with Zarathustra, or in the Avesta, delineating the sacred and divine in the world, the eternal cosmic truth and cosmic ordering, is but little understood by scholars and usually much too abstractly translated. It has another form, *ereta (öröta)*.[113] With this it is identical to the Indian-Vedic *rta*, which also signifies the sacred cosmic ordering and cosmic ritual, and already points linguistically to the Lat. 'rite' and to the Gk. 'rhythm'.[114] The great cosmic rhythm and cosmic ritual, seen as a round-dance of creative beings (*amöschaspönts* and *izeds*), was for Zarathustra the sacred and divine in the world.

Where do we find something of this also in Nietzsche's Zarathustra? We find it where we do not immediately recognize the connection, where we are inclined initially to take it as one of the arbitrary moods and inspirations of the lonely thinker, that is, where Nietzsche's Zarathustra in such a characteristic manner speaks of the *dance* and *dancers*. Here above all belongs the passage in the song of eternity, 'The Seven Seals' in *Zarathustra*:

> If ever a breath came to me of that creative breath and heavenly necessity that *compels even accidents [Zufälle—coincidences] to dance stellar round-dances*.[115]

and in the 'The Grave-Song': 'Only in the dance can I tell the allegory of the highest things.'[116]

In our studies, when we really penetrate to the depths, we shall also find in the passages where *Zarathustra the dancer* is spoken about, genuine Zarathustra spirit.

***

So there would seem to be more real Zarathustra-connections in Nietzsche's *Also sprach Zarathustra* than would appear to a mere superficial observation. And to what has been said some other things can be added. We breathe the spirit of the early Zarathustra where Nietzsche's Zarathustra in the song of eternity calls out before the ocean, '—boundless roars all about me, far and away space and time sparkle ...',[117] whereby we recall, that with Zarathustra, or in the Avesta, the 'sea' actually always signifies the *etheric ocean*. Also with Nietzsche who, as we know from his letters, was not particularly moved by the sea in the physical world, this feeling of the etheric lay in the subconscious. There in the subconscious, in the hidden star-depths of his being, there was illuminated for him 'the widths of space and the depths of time', there for him 'far and away space and time sparkle'.

***

The decisive thing of all contrasting the earlier and later Zarathustra is the relationship of the two to the tremendous *cosmic Sun-impulse*—which Nietzsche tragically did not recognize as the Christ-impulse. Zarathustra above all is the great Sun-initiate and carrier of the Sun-impulse. He still found the divine of the world in the Sun [sphere], which in the Mystery of the Sun connected itself to the Earth. What he venerated as divine was in actual fact not the physical Sun, but a spiritual-etheric Sun, the great Sun-aura—Ahura-Mazda. The Sun-experience of Zarathustra inspired all the subsequent Mysteries of humanity, right into the Egyptian Mysteries.[118] This concerns what was always called the 'beholding the Sun at the midnight hour'.[119] The earthly element, the Earth itself, becomes transparent for the beholder. In the darkness of the outer senses, in the deep midnight, he beholds the spiritual Sun unveiled in such a way that the mysteries of cosmic and Earth evaluation, equally the relationship of the Christ with what steiner calls Ancient Sun, are unveiled in this holding. He beholds the connection of the Christ to what Rudolf Steiner calls 'Ancient Sun'. Midnight becomes here an experience of initiation, the *Weihe-nacht*, the consecrated night [Christmas].

Not in pure inspiration, but in broken rays this Zarathustrian beholding of the 'Sun at the midnight hour' could reach Nietzsche's consciousness, which, being unprepared, could not yet bear it. The Sun for him remains completely the outer Sun. We find this radiant, beautiful experience of the Sun already in the opening words: 'Greetings, Great Star! What would your happiness be, were it not for those whom you illuminate!'[120]

And especially in the hymn 'Before the Sunrise', as if inspired by the Holy Spirit:

> O Heaven above me, so pure! so deep! You light-abyss! Beholding you I shudder with godlike desires. Into your height I cast myself—that is *my* depth! In your pureness I hide myself—that is *my* innocence![121]

And we think of the more naive yet still grandiose manner in which Zarathustra in the Avesta looks into the light-filled heaven and the heaven of stars. Genuine early Sun-symbols also live in what we find in Nietzsche's *Zarathustra* as symbolism of the Lion, and as the great Zarathustra symbols of 'eagle and snake'. In this picture of eagle and snake the transformation is expressed from lower into higher, physical into etheric forces. In this Nietzsche divines in depths of soul, the *magical* greatness of Zarathustra.

The 'beholding the Sun at the midnight hour', as we say, falls apart with Nietzsche's Zarathustra into the characterized Sun-experience, and into the perhaps deeper, still more moving and tangible *experience of the profound midnight*. The primal Zarathustra also knew Mysteries of the night and the miracle of its revelation of stars. In the Avesta something of this is reflected in the beautiful passages, where we read of the heaven of stars, the night adorned with stars. And in the experience of the night Nietzsche's Zarathustra reaches perhaps the poetic high point. We find something of it already in the 'Night-Song' [2, 9] and the 'Grave-Song' [2, 11]. Everything here admittedly carries a strong soul-felt colouring, originating in the personality of Friedrich Nietzsche and the modern consciousness of the age that has nothing to do with the spirit of the early Zarathustra. What we find in this may be, that the *spirituality* of Zarathustra with Friedrich Nietzsche, who could not yet produce it as spirituality, becomes an expression of *soul*.

However, it was something tremendous and profound, a real breath that wafts out of the primordial Mysteries of humanity that here reaches the consciousness of midnight of the recluse of Sils-Maria. We recall the moment when:

> Zarathustra put his hand to his mouth a third time and said:
> *'Come! Come! Come! Let us now wander! The hour is here: let us wander into the night!'*
> You superior humans, it is close to midnight: now I want to say something in your ears, just as that ancient bell said it in my ear—
> —as secretly, as terrible, as heartily, as that midnight-bell speaks it to me, which has experienced more than any human has:
> —which has already counted off your fathers' heart-pains' beats—ah! ah! how she sighs! how in dreams she laughs! the ancient deep, Deep Midnight!
> …
> —do you not hear her, how she secretly, terribly, heartily speaks to *you*, the ancient deep, Deep Midnight?
> *O man, take care!*[122]

Nietzsche could not yet find the pure spiritual element, because the soul-element was still too mighty in him: '—the bell now booms, the heart is still rasping, the woodworm, heart's-worm still burrowing. Ah! Ah! *The world is deep!*'[123] With these four last words we perceive again the genuine spirit of Zarathustra. The midnight experience embraces the soul of the poet ever deeper. The midnight experience becomes midnight blessedness, the midnight hope and midnight prophecy, in which there penetrates a delicate fragrance of 'blissful roses', linked with the presentiment of a new cosmic morning and cosmic day:

> An odour is secretly welling up,
> —a fragrance and odour of eternity, a rose-blissful brown gold-wine-odour of ancient happiness,
> —of drunken midnight-dying happiness, which sings: The world is deep, *deeper than day had been aware!*[124]

And even the 'experience of the Sun at midnight', of which Nietzsche certainly was not yet fully *spiritually* conscious, shines in as a delicate distant shimmer, when we read later in section 10: '… *midnight is also midday… night is also a sun…*' This is followed by words so characteristic of Nietzsche: 'be gone! or you will learn: a wise man is also a fool.'[125] Dimly he senses that there is a shift, a 'derangement' of the threshold of consciousness, which has nothing to do with the noxious, everyday meaning of this word.

The midnight episode reaches its climax perhaps where in the seventh section the saying comes that we can really understand in a perspective of Zarathustra's world, indeed, if we want, in a pure and elevated Christ-perspective, words that again could appear as inspired by the Holy Spirit:

> The purest shall be lords of the earth, the most unrecognizable, strongest, the midnight-souls, who are brighter and deeper than any day.[126]

(Cf. Rev. 3:5, 7:9ff., 14:1-5, 21.) What lights into Nietzsche's consciousness can suggest something like a Jupiter future of [planet] Earth, a New Jerusalem.

And like a Zarathustrian wake-up call out of the far past, there sounds to our ears in the words of the 'Midnight Song', with which Nietzsche closes the whole story, with which we, too, would like to end these thoughts devoted to Friedrich Nietzsche. These are the words that still today can move our hearts and which the mountain wanderer in the Oberengadin can read on the Nietzsche memorial on the isthmus in Lake Sils.

> *O man! Take care!*
> *What does Deep Midnight now declare?*
> *'I sleep, I sleep—*
> *From deepest dream I rise for air:—*
> *The world is deep,*
> *And deeper than day had been aware.*
> *Deep is its woe—*
> *Joy—deeper still than misery:*
> *Woe says: Be gone!*
> *Yet all joy wants Eternity—*
> *—wants deepest, deep Eternity!'*[127]

2. The First Zarathustra and Primordial Wisdom

For us today, the meaning of Zarathustra in the history of humanity is mainly that he stands before us as the founder, the inaugurator of that Mystery stream[128] which consciously looks towards and leads to the central event of the history of the Earth, the Mystery of Golgotha. In India there lived a stream in which one actually only looked at the primordial past, the paradisal childhood of the human race. Accordingly for the consciousness at the time, only the eternal Divine is the reality, and the sensory element of space and time is only illusion, maya. With Zarathustra there begins a beholding not only of the nature of the eternal Divine resting in itself, above space and time, but the soul takes an active part in the *revelation* of this Divine nature *in space and time*, through what unfolds and develops in space and time. The Indian only knows of a knowledge of the Divine (*brahmavidya*, theosophia), which is still completely a *living* in the Divine. Only with Zarathustra do we find a knowledge, which as knowledge of space and time, is already earthly wisdom, earthly knowledge, although this earthly knowledge still stands fully connected to a knowledge of the supersensible world. Out of this connection with the supersensible, thinking still draws its influential, active power, its power to direct the world and transform the Earth.[129]

Thus earthly knowledge becomes with Zarathustra also *earthly activity*, earthly creative power, the work of transforming the Earth out of the forces of the spirit, towards what is spiritually good. If we understand under 'magical' that working of the spirit that takes hold and metamorphoses the earthly element, then Zarathustra's basic impulse is in this sense a *magical* one, whereas the basic impulse of the Indians, which originally was not strange to a magic remaining more in the spiritual realm, increasingly becomes a *mystical* one, the path of a one-sided inwardness.[130]

The Indian is the archetypal mystic, Zarathustra the *archetypal magician* of humanity. In this sense Plutarch also calls him—and with this he means, as we have seen, the primal Zarathustra—the 'magician Zoroaster'. Zarathustra is the magician κατ'ἐξοχήν. The powerful earthly personality of Zarathustra, contrasts characteristically with the typical undefined and impersonal aspect of the Rishis and other wise men. If in a very spiritual sense we regard Indian culture as the child-hood of humanity, with Zarathustra we can see the full mature, male personality. The Indian still lives in a more heavenly element, whereas Zarathustra stands with both feet firmly on the Earth. The Indian is still completely given to the forces of birth, the cosmic primordial fem-inine and maternal, to the *Tree of Life*; with Zarathustra we already find a courageous coming to terms with the forces of death, with the *Tree of Knowledge*. Indeed we may say: the primordial Indian and primordial Persian spirits behave like the Trees of Life and of Knowledge.

***

In a deeper sense the figure of the primal Zarathustra is connected, as with the Mysteries of the widths of space, so too with the Mysteries of the course of time, of the cycle of the year and those more comprehen-sive ages of the Earth and ages of humanity of which the cycle of the year is a small picture and comparison. In a certain spiritual sense all Zarathustra-knowledge—as Steiner once mentioned—is 'chronology'. Thereby it is important to regard Zarathustra himself 'chronologically', in the sense of reckoning with cosmic cycles.

For this reckoning, as well as for reckoning Zarathustra's own time—as the further description will make clear—what today is known to us purely as an astronomical fact is especially important. This is the great course of the solar year, also known as the 'Platonic cosmic year'. This is like the annual course of the Sun through all the monthly zodiacal signs, but now not concerning a monthly progression. In a duration of more than 2,000 years the Sun's vernal equinox [the 'first day of Spring'] moves on to the subsequent zodiac sign. After 25,920 years the Sun's cycle (the cyclic precession of the vernal equinox) has passed through all the twelve signs of the zodiac. Today, or rather since the beginning of the fifteenth century, the vernal equinox lies in the zodiac-sign of the Fishes; at the time of the Mystery of Golgotha it lay (since BCE 747) in the Ram, before that (since BCE 2,907) in the Bull. In anthroposophical reckoning, this age of the Bull is the third of the seven post-Atlantean cultural epochs, what is called the 'Egyptian-Chaldean-Assyrian-Baby-onian' culture. This is followed by the time of the Ram as the fourth, the 'Graeco-Latin' cultural epoch. Our age today with the vernal equinox in the Fishes is the 'fifth post-Atlantean epoch'.

In this numbering, the primal Zarathustra's age is the second (pri-mal Persian) cultural epoch, embracing the age in which the Sun rose at the vernal equinox in the constellation of the Twins (sixth millennium before Christ), whereas the first (primal Indian) cultural epoch (vernal equinox in the Crab) is reckoned as the eighth to seventh millennium before Christ. (The age from which we receive the Indian, as well as the Avestan documents, is much later.) The Twins are the sign of the climax of the course of the Sun and of the Sun's impulse. Consequently, in terms of the history of humanity, we find the cosmic Sun-impulse at its height with Zarathustra. Moreover, the 'Twins' characteristically point to Zarathustra's teaching of duality. Because Zarathustra beholds the great cosmic polarity of *light* and *darkness*, he can raise himself from the mere undefined life of the Indian in the basic things of the world to *revelation*, which is only possible where the light is contrasted to the shadow of the light, the power of death of Ahriman. This power of death and of darkness of Ahriman is linked with Mysteries of the Sun's life and its revelatory knowledge that the Indian did not yet take fully into his consciousness. In a survey, anthroposophy shows us the great periods of earthly development, the correspondence of its great and small rhythms, how the primal Persian age is the mirrored repetition of an earlier condition of the Earth, which again presents as a repetition that far earlier condition in which the Earth itself was still Sun [the 'Ancient Sun' incarnation]. (By 'repetition' is always meant here only a picture, or comparison, as the repetition on a completely different stage and in a completely different form.)

***

Out of the substance of the Indian primordial Mysteries in a later period, at the beginning of the 'dark age' (Kali-Yuga), in the described time-reckoning, that is, already in the 'third post-Atlantean' period, the initiate *Krishna* appeared to the Indian people. Of his teaching and activities the Bhagavadgita gives an echo. In him, anthroposophy tells us, there lived that primordial childhood-soul of humanity. This soul lived a not-fully-realized, not fully earthly, *maya* incarnation, which had not entered the Fall of man and earthly incarnations. This soul was only really embodied in the great Mystery of Christmas, narrated in Luke's Gospel. This soul is really the actual being who overviewed and inspired the essence of the whole Indian Mysteries. And in a still later age when the ancient forces of humanity progressively dimmed and already were approaching their zero point half a millennium before the turning point of time, the Indian Mystery-impulse, the Krishna-impulse, in the weakened manner in which it was still possible then, was renewed through Buddha. With regard to the personalities of both of these great Indian initiates, we can also call the spirituality governing the being of the Indian Mysteries, the *Krishna-Buddha stream*. Not only for India, but for the whole development of humanity this stream is of a certain significance. Something of it has also flowed into Luke's Gospel and the figure of Jesus in that Gospel, and later again in Francis of Assisi.[131] (In a more outer manner, not penetrating to the spiritual backgrounds, these connections with Luke's Gospel were already seen by earlier philological research.)*

The *Krishna-Buddha stream* looked back, as it were, only to the origin of humanity, our 'origin in the light'. It saw the Christ, in as much and insofar as it did see Him, only in the eternal, in the world of pre-birth; it saw Him actually only through that being who stands in the midst of the Mystery of Christmas. It did not yet see Him as the Spirit, Who (to use Rudolf Steiner's words), 'went through the Mystery of Golgotha for the healing of the Earth, for the freedom and advancement of humanity'. (To speak in a prophetic sense, it would indeed have also been quite possible in the earlier Indian Mysteries, as in actual fact this did occur in the Zarathustra-Mysteries.) Christ's earthly deed, to which Zarathustra points so mightily, did not have a place in Indian culture. And only where Christ holding the balance between the bearer of light and the power of darkness in its earthly reality was seen, did He appear in His full reality. Only Zarathustra, who recognizing and struggling with the power of darkness, confronted Ahriman, could penetrate to behold this earthly reality of Christ.

In this sense we differentiate the *Zarathustra-stream*[132] from the *Krishna-Buddha stream* as that stream that first consciously took up the Earth, the earthly and human elements, the earthly-*historical* element and the determination for the future, the future of humanity with Christ. This stream takes us significantly out of the region of the simply eternal, of the world of pre-birth, into that of space and time, where the forces of death govern. From the appearance of Zarathustra this governs all the beings of the Mysteries (at least all the *higher, nobler* Mystery-beings) of humanity, insofar as this did not remain connected as in India with the Krishna-Buddha stream. All the higher post-Indian Mysteries of the pre-Christian cultural development are inspired by Zarathustra.

- The Krishna-Buddha-stream, as that of the forces of birth and the maternal forces, has flowed into *Luke's Gospel*. Its initial chapters help us to glimpse the maidenly-childlike mother of the Saviour.

---

*See the Bibliography and comments presented by Beckh in *Buddha's Life and Teaching*, Temple Lodge, 2019.

- Similarly, in *Matthew's Gospel* the Zarathustra-steam in which the forces of personality and the paternal forces have flowed right at the beginning helps us to glimpse no less significantly the *Father*, the fact of fatherhood.
- The Christ, by entering the bodily vessel of Jesus of Nazareth in the Jordan-baptism, brings the higher union, the synthesis of both streams. In the last resort, it is connected to the primordial opposition occasioned through the 'Fall of Man', with the contrast of Earth and cosmic heights, pictorially indicated in the Bible in the story of Cain and Abel. It is the contrast of the being which can only live in the spiritual heights, in the etheric heights, and of the other being who has mastered the earthly element, who has strongly united himself to the Earth, but has thereby lost the cosmic heights. Through the Christ this primordial human contrast is balanced out and transcended, and so balanced out that the being of the cosmic heights can exist again in the earthly existence and that the earthly element can be carried up into heavenly heights. And from here a significant light falls on that anthroposophical knowledge, which today still presents difficulties for the understanding of many people. The mystery is of the 'two Jesus children', whose differences are secreted into the differences of both gospel narrations of Luke and Matthew. Already the complete difference, with the pure and simple contradiction of both ancestral trees in Matthew 1 and Luke 3 (they deviate from David onwards) cannot be set aside by some sort of Bible exponent and apologist remaining somehow disposed to externals. Moreover, several other 'contradictions' can be added. The time is not far distant when, through such 'contradictions' in the gospel narrations and behind them, people will learn to become aware of deeper hidden spiritual connections. Only from these connections will the gospels be read and understood correctly one day.

But with that knowledge first made public by Rudolf Steiner in *The Spiritual Guidance of Man and Humanity* [GA 15], Chapter 3, it has above all to do not with something totally new but with a knowledge that was also present in earlier times at least here and there, where the sacred story was investigated with earlier powers of vision. From paintings from the Middle Ages examples can be mentioned how such visions entered the inspiration of the great painters.[133]

***

All this has to be mentioned here because it would not be possible to give a clear presentation especially of Zarathustra's being were the facts here not thoroughly looked at but avoided. For Zarathustra's being is the one which then really incarnates in the figure of the 'Solomon Jesus-child' of Matthew's Gospel, whereas [with] the 'Nathan Jesus-child' of Luke's Gospel that other being lived who never before had entered an earthly human incarnation, which, as it were, untouched by the Fall had preserved the human ether-substance, the life-Sun-ether, which had remained childlike, innocent (Adam before the Fall of man). The beginning of the Bible contains indications of all this in what is said there about the 'Tree of Life' in Paradise. In the Nathan-Jesus-child we can also say, there lives the *cosmic primordial child* who carries the power of the Tree of Life. The Solomon-Jesus child who carries the Zarathustra 'I' in himself carries the cosmic primordial wise man (in him the 'Tree of Knowledge'). The two gospels significantly express these contrasts. In Luke there are the childlike, humble shepherds, who in the simplicity of their hearts behold the realms of the angels. These beings —one thinks of the cloud background of [Raphael's] Sistine Madonna—at the birth full of grace in Bethlehem, have, as it were, taken on earthly substance. With Matthew the story of the three Holy Kings, the Wise Men from the East, behold the star of Zarathustra shining in the heavens that leads them to the one who is the new earthly incarnation[134] of the great Zarathustra. (That it really was the Star of Zarathustra who led the Magi to Bethlehem is not expressly stated in Matthew's Gospel, but it is suggested in the childhood gospel, the apocryphal Gospel of Pseudo-Matthew.[135] There the name Zarathustra, missing in Matthew's Gospel, is mentioned.)

It is something of great significance that the 'flight into Egypt', the journey of the child Jesus with his parents to Egypt [related] only in Matthew's Gospel, that is, only narrated with regard to that Jesus-boy who as the 'Solomon Jesus', is the reborn Zarathustra. The Zarathustra-youth is inspired by the leading of destiny, by the cosmic leadership of Christ, guided in early childhood to those countries whose primordial, sacred Mysteries he as Zarathustra once inspired in long past millennia through his exalted pupil (Hermes); to the same land of Egypt, in which also Moses, the preparer of the Christ, was led to become acquainted with Zarathustra's Mystery-impulses and the impulses of his law.

From the flowing together of both streams spiritual research reports the following: after the early death of the childlike mother of the one Jesus and the father of the other, both families lived together in Nazareth. The early maturing Zarathustra-Jesus youth is deeply drawn to the childlike loving being of the other, the individuality of the cosmic, primordial wise one feels he is mightily drawn to the cosmic, primordial child. So the event takes place that in the narration of Luke's Gospel is described as the sudden becoming-wise of the childlike boy, shocking the parents as it was revealed in the conversation with the teachers in the Temple: the passing-over of the Zarathustra-'I' out of the bodily vessel of the Solomon-Jesus boy into the bodily vessel of the Nathan-Jesus child (which up till then had lived simply as an etheric-soul being, instead of a fully developed human 'I'). The picture exists by Borgoganone (15th century), which as out of a dawning spiritual vision characteristically expresses the diminishing figure of the one boy (who after the event soon dies) before the youthful burgeoning figure of the other. And we can well imagine how the early maturing youth, carrying in himself the 'I' of the great cosmic wise one, cannot live much longer than those years during which, with puberty, in a certain way the entity of the Tree of Knowledge is taken over by the entity of the Tree of Life. However, the bodily vessel of the other youth burgeoning completely out of the Tree of Life was strong enough at this point to take into himself such a highly developed human 'I' as Zarathustra's.

Thus the beings of the two paradisal trees, as it were, penetrating and mutually embracing lived on in Jesus of Nazareth, until at the Baptism in the River Jordan through John the Baptist the decisive event took place. The Holy Spirit 'prepared the son of Mary to be the vehicle of the Christ', so that he really could take up the cosmic Sun-Being, the Christ, out of the cosmic heights. In order that this could happen the Zarathustra being, who, as it were, had already sacrificed his own earlier corporality in order to give his 'I' to the corporality of the beloved friend, had now also to sacrifice his 'I', in order to allow an entrance for the cosmic 'I' through providing its bodily vehicle. These processes show us, how—already mentioned in Chapter 1—Zarathustra's being truly was completely *bestowed virtue*. Such an exalted being, the great cosmic initiate, does not wish to gain anything for his own personality in this world-event, by completely merging into it, sacrificing his whole being for the development of the Earth and of humanity. And in the following we shall hear how beside his physical corporeality and his 'I', he still sacrifices his other supersensible members for the development of the world.

***

Before speaking of this great sacrifice for the development of the world, the devoted bestowal of Zarathustra himself that includes his supersensible members lying between the 'I' and the physical body, the nature of these members should first be discussed. An understanding will be sought for that which in anthroposophy is called the human 'etheric body' and the 'astral body'. People familiar with the liturgical treasures of The Christian Community can approach an understanding by recalling the words always spoken at the altar during the Offertory. These are words about the creation of man out of the *supersensible divine members* of the Ground of the World. We can imagine what is spoken here of the Being Who with its higher members reaches into the supersensible realm and how these members were embodied into the human being at the origin of the world. We may also recall how this creation of the world is presented in the story of creation in the Book of Genesis. It may be recalled how in *Our Origin in the Light*, Chapter 1 'Primordial Creation', these things were discussed. There it was attempted to show how all 'world creation' is actually *creation of the archetypal human being.* The still spiritual, primordial human being is the human-divine image that stands before us at the end of this chapter of creation.

Consequently, when plants, animals and stars are mentioned one should not think of the outer worlds of plants, of animals and of the outer world of the stars. All this only arises—and at first still completely etherically, supersensibly—in the 'creation of the Earth' of Genesis 2. Here in the becoming of the human being, it was pointed out, the picture of the plant world initially means the impact of the living element containing the forces of growth on what previously was bare lifeless physical materiality. And in the same way, the picture of the stirring animal world that is significantly connected to the shining of the stars in the firmament, initially shows in the biblical creation story the impact of the *feeling element* of the soul upon that which hitherto was only corporeality. This was enlivened in the sense of a plant filled with forces of growth, but not yet with a sentient, feeling soul. The essence of the human being is completed when to that which he shares in common with plants as a living growing being and with the animal realm as a conscious, feeling being, that element is added which he receives directly from the Divinity, which he shares only with the divine-spiritual world itself, the 'I'. This alone makes him a human being, [created in] the image of the Divinity.

- That human member connecting him to the sensory, material, mineral realm, is called in anthroposophy the *human physical body.*

- That member connecting him as a supersensible body of forces connects him with the living forces and forces of growth of the plant realm—which like the forces of growth of plants has consequently to be regarded as a entity of *time*—is called in anthroposophy the *etheric body*, or life-body.
- That member that in a higher spiritual manner connects him as a body of forces, with the forces of the stars, also existing with animals—of the feeling consciousness and conscious feelings, is called the *astral body*, or the sentient body. The whole human being consists of *physical body*, *etheric body*, and 'I'. What sometimes is presented as still higher members—Spirit-Self, Life-Spirit and Spirit-Man—are the astral body, etheric body and physical body transformed by the 'I'.

With our presentation of Zarathustra's being it is actually not that such concepts as 'etheric body' and 'astral body' are simply taken over and used as expected, known from anthroposophy. Rather these concepts—that are still imagined by many people too abstractly and in a physically material manner—especially through Zarathustra become for us in a deeper sense spiritualized. Zarathustra in quite a special sense becomes a teacher for the connection of what are called the 'etheric' and 'astral' bodies to the cosmos; in them 'space and time' are mirrored. The 'etheric body' is actually a time-entity and as such is connected with all the mysteries of the becoming and growing in time. The 'astral body' as a star-entity is connected to the mysteries of the 'widths of space' and stellar realms. This whole presentation dedicated to Zarathustra can and shall be a path for us, for the deeper grasp of the mystery of our 'etheric' and 'astral' bodies.

The whole question regarding how far Zarathustra, by sacrificing his whole being step by step for the development of humanity and thereby also allowing these higher 'supersensible members', the etheric and astral body, to flow into the development of humanity, leads to the significant connection of this primordial initiate and primordial Mystery teacher of humanity not only with the early Iranian Sun-Mysteries themselves but with the nature of the post-Indian Mysteries as a whole. In particular there is the connection with the time of its main blossoming in humanity, in early Egypt and the Hebraic Mysteries of Moses—again derived from the Egyptian Mysteries—all of which form a bridge to the Mystery of Golgotha. Here it is important to recall what already at the beginning of this section was said of the character of this wisdom compared to that of Indian wisdom. Indian wisdom, initially only a wisdom of the eternal-divine, faces—of course also rooted in the divine—the Zarathustra knowledge as a *wisdom of space* and as a *knowledge of time*. Rudolf Steiner has shown how:

- the wisdom of space and of the stars of Zarathustra was the basis of the Egyptian, or rather the Egyptian-Chaldean Mysteries, whereas
- the wisdom of time flowed into the Hebrew, Mosaic Mysteries.

Such an in-flowing should not only be imagined as undefined and abstract but in such a way that we recognize how the living essence of the great initiate in itself becomes sacrifice, how in a quite tangible sense it gives itself to humanity as something essentially real. In order to understand the initiate and the role he plays in mankind's becoming, we really have to raise ourselves above the everyday consciousness, have to move up to the Imagination so that not only the 'I' but the whole being of such a great personality as Zarathustra standing already on the threshold of the superhuman is directly important for the whole world, playing a role in world-events reaching far beyond the everyday. The 'greatness' of a personality is hereby decided by the measure of its selflessness, of its readiness for sacrifice, of its bestowing virtue, of the rising personal concern for the world.

So gradually we may understand when spiritual science finds that the etheric body of Zarathustra has later flowed into the substance of the Hebrew Mosaic Mysteries, and the astral body of Zarathustra with its star-wisdom into the substance of the Egyptian Mysteries. Zarathustra was incorporated in the founder of the Egyptian Mysteries—tradition names him as Hermes (Egyptian: Thoth)—who was a reincarnation of a pupil of Zarathustra.[136] He was that pupil who had assimilated from Zarathustra the wisdom of space and the wisdom of the stars. And the 'astral' body, the star portion of our being, is really the inner star-life; the 'heaven of stars' is but the outer reflection. The fact has become difficult to penetrate through the effect of the Fall of man; the human being's feeling for the heavens, linking him to the world of the stars, has become darkened through the earthly element. Thus the 'inner star-life' for human beings has become unconscious or subconscious. But in the age of Zarathustra the soul was much more conscious [of this] than it is today. And Zarathustra, the initiate, had brought the star-portion of his being, his astral body, to a highest degree of purification, so that in with it all the mysteries of the cosmic widths and the regions of the stars could come to light.

Today we comprehend the star 'scientifically' by projecting earthly concepts into cosmic space. Zarathustra experienced the star still *in essence* in such a way that the star revealed to him the mysterious connections of man, the Earth and the cosmos. He still experienced a star-consciousness lost to people today. He still read in the stars the heavenly script, still perceiving within them the revelation of the heavenly hierarchies. His knowledge was star-wisdom. In the innermost depths of his being he was, as it were, united, married to this star-wisdom. And this star-wisdom became the glory of Chaldean as well as the Egyptian Mysteries. Star-wisdom has flowed into those Mysteries, not merely through any tradition but out of Zarathustra's being itself, out of his 'astral body', the star-portion of his being. The star-wisdom, and with it the 'astral body' of Zarathustra, continues to live as an essence in the Chaldean and Egyptian Mysteries.

And this star-wisdom of Zarathustra still embraces the being of distant fixed-star worlds. Out of the brightest star of the fixed-star heaven, out of the cosmic-Sun Sirius connected with the seven stars of Orion that form the diamond-like shining adornment of our [Northern] winter sky, there shines for him the highest revelation of the World-'I', the cosmic Christ. He experiences this revelation as *his* 'I' connected with the soul of humanity. That each person really has his own star was still known to the human soul at that time. And the Star of Zarathustra, the Star of the great cosmic initiate whose 'I' was still one with the soul of humanity, was the brightest star, Sirius. Zarathustra, the initiate of primordial times, experienced his 'I', that part of his being connected to Christ, in the Star. Above the revelation of the earthly Sun stood the revelation of the cosmic Sun.

Thus for Zarathustra there existed above the Mysteries of the Sun and of the planets, a *wisdom of the fixed stars*. Wisdom of the Sun and the planets is connected to the soul, the astral element; the fixed-star wisdom relates to the 'I'. Right into the Avesta—which essentially is tuned to echoes of the wisdom of the Sun and the planets, beholding the Divine in the essence of the Sun and the planets—we still find echoes of this fixed-star wisdom, especially in the great hymn to the star Sirius (see Chapter 3, below). In this hymn, Sirius is still expressly called the Star of Zarathustra. Here he is called the Shining One and the *healing one*. Zarathustra still experienced the enlivening, health-giving, healing, star-etheric growth-forces, the life-ether of the stars as the *star-soma*, from which the soma plant (Avestan: *haoma*) is the earthly-cultic reflection. The Avesta is still penetrated by the soma-cult and soma mysticism. And this soma-cult and soma-mysticism express a living star-wisdom, which for Zarathustra was at the highest level still, *fixed-star wisdom*.

We find this too with Zarathustra, with the star-portion of Zarathustra's being, in the wisdom described in connection with the Egyptian Mysteries during the age of their earliest primordial blossoming as a wisdom of the fixed-stars. And this epoch of Egyptian fixed-star wisdom lasted during the time when the spring equinox took place in the Twins. (This is the time called in anthroposophy the 'second post-Atlantean cultural epoch', the primordial Persian age.) Also the later Egyptian planetary wisdom belongs for a large part to this primordial Persian age; only its final sounding out falls with the beginning of the 'third post-Atlantean, Chaldean-Assyrian-Babylonian culture', the time when the spring equinox occurred in the Bull.[137] Consequently, when the actual Egyptian cultural epoch began, star-wisdom was already in decline. Yet it lived on as a veneration of the stars in religion and the world of the Mysteries. The highest veneration was always enjoyed by that brightest star about which we know that it was the Star of Zarathustra, the cosmic Sun, in which Zarathustra experienced his 'I' united with the entire soul of humanity. With the rising of this star (Sirius) the Egyptians reckoned their calendar, also ordering the greater ages encompassing 1460 years (Sothis periods), the calculation of which gives the result that the Egyptian primordial Mysteries reach back into the age of Zarathustra.

Still in the later Egyptian age Sirius for the Egyptians was the soul of the goddess Isis, the soul of humanity and the essence of the star-wisdom, that soul of humanity and wisdom of the stars with which Zarathustra in the depths of his own being, was as though married. And so for the Egyptians the Star of Zarathustra was the Star of Isis. Zarathustra bore essentially in himself the Eternal Feminine of the world, which stood for the Egyptians beside the 'I'-imbued Masculine, Osiris. Rudolf Steiner emphasized the purity of Zarathustrianism, which lies in the fact that the cosmic polar opposites were not yet seen in Masculine and Feminine, but still purely as the contrast of light and darkness.

The early star-wisdom in Egypt still echoed on, likewise with the Chaldeans, where the spiritual essence of the stars only gradually disappeared. Outer sensory appearance, astronomy, took its place. So it is interesting to see how in the Hebrew revelation in the Bible, in the age of Moses, it became completely lost. The story of creation in Genesis, which still links to Egyptian Mystery-wisdom, refers to the stars with a still completely spiritual meaning, where (followed up in a deeper exposition[138]) it is mentioned that into the becoming human being the star-life of the feelings enters, the sensitive supersensible member, the star-body, the astral body.

Then we find the stars with Abraham, who comes from the land of the ancient star-wisdom, from Ur in Chaldea, where later the star-prophecy given to Abraham is mentioned, 'your descendants are to be organized according to the sacred order of the heaven of fixed-stars'[139] (that is, according to the Mysteries of the zodiac) and in the dreams of Joseph (Genesis 37:9), who is repellent to his brothers by his still possessing early star-clairvoyance. Then probably still here and there with the prophets (who according to their nature maintained a certain connection to star-wisdom and early clairvoyance), in the Psalms and in the Book of Job and Ecclesiasticus, as if wafted in from the world prior to the Hebrews.[140] But with Moses it appears character-istically only in the prophecy of Balaam (Numbers 24:17), who is the representative of the early Egyptian star-wisdom, which was disliked by the Hebrews and is mentioned in this sense in the Apocalypse (Rev. 2:14). The stand Moses himself took to the stars and the star-wisdom is revealed almost astonishingly in Deuteronomy 4:[15 &]19:

> Take then good heed unto yourselves... And lest thou lift up thine eyes unto heaven, and when thou seest the sun, and the moon, and the stars, even all the host of heaven, shouldest be driven to worship them, and serve them...

Moses, who himself was initiated in the Egyptian Mysteries, belongs to a time when even in Egypt the pure and exalted star-revelation, the actual star-wisdom had for a long time receded; what he does not experience there is wisdom of the elements, the revelation of the etheric, living element of the Earth. And these, too, were receding at this time, when he led the Hebrews out of Egypt, and only sensory knowledge, the revelation of death, remained at the ancient Mystery-centres. What could still be found there concerning the reverence of the stars was no longer pure. Moses had to be concerned that it would distract his people from the pure veneration, without images, of Yahveh, the divine 'I'. A demonic element had entered everywhere into the heathen veneration of the stars; Moses wanted to keep his people, who were called upon to prepare the earthly bodily sheaths for Christ, free from these demonic elements. The struggle against this heathen-demonic element fills the whole story of the Old-Testament people. And so it happened, that the stars, at least in the historical part of the Old Testament, are no longer mentioned at all.

Where in the New Testament does the star appear again? Right at the beginning of Matthew's Gospel, where the story is narrated of the Christmas star, the birth-star of Christ Jesus. But who sees this star, who recognizes the star's revelation of Christ? Not the Jews, not the wise men of the Hebrews, but the Wise Men from the East, the distant Magi, the representatives and guardians of the ancient Oriental star-wisdom. It has been suggested, and apocryphal gospels give glimpses of the fact that the Star which they saw is indeed the Star of Zarathustra, Sirius, not as seen by the normal eye, but as the eye of the Mysteries saw it pictorially in essence, carrying in itself the picture of the divine Virgin with the Child, Isis-Sophia. Moreover a special constellation of planets and several other things were still connected at that time with the appearance of this Star.

And so in the beginning of the New Testament, the Star of Zarathustra appears significantly, but now linked to the revelation of Christ. The Child itself, to which it points the Wise Priest-Kings, is indeed none other than the reborn Zarathustra, chosen by the Holy Spirit to offer in the above-described manner the earthly vessel for the Christ.

We do not find the Star again—apart from *one* characteristic exception soon to be mentioned—in the gospels, not even in John, but only again in the Apocalypse, where the resurrected Christ himself holds the 'seven stars' in his right hand, where all kinds of revelations of the stars take place. In the three other gospels, the chapters known as the 'little apocalypse' is a kind of reflection or preview of the Apocalypse of John (Matt. 24, Mark 13, Luke 21). The final saying of Christ in the Apocalypse of John [Rev. 22:16] significantly contains the *star*: 'I am the root and offspring of David, the bright morning star.' The Star that once fell to the adversary, about revering which Moses had to warn the Hebrews, has become sacred again and is spoken of as sacred through *Christ*. Christ brings back into the future of humanity the lost consciousness of the star, the early star-wisdom and knowledge of the star-script of mankind. He is in this sense also—prophesied by Zarathustra himself—the Fulfiller of the great star-initiate, of Zarathustra.[141] And spiritually led by Christ, we may also regard Zarathustra again as, of all humanity, the great Wise Man and initiate of the stars. In the Christian era Zarathustra may tell us of the ancient—and in the future freshly achieved—human consciousness of the stars (against which Moses had to warn the Hebrew folk).

And Zarathustra can reveal to us—when we learn again to behold him in this future sense and Christ sense—something concerning that life of the stars hidden in the depths of our soul, concerning the star-portion and the star-mystery of our being, the *astral body*.

***

The wisdom of space and of the stars carried by the 'astral body' of Zarathustra, a knowing of the mysteries of the stars, flowed into the Egyptian (and Chaldean) Mysteries. The ether-body that carries the *wisdom of time* flowed into the Hebraic Mysteries. It was incorporated in Moses, who was the reborn pupil of Zarathustra, to whom Zarathustra had once bequeathed the wisdom of time. Zarathustra's wisdom of space and of the stars inherent in his sentient body, the astral body, passed on to Hermes, the Egyptian primordial teacher of the Mysteries. Zarathustra's wisdom of time inherent in his life-body, in the etheric body, passed on to Moses in that he himself received the ether-body of the great initiate. And Rudolf Steiner's[142] researches point out how and where the Bible indicates this event. It takes place in that remarkable story of the basket floating on the water, in which the child Moses is drawn to land by the daughter of the Egyptian Pharaoh. The picture points to mysteries of the etheric (water) and to ancient initiation events. They express that already with the birth of the child this contact with Zarathustra's being, the incorporation of Zarathustra's etheric body, takes place.

Because he receives the etheric body of the great teacher which carries the wisdom of time, for this reason, Steiner reports, he was able to speak in the Book of Genesis in such tremendous pictures of the evolution of the Earth and of mankind. In the astral body the *feelings* —predominant in ancient Egypt—are inherent; in the ether-body it is the *thinking*, to which Moses had to introduce humanity. His great task was to lay in the earthly thinking, in the intellect, the seed of the earthly 'I', to lead humanity from the Tree of Life to the Tree of Knowledge. To Moses, like Zarathustra, belonged this entity, the Tree of Knowledge. As with Zarathustra, Moses appeared to his people as the great lawgiver, who out of knowledge of the divine set up over them the tablets of good and evil (thereby, we feel the 'Tree of Knowledge of Good and Evil'). And the Bible shows the whole context existing between Moses and Zarathustra. It also indicates, soon after the story of the basket, once again in Mystery-pictures, the relationship Moses had to the priest of Midian, initially called Reguel, then Jethro, the father of 'seven daughters' (Exodus 2:15ff., 3:1). It must have been Zarathustra-wisdom that Moses met at this time. And perhaps in the name Jethro can be found an echo of the name Zarathustra, as indeed in the ensuing age in actual fact it was borne by others, especially by the inspirer of the Avesta.

Once again it is one of the bequeathed spiritual members of Zarathustra that through Moses and the Mosaic Mysteries served directly towards the preparations for the Mystery of Golgotha. The whole manner of the sacrifice of Zarathustra being poured out through the course of time appears to be arranged for Christ and for the cosmic sacrifice of Christ.

***

We may look back on the many initially difficult insights of the spiritual researcher concerning the bestowal of the etheric body of Zarathustra to Moses. Through his relationship to spatial orientation and star-wisdom Zarathustra gave us access to the mystery of the 'astral body'. Now also through his relationship to the course of time and to the wisdom of time, he can reveal to us something concerning the mystery of the etheric, of the etheric body. Many object to this 'etheric body', because they imagine it too one-sidedly as spatial. Zarathustra teaches us that the 'etheric body' is a time-entity. The Avesta knows the picture of the etheric archetypal plant, the 'hvapi tree'. By regarding the plant and its processes of growth in time, something of the mystery of the etheric body can be revealed to us. In the metamorphosis of the plant, in its development out of the seed through shoot, leaf, blossom to fruit, which again encloses the seed, in all these stages of blossoming and withering, in the whole circulation of its juices—as in the blood of the human body[143]— the essence of the etheric body is revealed as an entity in time. And we can imagine how the etheric entity, the 'ether-body' of the primordial teacher of humanity, was united at the great turning point of time with the whole evolution of the Earth and mankind and of cosmic evolution. And so Zarathustra becomes the teacher of the great cosmic year. And as the metamorphosis of plants is a cycle, which from the fruit leads again to the seed, from withering and death to new growth, so Zarathustra as the teacher of the great cosmic year also becomes the 'teacher of the eternal return', the 'recurrence of all things'. But not in the sense that Friedrich Nietzsche meant as a mere eternal return of the same, but in the sense of a new ordering of the world on a new, higher, spiritual stage. This sounds through the prophecy of Christ in the Avesta.

Moreover, the great cosmic year of Zarathustra is not merely the pale, uncontoured and insubstantial 'monster of the great year' about which Nietzsche speaks, but, as anthroposophical research shows, it stands connected with the great astronomical cosmic year that arises through the gradual precession of the spring equinox. In about 25,900 years the Sun in a comprehensive sense completes its circuit through all twelve signs of the zodiac, as it describes it in small during the course of a single year. And according to a statement of spiritual research, as well as what is found in the Persian documents, a Zarathustrian cosmic year takes about half of such a period of time. At the beginning of such a period, 6000 years before Christ, the great Zarathustra appeared. 6000 years after the turning point of time, somewhat more than 4000 years from today, such a greater Zarathustra-circle of return will be closed. What will then return?

What then returns is not simply the same, as Nietzsche thought, but a more specific stage of human consciousness, one on a new and higher stage of 'I'-consciousness achieved through Christ, out of this 'I'-freedom of Christ, about which Zarathustra himself had already prophetically spoken.

Here it may be permitted simply to take words that Rudolf Steiner spoke in a New Year's lecture on New Year's Eve, 1915,* where much was said on the subject of Zarathustra and the Zarathustrian cosmic year. Dr Steiner, proceeding from growth and the consciousness of plants, points to the most significant connections of plants with the etheric nature and of the nature of time. He explains how the consciousness of plants is admittedly more dull, but for this reason much more comprehensive than human consciousness. The human being thinks initially only of his earthly surroundings; the plant, however, 'thinks'—if we can use this word in an analogous sense—of cosmic things. And its consciousness embraces the solar system. It thinks, as it were, 'planetary wisdom'. This regulates its processes of growth. Only at a quite specific time of the year is its consciousness comprehensive. This is the time of the shortest days, after the winter solstice, the period one also calls the Twelve (or Thirteen) Holy Nights (from Christmas to Epiphany), the time when the outer plant growth has entered most deeply into the winter torpor. During this time, Steiner says, not only does the plant have its otherwise Sun-and-planet consciousness, but it goes through this to a still more comprehensive though more dull consciousness of the mineral world.

---

*'The Year as a Symbol of the Great Cosmic Year'; in GA 165.

As the consciousness of the plant world embraces the solar system, so the still duller consciousness of the mineral world embraces the whole cosmos of stars. The plants, as it were, 'think planetary wisdom'; the stones, even if in deadly torpor, 'think' something like 'fixed-star wisdom'. We sense profound mysteries in the words of Novalis: 'I know not whether anyone ever truly understood the rocks and stars, but any such must have been a sublime being.'[144] The plants go through this New-Year period, through this more comprehensive consciousness of the mineral world embracing the cosmos of stars. Every year the plants go through the cosmic consciousness of the mineral world embracing the star-cosmos. The consciousness of the human soul is also united to the cycle of the great cosmic year with the comprehensive consciousness of the astral body. This—as we have already seen—is a star-consciousness, a consciousness embracing the regions of the stars.[145]

The age of Zarathustra was such an age of astral consciousness. For this reason the great initiate of the human race, with such a comprehensive star-consciousness, could proclaim such a sublime star-wisdom in the Mystery-centres. What the form of consciousness of the whole age was, appeared with Zarathustra in its highest purity and completion. 6000 years before Christ such a comprehensive consciousness of mankind, of stellar space and stellar mysteries, was present. 6000 after the turning point of time, when again a transition of human soul-life through the astral body will take place, it will be able to be present once more, but then on a higher, Christened, 'I'-conscious level. In his New-Year lecture 1915,[146] Steiner says:

> Twelve months of the year pass by from the one union of the earth's plant consciousness with the mineral consciousness, to another [subsequent] union. Twelve millennia pass by from one cosmic New Year to another cosmic New Year of the Earth, from one passage of the human soul through the astral world to a new passage of the human soul through the astral world.

The lecturer concludes with the words:

> The year is an image for the aeons. The aeons are the reality of those symbols we encounter in the course of one year. If we really understand the year's course, we will be penetrated during this worthy night marking the beginning of a new year by the concept of the mysteries of the cosmos. Let us try to attune our soul so that it can look into the new year, conscious of the fact that it can bear within it the year's course as a symbol for the great *cosmic course*, which encompasses all the mysteries pursued by the divine beings

who surge and weave through the universe from aeon to aeon, just as the lesser gods pursue the mysteries connected with the development of the plant and mineral kingdoms during the course of a single year.

Words, as spoken here, help us to think again the great *Zarathustra concept* in a new and sublime, Christened manner, different from the way Nietzsche did, especially when he speaks of the great year and the eternal return. He speaks sublimely, yet so that initially only a caricature of what is true and correct comes across. Yet right through this caricature we always feel something of the greatness and sublimity of Zarathustra's concept. And if we may add something out of the really ancient wisdom of Zarathustra it would be this, that also for this great Zarathustra-cosmic year, pointing us to the future of humanity with Christ, the Star we recognized as the Star of Zarathustra, the Christ-star Sirius, is significant.

Around the turning point of time the Star of Christ's birth appeared in a specific constellation—or in connection with other constellations. When the great 'circle of recurrence' of the star-consciousness closes, such a constellation will be present again. Details concerning this can be found in early sacred texts.[147] For the ancient Egyptians Sirius was that Star whose rising in the morning sky gave hope of the flooding of the Nile, and through this introduced the beginning of the year. Sirius was the star that for those in the Mysteries, was the regulator of greater periods of time. It was for Zarathustra the great Star of Hope that for him also announced prophetically the great cosmic New Year, the reconstitution of all things and of the ancient vision in *Christ*. And when the human soul through Christ learns again to read the secrets of the star-script, it will also learn to regard the star Sirius—which rises for us so promisingly in the night sky, every year towards Christmas, as a bearer of the hopes of the year and of the New Year—as the cosmic Star of Hope and cosmic Star of Grace. This star helps us so to sense the future of the Earth and mankind with Christ. In the midst of everything surrounding us of decline and all the destructive hopes for the Earth, we preserve this great cosmic future hope with Christ as something indestructible.

3. Avesta

It has to be repeatedly emphasized that the religious document coming down to us in fragments as the *Avesta* at the most contains only echoes of the teaching of the original Zarathustra that we attempted to describe in the previous chapter. The writer or inspirer, even if, as one assumes, he bore the name Zarathustra, belonged to a much later age than the original Zarathustra. He is to be placed, at the most, in the second (even if, as philologists think, in the first) millennium before Christ. He does not belong, like the earlier Zarathustra, to the 'primordial Persian' epoch, but, at the most, to the third, the Egyptian-Chaldean-Babylonian, cultural epoch. In the Avesta we actually meet—even if in a certain continuing connection with the activities of primordial Zarathustra and the actual Zarathustra Mysteries—what was contained in a later age in the Iranian people as the religion of Zarathustra. Today the followers of this religion are called *Parsees*. In India there are today [1926] about 80,000 Parsees who believe in Zarathustra,[148] in particular upholding the purification laws of their religious founder.

Concerning this religious founder, about whom apart from some contemporary kings' names we do not know very much, we may imagine that he appeared as the renewer of the old Zarathustra-impulse. Something from the first Zarathustra lived in him. But he had naturally adapted all he had learned and practised to the needs of his later age. Hereby not the whole Avesta originates from his direct inspiration, but only its oldest part, what are called *Gathas* (that is, songs, mantric verses). They are differentiated linguistically from what is called the younger Avesta, that in this connection carries the stamp of a still later age. The Gathas of the Avesta have the greatest similarity with the languages of the oldest Vedas, the Sanskrit of the Vedas. Hereby lies a main reason that speaks for an older age for this part of the Avesta along with that of the oldest Vedas (second millennium before Christ).

The mantric character of language appears strongly in the Avesta, especially in the Gathas of Zarathustra. The difference between this language from the otherwise similar ancient Vedic [Old Sanskrit] is especially the larger richness of vowels. Compared to the polished vowels of Sanskrit, it is regarded as the more original and more ancient language. The language thereby contains a strong feeling-element compared to the thinking-element more apparent in Sanskrit.

Feelings of religious devotion and reverence come to expression more purely and strongly than in hardly any other language. Something of the mighty earthly personality of Zarathustra lives in this language. Within this there lives the strong spirit of an ancient ruined Aryan civilization.[149] Even today these ancient religious documents can convey much joy, can stimulate enlivening forces of courage and hope, thereby stimulating in us healthy, unsentimental religious feelings. And all this would not be so were not something of the early, genuine spirit of Zarathustra alive in it.

**

For the first Zarathustra there was the characteristic new impulse to behold the revelation of the eternal Divine in space and time, in the *ordering of space* and the *course of time*. He expressed this on the one hand as the *wisdom of space* and *wisdom of the stars*, and on the other hand as the *wisdom of time*, as the teaching of the great cosmic year. This is echoed in the Avesta in the whole manner of the dual presentation of the *eternal, heavenly region grounded in itself—thwasha hvadhata*; then the *infinite, boundless time, zarvana akarana*, the primordial eternity, resting in itself—*zarvana daröghohvadhata*. This last expression means, literally, 'from time immemorial founded in itself'. In these two words something completely different lives than in the 'concepts' of, for instance, Kantian philosophy. Space and time are not abstract 'forms and concepts', but something still completely spiritually tangible and substantial, real factors of creation and of the cosmic powers. One would rather recall the words of Novalis, when he speaks of Christianity as the '*Grundlage der projectierenden Kraft eines neuen Weltgebäudes und Menschentums… eines* lebendigen, moralischen Raumes', the 'foundation of the projective power of a new cosmic structure (edifice) and [new] humanity… a *living, moral region*'. He then continues:

> Hereby, this excellently links to my ideas of the failure hitherto to recognize space and time, *whose personality and primordial power* has become indescribably clear. The *activity of space and of time is the creative power*, and its connections are the crux [*die Angel*] of the world.[150]

Moreover, the Indian word for space—*akasha*—has nothing to do with today's abstract concept of space; it signifies at the same time the living ether, bearing in itself the physical formative forces. In this ether the creative powers of the divinity live and work. Likewise, with Zarathustra space and time are creatively working and fashioning entities.

Zarathustra's 'boundless time', *zarana akarana*, Rudolf Steiner points out, essentially contains the viewpoint of the highest divine Unity above the duality of the light and the dark, Ahura Mazda-Ormuzd and Angromainyush-Ahriman. Even if in the Avesta not overmuch is said in detail concerning space and time, it is nevertheless significant that in the oldest part of the Avesta, the Yasna, both these cosmic mysteries resound; it ends with an eulogy to the heavenly region, grounded in itself, and boundless time, resting in itself.

***

What we found with the primordial Zarathustra as the wisdom of space and of the stars and of the wisdom of time, which met us in its connection on the one hand with the mystery of the astral body, then with that of the etheric body, is at play in the Avesta in particular in the whole way two words are used which we could feel as characteristically important for Zarathustra. The two words are *star* and *year*, which also in Avestan so sound that the primordial connection to the Germanic languages can come to consciousness. The word for star in Avestan, *star*, also roughly shows the form which this primal word still has in English. And the Avestan word *yār* is exactly the same as the German word *Jahr*, not only in meaning but also in the way it is pronounced. Precisely when we glimpse Zarathustra as the proclaimer of the great cosmic year and of eternal recurrence, as the exalted founder of the mysteries of the cycle of the year and the course of time, it can awaken in us a deep impression that our New High German word today for 'year', *Jahr*, is still the same word with which Zarathustra named the year and its mysteries. This is not the only echo between the language of Zarathustra and our language today. Nietzsche would have been able to say—though he probably didn't know it—that single sayings that he makes his Zarathustra speak, right into the language, could have been spoken out of the mouth of the actual early Zarathustra.

The linguistic relationships between the language of Zarathustra and the Germanic languages appear all the more significant than those even with primordial Sanskrit, otherwise so closely related to Avestan. Sanskrit has already lost both primordial words. From the word *star*, *str*, only scanty residues—some plurals in a few places—are to be found in the earliest Veda; the word *yār* does not appear in Indian, also not in the Vedas. The words with which the Indian expresses both concepts have nothing more to do with the early primordial words. And for the Indian both 'star' and 'year' no longer contain the intimate relationship as for Zarathustra, because according to his nature the Indian is given more to the eternal divine, not yet so much to the ordering of space and the course of time.

**

In the Avesta, in the whole manner Zarathustra looks up to the heaven of stars, we still breathe a nature-related existence. We feel how his gaze is still drawn into the boundless distances of space and thereby how for him the soul follows into the distances of space whence a warm breath of cosmic love from the stars streams towards him. He feels the 'essence of his own being' in them, divining in them the deeds of the hierarchical creative powers. Under the shining heaven of stars Zarathustra holds discourse with the 'Lord of Life', the 'Master of Wisdom', the Cosmic Master Architect and Cosmic Artist who created it all, with Ahura Mazda. And Ahura Mazda tells him[151] how the realm of the angels were helpers in unfolding the bright tent of heaven:

> Through their lustre and glory I unfolded, O Zarathustra, that sky up above, the shining sky, which allows us to gaze into distances of worlds that surround this Earth, as it seems like a stronghold... Thus it stands, placed there by the spirit, firmly founded and with its border in the far distance with a body like shining ore radiating into the three realms into which Mazda clothes himself as into a garment, woven by stars, fashioned by spirits.

Here no abstract 'empty space' is narrated, but a radiating heavenly ether, which is the garment of light of the Godhead. The life-ether of the Sun, originally also that of the fixed stars, is the radiant garment of Ahura Mazda, the great 'Sun-ether-aura'. What we today call the 'etheric formative forces'[152] is the realm where, out of the life-forces of the Sun and the forces of the stars, the 'Cosmic Artist' at work sculpturally forming becomes visible to clairvoyant vision. The stars are frequently expressively called the 'lights without beginning' and the angelic hierarchies are spoken about, as 'the stars, the Moon and the Sun, which the lights without beginning direct on their rhythmic courses'.[153] And it is told how also these sacred, rhythmic courses have to be wrested by the good powers of the light from the resistance, the hate, the disturbance of the dark demonic powers of the adversary.

More than all this, sounding like a distant recollection of early fixed-star wisdom, the great hymn to the star Sirius[154] (*Tishtriya*)[155] begins:

> We revere devotedly Sirius, the Shining One, with sunlike radiance, in whom lives the peace, the blessed tranquility, the golden shining Bright One, who allows us to look into the cosmic distances, the Shining One, the Healing One.

This is the star which to the Egyptians then became the star of Isis, in which the healing forces of Isis, the forces of the light-ether in particular were experienced.[156]

> Him, the Sublime One, the One who hastens along in quick flight [correctly, probably: 'bringing forwards'], who shines from afar with his rays, the Bright One, without stains, who allows the waters to flow on and the healing stream which pours along from afar.

This could remind us of the Milky Way, which the early peoples called the heavenly stream—in Indian the 'heavenly Ganges'—yet is related to earthly situations if we recall how in Egypt—which took over its star-wisdom from Zarathustra—linked the rising of Sirius with the fruitfulness of the land, with the flooding of the Nile. Just as today towards Christmas and New Year when we look up to the evening sky or early night sky where Sirius shines as the 'New Year star', so in a later section of the 'Hymn to Sirius' in the Avesta it is said how the human being, approaching the turn of the year, looks towards the rising of Sirius. The hope is added that Sirius may send to the Aryan realms a 'good year' (a good harvest), may be to them the bringer of a 'good new year' (*huyairyao*). This very much recalls the Egyptian situation, where the observation of the rising Sirius after the summer solstice in the morning sky was made a festive, cultic occasion through the priests. And, to return to the beginning of the 'Hymn to Sirius', we could also find Egyptian elements in it. In the way the Avestan singer venerates the 'divine created name of the cow' recalls the Egyptian Isis-mysteries and titles of Isis. And he venerates the star as the 'exalted and mighty, sovereign Sun-ether-aura (*hvarōno*) bearing promise, as the angelic genius of the sacred (actually 'bearing the sacred cosmic rhythm in itself'[157]) Zarathustra Spitama'.*

Besides the fact that here we experience that Sirius is the Star of Zarathustra, the word *hvarōno* is significant. It describes the fixed-star wisdom being recollected here, still with the cosmic Sun, of the bright

---

*'Spitama' is recognized today as the name of the family or clan into which Zarathustra was born.

beam of the Sun-life-ether connected with Sirius, the Sun-ether-aura, the heavenly radiant glory, still borne by the bright King of the Golden Age gifted with early clairvoyance (*hvarödaröso*), called in Iranian Yima and in Egypt called Osiris. And in the great prophecy of Christ, which in conclusion we shall get to know, the word means the same, with the same addition,[158] 'the sovereign promise bearing Sun-ether-aura, or radiant glory', the being who descends on the future healer, Saoshyant—Jesus.[159] Thus for us today the Avestan word *hvaröno* (Sun-ether-aura, ether-radiant glory), even if not expressing the most inner nature of the Christ, yet points to Christ, to that Christ-Sun-aura that Grünewald's picture of the resurrection[160] so expressively portrays.

In the Avesta we still experience that this radiant glory, *hvaröno*, when no earthly bearer is available for it, rests in the 'cosmic ocean', *vourukasha*. This cosmic ocean—about which philologists argue whether it is the Caspian Sea, the Aral Sea, or some other lake—is the *etheric ocean*. Therein is found the (etheric) archetypal plant, the mystic tree *hvapi* or *vispobish*, 'the Tree of the Eagle, containing the good and strong healing remedy, in which all plant seeds are placed'.[161] The picture recalls the world-ash Ygdrasil of Teutonic mythology. We think of the 'archetypal plant'[162] and at the same time of Genesis 1:11, 12 (cf. *Our Origin in the Light*, Germ. ed. 18f., p. 17f. above), when in the Avesta, it says[163] of this tree: 'Out of it all my plants grow and all kinds of plants in hundreds and thousands and myriads.' And we recognize how the *Urfplanze* coming to light again in Goethe's thinking was already present in the pictures of early clairvoyance, particularly where this clairvoyance, as with Zarathustra, was a Sun-clairvoyance.

A certain inner relationship exists to this etheric ocean, vourukasha, with the other often mentioned Lake of Kansaoya/Kansava (Lake Hāmūn) [in S.E. Iran on the Irano-Afghan border] (it is said to relate geographically with Lake Hāmūn, yet the meaning of the name is not exhausted in a geographical sense). In this, the profound saga says, there rests until the great turning point of time the sacred seed of Zarathustra, out of which the future Saviour is to be born. And when it says[164] that three sons shall arise out of this seed of Zarathustra, we are to think of reincarnations.[165]

- With the first of these reincarnations, a connection to that personality is thought, met in the story of Moses as Jethro.
- The second was that initiate with whom the Jews were together in the Babylonian captivity. (In Egypt as in Babylon *Zarathus-*

tra's being prepared the Hebrew folk for its tasks, to provide the paternal vessel for the Christ.)[166]

- The third of these 'sons', the third of Zarathustra's re-embodiments, is the future great World-Saviour so expressively prophesied in the Avesta, who brings the resurrection of those who have died, the 're-enlivening of the dying Earth-existence', the Saoshyant-Jesus, to Whom passes the great Sun-ether-aura *hvaröno*.

It is told how this Sun-ether-aura (*hvaröno*) slipped away from the king of the primordial time, Yima, whom it once adorned, when he was false to the truth, succumbing to a kind of Fall through lying. Then, it is removed from his subjects by Ahura Mazda, as the bearer of its essence,[167] and confined to the bed of the Vourukasha Sea. Three times an adverse Turanian dived for it, but it repeatedly evaded him—behind these pictures are hidden the whole struggle of a decadent Mystery-being, adverse to the development of the 'I', against the progressive Sun-Mysteries. Finally it hid itself in the Kansaoya Sea.[168] From there it passed to the one destined to be the bearer of the Christ—the future Saviour of the world, the wakener of the dead. We are dealing here with all that not only concerns a prophetic vision of the turning point of time, but probably also that event of the future we call the 'reappearance of the Christ in the etheric body'.

***

Before we proceed with these things, something should be said concerning the whole relationship of the Avesta to Christ and to the divine. Christianity as a stream of life can first be present from the moment the Christ-Sun-being in the Mystery of Golgotha had united Himself with the Earth. When one speaks of the relationships of the pre-Christian Mysteries to Christianity, something different is meant. The Christ, Who through Golgotha united Himself with the aura of the Earth, *before* this moment had to be encountered in the aura of the Sun. Zarathustra also sought Him there. And when he looked to the highest divinity, to *Ahura Mazda*, the 'great Sun-ether-aura', the indication points, corresponding to the conditions of the age, to the Christ-Sun-being,[169] even if the distinction between the Christ and the 'light-bearer' in the Avesta is still not completely clear. (Between Lucifer and Ahriman, Christ stands in the middle.) Nevertheless, Ahura Mazda is without doubt strongly presented as the representative of the True and Good. Evil is characterized for Zarathustra mostly in that which resists the truth, in lies, deception and denial. This being of deception, lies and denial is called in the Avesta Drug (pronounced 'Drudsh'), a nightmarish female demon. Followers are called 'delighters in deception' (drögvant), who will be turned out at the great divorce at the end of all things.

The direct dictionary meaning of the words Ahura Mazda is 'Lord of Life, Master of Wisdom' (or 'Spirit of Wisdom'). With 'Lord of Life', by thinking of an etheric Sun-life, the life-ether of the Sun, there is the connection between Ahura and 'aura'. (In Persian the word *Ahura* really became 'aura'.) And the word *Mazda* is somehow related to the word *Meister*, 'master' (even if not in the sense of [what Novalis termed] 'pragmatic' etymology). It delineates the spirit-power of wisdom and prudence—in a quite special sense also the 'power of divine recollection'. Different from what we are able to imagine today, *spirit-power* in earlier times was the power of memory. The spirit-power expressed in clear, bright thoughts, the streaming wisdom of the cosmos, is above all what lives, sounds and shines in the Sun-spirit Ahura Mazda.

Alongside this viewpoint, the *artistic element* appears very strongly in the Avesta.[170] Ahura Mazda is the great cosmic artist, to whom the Gatha verses[171] refer, when they ask:

> What artist created [in the beginning] the light and the darkness, what artist created sleeping and waking, what artist created the becoming of morning, midday and night that are the insightful warners of the great divorce [the Last Judgement, or the world's turning point]?

Terms for space, consciousness and time here are significantly placed alongside each other. And we always see how in Zarathustra's teaching all thoughts on time and conceptions regarding time predominate. The thoughts of periods of time approaching the given everyday consciousness are raised to cosmic time-periods and distant cosmic ages, thereby glimpsing more clearly the image of a more distant, more comprehensive viewpoint (as in the earlier section the customary year is presented as an image of the great cosmic year).[172]

Furthermore, Ahura Mazda's being is proclaimed in the question (the answer once again means Ahura Mazda):[173]

> This I will ask you, tell me truly, O Lord of Life: Who in the primal beginning of creation was the Father of the sacred cosmic rhythm? Who showed the singing Sun and the stars their course? Who made the Moon periodically to wax and wane? This, O Master of Wisdom, and other things I would like to know.

Ahura Mazda, as the Sun-spirit of wisdom, is rightly the bearer of the cosmic rhythm. The word *ascha* (discussed in Chapter 1, above) would probably be translated by a philologist as 'cosmic ordering'). It can clearly be seen, however, that it is related—through its secondary form öröta = Indian *rta*—with the Lat. *ritus*, as with the Gk. *rhythmos*, where it expresses the sacred rhythmical movement in which something like a cosmic-cultic round-dance of creative beings results. And to the rhythmic element the musical element is added. It seems significant how in the early Gatha-Avesta the word for Sun, which in the later language with the consonant 'r' (*hvar* = Heb. *or*, 'light') is clearly a word for light, still with the consonant 'n' (*hvan*, here especially expressive in the genitive form *hvöng*) makes its effect as a word for sound. It points to an age of human consciousness in which the spiritual music of the Sun was perceived. 'The Sun makes music as of old/ Amid the rival spheres of Heaven'[174] was still experienced. For Zarathustra, the sound-ether was still united with the life-ether of the Sun-aura (Ahura Mazda).

The following words[175] point to the spiritual, moral element in the activities of Ahura Mazda:

> And as the Holy One I met You in spirit, O Master of Wisdom, Lord of Life, as I beheld You in the creation of the primordial Life in the beginning, when You created the destiny-imbued arrangement for words and deeds, through Your might allotting evil for the Evil, good for the Good for the final end of created existence.

It is to be considered everywhere that the translation gives only a weak notion of the strong ('mantric') power of the words of Avestan. *Mantra* in Indian means, through a rhythmic and musical harmonizing adjustment of the speech sounds, the word produces a spiritual strength. In Avestan *manthro* (= Indian *mantra*) means 'the sacred word', indeed 'word' in general, yet only because the word itself is felt as holy and mantric. And it is said that through the sacred word sounding in the sacrificial rites, the soul would be 'bright, shining, thoroughly radiant', the imperishable principle of life—*urvan*—Ahura Mazda.

Some of the prayers directed to Ahura Mazda almost recall the style of saying Mass, indeed precisely the form of the words, as freshly discovered in the Act of Consecration of Man out of the primal language. One can compare, for example, words at the beginning of the Offertory of the Act of Consecration of Man, that it be received 'from our pure thinking, loving heart and willing devotion', and 'Christ's light in our daylight', with the following passages from the Avesta:[176]

> We revere You, we thank You, O Spirit of Wisdom, Lord of Life, *we approach You with all our pure thinking, with all our true words, with all our good deeds*, we consecrate for You the most noble body of all bodies, O Spirit of Wisdom, Lord of Life, *to You this daylight*, to you the highest heights of the Sun.

One day when it will be possible to show more clearly than can be done today, how via the Mithraic Mysteries early sequences of words, partly traceable to the Avesta, are present in the earlier Mass, it will perhaps be recognized how the Act of Consecration of Man here and there stands closer to the primordial word and to the word of the first Zarathustra than do the corresponding words in the Latin Mass. As is frequently the case, that which is historically later is inwardly closer to the primordial word.

Moreover, the 'Holy Spirit' is already addressed in the Avesta, in connection with Ahura Mazda:[177]

> Grant to me, You who creates the cow and the water and the plants, the indestructible salvation through Your most Holy Spirit, O Mazda, and rejuvenating strength through the Spirit of the Good at the great decision.

***

It is not possible to examine the being, the rulership and the activities of Ahura Mazda in the Avesta without referring to the power of darkness, the dark adversary who always crosses the intentions of the bright spirit, *Ahriman*, or as he is called in the language of the Avesta, *Angromainyush* (Ahriman is the later Persian form); *mainyu(sh)* is spirit (Indian *manyu*, related to *manas*), *angro* is linguistically like the meaning of the German 'arg', Eng. 'angry'. It is a delight that Avestan stands so close to much in our language today.

Great and majestic is the teaching of the first Zarathustra, the teaching of the tremendous contrast of light and darkness projecting out of distant prehistoric times into the present. We sense how in the future it will achieve a towering significance when it comes to deal with transforming the darkest evil in the world, grown to its height, raised through a higher power of the Good to the light. The splendid Manichaean legend in which the light sacrifices itself into the darkness, points to how what once was fallen light is drawn up again into the heights of light. Such a Manichaeism, arriving at its height and practical significance, will one day be there. With this, today still in the far future, with the re-emergence of a Zarathustrian cosmic year, there will be a new *Christened* Zarathustrianism. And we have to think that Zarathustra, the first Zarathustra, had prophetically glimpsed this future of mankind. In the light of this future, he also saw the primordial mystery of the contrast of light and darkness.

Yet of all this the Avesta hardly shows echoes. In contrast to what the teaching of Zarathustra and the will-impulse of Zarathustra once was in the primordial past, when what today is still a far future of humanity it will once again exist in the light of Christ—the Avesta remains in a certain way very reticent, especially when it has to do with that basic teaching of good and evil, of light and darkness. However much we could rejoice concerning the strong way with which in the Avesta Zarathustra reckons with the adversary of the Good, thus much we can still feel, that it does *not* contain some kind of decisive final and highest revelation.

Famous Gatha words in a translation by Rudolf Steiner[178] run as follows:

> I will speak! Harken, you who journey from afar, and you that come from near at hand, with longing to hear. Mark well my words! No longer shall the Evil One, the false leader, conquer the Spirit of Good. Too long has his evil breath permeated human speech.

Then we hear out of Zarathustra's mouth the spirit of light, Ahura Mazda himself, speaking about his dark adversary:[179]

> I will speak of both spirits in the primal beginning of the world, concerning which the Holy One also spoke of bad things: Our thoughts do not agree, neither our teaching, neither our decisions of will, neither our convictions of belief, neither our words nor our deeds, nor our whole beings and souls in any kind of harmony.

In another Gatha[180] Zarathustra airs his views concerning the adversary:

> The arch polluter always works against me; I see to make good again his evil intentions *through the sacred cosmic rhythm* [in the strength of the True and the Good].

The word *asha*, translated here as 'the sacred cosmic rhythm', has already been discussed. Ahriman, the spirit of darkness, is the one who always wants to disturb the sacred cosmic rhythm—which is also revealed in the fixed courses of the stars—wanting to place arbitrary will and arbitrary meaning in place of the eternal rhythms and eternal harmonies. The spirit of light is the one who sets everything right again through *rhythm*. In this sacred cosmic rhythm rests essentially the power of the True and the Good. And this sacred cosmic rhythm, this power of the True and Good in the religion of Zarathustra, is really regarded as a great cosmic ritual, a religion of sacred, creative beings.

The one next to Ahura Mazda himself—which we in the sense of the Christian nine hierarchies[181] allocate to the 'Spirits of Wisdom', the highest of these beings are called in the Avesta the 'eternal sacred ones', amöshaspönts.[182] And it is said these are the bodily forms in which Ahura Mazda invests himself, 'the beautiful bodies of the amöshaspönts, the exalted bodies of the amöshapönts'. These 'immortal holy ones'[183] serve, as it were, as Ahura Mazda's raying, etheric garment ('the living garment of the Godhead').

Six or seven bright amöshaspönts are named in the Avesta (the number seven comes about when Ahura Mazda once more as in a mirror reflection appears in this lower hierarchy), to which are arrayed five spirits as mights of the adversary, so that in this sense also the number twelve arises. The essential and decisive thing, however, in the Avesta is the septenary. They are spoken of[184] as those:

> who are all seven like thinking, who are all like words, who are all like activity, whose thinking is the same, whose words are the same, whose activity is the same, who all have the same father and mother, namely, the Creator Ahura Mazda.

We are reminded of Friedrich Doldinger's poem:[185]

Seben sind sie, sieben sind.	They are seven, are seven.
All sind sie von dem Einen.	They are all in the One.
Sieben sind sie, sieben sind,	They are seven, are seven.
Alle gehn sie zu dem Einen.	They all go to the One.
Sieben sind sie, sieben sind.	They are seven, are seven.
Alle loben sie den Einen.	They all praise the One.
Sieben sind sie, sieben sind.	They are seven, are seven.
Alle sind sie nur der Eine.	They all are but the One.

So we can understand why the name Ahura Mazda standing over them also stands under them.[186]

From here we already have a presentiment that in a certain sense with the septenary of *amöshapönts* we have to do with the 'Spirit of the seven planets'—amongst which Sun and Moon always appear. And there would be—in order also to add the names of the individuals:

- Ahura Mazda himself the Spirit of the Sun,
- Vohu Mano 'the Spirit of the Good', that of the Moon. Between *manas*, Avestan *mano* 'spirit' (from *man* 'to think', from which also Indian *manushya*, Germ. *Mensch*, 'the human being') and the Indo-European words meaning the 'Moon', a linguistic connec-

tion exists, which in the light of esoteric research (see Steiner's *Esoteric/ Occult Science*) also proves the prehistoric connection. To *Vohu Mano* there stands opposing—amongst the five counter-forces—a dark Moon-spirit Aka Mano 'the bad spirit' as the evil antagonist. Evil in the sense of Zarathustra is quite rightly the 'bad one'. The other names are:

- *Khshathra* 'lordship, warriorhood': the spirit of Mars,
- *Armaiti* (related to 'harmony') 'divine thinking, pious devotion': the spirit of Jupiter (*sophia* ['wisdom'] in the sense of Rev. 5:12),
- *Haurvatat* '': the spirit of Saturn (*plutos* ['riches'] in the sense of Rev. 5:12),
- *Amörötat* 'indestructible life', as the spirit of Venus a kind of goddess of the Tree of Life and genius of the plant world, her healing and rejuvenating forces, and finally,
- *Asha*, the 'sacred cosmic rhythm' itself as a 'being': Mercury, who holds the rhythm and balance expressed in the cosmic scales (for this reason, too, 'at home' in the zodiacal sign of the Scales, *timé* ['honour'] in the sense of Rev. 5:12).

To the *amöshaspönts* there is added in the series of hierarchies the beings called *Yazata* (Persian *Izeds*) in the Avesta, the 'archangel' of Zarathustra. Here, too, various names like *Sraosha*, 'hearing sense' and others are mentioned. A main role is played by the great Sun-archangel Mithra, the Zarathustrian Michael,

> who as the first of the archangels rose over the high mountain Hara [the Caucuses], whereby the indestructible Sun with the swift steeds, who as the first in the golden shimmer gained the splendidly adorned heights, from there he, the strong hero, surveyed the whole land of the Aryans.[187]

Zarathustra's feeling for the splendour and holiness of the mountain heights comes mightily to the light of day in these words. The struggle of Mithra-Michael with the demon of darkness is clearly and impressively described:[188]

> The evil one came rushing by, the miscreant of rash courses; then Mithra Lord of the rich pasture-lands quickly harnessed his chariot, and Sraosha, the holy hero, smote him in the fight or in single combat.

The next hierarchy, that of the *angels*, is the *fravashi*, which as such present the connection with the Earth and the earthly element. Here it is shown again how Zarathustra, who knows how to look out deeply into the depths of the cosmos and the regions of the stars, equally stands firmly on the Earth and at the same time loves the Earth and its beauty. These are authentic words of Zarathustra, which—apart from a special place taken by the Atharvaveda,[189] where a beautiful hymn to the Earth is handed down—are found nowhere in India in this way, where an angel and its connection to the earthly element is narrated:[190]

> Through your lustre and your glory, O Zarathustra, I unfurled this broad, divinely created Earth, which is the bearer of much beauty, which carries every physical [actually: 'invested with a skeleton'] being, the living and stirring and the form numbed in death, and the high ranging mountains, rich in grazing pastures and flowing water.

And it is told how these angelic beings (*fravashi*) out of the ether-sea *Vourukascha* bring water, that is, enlivening etheric forces, to the people linked to them and the Earth.

***

Thus we are led down through the series of hierarchical stages (of the nine, four are recognizable in the Avesta), from cosmic heights, the starry heights and the heights of the Sun, down to the Earth with its tasks, whose care and development is so mightily understood by Zarathustra. A strong echo of what was said in an earlier chapter lives in how Zarathustra is spoken about in the Avesta as 'the first Priest, the first warrior, the *first cattle-breeder*'. With Zarathustra the priest is at the same time warrior, a champion against hostile powers, also where, as for Zarathustra with the Turanian people, they are quite tangibly incorporated in human beings. And he taught the people in the struggle against all possible noxious plants and animals and oppressive natural influences, to work on the Earth and to cultivate, establish agriculture and raise animals. It would be unthinkable if, for instance, one of the great Indian wise men was addressed as a 'cattle-breeder' or 'stock-farmer'. With Zarathustra, however, these things are meant in a completely real, earthly sense. He tamed—or taught to tame—the wild nature of the wolf, so that in dogs the human being gains the friend and serving companion. And similarly with other domesticated animals.

And yet we would not light upon the whole meaning if with 'Zarathustra the cattle-breeder' we thought only of earthly cattle. Early star-wisdom also still lives in this word, a star-wisdom and parabolic star-language in which the '*Tiere*', the 'animals'—one thinks of the '*Tierkreis*', the Zodiac with its animal images—yet at the same time depict the human passionate nature, the 'astral' nature. The great initiate Zarathustra tamed this human passionate nature, cleansing and changing it in himself; he raised it again to its pure star-origin, freed the heavenly 'astrality' from its earthly darkening and impurity. That is why his aura shone, still visible for an early clairvoyance, the 'golden star', the purified astrality, *manas* (Spirit-Self) hovered as the star—visible to higher sense—above his head. This star of *manas* is also the picture for that which in the Avesta is delineated as the genius or angel (*fravashi*) of Zarathustra. Its mirror reflection in the outer heaven of stars is the bright star Sirius. Thus also with the 'cattle-breeder' Zarathustra we are not so far removed as it initially could appear from the stellar heights of the beginning.

This 'golden star' can also lead us to the right interpretation of the name Zarathustra. Already the Greek form of the name Zoroaster shows that the name was understood in this sense, for *aster* means 'star', *zoros* the pure mixture in the mixing-jug,[191] or if one seeks to explain the word as an old Mystery-word out of its sounds and its relationship to *zoos*, 'living'—'the living one radiating light'. With the form of the name Zarathustra, or Avestan, 'Zarathushtra' the scholars are admittedly taken aback, that *ushtra* in Avestan means 'camel', and that *zarath*, a word not really existing in Avestan (but only to be unravelled indirectly out of Sanskrit), if it did exist, would mean 'old'. One should not immediately dismiss such things with a laugh before one knows exactly what role some animal or other played in the esoteric imagination of the early peoples. And with 'camel' one appears to have felt in the early Mystery-language—it even has echoes in the New Testament—a connection with the cosmic powers of the Scales, of the inner balance in the Spirit-self. In earlier times this balance was still determined from the cosmos; in modern times it has to be found afresh out of the 'I' (through Christ). With Zarathustra the 'old' forces were still active.

But it is more obvious to think with *stra* of the word *str –*, star 'star' (= Gk. *aster*). Nevertheless, a word *zarathu* does not directly come in the Avesta, yet the beginning of this word does clearly sound in various words, which in the Avesta means 'gold' or 'golden' (e.g. *zaranya*, gold); still in New Persian *zar* means 'gold'. And that in still earlier times there was a primordial word *zarathu* 'gold', it seems fair to assume this word according to its sound exactly corresponds, when one is clear that especially the Assyrian *churasu* 'gold' (from which Heb. *charts*, Gk. χρυσός) is directly related. And considering that in the Avesta *r* always replaces the *l*, and a Teutonic *g* (Skt. *h*) frequently corresponds to Avestan *z*, then the comparison *zarathu* = Assyrian *churasu*

= Gothic *gluth* 'gold' is acknowledged. *Zarathu* then *means* not only 'gold', but it is in origin, right in the sound, completely the same word. And the name Zarathustra, like the Gk. Zoroaster, would then mean 'star of the shining', or 'golden star'.

***

That element in which the connection of the super-earthly with the earthly, such a decisive one for the 'Magus Zoroaster', comes especially to expression, is *fire*. In the fire, in the warmth-ether, the spiritual element of the higher ether finds its transition into the physical world.[192] Heraclitus, the initiate of the Ephesian mysteries, intuited the origin of everything physical in this etheric fire. In this sense the flame on the earthly sacrificial altar is a picture of the cosmic sacrificial flame at the focus or hearth of the fire of creation; the earthly ritual is also a picture of the cosmic ritual. For this reason in all early cults and Mysteries there is the revering of the 'sacred fire'. But none of the great religious founders felt this sacredness of fire more than Zarathustra. This is clearly to be felt right into the Avesta. And always the earthly fire is thereby a picture of a higher, etheric fire, the sacrificial glow of creative being. Already the Avestan word for fire, *athar*, recalls the Greek αἰθήρ 'ether', that is again connected with αἴθω 'to burn'.

Fire was felt by Zarathustra as pure and sacred, the cleanser and purifier. For this reason the religion of Zarathustra does not cremate, because the dead remains, the impure corpse, should not come into contact with the sacred and pure element of fire.

The sacred and cleansing fire is especially evident in the fire ordeal in the cosmic assizes. As everything earthly—this was common knowledge of the primordial Mysteries—arose out of the higher ether right through the warmth-ether, the fire, so ultimately, as expressed by Jakob Böhme, it has to 'return into its ether'.[193] This is also the deeper meaning of the great fire-ordeal with Zarathustra, the cosmic crisis in the cosmic fire. It is the greatness of Zarathustra's teaching of the last things eschatology that it does not reckon in the lower sense with rewards and penalties, but with the fact that to one and the same element, to the same etheric-supersensory element, all souls will one day be led, that all have to enter the same element. For those correspondingly inwardly prepared this element becomes a refreshing stream of milk, for the others a stream of consuming fire. These are the pure ether-spheres, mentioned in the St John's-Tide Epistle of the Act of Consecration of Man, whose 'glancing rays' bear only what is 'guiltless'. The great fire trial in the Avesta is experienced and described as an initiation event. Before passing through the fire, prayers are directed to Ahura Mazda:[194]

> Through the effect of this fire we approach you, O Master of Wisdom, Lord of Life, to you through your most holy spirit reigning in the fire, which becomes pain for the one whom you deem for pain. As the most blissful thing, you may approach us, O fire of Ahura Mazda, at the trial, with the bliss of the most blissful, with the reverence of the most reverential, you may approach us at the greatest of events.

All this was presented by Zarathustra not only as a future prophecy of humanity, but was experienced as an initiation event in the present. And as far as it relates to the future of humanity, as seen from today no longer the most distant future is meant, but as the near future that is already being prepared today as the 'return of Christ in the etheric body'.

***

Besides fire, as the element in which the spiritual-etheric is connected to the earthly element, the higher ether of life containing the enlivening, healing, health-giving and rejuvenating forces is revered by Zarathustra in *soma* (Avestan *haoma*). It is shown how soma, originally soma of the stars, then appears as the enlivening ether, as the enlivening essence of the plant world; the enthusing drink gained out of the milky juice of the earthly soma plant pictures the higher, the spiritual soma. Like a living being, this soma, or *haoma*, appears in the Avesta before Zarathustra at the soma sacrifice. Already in the Indian Vedic rituals, also with Zarathustra, the soma cult presents the innermost centre of the sacrificial cult; the soma mysticism presents the centre of the Mysteries. In the Avesta soma is called the sacred one keeping death at bay (actually,[195] 'carrying in itself the sacred rhythm of the world'). In expressive hymns the soma and everything that plays a role during the soma sacrifice, including the wood of the press, is glorified:

> I praise the high mountains upon which you, *haoma*, have grown. I praise the wide, extensive Earth that possesses a wide conscience, the benevolent one, your mother, O sacred *haoma* [bearing the sacred cosmic rhythm]. I praise the fields of the Earth where you grow as fragrant one ...[196]

Any other intoxication, it is said, makes one heavy and angry, soma 'carries one lightly upwards'.[197]

Also in the Mysteries that still shine through in the Rig-Veda, the mysticism of soma always stands directly besides the mysticism of the fire. Fire (*agni*) and soma are addressed like a twin pair of divinities. The soma mysticism runs through all the pre-Christian Mysteries. From the soma of the stars and the bread of the stars, which it originally meant, the soma descends via the stages of the Moon-soma (soma in Indian also means 'Moon') and the etheric plant-soma, down into the physical element. In Greek, soma is the earthly human body. In the body of Christ-Jesus, soma has become the earthly human body. In the body of Christ-Jesus the soma of the stars, the bread of the stars, has become earthly. And the pre-Christian Mystery of *agni* and soma, of soma and fire, appears on the Christian level as the Mystery of bread and wine, of Body and Blood.

***

On this Christian Mystery, which as such could not yet be there for Zarathustra, yet a prophetic beholding can be found right within the Avesta (already mentioned earlier). And we are not able to end these observations devoted to Zarathustra and the Avesta more worthily than finally to bring the text of the great prophecy of Christ in the Avesta. It is probably one of the most tremendous prophecies of Christ that sounds to us out of the pre-Christian ages—with the exception of the prophets of the Old Testament, surely the mightiest. That the Avestan *hvaröno* does not yet express the most inner 'I'-viewpoint of the Christ-being, was already emphasized. It is the light-aura of the paradisal Sun-life-ether, which still shone in the primordial time of humanity still adorning the king of the old 'golden' age of Sun-clairvoyance like a heavenly radiating crown. Also in the whole connection of the Christ-prophecy, *hvaröno* relates not only in the limited sense to Christ, but also to everything lying between Christ and the disciples, which however then increasingly is concentrated on the one John. But the great Christ-event of the turning point of time is surely meant with all this. And that the Christ-Sun-aura is differentiated from the personality of the Saviour, over to Whom it passes, appears deeply significant for a spiritual viewpoint. The Avestan *Saoshyant* 'Saviour' is essentially the same word as the Hebrew Jehoshuah-Jesus.

The prophecy speaks in a tremendous manner of the resurrection of the dead and the whole 'rejuvenation of the dying Earth-existence'. The way the thought of resurrection is set forth would in Indian culture be not yet conceivable. It only appears possible where, as is the case with Zarathustra, the spirit strongly grasps the earthly element. And in it the Christian element sounds within it in an unheard of strength for this early time. Likewise in the way the development and advance of the world is mentioned. Here too one does not find similar things in early India. At all events the concept of development here sounds gently, as in Yoga, where it concerns the development of the individual. The main concern with Zarathustra is the development of the Earth and human development. And almost modern there sounds in the Christ-prophecy of Zarathustra the suggestion of freedom of the will and the sovereignty in the will of that which we today call the 'philosophy of freedom', and how all this is linked to the fact of Christ.

The 'birth of the will':

- as in a certain sense it is already linked with the Zarathustra-impulse,
- as we already encounter it as the ideal concept also in Nietzsche's *Also sprach Zarathustra* in such an impressive and majestic manner,
- appears here in a more elevated stage filled with reality, of the impulse of Christ.

The prophecy runs:

Yasht 19, 89
The mighty, the kingly Sun-ether-aura bearing prophecy,
the divinely created one,[198]
we venerate in prayer,
which will pass over to the most victorious of the saviours,
and to the others, his Apostles,
which will bring the world forwards,
allowing the world to overcome age and death,
decay and purification,
which helps the world to eternal life,
to eternal prosperity,
to free-will ['to govern the will']
when the dead will arise again,
when the last conqueror of death comes
and through the will the world will be brought forwards.[199]

Appendix

In order to give an extract from the ancient Avestan, we also reproduce here the version in the original language related to the translation of the Christ-prophecy. With the transcription the attempt is made for the most possible general understanding. Certain finer differences of the single sound, as they appear in the Avesta, are ignored. Thus *ao* is only a wide, open, an *a* tending towards o (whereas ao diphthong is similar to au). a' is nasal a (like Fr. an), ö like Fr. in e in 'le', kh is like ch, gh as the corresponding weak spoken sound. th corresponds to the hard, dh to the weak English th, y is Germ. j, sh (in Avestan differentiated threefold) Germ. sch, z is voiced weak s, v spoken as in Fr. and Eng. The vowels in italics are long and emphasized. ae is not Germ. ä, but a diphthong similar to ai.

The correct emphasis in speaking is approached when one really prolongs the longs and the shorts are made very short.

ughröm kava*e*m hvarön*o* mazdadh*a*töm yazamaide
yat upanghatchat saoshyant*a*'m vöröthr*a*dschanöm
uta any*a*ostschit hakhay*o*
yat körönav*at* frashöm ah*u*m
azarshöntüm amaröshöntöm
*a*frithyantöm apuyantöm
yava*e*dsch*i*m yav*a*esum vasokhshathröm
yat irista paiti-usöhisht*a*t
dschas*a*t dschivay*o* amörökhtish
dathaite frashöm vasna anghush.

III.

FROM THE WORLD OF THE MYSTERIES

(Translated by Maren & Alan Stott. Ed. N. Franklin)

Introduction to *From the World of the Mysteries*

A glance at the situation when Beckh was writing is helpful to lead to a radical re-assessment of his achievement. It would be useful to start by tracing the development of his friend and colleague Friedrich Rittelmeyer.

In 1912 when Friedrich Rittelmeyer, Pastor at the Evangelical-Lutheran Heilig-Geist Church in Nuremburg, was first discovering something about Rudolf Steiner and anthroposophy through his acquaintance with Michael Bauer, he presented four talks for his community on the subject 'Jesus'. These were shortly afterwards worked up into a small book *Jesus. Ein Bild in vier Vorträgen.*[200] It is a splendid, brave, heartfelt book aglow with the author's love of the Jesus in the Gospels. Yet at the time, age 40, he could profoundly sense in himself that the talks and the book were not getting close to the real subject. Seventeen years later, in 1929, he came round to writing the autobiographical *Rudolf Steiner Enters My Life* where he explains with regard to 1912:

> When I tried to form a conception of the personality of Jesus from His words and acts, linking it up with the results of modern theological study, I kept coming across an incomprehensible mystery. A voice was always whispering: 'This Jesus is not Jesus... What is the real truth about this Jesus? As men of the modern age can we not get to the reality which there confronts us? In what way must we think differently, learn differently, in order the better to understand this reality?' The whole impotence of current scientific theology revealed itself to me in the face of the mystery of Christ.[201]

Twenty-four years after *Jesus* he had to try to resolve the issue, never having forgotten the original shortcomings. The result was a new book simply entitled *Christus*.[202] At the very beginning Rittelmeyer wants to make two points clear. The first regards the change from 1912 to 1936:

> The writer has repeatedly shied away from writing a book about Christ. With the best-intended speeches concerning Christ you can simply block people's way to Christ. A human shadow blocks the light. However, when we consider to what extent humanity today has turned away from Christ, when

we daily experience what shocking blindness to Christ is spreading, what consequences follow from not recognizing the most decisive appearance of our earthy history, then everyone who has something to say should feel called to do so. Especially when he is aware that he himself had to struggle to gain a new view of Christ and that the deepest need of the present-day consists in a new view of Christ ...

The writer brought out a book on *Jesus* in 1912. Up to about his fortieth year he searched for Jesus. But he came to a great and mysterious barrier. He repeatedly stood before this mystery. 'This Jesus is not Jesus ...' Now, about twenty-five years later, by bringing out a book about *Christ*, both titles indicate the author's own path. It was a way 'from Jesus to Christ'.[203]

The second observation is that Rittemeyer has broadened his approach. In 1912 the Evangelical-Lutheran understandably focused on the Gospels, on Luther and the German inheritance. In 1936 the author of the new *Christus* could begin his renewed appeal by pointing towards Ancient Egypt, the Avestan texts, Sumerian and Babylonian records.[204] What has changed? Friedrich Rittelmeyer experienced three momentous events in his life after 1912 following an experience in 1893 when he experienced something from his previous life. (i) He met Rudolf Steiner and was convinced by anthroposophy, (ii) he nearly died in an accident in the summer of 1918 while walking with his son in the French Alps and (iii) he was consecrated at the foundation of The Christian Community. Still, none of these, I think, sufficiently explain why the Oberlenker in 1936, writing *Christus* as the fulfilment of the 1912 *Jesus*, would immediately begin the new book by appeals to ancient civilizations and their sacred texts.

When The Christian Community began in 1922, the Stuttgart Seminary building at 41 Urachstrasse housed the Rittelmeyer family on the ground floor, the Bock family on the first floor and Hermann Beckh in the attic. Rittelmeyer, as the leader of the community, found himself in the role of proclaiming the Christian kerygma—something he was very well capable of doing. Bock, the youngest of the three, could put colossal energy into community-forming, anything from buying huge rolls of lino for the building to re-translating the New Testament. Beckh was given the task in the seminary of relating Christianity to the older religions. All three performed their tasks in an exemplary way. But which role could be the more transformative?

Late in 1925 the editors of *Die Drei*, also in Stuttgart, Dr Kurt Piper und Dr Erich Schwebsch, realized that it was both a possible and highly attractive proposition to produce a whole series of sequential monthly issues in the first half of 1926, each focusing on a major figure or theme from world religions. Each issue would be led by a lecture by Rudolf Steiner from the public lectures in Berlin, 1911, with a good half-dozen contributions from prominent representatives of anthroposophy. The editors were in no doubt that the person to shoulder most responsibility for contributions was indeed the Reverend Professor Hermann Beckh. One would like to know how contact was made—did *Die Drei* send a letter of invitation or was there a face to face meeting in the nearby office? However it was, Beckh agreed.

As the plan became more concrete, the editors were aware that Steiner's public lectures in 1911 did not reach back to Sanskrit sources; historically, the earliest figure represented was Zarathustra. Here was a fortuitous coincidence or a working of destiny. Whether it was just before or just after the invitation from *Die Drei*, Beckh was working on a small book entitled *Zarathustra* to be published by The Christian Community (editor, Fr. Rittelmeyer) from the press installed in the basement of 41 Urachstrasse. The Foreword to this book was written 'In Advent 1926'. Other than Beckh, who could read Avestan fluently, there was no ordained priest in The Christian Community in 1926 and no writer for anthroposophy at the time able to quote extensively from the Avestan Gathas in the original language with transcriptions and philological observations.

Piper and Schwebsch had made the right choice. In 1926 Beckh had two distinct sources of love and wisdom. The first was unarguable: Beckh was a professor totally at home in Sanskrit, Tibetan, Pali, Avestan and Hebrew. His room in the attic of the seminary was piled high with primary texts in all the languages; his authority on Tibetan texts was recognized by all European universities. The second source has to be approached with rather more care and tact.

Once it has been acknowledged to a greater or lesser extent that the life and work of Rudolf Steiner reveals a progressive deepening of spiritual and aesthetic realizations, especially with regard to the analyses of Sergei Prokofieff, and that the path to such accomplishments was open to all through *Knowledge of the Higher Worlds*, *Occult Science* and the First Class of Spiritual Science, is it not *probable* that certain individuals after 1924 would follow after Steiner in the most realistic sense? Or are we to believe that such personal development was *beyond* anyone's reach? A re-consideration of Beckh's *oeuvre* would indicate otherwise.

With his scholarly work on *Buddha's Life and Teaching* Beckh analysed the stages of higher knowledge—or rather realization—in primary Buddhist texts. (i) With his lectures and publications on speech in the early 1920s we find that apprehension crosses over to a borderland between the Mystery of 'wake and sleep' where the origins and power of speech sounds are directly experienced. (ii) Shortly afterwards Beckh crossed a threshold to perceive the relationships between music and the zodiac signs relating to the Earth. (iii) By 1925 he had moved further in: there was an area of perception that was revealed when the musical keys and the stars of heaven vanish, leaving (as in *The Magic Flute*) total darkness. But in this darkness—the depths of sleep—a great radiance appears behind all manifestation. Beckh, as others, came to recognize this radiance as the Divine Feminine. Five years later—beyond the scope of this brief account—Beckh could write of the mystery of substance. Given all of this, Piper and Schwebsch had certainly made the right decision.

Die Drei duly appeared in 1926 and its potential impact on the Anthroposophical Society and The Christian Community should not be underestimated:

- In January came the 'Zarathustra number' led by Steiner's lecture, 19 January 1911 (GA 60, lect. 9);
- February saw the 'Egyptian issue' led by Steiner's 'Hermes' (GA 60, lect. 12), 16 February 1911;
- in March there appeared 'Buddha' with Steiner's lecture on the subject (GA 60, lect. 13), 2 March 1911;
- April was celebrated by the 'Moses' issue headed up by Steiner's lecture of 9 March 1911 (GA 60, 14);
- May was dedicated to Steiner's 'Elijah' of 14 December 1911 (GA 61, 7) which Beckh had attended and never forgotten;
- in June the series came to a triumphant conclusion with the 'Christ' lecture of 25 January, 1912 (GA 61.10) 'Christus und die zwangzigste Jarhundert', bringing the reader to the present day.

For the editors and contributors it must have been clear that the six issues had achieved a very high degree of professional excellence. In turn, Beckh's seven articles—there were two pieces on Isis for the Egyptian issue—had set a new standard of profound wisdom and insight which caught the eye of the publisher Rudolf Geering in Basel. So it was that *Aus dem Welt der Mysterien. Sieben Aufsätze von Prof. Dr. Hermann Beckh* was compiled and published 1927, now for the first time translated into English. Beckh had made only a few slight changes from the articles in *Die Drei*, re-arranged their order, and found that the publisher Rudolf Geering would enter areas which, significantly, neither Friedrich Rittelmeyer nor the basement press in Urachstrasse would countenance. Geering dropped the 'Rev.' from Beckh's titles. At that time neither Beckh nor Geering could have guessed that their destined partnership would shortly lead to the publication of Beckh's masterpieces on *Mark's Gospel, the Cosmic Rhythm* (1928), *John's Gospel, the Cosmic Rhythm* (1930) and *Alchymy: the Mystery of the Material World* (1932).

From the World of the Mysteries in fact occupies a sequestered borderland where readers discover that accustomed boundaries are dissolving and, perhaps like Tamino, find themselves in an imposing study or library when all the lights are extinguished. Beckh was always delighted to find that Novalis had preceded himself and Rudolf Steiner into the Mysteries of the night, an area indeed where Buddhist texts come into their own. Yet Beckh did not turn to the levels of consciousness which he had analysed in *Buddha's Life and Work*, nor was the real centre of his concern Zarathustra, the Old Testament or even The Mystery of Golgotha. What particularly occupied Beckh in 1924-27 was the perception of the Divine Feminine, especially in ancient Egypt.

As we have seen above, Beckh's small book on Genesis for *Christus aller Erde* (1924) was composed with an eye for a sevenfold lemniscate with its centre (Chapter 4) devoted to Eve. This was no haphazard structure. With *Aus dem Welt der Mysterien* we find once again that the central piece of the seven articles concerns 'The Name Eve', immediately preceded by the work on Isis: the extraordinary *two* articles submitted by Beckh for the 'Egyptian' number of *Die Drei* in February 1926. One might find this a little unexpected as the professor was a master of several ancient languages and had a very good knowledge of Old Testament Hebrew but had no academic credentials in Egyptian hieroglyphs or Coptic. Instead he turned to three books: Friedrich Creuzer, *Symbolik und Mythologie der alten Völker* (1810-12, 2nd ed. 1819, 3rd ed. 1837); Rudolf Falb, *Das Land der Inca in seiner Bedeutung für die Urgeschichte der Sprache und Schrift*, Leipzig 1883; Heinrich Karl Brugsch, *Religion und Mythologie der alten Ägypter*, Leipzig, 1887. These heavyweight volumes, however, were only consulted to find some further evidential support for what Beckh had personally experienced in deep meditation following Rudolf Steiner, and could also conceptualize out of the primary Buddhist texts.

One can have some sympathy with Friedrich Rittelmeyer and Emil Bock at this time. Both were entirely committed to the vision that the Bible, Luther, Germany and Rudolf Steiner had established as the parameters of The Christian Community. While accepting this, Hermann Beckh *knew* the importance of the Divine Feminine, which he recognized as Isis-Sophia. There was some hesitancy at 41 Urachstrasse: the leadership wanted to avoid any revival of a veneration of Mary. When Beckh went on to introduce the blazing star Sirius as the representative of Isis-Sophia their consternation can be imagined.

Five years later, Beckh published a long series of contributions to the Priests' *Rundbrief* concerned with the stars and the Eternal Covenant found in the visible heavens. This was in response to work by Rudolf Frieling, who, taking up Beckh's approach to the 'cosmic rhythm' in his studies on Mark and John, presented his own exegeses of the relationship between the stars and the Creed of The Christian Community. Beckh was enthusiastic and, as he writes, took up his pen 'this very day'. The result is the first attempt to sketch a new wisdom of the stars, astrosophy based on Steiner's spiritual science, that should be more known today, nearly one hundred years after it was written.

Today, too, the presence of the Divine Feminine in both the Old and New Testaments has become an unassailable fact through exemplary studies, for example, Margaret Barker D.D. In place of the nineteenth-century volumes to which Beckh appealed, today we have Robert Powell's *The Sophia Teachings: The Emergence of the Divine Feminine in Our Time* (2001); Caitlín Matthew's *Sophia. Goddess of Wisdom, Bride of God* (2001) and the compilation of Rudolf Steiner's writings on the same subject made by Christopher Bamford, *Isis Mary Sophia: Her Mission and Ours* (2003). Even in his own time, although he was no doubt unaware of it, Beckh's contemporary Father Sergei Bulgakov, living as a Russian émigré in Paris within the Orthodox Seminary St. Serge, founded 1925, was challenging his own clerical hierarchy with *The Wisdom (Sophia) of God* and *The Burning Bush*, a study of the Mother of God.

Hermann Beckh's *From The World of the Mysteries* stands before a reader today as the clearest evidence that the greatest pioneers and pathfinders within Christ were not afraid to challenge the status quo among their own hierarchies. They could remain entirely true to their own vision and conscience and, although a century might pass, remain assured that the living spiritual truth will in time be recognized.

N.F.

Foreword

The articles collected here first appeared in German in the anthropo-sophical monthly *Die Drei* from January to June 1926:

- The Zarathustra-article appeared in January, Vol. V, No. 10 ('Zarathustra-number'), 751-74; Postscript, 783f.
- the two Isis-articles in Feb., Vol. V, No. 11 ('Egyptian-number'), 827-49 and 861-67,
- the Eva-article in April, Vol. VI, No. 1 ('Moses-number'), 50-60,
- the Buddha-article in March Vol. V, No. 12 ('Buddha-number'), 917-34,
- the article 'The Tree of Life' in May, Vol. VI, No. 2 ('Elijah-num-ber'), 96-119,
- the article 'The Christ-Mystery of the Early Mysteries' in June Vol. VI, No. 3 ('Christ-number'), 177-92.

This chronological sequence has been retained; the two articles 'Bud-dha's Passing' and 'The Name Eva', however, have moved places because of the inner connections and historical context.

It is intrinsic to such publications that a connection between the individual articles was not the original aim. In each case they came about independently out of the requirements of the journal with ref-erence to the planned content of the respective issue. The first article (on Zarathustra) was initially submitted as a kind of linguistic-philo-logical supplement to what the other articles contained on Zarathus-tra, pre-eminently the report of a lecture of Dr Rudolf Steiner [Berlin. 19 Jan. 1911. GA 60]. Excerpts from the early original language of Zarathustra, Avestan, were to be included. Only in the Isis-article of the Egyptian number did the occasion arise to return to the actual issues of the first Zarathustra and to present the connections to the early Zarathustra star-wisdom with the Egyptian Mysteries. Only with the progress of the work did there gradually result as if by itself something more like an inner connection of the individual articles. The connection of the individual pre-Christian Mysteries with the Mystery of Golgotha as the central Event of the history of the Earth increasingly stepped into the foreground; the content of those Mys-teries led increasingly towards the Mystery of Golgotha [the central Easter-event of death-resurrection of Christ Jesus].

The first Isis-article attempts to shed light on an area where hitherto little attention has been directed with presentations of Egyptian matters, that is, to the distant past and original flowering of the essential Egyptian mysteries. It is supplemented from the linguistic side by the article 'On the Name of Isis'. Here especially significant connections are revealed between the Egyptian (and Peruvian) Mysteries and their hieroglyphics and the results of anthroposophical research on the 'form tendencies' of the etheric formative forces, published by Dr Günther Wachsmuth in his *The Etheric Formative Forces in Cosmos, Earth and Man*.[205] The article 'On the Name of Isis' moves on to the closely related article on the name Eva. Here connections of the Egyptian mystery-wisdom with the Hebrew Moses-wisdom—which then provided transitions to the Mystery of Golgotha—become clear.

With the article 'Buddha's passing' we enter the realm of Indology. For a complete presentation of the essence of the pre-Christian Mysteries—which in this short series of articles is neither the aim, nor would it be possible—we would have had to preface descriptions of India and the original Indian Mysteries. From this viewpoint, however, it became of itself ever more clearly relevant to present Zarathustra as the inaugurator of that great Mystery-stream which then led to the Mystery of Golgotha. To this stream a certain early Indian counter-movement was a sub-theme. The article 'Buddha's Passing' offered a good opportunity also to show how and to what extent specific connections exist to the Mystery of Golgotha from the Indian side (Krishna and Buddha).

The various motifs touched on in the first five articles are combined in the last two in such a manner that new cohering viewpoints arise. The essay on 'The Tree of Life' initially helps us to look back to the primal past. Linking to India, Persia, Egypt, Assyria, and the Hebrews, the essay takes into account in the Indian realm, besides Buddha, the original Indian culture, or its echoes in the Veda. Only the last section of the essay, dedicated to Novalis, allows us to look more towards the future in Christ, whose connection with the Indian, Persian, and Egyptian Mystery-past then forms the theme of the final essay 'The Christ-Mystery in the Early Mysteries'.

The single essays are essentially printed unchanged. Only a few internal details are changed, added, or omitted. Certain changes that have arisen in the transition from journal to book-form are naturally of a purely formal nature.

Hermann Beckh

The Sacred Primal Word of Zarathustra
with excerpts from the Avesta

The documents relating to Zarathustra retained in the Avesta (Zend-Avesta) may be of later origin; they may derive from a later successor of the first Zarathustra, who in the first, if not in the second, millennium BC (philological research assumes the fifth or sixth century)[206] carried the name again of Zarathustra and renewed his influence. Nevertheless, they contain many things that point to the great age of the primal Zarathustra presented to us by spiritual science. That distant age is already mentioned by the Greek historian Plutarch, when he proclaims him to be the 'magician Zoroaster'[207] (this is the Greek form for Zarathustra of the Avesta) who lived 5000 years before the Trojan War. A breath from the true primal time of the early Aryan age reaches us from the Avesta—initially from the most ancient part according to its language and content, what is called the Gathas of Zarathustra [or the Zoroastrian Gathas—Avestan: *Gāθās*: the 17 hymns believed to have been composed by Zarathustra himself], but even from the later Avesta. However philological research judges the age and origin of the texts of the Avesta that have come down to us, there still lives something of the spirit of the primal Zarathustra in this most beautifully human and powerful religious document of early Aryan humanity.

Above all there lies over the language itself the mood of this distant age, the spirit of the first Zarathustra. It is not identical with the language of ancient Persia. Philology can only guess where it was spoken. Important researchers[208] seek its origin in the region of the Lake of Kansaoya / Kansava (Lake Hāmūn) in S.E. Iran on the Irano-Afghan border. In this lake, according to an ancient Iranian legend, lies the ancient seed of Zarathustra out of which the future Saviour of the world is to be born. Such pictures, as well as in other places of the Avesta, gently hint towards mysteries which at that time still rested in the lap of the future, today freshly opened up to anthroposophical research as connections to Christ and Christ-mysteries. When linguistics today always ask: where were the ancient Vedic Sanskrit and ancient Avestan actually spoken? then this is actually a wrongly formulated question. In the way this research imagines it was 'spoken'—that means, used as an everyday language—does not at all apply to early Vedic Sanskrit or

Avestan. These were purely the languages of the priests, languages in which the word completely contained the memory of the sacred origin of all speech, of which Rudolf Steiner tells us in a beautiful and gripping manner in an essay in the journal *Lucifer-Gnosis* [see 'The Lemurian Race' in Rudolf Steiner, *Cosmic Memory. GA* 11]. Towards Avestan it can be felt that it is still a completely sacred language, that it is *through and through nothing but mantra. The word* itself in Avestan is *mantro*, which is nothing else than the Iranian form of the Indian word *mantra*. Only out of the essence of the *mantram*, out of the primal meaning of the sounds and of the effects of the rhythm, of the forming element of the consonants and out of the musical quality of the vowels, which is developed especially in the Avesta, can the sacred primal word of Zarathustra be understood.

In contrast to the *thought*-element in Sanskrit, which is formed by the consonants, there lives in the rich vocalizing of the Avesta a strong element of *feeling*, especially the feelings of deepest religious devotion that intensify up to true ecstatic devotion. Through word and sound we are carried on the wings of devotion into cosmic widths and the starry realms. No other language through its mere sounds already conveys so strongly this mood of devotion as early Avestan. A mere translation according to the dictionary would give no idea of this. With a correct living into the spiritual essence of the language, one will have to get beyond the premature assumption that a real 'translation' from one language into another, especially from an early mantric to a modern language, would be at all possible. And in the place of a dictionary-inspired translation there has increasingly to appear the fresh artistic creation out of the spirit of the other language (into which it is to be 'translated'). In such a difficult and unique, early and most remote language as early Avestan *every* attempt will always remain somewhat incomplete. Consequently, if extracts out of the Avesta are to be an accompaniment here, it appears necessary to add the original text. The words and sounds of Avestan have to convey something of the spirit of Zarathustra. In this language we strongly and miraculously feel the ease of expression, the living element of discussion, of which the Old Man with the Lamp speaks in Goethe's fairy tale 'The Green Snake and the Beautiful Lily'.[209] In contrast to Vedic Sanskrit that loves the exalted, abstract heights lying far removed from natural speech, we always find in Avestan, where devotion is raised into cosmic widths and the starry realms, a solid and secure standing on the Earth, a solid connection with the Earth. This makes possible a real *beholding in the cosmic widths*, not a mere dreaming in mystic depths.

In his public lecture on Zarathustra held in the Architects' House, Berlin 19 Jan., 1911 [in GA 60], Rudolf Steiner points significantly to the *purity* of Zarathustrianism, based on the fact that it views the primal duality, the primal polarity of the world not in the picture of gender difference, but in the pure picture of *light* and *darkness.* The good spirit of light, Ahura-Mazda (Persian *Ormuzd*), is opposed by Angromainyusch (Persian *Ahriman*). Right at the end of the lecture, the famous Gatha passage was quoted (Yasna 45), where Zarathustra proclaims the doctrine of the two spirits: 'I would speak! Come and listen to me ...' Directly following this come words in which the spirit of light, Ahuramazdau, himself struggles with the dark adversary, Angromainyusch, or Ahriman.[210]

> At fravakhshy*a* angheush mainy*u* pouru*ye*
> Yay*ao* spany*ao* *uiti* mrav*at yöm* angröm
> n*o*it n*a* man*a*o söngh*a* n*o*it khratavo
> na*eda* varana n*o*it ukhdh*a* na*eda* shyaothan*a*
> n*o*it da*enao* n*o*it urv*a'* n*o* hatschaint*e*

> And I will speak of the two spirits in the primal beginning of the world,
> and of those two the more sacred one spoke to the evil one:
> Neither our spiritual selves, nor our doctrines,
> nor our decisions of will, our convictions of belief,
> neither our words, nor our deeds,
> neither our whole being, nor our soul do
> correspond in any kind of harmony.

In the Gatha Yasna 49 Zarathustra himself speaks in a similar manner of the eternal adversary Ahriman:

> at m*a* yav*a* böndv*o* pafr*e* pafr*e* mzishto
> y*o* duzhöröthrish tschikhnush*a* ash*a* Mazd*a*
> vanguh*i ada* gaid*i* m*o*i *a* m*o*i arap*a*
> ahy*a* voh*u vida* manangh*a*

> And always working against me [crossing my intentions], the arch-defiler,
> whose evil intentions I seek to make good again through the power of truth,
> O Mazda;
> may a just balance come to me,
> be my support and security, and through the spirit of the good, cause his
> downfall.

Ahura Mazda appears in the Gathas as the Lord of eternal, cosmic order and of karma. The word in Avestan for this cosmic order, *asha* (spoken: asha), is actually one of the untranslatable words, whose nuances are not contained in a modern word. According to its sounds and its meaning it corresponds to the Vedic *ta*, to that word which actually means the *great rhythm*, the cosmic rhythm. On the one side this rhythm is revealed in the lawfulness of nature, in the fixed, ordered courses of the stars and in the course of the year; on the other side is reflected the order of the public cult and cultic ritual (*rta* = rite). We can feel the *rta* (Avestan *asha*) as the great *cosmic ritual*, of which the earthly cultic rites are a reflection. In all this, such names as *asha* are not at all the mere abstract concepts as they appear to be when we translate: eternal cosmic order, sacred truth, sacred right, and so on, but they are basically *entities*, felt as divine beings, to whom certain prayers are directed. Ahura Mazda is the creator of this *asha*, of this eternal cosmic order, this great cosmic rhythm and cosmic ritual. He does not create it as some kind of abstraction, but as a being or a ring-dance of creative, rhythmically fashioning beings. In this sense all the questions are to be understood, which in the Gatha Yasna 44 Zarathustra directs to Ahura Mazda, where always the answer is to be thought, 'Ahura Mazda himself':

> tat thwa pörösa örösh moi vaotscha Ahura
> kasna zántha pata ashahya pouroyo
> kasna hvöng staröm-tscha dat advanöm
> kö[211] ya mao ukhshyeiti nöröfsaiti thwat
> tatschit Mazda vasömi anyatscha viduye

> This I will ask you, proclaim it rightly in the word, O Lord of Life:
> Who in the primal beginning of creation was
> the Father of the sacred cosmic rhythm [of the *asha*]?
> Who showed their courses to the harmoniously sounding
> Sun and the stars?
> Who caused the Moon to increase and [periodically] decrease?
> These things, O Master of Wisdom, and still more I wish to know.

The third line would be simply translated by the philologist as 'Who showed the Sun and the stars their path'. Now the word for Sun (here in the genitive form '*hvöng*') in the Gatha-Avesta shows a remarkable physiognomy. It is otherwise *hvar*, and this form in the later, more recent Avestan, *hss* became the only form. This *hvr*, corresponding to the Sanskrit *svr* (related to this, also Skr. *surya* 'Sun') is clearly a word for light, related in the primal language to the Heb. *hor*, '*or* 'light'. It is quite remarkable that in the earlier Gatha-Avesta, besides this word for light with *r* another word with *n* appears which also means 'Sun': *hvan*, gen. *hvöng*. *Hvr* corresponds to the Skr. *svr* ('heavenly light'), *hvan* corresponds to Skr. *svan*, 'to sound'. In *r* lies the raying light, in *n* the sounding element. That means, besides the actual light-word for 'Sun', yet another earlier word that through its sounds clearly says that in times of an earlier human consciousness the Sun was not only experienced as an appearance of light but as still sounding. We may recall Goethe's Faust:

> The sun intones in ancient fashion
> mid brother spheres a rival song.[212]

Also the Germ. *Sonne* (cf. Lat. *sonus* 'sound') contains a memory of these connections. No longer during the time of the inception of the Gatha-Avesta assumed by the philologists, though certainly during the time of the first Zarathustra, of whose spirit a breath still survives in the early Gathas, there Man, especially a great leader and inspirer of the entire cultural epoch like Zarathustra, still lived in such a consciousness of the Sun and the planets that the astral body still experienced the great rhythms of the Sun and planets as 'sounding'. The consciousness of inspiration, of perceiving the spiritual, cosmic sounding still existed. Out of such a consciousness the Sun was depicted, besides the word for light, with a unique sound-word, which here in the genitive form *hvöng* makes a very characteristic effect as expressing immediately through the sounds, the great Sun-harmonies, mantrically and musically. Consequently, the translation could be given away from the dictionary but in accordance with the original revelation of the sounds, 'Who showed their courses to the *harmoniously sounding* Sun and the stars.' A further verse follows:

> tat thawa pörösa örösh moi vaotscha Ahura
> kö huapao raotschaos-tsha dat tömaos-tsha
> kö huapao hvafnöm-tsha dat zaema-tscha
> kö ya ushao arömpithwa khshapa-tscha
> yao manaothrish tshazdonghvantöm aröthahya

> This I will ask you, proclaim it rightly in the word, O Lord of Life:
> which artist created the light [the worlds of light, the dreams of light, the beings of light] and the darkness,
> which artist created sleep and waking,
> which artist [created] the progress of the morning, midday, night, which, to him who knows decision-making,
> who are admonishers for the great decision?

Ahura is here the great *cosmic artist*, a thought which plays a great role with Zarathustra, whereas this thought is hardly found in Indian culture, except where it is concerned with that divine figure, behind whom stands hidden the creative Christ-figure *Vishva-karman* or *Tvashtar*, the great cosmic artist, or cosmic carpenter. The Avesta-word hu*a*pao (quite literally: 'the one who accomplishes beautiful works, the maker of beauty') points still more directly to the *artistic* moment in the divine creation.

That Ahura Mazda is especially the creator of the moral world-order and the balance of destiny, karma, is expressed in the following Gatha (Yasna 43), where Zarathustra out of his spirit-vision speaks, raising himself to the cosmic primal beginnings.

> Spöntöm at thw*a* Mazd*a* möngh*i* Ahur*a*
> hyat thw*a* angheush za'nthoi darösöm paouruyehy*a*
> hyat d*a*o shyaothan*a* m*i*zhdava'n ya-tsch*a* ukhdh*a*
> aköm *aka*i vanghuh*i*m ash*i*m vanghaov*e*
> thw*a* hunar*a* d*a*moish urva*e*se apöm*e*

> And I recognized You in the spirit as the Holy One,
> O Master of Wisdom [Mazda], Lord of Life [Ahura],
> when I beheld You at the creation of the primal beginning of life,
> when you for deeds and word created there balance of destiny,
> and through Your mighty ability [return] the bad to the bad
> and the good to the good at the Last End of earthly development![213]

***

In his lecture-cycle *The Spiritual Hierarchies* [Düsseldorf. 12-18 April 1909. GA 110] and the book *Esoteric/Occult Science* [GA 13], Rudolf Steiner has shown how fire, the warmth-ether, in a certain sense stands in the centre of everything to do with world-becoming—tending on the one side towards the physical, material element, and on the other to the spiritual element of soul—in itself the immediate outpouring of the tremendous cosmic sacrifice at the altar of creation. We also find the sacred fire, the flickering sacrificial flame in the pre-Christian religions, Mysteries and cultures. In this, too, the earthly ritual element is a mirroring of the great cosmic ritual; earthly fire is a mirror of the cosmic, sacrificial fire. Everywhere in the early Mysteries and cultures we find veneration of the sacred fire. Nowhere, however, is the sacredness of fire felt more than in the religion of Zarathustra. It is the fire-ritual, the veneration of fire κατ'ἐξοχήν [to the highest extent]: in no other religion is the sacred and purifying effect of the fire so emphasized. Consequently, especially in the religion of Zarathustra they do *not* burn their dead because the remains, the impure parts of the corpse, should not come into contact with the sacred and pure element of fire.

Ultimately Zarathustra intended with the sacred fire not only the physical but a higher etheric fire. Already the Avestan word *athar* 'fire' points to the Gk. *aither* 'ether' (whereas in Indian culture and language we look more from the etheric towards the physical, we find with Zarathustra as well as in Egypt the beholding of the etheric element). The sacred and purifying [force] of the element of fire appears especially where the great fire ordeal of the Last Judgement, the great decision at the end of the cosmic-era is mentioned. The thought is worked out wonderfully in the teaching of Zarathustra that a difference of reward and punishment does not exist, award for those who are good and punishment for those who are bad, and so on, in the great cosmic crisis. It will, however, be the one and the same element, the same etheric-supersensory element that the two groups of souls will meet, into which they both have to enter. For those who are good, who have been properly inwardly prepared throughout their life, this element will be a stream of quickening milk, for the others it will be a consuming stream of fire. There are, to speak with the word of our ritual today [Epistle for St John's-Tide in The Act of Consecration of Man], the 'pure ether-spheres, that alone can bear the guiltless on the glancing waves of spirit'.

Already in the early Gathas of Zarathustra we find meaningful indications of the great fire ordeal at the end of time, and the two groups, those who have reached the goal of development and those who have not, will then face each other, in Gathas Yasna 51:9:

> ya'm khshnutöm ranoibya dao
> thwaa athra sukhra Mazda
> ayangha khshusta aibi ahvahu dakhstöm davoi
> rashayenghe drögvantöm savanyo ashavanöm

> The ordeal, which You will place before the two parties in your pure fire, O Mazda,
> with liquid ore in order to accomplish the testing of souls,
> that it may damage the companion of deceit, that it may heal the pious [the companion of truth]…

The word *drögvant*, Germ. *Truggenosse* 'companion of deceit' as the evil ones are called here, is derived from *drug* or *drudsch*, Germ.

Lüge, Trug, Verleumdung 'lie, deceit, calumny', most likely etymologically connected to the Germ. *Trug* (we are also reminded of *Druck*, *Albdruck* 'pressure, nightmare', *Trud*, etc., for also the *Drudsch* is seen as in a nightmare apparition as a female demon). *Drudsch* is the opposite of the good genius *Asha*, 'sacred truth, sacred order, sacred right'. In his lecture on Zarathustra, Rudolf Steiner points out how evil for Zarathustra is especially embodied in that which opposes truth in lies, deceit and calumny. This being of deceit, the lie and calumny, bringing death and destruction is called in the Avesta *Drudsch* (*Drug*); whoever follows it is *drögvant*, a companion of deceit, who at the Great Decision at the end of all things, is excluded.

A prayer which, with regard to the Great Decision in the fire-trial, the Zarathustrian believer would direct to Ahura Mazda, can be found in the above-mentioned Gatha, Yasna 51:7:

> Daidi moi yo ga'm tasho apas-tscha urvaraos-tscha
> amörötata-haurvata spönishta mainyu Mazda
> tövishi utayuiti manangha vohu sönnghe

> Give me, You who created the cow and the water and the plants,
> the immortal salvation through your sacred spirit, O Mazda,
> and the rejuvenating power through the spirit of the Good at the Great Decision.

Other places can also be found where the walking through the fire, *the trial by fire*, is lived through like an initiation process and Yasna 36 contains prayers directed to Ahura Mazda before passing through the fire.

> ahya thwa athro vörözöna paouruye
> pairidsch asamaide Mazda Ahura thwa
> thwa mainyu spönishta yo a akhtish
> ahmai yöm akhtoyoi daonghe
> urvazishto hvo nao yataya
> paitidschamyao atarö Mazdao Ahurahya
> urvazishtahya urvazya na'mishtahya
> nömangha nao mazishtai yaongha'm paitidschamyao

> Through this activity of the fire we first approach You,
> You, Master of Wisdom, Lord of Life,
> to You, through your sacred Spirit, [which lives in the fire],
> which is pain for the one
> whom You choose to undergo pain.
> As the most blissful [experience] may You meet us,
> O fire of Ahura Mazda, at the Trial

with the bliss of the most blissful One,
with the reverence of the most revered One
may you approach us
to the greatest of all events.

Later passages in the same Gatha sound already like a Christian Mass text.

nömah yamahi ishuidyamahi thwa Mazda Ahura
vispaish thwa humataish vispaish hukhtaish
vispaish hvarshtaish pairidschasamaide

We venerate You, we render our guilt-laden gratitude,
O Spirit of Wisdom, Lord of Life,
we approach you with all our pure thoughts,
with all our right words,
with all our good deeds.

sraeshta'm at toi körhrpöm köhrpa'm
avaedayamahi Mazda Ahura
ima raotschao barözishtöm barözimana'm
avat yat hvaro avatschi

We consecrate to you the noblest body[214] of all bodies,
O Spirit of Wisdom, Lord of Life,
to you this daylight,
to you the highest of heights
up above, what we call the *Sun*.

***

Hitherto only Gatha passages have been chosen, that is, passages from the oldest, and also most difficult sections of the Avesta, which still reflect in the purest way the spirit of the first Zarathustra.

With the later Avesta this spirit appears in the artistic form of a later age which lies nearer to us. More clearly than in the Gathas there appears here the view of the hierarchical beings (probably the Spirits of Form) surrounding the highest divinity, Ahura Mazda, of what are called 'immortal holy ones, of the Amösha-Spönta, or Ameshaspents, also mentioned in Steiner's Zarathustra-lecture. Six of these beings appear in the Avesta, or seven if we include the divinity Ahura Mazda who is above them, a kind of reflection amongst them. The already-mentioned godhead Asha belongs to them, also Vohu Mano (the 'spirit of the good'), Khshathra (rulership, kingdom), Armaiti (the pious, devotional thinking), Haurvatat (fullness of healing) Ameretat (immortality, especially the genera of the plant world, of its healing and rejuvenating forces). The number twelve, of which the lecturer speaks, arises, when to the six spirits their six dark antipodes are added, whose names also appear in the Avestas.[215] Yasht 13:81 speaks of the relationship of these Ameshaspents to Ahura Mazda:

> yenghe urva ma'nthro spönto
> aurusho raokhshno fradörörsro
> köhrpas-tscha yao raethwayeiti
> srirao Amöshana'm Spöntana'm
> vörözdao Amöshana'm Spöntana'm
> hvarökhshaetöm aurvat-aspöm yazamaide

> Whose ether-soul [Life-spirit] is the holy
> word of sacrifice [mantram],
> the bright, shining, widely-raying One,
> whose bodily figure in which he clothes himself
> are the beautiful bodies of the 'immortal holy Ones' (Ameshaspents),
> the exalted bodies of the 'immortal holy Ones',
> Him the radiant Sun-spirit [Ahura Mazda]
> with the swift steeds we venerate in prayer.

The word *raokhshno* in the second line is one of numerous words for light or shining in the Avesta. Compared to the richness of the nuances of light and shining which this language expresses, any translation appears poor. The language itself shows here its aura, and what it expresses are not the physical contours of the things and beings, but more their etheric being, their aura. The word *raokhshno* (*ao* is like a diphthong, *kh* like 'ch' [as in 'loch'], *sh* like 'sch') corresponds according to its sounds exactly to the Indian *rukshna*. For the philologist these two words are identical, but whereas a spiritual experience of the sounds with *rukshna*, has so to speak only the physical contours of the shining object before it, we feel in *raokhshno*, as it were, its ether-aura lighting up, we think of the fine, mist-like, formations of light which clairvoyants and sensitive people perceive around crystals, plants and human hands, etc. of the phenomena 'Od ' which Reichenbach named and illustrated [Karl von Reichenbach, 1788-1869].

Further on in the verse the strongly active far-penetrating (*vörözidoithra*) eye of the Ameshaspents is mentioned and their united harmony.

> yoi hapta hamomangho
> yoi hapta hamovatschangho
> yoi hapta hamoshyaothnaongho

yaescha'm asti hamöm mano
hamöm vatscho hamöm shyaothnöm
hamö pata-tscha frasasta-tscha
yo dadhvao Ahuro Mazdao

All seven who are of the same thinking, all seven who are of the same word, all seven who are of the same activity, whose thinking is the same, whose words are the same, whose activities are the same, who all have the same Father and Master, namely, the Creator Ahura-Mazda.

***

A further category of beings is the *Izeds* (the Persian word), the Avestan word is *Yazata* (first syllable stressed). These are the *archangels* of Zarathustrianism. Some are named and especially celebrated, for example, Sraosha ('sense of obedience'), then especially the Archangel of the Sun, *Mithra*, whose name is linked in a later cultural period to the Mysteries of Mithras. In the form *Mitra* the name also appears in the Rig-Veda; it delineates the Sun-god, the godhead of the light-filled sky of the day.

In the Avesta generous hymns are directed to the Archangel Mithra. The song of praise in Yasht 10:13, is in his honour.

yo paoiryo mainyavo yazato taro Hara'm asnaoiti
paurvanaemat amöshahe hu yat aurvat-aspahe
yo paoiryo zaranyopiso srirao baröschnava göröwnaiti
adhat vispöm adidhaiti airyoshayanöm sövishto

The one who as the first spiritual angel-being rises above the high
Hara Mountains [the Caucasus], in front of the immortal Sun with the swift
    steeds,
who gains as the first one the magnificent heights which are adorned in
    golden splendour,
from there he overviews the whole land of the Aryans, the strong hero.

The name for the mountains, Hara, recalls the Hebrew *har* 'mountain'. Still more strongly than the Indian, and again with a different nuance from the Hebrew, the Aryan Iranian experiences the sacredness and splendour of the heights of the mountains. The Avesta in many places calls the mountains: ashahvathra, which means 'where one can breathe comfortably again in the great cosmic rhythm'.

The early Iranians also felt that the gods live in the mountain heights which are not reached by the foot of man. Up there is the home of Mithra. From here he fights the adversary of the gods, Ahri-man, Yasht 10:52.

aot yat duzhdao fradvaraiti
yo aghavarösh thwashagama
thwashöm yudschyeiti vashöm
Mithro yo vouru-gaoyaoitish
Sraoshas-tscha ashyo suro
… rasmodschatöm va dim dschainti amodschatöm va

If then the evil one comes rushing forth,
the wrong-doer in speedy advance,
then in haste he harnesses his carriage,
Mithra, the Lord of the rich pastures,
and Sraosha, the sacred hero,
… and slays him in battle or in single combat.

Directed towards a third group of beings, to the Fravashi (angels, special guardian angels), is the hymn Yasht 13 (Fravardin-Yasht):

mraot Ahuro Mazdao Spitamai Zarathushtrai
aeva te zavarö aodschas-tscha
hvaröno avas-tscha rafnas-tscha
framrava örösvo Spitama
yat ashaona'm Fravashina'm
ughrana'm aiwithurana'm
yatha me dschasan avangh yatha me barön upasha'm
ughrao ashaona'm Fravashayo

Thus spoke Ahuro Mazda to Spitama Zarathustra:
Therefore I proclaim to you, O Zarathustra,
the power and the strength,
the shining glory and the protection and guarding
of the sacred angels, of the powerful supra-mighty ones,
as they came to my help,
as they gave me support,
the strong guardian angels of the pious ones.

aongha'm raya hvarönangha-tscha
vidharaem Zarathshtra aom asmanöm
yo ustscha raokhshno fradörösro
yo ima'm za'm atscha pairitscha buvava ma'nayön ahe yatha vish

aem yo hishtaite mainyustato
handrakhto duraekarano
ayangho köhrpa hvaenahe

raotschahino aoi thrishva
yim Mazdao vaste vanghanöm
stöhrpaesanghöm mainyutashtöm

Through their shining and their glory
I, Zarathustra, surveyed that heaven above,
the radiant being that allows us to behold world-distances,
who surrounds the Earth from all sides,
one could say, like a stronghold,
he, standing there held in balance by spirits,
firmly grounded, bounded in the far distances,
with a body equalling transparent ore,
radiating into all three realms,
into which Mazda clothes himself as with a garment,
which is star-wrought, carpented by spirits.

Heavenly distances and starry realms shine before us in this verse, even though the translation only dimly renders the shining power of the Avestan words. The word for heaven *asman* in the third line of the second verse is remarkable (here in the accusative case *asmanöm*); in the first instance it means 'stone' and from there has come to mean 'heaven'. We feel transported into primal ages of human consciousness, where people still clairvoyantly experienced the connection of the cosmic, starry influence on the mineral, stony element. That connection Novalis helps us to experience when he speaks of the heaven of stars as the sublime dome of the realm of stones,[216] or in other places connects the mysteries of the stars with those of the stones. A relationship, too, of the spark in the stone to the lightning spark in the clouds of heaven may have played a role in his consciousness. In any case, we recognize how far the nuances of our words today are removed from those of the Avesta.

An important viewpoint in Steiner's lecture on Zarathustra [Berlin, 19 Jan. 1911, in GA 60][217] is the indication of the difference between Zarathustra's view and the mystical stream of early India. In India there is predominantly a looking within the depths of the soul, whereas with Zarathustra, 'the forces which are strengthened in our soul penetrate behind the veil of the outer world into the supersensory realm, which spreads into infinity—one would like to say: into immeasurable distances'. Quite differently from the early Indian, we might feel, Zarathustra and the one venerating Zarathustra experience the *stars*. Certainly, the Indians had words for the stars, but they are more abstract words; he has the concept 'star', yet he does not live with the essential nature of the stars. The Zarathustrian feels in the stars 'the essence of his own being', his heart becomes warm when the stars light up before him. On the wings of devotion, he himself will be carried as into the widths of the world. The star becomes for him the awakener of clairvoyant (astral [= starry]) vision. The early Iranian still had the really ancient primal word for 'star' which the Indian had already lost during the time of Sanskrit; this primal word is none other than [what] we have in German as *Stern*—here only strengthened by the final sound *n*—appearing again in the English 'star', reduced to the word's original primal form. In early Avestan *star* means 'the star', only the vowel changes or is omitted in compound words. In the verse quoted above the word appears as *stöhr* at the end—*stöhrpaesanghöm* 'star-wrought' .

The more we study Avestan, the more we recognize in it something of the early star-wisdom, and in the language itself this star-element is expressed. The innermost soul of Zarathustrian wisdom is the *star*, and with the name 'Zarathustra' those people who find in it the word 'star' (*star*, *str*) will be correct. In 'star' Zarathustra looks up to the *higher* 'I'. He does not speak any abstract teaching about this higher 'I', but about the 'star'. With Zarathustra, as already mentioned, there ultimately lies the seed for the starry wisdom of early Egypt which stems from that far-distant primal age that reaches far beyond the actual 'Egyptian-Chaldean cultural epoch', into the age of Zarathustra. And in later Egyptian times, this wisdom of the stars and reference to the stars is still mirrored especially in the narrative of the star Sirius and the constellation of Orion connected to it. In Sirius (*Sothis*-star), the soul of Isis was seen, and the soul of Osiris in Orion. Consequently, it appears especially significant when we also find in the Avesta (Yasht 8) a great hymn to the star Sirius (Avesta: *Tishtrya*) spreading out the whole abundance of Avestan words for 'light'.

**

In a genuine spirit of Zarathustra, the Fravardin-Yasht returns from the cosmic distances and starry heights back to the Earth on which the early Iranian stood much more firmly, ready for battle, than the Indian. The eye of Zarathustra also sees in and behind the Earth the spiritual essence, upon whose becoming and further activity the angelic hierarchies have taken and continue to take part, Yasht 13:9:

za'm pöröthwim ahuradata'm
ya'm masim-tscha pathana'm-tscha
ya baröthri paraosh srirahe
ya vispöm ahum astvantöm

baraiti dschum-tscha iristöm-tscha
garayas-tscha yo börözanto
pouruvastraongho afönto

Through its shining and its glory, O Zarathustra, I unrolled this wide, divine-ly-created Earth, the great expanses, who is the bearer of many beautiful things, who carries all physical beings [literally: 'those invested with a skel-eton', *astvantöm*], the quick and the dead ['that which has become rigid in firm form', *iristöm*], and the high-reaching mountains, rich in pastures and running water.

Zarathustra is the first great initiate of humanity who stands in such a way firmly grounded on the Earth, the first to tell humanity of the *meaning of the Earth* (here one of the few connecting points lies which lead from the first Zarathustra of the Avesta into the otherwise quite remote thought-world of Friedrich Nietzsche). From none of the great wise men and leaders of India, least of all the Buddha, are we able to think of a characteristic attributed to Zarathustra in the same Yasht (13:88), where Zarathustra is called in one breath the first priest (*athaur-van* 'fire magician'), the first warrior (*rathaeshta* 'chariot warrior'), the first *cattle-breeding farmer (vastryo fshuya'ns)*.

The opponents, in this Yasht singing of the angelic hierarchies (Fravashi), are the demons, the *Daevs* or *Devs*. In his lecture on Zarathus-tra, Rudolf Steiner speaks of the reasons that have led to the fact that the same word in Indian characterizing the bright spirit-being *deva* (= *deus* [Lat. for 'god']), in its Avestan form *Daeva* expressess the demonic adver-sary, whereas the Indian *asura* expresses seldom the divine, mostly the demonic element of the opponents of the divine, for in its Avestan form *Ahura* becomes precisely the name of the divine. The whole difference between the state of consciousness peculiar to the early Indians and the early Iranians, and the Indian and Iranian paths of initiation plays a role here. These *Devs* or *Daevs*, adversaries of the gods, are brought into interesting astronomical connections in the Fravardin-Yasht, when later it is said of the angels (13:57, 58):

ya'o stra'm maongho huro
anaghrana'm raotschangha'm
patho daeshayön ashaonish
yoi para ahmat hame gatvo daröghöm
tishtönta afrashimanto
daevana'm paro tbaeshanghat
daevana'm paro draomohu.

Those who govern the sacred, rhythmical courses of the stars, the Moon and the Sun, and those lights without beginning, those who before the fiend-inspired hate of the *Daevs*, formerly stood still on the same spot, in fear before the fiendish assaults of the *Daevs* [*ae* spoken as a dipthong, like *ai*, not like ä].

aat te nuram fravazönti
duraeurvaesöm adhvano urvaesöm nashömna
yim frashokörötoit vanghuyao

And hereafter they stride forwards, till they one day achieve the far-off aim of their path to renew the Earth out of progressive development.

Endlessly significant for the whole teaching of Zarathustra is the *concept of development* lying in the word *frashoköröti* (usually literally translated 'newly fashioning' or 'world-renewing': 'progressive steps', that is, advancing creation and development in the sense of cosmic renewal). This concept, so important for us today, we do not find clearly in India. It is of great significance with Zarathustra that he and his language have this so clearly. The whole Zarathustrian religion bears the imprint of progress, still today in the good sense 'modern'; we always find the active working towards the renewal and re-fashioning at the end of things (that is, of the present [incarnation of the] Earth), for that which in [the Creed of The Christian Community] the Christian ritual we call the 're-enlivening of the dying Earth-existence'. It also prophetically points towards the coming Saviour of the world (*Saoshyant*), the *Christ* (initially the Solomon-Jesus[218] child).

Before we quote relevant passages here, as the counterpart to this a religious-historical description of the primal age of humanity (i.e. in this case, of the *first post-Atlantean cultural period*, of the 'golden age') has to be mentioned, especially important also to illuminate the Egyptian age.

***

This description can be found in the presentation of the mystical Soma (Haoma) ritual, which along with the fire-cult stands at the centre of the Zarathustrian cult. Soma, Avestan *Haoma*, is a certain sacred plant, the milky juice of which, pressed and distilled, produces the famous drink that awakens the ecstasy of high consciousness. This higher ecstasy is clearly distinguished here from a lower intoxication, as also in India. Indian culture and Avestan culture closely meet in the mystical Soma. The outer plant and the outer drink are pictures for a spiritual reality.

This appears most clearly with Zarathustra, who everywhere looks at the etheric side of things. He knows the etheric *archetypal plant*, the tree Hv*a*pi (Vendidad 5:19): 'Out of this [tree] all my plants grow [athra me urv*a*r*ao* raodhönti visp*ao*] and all plant species [visposarödho, that is, as in Genesis 1:11, 12] the hundreds and thousands, myriads upon myriads.' Thus the Soma in the star-wisdom of Zarathustra is ultimately the cosmic essence of the stars themselves, the enlivening dews of the stars that awaken in the human soul the astral clairvoyance, which in the epoch of Zarathustra was a true Sun-clairvoyance. What existed in the time of the first Zarathustra as a reality, lived in later epochs as a memory. During the time when the documents of the more recent Avesta were written, during the time of the later Zarathustra, people still lived in the memory of the great times of the early clairvoyance, of the ancient Sun-seer power which was linked to the name of the great Zarathustra, and to certain others, which is highly interesting for the history of religion and of human origins.

In Yasna 9 we hear how Zarathustra one morning met the Soma (Haoma). Haoma as a being appears before him during the ritual. 'Who are you, whom of all embodied life I see as the most beautiful, who contains in himself his own Sun-like immortal life?' The Soma being answers him, 'I am, O Zarathustra, the sacred Soma holding death at bay [azöm ahmi Zarathustra haomo ashava duraosho]. Take me, press me into the drink, sing my praise, as also the future saviours will praise me.' When Zarathustra responds, 'Praise be to Soma' (nömo haom*a*i), and asks him who among mortals was the first to have extracted him, the Soma (and thereby opened to himself the sources of the Sun-clairvoyance), 'the sacred Haoma who keeps death at bay' answers him:

> *Vivanghvat* was the first human being [mortal] of the physical world who extracted me. He was blessed that a son was born to him, *Yima*, the light-filled, the good shepherd, who amongst the Earth-born [hvarönan-guhastömo zatan*a*'m] possessed the most sublime, bright Sun-ether aura [hvaröno], *who amongst the mortals possessed the Sun-eye* [hvarödaröso mashyan*a*'m]. This had the effect that man and animal did not die, water and plants did not dry up, and nourishment did not diminish. In the realm of the hero Yima neither cold nor heat existed, neither age nor death, no infection of sickness and illness of evil demons. Like fifteen-year-olds in appearance, father and son went their ways as long as Yima ruled, the good shepherd, the son of Vivanghvat.

Here we meet the 'legend' of the 'golden age' found in so many peoples (the Indians speak of 'Krita Yuga'). But in these legends real human memories live, not of the actual 'age of Paradise' before the 'Fall of Man'—this would be, in anthroposophical terminology, the 'early Lemurian age'—but its later reflection. Such a reflection initially takes place during early Atlantis, after the Lemurian fire-catastrophe, with the first Atlantean root-race. This completely childlike race, possessing a high and pure clairvoyance, was not yet connected so deeply with the physical element that they would have experienced (objectively existing) the discarding of the body as death as we do today. And this early Atlantean period is not meant here, but these conditions are mirrored once more in a later time, even though weaker, after the Atlantean catastrophe in the first 'post-Atlantean epoch' in the *primal Indian age*. The human being is now quite far removed from 'Paradise', yet that part of humanity that was saved out of the Flood still lived in an exalted spirituality, for today's conceptions unimaginable, still lived more in the memory of Paradise than in a full consciousness of what the Earth has become in its physical state through the Fall. At that time the discarding of the physical body is not yet experienced as death as is known today. Hunger and thirst, heat and cold, all physical suffering is not yet experienced as it is today, because consciousness lived still more in the spirit. An exalted and pure Sun-clairvoyance is the inheritance of this race.

In the Mysteries of the various peoples the memory of this Sun-clairvoyance continued. The splendid primal time of this existence out of the Mysteries prevailed, which then increasingly declined until the great turning point and ascent of a new Mystery-existence in the Mystery of Golgotha. We should not imagine this first post-Atlantean time geographically limited only to ancient India; yet at least an influence raying out from there, a ray of the early Sun-clairvoyance, reaches the epoch of Zarathustra and his realms, and from there to Egypt (whose Mystery-existence in the primal time of its development—around BCE 6000—belongs at least to the Zarathustrian epoch).

When we take note of all this, then the significant connections arise to which the short narration of *Vivanghvat* and *Yima* in Yasna 9 can lead us. Firstly, *Yima* purely linguistically—this is also quite certain for mainstream linguistics—is nothing other than the Indian *Yama*. Yama and Yami in the Rig-Veda are the first human pair, Adam and Eve of Indian culture. Through the Fall of Man (in which the Rig-Veda, more than in the Bible, preserves a strange recollection drawn more into the sexual sphere) Yama is the first mortal, the first human being to descend into the realm of death. There he immediately takes on the role of ruler; Yama becomes for the Indian the god of death. The father of this Yama is *Vivasvat*, the divine Sun-being. This word, out of the lawfulness of the sounds, corresponds exactly to the Avestan Vivanghvat, which we have met as the father of *Yima*. The difference is only that with Yama the Indian thinks of the real age of Paradise, the Iranian with Yima of the later mirroring in the 'golden age' of the first post-Atlantean cultural epoch. But in a not-quite-fully-conscious clairvoyant *Rückshau*, or retrospective vision, these things coincide. Also concerning the Iranian Yima, the Avesta tells of a kind of later Fall; through lying he loses his Sun-ether-aura, *hvaröno*, so that the splendour of that age disappears.

With this, the relationships are not exhausted. Vivasvat is not only the divine Sun-being, but also the Atlantean divine Sun-initiate, the *Manu* of the contemporary cultural-epoch, who after the Atlantean Deluge establishes the primal Indian culture of the seven Rishis. His biblical mirror is Noah; his Assyrian-Babylonian mirror is Xisuthros-Utnapishtim of the Gilgamesh saga. Thus we would have in Vivanghvat the Avestan Manu-Xisuthros-Noah. Besides Vivasvat there appears in India the figure Vaivasvata as the name of Manu. And this Vaivasvata, meaning 'son of Vivasvat', is also the name of Yama. This is how things merge. The most significant thing in the Avestan Yima-narration is that Yima is called *hvarödaröso*: 'The one who possesses the *Sun-eye*', i.e., the ancient Sun-clairvoyance. The decisive thing about the narration is not that this or that king once lived, but the recollection that in the consciousness of humanity there was once a Sun-clairvoyance, and this is linked pictorially to the personality of a partly mystical, partly historical, original king.

From here there now opens a quite meaningful glimpse towards Egypt, since this *hvarö-daröso* 'with the Sun-eye' is according to its significance nothing other than the Egyptian *Osiris*. Already in the hieroglyph for Osiris we see the eye, *iri* (cf. Gk. *iris*). There in Egypt the same saga of the original King of the Golden Age, who reigns happily in whose realm people do not know death, until dragon-powers (Typhon) gained the upper hand, who kill Osiris, the Sun-eye of early clairvoyance. Osiris, once the bright day-time Sun-consciousness of man, now lives as ruler in the realm of the dead and is met by the one who descends, who enters into initiation, in the depths of soul. As has been said of Yima *hvarö-daröso* ('with the Sun-eye') of the Avesta, equally the name of Osiris guards the memory of the Sun-clairvoyance of humanity's primal age. As Yama, Osiris is the inaugurator of a human epoch, and consequently ruler in the realm of the dead. Like the father of Yama and Yima, Osiris is at the same time the divine Sun-being (for more details, see the essay [below] on 'Isis' in which the Egyptian context is investigated).

***

From these pictures from the past, let us turn briefly to Zarathustra's prophecy of the future, which we find in the final, closing Yasht 19. Everywhere and more clearly than the other pre-Christian religions, more clearly especially than the Indian religions, the religion of Zarathustra contains the indication of the Saviour of the future, and more clearly than in other religions this prophecy bears the character of a prophecy of *Christ*, indeed of pointing to the return of Christ in the etheric body—whereas in Buddhism we find something similar, not Christ but the Buddha of the future, Maitreya, is meant. According to the picture of the early Iranian saga, out of the seed of the old Zarathustra kept in the Lake of Kansaoya/Kansava (Lake Hāmūn), there should appear three sons (that is, reincarnations) of Zarathustra. The first of these re-embodiments would be the later Zarathustra, the inspirer of the Avesta; the second the initiate Nazarathos; the third the Solomon Jesus, from whom the 'I', or ego, of Zarathustra went over into the Nathan-Jesus, in order to sacrifice himself for the Christ-'I' in the Baptism in the Jordan. In the Avesta this third embodiment is called the actual future Saviour (saoshyant): *Astvatöröta*, that is, quite literally, 'the great cosmic rhythm incorporated right into the skeleton' (*öröta* = *asha*, Skr. *rta*), a wonderful expression for the mystery of Christ! And just as wonderful in the concluding 19th Yasht containing a future prospect, is the way how actually already the Zarathustra incarnation of the future saviour (*Saoshyant* 'the healer', purely linguistically = Jesus, the Solomon-Jesus) is differentiated from the Sun-ether-aura (*hvaröno*) of the Christ, which (in the Jordan-baptism) descended on him (19:89), and which alongside the resurrection-impulse, emphasizes the '*re-en-livening of the dying Earth-existence*', this as the Christ-impulse is already recognized by Zarathustra as the 'I'-impulse of freedom:

Yasht 19

ughröm kavaem hvaröno mazdadhatöm yazamaide
yat upanghaschat saoshyanta'm vöröthradschanöm
uta anyaostschit hakhayo
yat körönavat frashöm ahum

azarshöntüm amaröshöntöm
afrithyantöm apuyantöm
yavaedsch*i*m yav*a*esum vasokhshathröm
yat irista paiti-usöhisht*a*t
dschas*a*t dschivay*o* amörökhtish
dathaite frashöm vasna anghush.

The mighty, the kingly Sun-ether-aura bearing prophecy,
the divinely created one,[219]
we venerate in prayer,
which will pass over to the most victorious of the saviours,
and to the others, his Apostles,
which will bring the world forwards,
allowing the world to overcome age and death,
decay and purification,
which helps the world to eternal life,
to eternal prosperity,
to free-will ['to govern the will']
when the dead will arise again,
when the last conqueror of death comes
and through the will the world will be brought forwards.[220]

Postscript on the name Zarathustra²²¹

The attempts to interpret the name 'Zarathustra' are in a certain way symptomatic of the nature of research today. The name does present undeniable difficulties for its philological explanation. It cannot be clearly derived from Avestan itself, even though the beginning of the word points to gold (*zaranya*) or golden shine (*zairi, zaray*), and the last syllable of consonants does contain the word for 'star' (*star, sir*) (according to linguistic laws, through the influence of the previous *u, s* becomes sh). Bartholomae's interpretation, that 'camels are old', is found to be both artificial and senseless [Christian Bartholomae, 1855-1925, *Das Altiranisches Wörterbuch* (1904) and its supplementary volume (1906)]. In Avestan *ushtra* certainly means 'camel'. A word *zarant* 'old' or 'become old', however, does not exist in Avestan. The Indian word *jarant*, which has that meaning, and which if it appeared in Avestan (which it does not) would be transformed, according to the sounds, into *zarant*, is but artificially construed. An artificial word that does not exist in reality is construed, in order with its help to come to such an endlessly meaningless interpretation. If the word *Zarath-ustra* could really be resolved in such a way into *zarath* = 'old' (but the word does not exist) + *ushtra* 'camel', then the solution of the construction would be linguistically possible as 'old camel', in the same way as the one that sees the construction as a so-called 'construction of determinism' (that is, 'Redbeard' means 'the one who has a red beard'): 'that camels are old'. Only because to him '*old* camel' itself appears too crass, Bartholomae (whose extraordinarily high achievements in Avestan research in general should be recognized in full gratitude) chooses the other kind of solution '*that* camels are old', which is without any reasonable sense. It can clearly be felt that these attempts to explain do not lead to any useful result.

The Greeks were certainly nearer to the true recognition of the name Zarathustra when out of Mystery wisdom they brought into it their 'Zoroaster', or 'Zoroastris', the 'gold-star', or 'star of shining'. When Rudolf Steiner speaks of the meaning of the 'gold star',²²² he always directly relates to the form 'Zoroaster'. *Aster* in Gr. means 'star'; concerning *zoros*, Dr Stein's article contains the details [the previous article in *Die Drei*, January 1926. 775-82]. It appears to have been a word from Mystery-language, whose deeper sense has to be read out of its sounds. [Gk.] *Zoos* means 'living'; if the etheric element of life connects to the purified, star-radiant astral part of the personality, then *zoos* becomes *zoros*. Philologists like Pape [J.G. Wilhelm Pape, 1807-1854] in the dictionary also point towards the possible relationship to *zoos*.

The difficulty concerning the interpretation of the Avestan name Zarathustra lies in the syllable *thu*. A '*zarathu*' is not found in the Avestan dictionary. We can certainly clearly feel, if we ignore all philological interpretation, all 'pragmatic' etymology, and listen to the revelation of the speech sounds, how precisely this *thu* is contained in Zarathustra's name. In it lies the whole earthly might of the name Zarathustra. In Sanskrit a root-word exists √*tu*, which means 'be strong, be mighty, have authority or power'. The German [and English] words '*tausend*—thousand' are related. All this is to indicate a fact, not at all to be directly utilized to establish the etymology of 'Zarathustra', although the transition from the Indian *t* into Avestan *th* is something quite normal, linguistically established.

In fact it is revealed that in *zarathu* we have an older word-form, no longer to be derived directly merely out of Avestan. With names it is generally the case that older forms of language are contained. In German, English, and so on, names can in many cases not be simply explained out of the modern form of these languages. The Avestan form for gold, *zaranya*, appears in Sanskrit as *hiranya, zairi*, or *zaray* 'gold colour' as *haari* or *harita*. If we are courageous to look from the Indo-Germanic languages towards the Semitic, then we come a step nearer to the primal language. Hebrew and Assyrian here offer valuable service (initially Sumerian leads us to the primal, root language). Precisely Avestan, more than Sanskrit, is clearly related to the Semitic tongue. Now, in Assyrian 'gold' *hurasu* or *churasu*, contains a clear echo to the Indian *hiranya* as to the Greek *chrysos*. In Hebrew the word appears in the form *charus*. Taking into account the laws of speech sounds, whereby Indian *h* (Semitic *ch*) in Avestan as *z* (sounding *s*), in German frequently appears as *g* (e.g. Skr. *hansa* = *Gans*, 'goose') and *l* in Avestan is always replaced with *r*, and the *th* is a kind of transition sound between *s* and *t* (cf. Indian *harita*), then it appears everywhere relevant to suspect an older form of the word for 'gold' in *zarathu*, which with the transition of the Assyrian *hurasu, churasu*, is presented in the language of Zarathustra. Indeed, *zarathu* then *means* not just gold, but linguistically and according to the history of the speech sounds in general *is the same word* as the Gothic *gulth*, New High German *Gold* [Eng. 'gold']. Zarathustra remains for us the 'golden star', the 'shining star', Zoroaster.

ISIS—the star-wisdom of the early Egyptian Mysteries and its connections with Zarathustra

Isis-Sophia	Isis-Sophia
Des Gottes Weisheit	Wisdom of God
Sie hat Luzifer getötet	Lucifer has slain her
Und auf der Weltenkräfte Schwingen	And on the wings of World Powers
In Raumesweiten fortgetragen.	Carried her forth into the widths of space.
Christus-Wollen	The Will of Christ
In Menschen wirkend	Working within humanity
Es wird Luzifer entreißen	Shall wrest from Lucifer
Und auf des GeisteswissensBooten	And on the sails of Spirit-knowledge
In Menschenseelen auferwecken	Raise up in human souls
Isis-Sophia	Isis-Sophia
Des Gottes Weisheit.	Wisdom of God.

Rudolf Steiner

1.

There are two words which in the sacred, primal language of Zarathustra appear especially meaningful because they are no longer to be found in Sanskrit which otherwise mostly coincides with its vocabulary. Only scarce remnants of the word *str* 'star' are still found in the Vedas; in classical Sanskrit this primal word has completely retreated in favour of other words, such as *tara*, *nakshatra*. These two words, on the other hand through their relationship to Germanic, present their primal-word character: the Germ word. *Stern* (Avestan *star*) 'star', and the Germ. word *Jahr*, Avestan the same-sounding *yâr* 'year'.

What in the primal consciousness of humanity lived as mysteries of the stars and of the year, of the cycle of time, has given the primal wisdom of the first Zarathustra its quite special stamp, even though the Avestan documents that have come down to us only contain echoes of this. It is at least meaningful that the oldest part of the Avesta, the Yasna, ends with these two great mysteries (Yasna 72:10) with an apostrophe to the eternal heavenly space, founded on itself (thwasha hvadhata) and eternal time (zarvana akarana), the primal eternity, resting in itself (zarvana darögho-hvadhata).

If we translate all this into the language of spiritual science, then we find in this wisdom of space and the stars a mystery of the *astral world*, in the wisdom of time a secret of the *etheric body*. Human beings in Zarathustra's time experienced their astral bodies differently from people of today. The human soul—here Rudolf Steiner gives meaningful insights in the New Year lecture, Dornach, 31 December 1915 [in GA 165]—was then just united with the embracing consciousness of the astral body that knows the secret of the stars. This, for the human being today in the time of the consciousness-soul, has become subconscious. Between that far-distant age of the astral body (c. BCE 6000) and the age of the consciousness-soul today lies the age of the sentient soul (Egyptian-Chaldean cultural epoch) and of the mind-soul (Graeco-Latin age). In his lecture-cycle on Matthew's Gospel, Steiner mentions how Zarathustra passed on these secrets to two of his pupils. To the one he predominantly revealed the wisdom of space, the mystery of what is spread around us as a simultaneous moment. To the other pupil he revealed the mystery of the flow of time. And the consciousness of the astral body that encompasses the widths of space and knows about the mysteries of the stars was with the great Sun-initiate so fully conscious and highly developed that we can understand how this astral body in its individual fashioning means something for the world. We read about this in the above-mentioned lecture-cycle (Lecture 2).

The astral body of Zarathustra was sacrificed to his pupil who received the *wisdom of space* and thus passed over to the Egyptian Hermes; the ether-body, in which the element of time lives, passes over to the pupil who receives the *wisdom of time*, who was incarnated in Moses. (Further details in the lecture-cycle on Matthew's Gospel, Bern, 1-12 Sept. 1910. GA 123, and Lecture 5 (19 Sept. 1909) of the lecture-cycle on Luke's Gospel, Basel, 15-26 Sept. 1909. GA 114). The power and activity of such a mighty, such an overwhelming personality on the threshold of the super-human as Zarathustra is not exhausted in one swiftly-passing earthly life. The personality means something for the whole development of the Earth and humanity and it remains connected with this development. The 'I' which returned in the initiate Zarathas, or Nazarathos (with whom the Jews in the Babylonian Captivity came into contact), and before this already in another personality about whom it is not possible with full certainty to say whether it was the later, second Zarathustra (who inspired the Avestas). The Zarathustra entelechy, when this being was re-embodied in the Jesus-child of Matthew's Gospel [the Solomon-Jesus] of the royal lineage, sacrificed this most tremendous of all human 'I's, for that other 'I' that was no human-'I' but the cosmic 'I' itself, in that it gave the *Christ* its earthly vessel at the Baptism in the Jordan. And this last decisive sacrifice of the 'I' was but the ending of a sequence of sacrificial deeds running through the development of the Earth. Zarathustra's being not only sacrificed its 'I' during the becoming of humanity, but *its whole human nature*, and each of these sacrificial deeds is intimately connected with the mystery of Christ who governs and works in the whole of earthly history. To show this in detail in the case of the Egyptian Hermes is the task of the following contemplation.

***

After what has been said about the relationship of the 'astral body' to the mystery of the realms of the stars, we should look on a sentence, such as, '*the astral body of Zarathustra passed over to the Egyptian Hermes*' as an 'esoteric fact' which is not provable with the usual means of understanding. However, *within the whole context that can be shown between the star-wisdom of Zarathustra and that of Hermes in the Egyptian Mysteries this esoteric fact is mirrored* (which as such is only directly accessible to actual spiritual research) in such a way that an unbiased thinking can find access to it.

Like the figure and personality of the first Zarathustra, the figure and personality of the Egyptian Hermes that we have first to investigate is concealed in the mists of legend from a far-off, prehistoric age. We looked at some aspects of the legends in the previous article on Zarathustra. We pointed out *Yima*, the son of *Vivanghvat*, the King of the *Golden Age*, when people did not yet know death nor burden of old age. It was shown how the name *Yima* points towards the Indian *Yama*, and the epithet *hvarö-daröso* ('gifted with the Sun-eye', that means, the early Sun-clairvoyance) points to the Egyptian *Osiris* (p. 145 above). With the Indian [traditions], we saw memory of the paradisal age and the early Indian age (first post-Atlantean epoch) flowing together. In a *Vivanghvat* (= Indian: *Vavaspat*) the memory lives of the divine initiate, of the Atlantean Sun-Mysteries, of Manu (Xisuthros-Utnapishtim of the Gilgamesh saga). As in the Egyptian saga *Osiris*, in the Indian saga *Yama* is the first mortal who arrives in the realm of the dead. *Osiris* and *Yama* become rulers in the realm of the dead.

The story told in the Indian Kāṭhaka-Upanishad is worth noting, of the Brahman youth who as a consequence of his father's curse steps into the realm of the dead and there is reverently greeted and hosted by the god and ruler of death, *Yama*, and then is *initiated into the Mysteries of Yoga*. It is significant how here *death* itself stands before us as the *original priest* and *original initiator*, as the original teacher of Yoga. The *secret* knowledge is revealed to the pupil at the *gate of death*. Whereas the Persian Yima is *king*, the Indian Yama shows more priestly traits. The being *Yima-Yama* appears in Iranian history as the primal king, in India as the primal priest and primal initiator. In Egypt both separate: *Osiris* appears as the primal King of the Golden Age (who, like Yima, possesses the 'Sun-eye'), his priestly right hand—the word for hand in Egyptian is *thoth*—is *Thoth*, which the Greeks called *Hermes*.

For someone imbued with the primal sounds of language the sound of *Thoth*—and if s/he knows the word initially means 'hand'[223]—it seems no coincidence that is sounds like the Germ. *Tod* ('death'), especially when s/he considers all the relationships to Yima and Yama. The highly interesting book by Rudolf Falb on the land of the Incas is worth mentioning for its significance for the primal history of language and the written script (*Das Land der Inca in seiner Bedeutung für die Urgeschichte der Sprache und Schrift* ['The land of the Incas in its significance for the prehistory of language and writing']).[224] On p. 61, amongst other things, it is pointed out that *Thoth* is the *hand with the sickle*, like the picture of the *scythe in the hand of death* which is hidden in the name of the Egyptian *Thoth-Hermes*.[225] And the Greek name *Hermes* goes back to a Hebrew word *hermes* [חרמש] (spoken 'chermesh'), which means 'sickle'. The Greek Hermes is *psychopompos*, leader of the souls into the realm of death. As in the Indian Kāṭhaka-Upanishad the god of death *Yama*, so also in the Egyptian Mysteries *Tod*, death, which is concealed in the name *Hermes-Thoth*, is the great leader in the Mysteries, the primal priest and prime initiator. Especially in the Egyptian Mysteries, which sank down step by step more deeply into death and the grave, the concept in its full seriousness had to be worked out. It was increasingly the darkness and loneliness of death that was experienced in the Mysteries when from period to period Egyptian Mystery wisdom entered into decline.

Here we stand at that point where we have to look at the periods of time in [the progress of] the Egyptian Mysteries themselves. The connection of Egyptian Mystery wisdom with the star-wisdom of Zarathustra is hereby brought into a clear light. We shall see in what way the stars influenced this periodic development. From that which once existed in primal times as real *star-wisdom* there remained a certain reverence for the stars in the later cultural periods which fell into the actual (Egypto-Chaldean) third post-Atlantean cultural epoch. The brightest star of the fixed-star heavens Sirius (*Satit-Sothis*) enjoyed a special veneration with the early Egyptians. The outer reason for this veneration was the coincidence of the first re-appearance of Sirius over the horizon in the morning sky after the summer solstice (19 or 20 July) with the flooding of the Nile, on which the fruitfulness of the ground of Egypt depended. Thus, for the early Egyptians, Sirius was the star of healing, its rising originally determined the beginning of the new year, the calendar, and counting the years.

Friedrich Creuzer, *Symbolik und Mythologie der alten Völker* (1812, Vol. II, p. 104) expressively describes how at the summer solstice, when one knew that the Sun had reached its highest point and had begun to descend, the Egyptian priests gathered at night in festive garments in the halls of the temple. After they had carried out their sacred customs, and the expected moment approached, the Stolist led in a gazelle, took it between his knees, observed between its horns Sirius just rising into the firmament and thus made the horoscope for the whole year. According to whatever circumstances occurred at the rising of the star he judged whether the year would be fruitful or barren, whether the Nile whose waters swelled during that season would reach a high water-level, or would only bring a sparse flooding. Thus the heliacal rising of this dog-star, Sirius, was connected to a number of hopes and fears; blessings and joys, or dearth and cares, according to the Egyptian belief, which were decided in those hours. With the ancient Egyptians, as by the way also with Zarathustra, the year was calculated with 360 days (twelve months each of 30 days) with leap days added. With this the extent of a quarter of a day remained unaccounted for; by so much the reckoned year was lacking with regards to the course of the Sun. Consequently, the astronomical beginning of the year shifted annually; only after $4 \times 365 = 1460$ years (1461 Egyptian years, 1460 Julian years) was the shift of a quarter of a day evened out; the beginning of the calendar year corresponded again with the Sirius-year. For the Egyptians there stood behind the 'annual' year the great year, a Sirius (Sothis)-period of 1460 (1461) years.

Thus far regarding the outer connection, behind which is hidden another, deeper, esoteric one. In his lecture on Hermes, Rudolf Steiner points out how these Sirius-periods, or Sothis-periods stand intimately connected with the whole Egyptian development of consciousness and that of the Egyptian Mysteries. A crisis for the development of these Mysteries means, according to Steiner, one year in which such a Sirius-period concluded, the year 1322 BCE (according to other indications 1324), when Moses led the Hebrews out of Egypt. Himself deeply initiated into the Egyptian Mysteries, Moses took these Mysteries to Palestine, and with them the great divine Mystery which had been revealed to him in the etheric element of fire, of the flaming thorn bush, the Mystery of the 'I' (I–H–V–H), before whom the Egyptian consciousness was afeared, as the Pharaoh stories in Exodus show. In this Mystery there was a level beyond the reach of the ancient Egyptian consciousness. Around this time the ancient Egyptians lost their clairvoyance, which until then had still existed as a *knowledge of the elements*, as the beholding of the elemental-etheric in water, fire, air and earth, in plants, animals and minerals. The year 1322 meant the transition of the knowledge of the elements into a knowledge of the senses, into that beholding that only sees and comprehends the physical. It is the period of the *grave* in the Egyptian Mysteries, of the grave, the secret of which speaks to us so impressively in the Egyptian *pyramid*.

In the 1460 years, which preceded this crisis, the ancient Egyptians, especially the initiates in the Mysteries, still possessed a *knowledge* of the elements, an etheric vision; in a still earlier time, which again embraces such a Sirius-period, or Sothis-period of 1460 years, a planetary clairvoyance, a *planetary wisdom* existed, that is, a consciousness which went beyond the borders of the immediate earthly sphere. This consciousness extended back to an even earlier period, to a primal time whose splendour can hardly be imagined today. There the human being still felt his being connected to the distances of the world—as was possible during the time when the soul-element coincided with the consciousness of the astral ['starry'] body. A wisdom of the *fixed stars* still existed, embracing the widths of the world and the stellar regions. From Steiner's indications one can calculate dates for the Sothis-periods:

    5702 BCE until 4242 a wisdom of the fixed stars
    4242 until 2782 a wisdom of the planets
    2782 until 1322 a wisdom of the elements
    1322 BCE until 138 CE a knowledge of the senses.

These periods are connected to the name *Hermes,* as Rudolf Steiner shows in his lecture (Berlin 16 Jan. 1911. GA 60). In earlier times he is called *Hermes Trismegistos,* the 'thrice-greatest', whereas in later times he was called the 'twice-greatest'. Like Zarathustra, the Egyptian Hermes is not a single physical personality, but a being who supersensibly overshadows the whole development of the Egyptian Mysteries, revealing himself afresh to each age. The most magnificent and powerful revelation took place in primal times of the earliest Sirius-period; in each following period, with the decline of the Mysteries, the Hermes-revelations became paler. So a later time regarded the primal Hermes as the 'thrice-greatest' and the Hermes of the ensuing times as 'twice-greatest', and finally as 'the great'. What was meant is the splendour of the ancient fixed-star wisdom when speaking of Hermes Trismegistos. And the Ancient Egyptians see in him the genius of Sirius, the leader of the Sirius stars. 'Sirius on the pinnacle of the firmament guards the creatures of light of the heavens; he guards and warns all creatures' (Creuzer. 108).

> He is the wise priest, the father of spiritual treasures. He is the bearer of the word and of writing; he is the sublime starry script itself. He is the embodied logos, the embodied intelligence, the word of life, the eternal bread ... the one to whom his light shines lives in the light; the one who looks into his mirror can see into all natures and creatures. Such a one is simply *the* priest, is Hermes. He reads in the stars, he writes the script of heaven, the hieroglyph, he interprets it into common script for the people. He advises the people, he helps them in body and spirit. He is physician, teacher of the law, judge, the one who sacrifices and prays, who prophesies. The priest is in and through Hermes, from and to Hermes (Creuzer. 116).

The above-listed Sirius-periods and their relationship to the development of Egyptian Mystery-wisdom is important in as much as this table shows that the period of time of this development surveyed here by the spiritual researcher in no way coincides with what is called the Egyptian-Chaldean-Babylonian-Assyrian cultural period, the third post-Atlantean cultural epoch. This cultural epoch lasted from 2907–747 BCE (the ensuing fourth [post-Atlantean] cultural epoch took place until 1413 CE). Only the time of the wisdom of the elements and of the last echoes of planetary wisdom falls within this period, in which the darkening of the early clairvoyance is already beginning. The time of the Egyptian culture is already the *grave of Egyptian Mystery knowledge. The unique high flowering of this Mystery knowledge,* that is, the whole early wisdom of the fixed stars and also nearly all the planetary wisdom, belongs to another, earlier cultural period, to the second post-Atlantean culture period, the age of Zarathustra.

From this point it becomes immediately clear what, for example, in his lecture-cycle on Luke's Gospel [GA 114], Steiner says about the influence and inauguration of the Egyptian culture through Zarathustra. Although the inner nature of this process, the *transition of the astral body of the first Zarathustra to the Egyptian Hermes* can only be researched spiritually, documents however do show traces of these connections, especially the Avesta, in which we find today all outer accounts of the tradition of the wisdom of Zarathustra.

This is shown especially for that star regarding which we have seen how it becomes the regulator of their yearly cycle and, beyond the yearly cycle, those greater epochs of human history which as *Sirius-periods* or *Sothis-periods* are so meaningfully connected to the development of human consciousness and the essence of the Egyptian Mysteries. Already what is given here in the purely outer facts helps us to divine, *how Sirius may once have stood at the centre of an early fixed-star wisdom* (in the same way as the Sun-Mysteries stood at the centre of planetary-wisdom). If we can accept this, it can awaken a deep impression when in the Avesta—which, of course, only contains echoes of ancient Zarathustra-wisdom (Yasht 8)—we find a tremendous, encompassing *hymn to the star Sirius* (Avestan *Tishtriya* = Persian *Tashter*), which is especially surprising through an abundance of details that seem to point towards Egyptian conditions (Nile and Nile-flooding, and certain names for Isis). Only the beginning of the (very comprehensive) hymn can be given here.

> Tishtrim staröm raevantöm
> hvarönanguhantöm yazamaide
> ramashayanöm hushayanöm
> aurushöm raokhshnöm fradörösröm
> vyavantöm baeshazim
> ravofraothmanöm börözantöm
> durat vyavantöm banubyo
> raokhshnibyo anahitaebyo
> apömtscha pöröthuzrayanghöm
> Vanghuhimtscha durat frasruta'm
> geushtscha na'ma mazdadhatöm
> ughrömtscha kavaem hvaröno
> Fravashimtscha Spitamahe
> ashaono Zarathushtrahe.
>
> We devoutly revere
> the star Sirius, the Shining One with sun-like rays,
> in which peace lives, blessed rest,
> the golden shining one of light, who enables us to see into cosmic distances,
> the radiant, *Healing* One,

the one who quickly carries forward [development], the Exalted, Sublime
   One,
who shines from afar with his rays,
the Being of Light without stain,
who permits the waters to stream abundantly
and the health-giving stream, which streams in from afar,
[he who carries] the divinely-created *name of the cow*,
the tremendous one, the Sun-ether raying glory carrying sovereign prophecy,
[we revere him] as the Genius [*Fravashi-Angelos*]
of the sacred Spitama Zarathustra.

***

Out of this hymn there speaks the consciousness of an age that still
looks up to the stars completely differently from our consciousness
today. Zarathustra's whole reverence for the stars is revealed here,
especially when we allow the early, sacred primal language in the
strength and fullness of its words for light to affect us. Translation
can but reproduce incompletely. Besides those places mentioning
the great stream of water, it is especially interesting (on the one hand
reminding us of the heavenly Milky Way, and on the other hand of
the sacred Nile, reminding us of Egyptian conditions), at the end
of the first verse, where Sirius is venerated and appealed to as the
Genius or *Guardian Angel (Fravashi)*, or, as we can say anthroposoph-
ically, as the *Spirit-self* of Zarathustra. (A lecture by Rudolf Steiner,
4 June 1924 [in GA 236], explains how behind the cosmic astrality,
which is shown in the picture of the stars, the 'cosmic Spirit-self-
hood' is inwardly experienced.) *Sirius is the star of Zarathustra*—this
is clearly expressed in the Avesta. The 'I' (unlike in our age of the
consciousness-soul when it is deeply immersed in physical corporeality) as the *star* shines out of cosmic distances to the consciousness
of cosmic widths of the primal time of humanity, and with the 'I'
there still shines the Mysteries of the human future. The *Mystery of
the course of time* links to the *Mystery of the widths of space*. Here Sirius becomes the star which not only prophesies to the human being
the 'annual' New Year—today we can perceive Sirius that begins to
shine towards Christmas and the New Year in the evening sky as
the star of the 'New Year'—but beyond that of a greater New Year of
humanity, a New Year of humanity's future.

In this connection what Creuzer has expounded (I. 250—the chapter on the Mithras Mysteries) on the *Mysteries of Sirius* in ancient
Persia appears significant. Hereby the name of the star Sirius plays a

role, which again with the Greeks appears as a decadent distortion,[226] or as an intentional occult veiling of deep esoteric backgrounds, but which, in what Creuzer narrates of the Persians, nevertheless appears meaningful. (The popular conception today of the Dog-Star sees the dog walking behind the hunter Orion, 'the guardian of the heavenly herd'.) In the Mithras-Mysteries the primal Bull is the concern, who through the Scorpion (or rather through the Snake, Scorpion and Ant,[227] the animals of ahrimanic darkness) receives the sting of death. (This scene is often represented pictorially.) But besides them exists as a being belonging to the good spirit, a 'dog of comfort', reminding one who is dying of the *Tashter* (Persian = *Tishtriya*, Sirius). According to Creuzer, he is the 'image of Sirius', of the Dog-Star (*Sothis* with the Egyptians, *Tashter* with the Persians). When one day in the *fullness of time* the Star of the Dog looks again on the world, then the Great Day of Re-enlivening breaks. Consequently, the custom of the Persians at the death-bed: when their end is approaching, a dog is led to them, who receives from their hand something to eat. This action was called *Sagdid* 'the dog sees'[228]—a comforting picture of the ardently hoped-for immortality. And so [in the Mithras-Mysteries] the Dog looks here at the dying Bull. The Dog prophesies the better future and consequently is itself the picture of re-enlivening.

All this is brought into a tremendous context when we absorb what has been said on the great Cosmic Year and Cosmic New Year in the already-mentioned New Year lecture by Rudolf Steiner. 6,000 years BCE there occurred a great Cosmic New Year in which the soul-element in man united with the consciousness of the astral body spanning the cosmic spaces and star-mysteries (as the consciousness of the plants during the time of New Year—during the nights around Christmas and New Year—connects with the mineral, although dull, consciousness of the Earth that spans the cosmic realm). Similarly, 6,000 after Golgotha, c. 4000 from now, such a Great New Year will occur. Again, such a passage of our soul-consciousness will take place through the astral consciousness, but on a higher ego-level. *Men will again enter into a cosmic star-consciousness.* 'And for this,' says Rudolf Steiner, 'we want to prepare ourselves through spiritual science, so that there are people prepared for this ....' He goes on to say:

> Twelve months of years [Jahr-Monate] will flow past from one merging of the plant-consciousness of the Earth to the mineral-consciousness to the next merging. Twelve millennia will pass from one Cosmic Earth New Year to the

next, from one astral passage of the human soul through the astral world to the next passage of the human soul through the astral world.

Here we are directed to a still more comprehensive period of humanity, of a still more embracing 'Great Year' than the Sothis period of the ancient Egyptian, a 'Great Year' for which—if there is any reality standing behind what Creuzer relates of the Mithras Mysteries—also, as for the Sothis period, Sirius would be important. We always see how out of the wisdom of the first Zarathustra looking into mysteries of the *stars* and the *year* the vision of such a *Great Year* arises (of which Friedrich Nietzsche's 'monster of the Great Year' in *Thus Spoke Zarathustra*, is a modern caricature pointing incorrectly to the concept of the Cosmic Year as an eternal return of the same).[229]

Also Egyptian concepts, which Creuzer (106) mentions, lead towards the connection of Sirius with world-renewal, the great Cosmic New Year. It is announced when, with the appearance of Sirius, a specific constellation links to it. Creuzer explains: 'When at the next summer solstice the Sun stands in the Lion, the Moon in the Crab, the planets in their houses and the Ram in the middle of the firmament, then *Sothis* (Sirius) appears again and in rising greets the new order of things and the new time, which begins now. *Every year presents in small the Great Year*: for every year, when the hot season comes in Egypt and everything dries up, shows, as it were, the burning of the Earth. Then the whole country would become a desert and go up in flames unless Sirius appears and with him the saving flood of the Nile, and now under the water the Earth is born anew.' Also in the Avesta with Zarathustra, Sirius is called *afshtshithra*, 'the one who contains the seed of the waters'. The key for the meaning of the *world-fire* we find with Zarathustra as well; cf. the previous article on Zarathustra. An indication of going over into the ether—in the article the connection of the Avestic atha-fire with the Greek *aither*, ether, was mentioned—lies in this, and therewith also the 're-appearance of Christ in the ether-body'. We divine how these Mysteries here are seen from the Egyptian point of view in the light of the fixed-star wisdom.

Creuzer (Vol II. 112) says that Hermes-Sirius (in the context of Egyptian wisdom) is the Spirit of all spirits; he guides the spirits, the souls, up and down through all cycles.

He stands at the beginning and end of all time. 3000 (4 x 3000?) years are allocated to the world and the spirits; then the Great Year is completed; then everything finds its meaning; then all life-cycles converge in one point and all purifications are ended, everything arrives at its place. [The query is Beckh's interpolation.]

In recalling the fixed-star wisdom in Egypt, the way Sirius is connected with the thought of world-renewal, the great renewal at the end of things, his connection with the phoenix can also be understood (Egyptian: *benu*), about which Creuzer reports (165). The phoenix, rising rejuvenated out of the ashes, is the great symbol of renewal. Consequently:

> he does not come every year; he comes in the Great Year; consequently he is the bird of the star with whose strange constellation he ascends. With him comes the picture of the star of the Great Year, the picture of Sirius [Sothis].

***

To these indications on Egypt, a passage on Greece may still be added (also mentioned by Creutzer, Vol. 4. 64). He mentions that among the Greeks Pan is promoted to the fixed star-heavens. As Sirius, he is supposed to describe the course for the other spheres, to describe in this stellar script the character of the heavens, to order the year, as an exalted disciple to rehearse and direct the choirs of the planets and in this capacity to accompany *Rhea*, the great Mother of the gods. In all this we feel and divine the decadent expression of ancient fixed-star wisdom, which in its pure form even today cannot be reached by human consciousness. And yet, in this conception, in the no doubt decadent expression of the Greek Pan-Sirius, we find again a thoroughly meaningful transition to Egypt when we first think of the meaning of *Pan*, pan = 'everything, the universe', and then think on the Egyptian goddess of Sais (*Neith-Isis*), who in her famous inscription says of herself, '*I am the All [Everything/the Universe], I am everything that was, that is and that shall be*. No mortal has lifted my veil',[230] reminding us hereby that for the Egyptians Sirius is the soul of the goddess Isis, and still was in later historical times. Isis and Osiris, the ruling couple of the golden age shine in the starry sky as Sirius and Orion.

2.

And here we come to the *soul of the Egyptian Mystery-wisdom and star-wisdom*. Everything that could be said here on this Mystery-wisdom and can be said, everything that has been said about Sirius is embraced in the consciousness of the early Egyptian Mysteries by the regal, virginal name of *Isis*. Thoth-Hermes is the *spirit*, Isis the *soul* of the early star-wisdom, and *Sirius* (Sothis) itself is again the *soul of Isis* (the soul, the inner centre of the ancient star-wisdom.) The goddess Isis, so rich in mysteries, has gone through many metamorphoses in the Egyptian Mystery knowledge; in each Sothis-period she reappears in a different picture. All these pictures retain some connection to the ancient star-wisdom that in the Egyptian Mysteries finally declined, descending as into a grave. In his lecture-cycle *The Mysteries of the East and Christianity* (Berlin. 3-7 Feb. 1913. GA 144; cf. the lecture-cycle *Christ and the Spiritual World*. Leipzig. 28 Dec. 1913—2 Jan 1914. GA 149), Rudolf Steiner mentions how the star-wisdom of Ancient Egypt, declining in the crisis of the Egyptian Mysteries, comes again to the light of day through the Mystery of Golgotha. But this occurs only at the beginning of the fifth post-Atlantean epoch, approximately as many centuries *after* Golgotha as the crisis of the Egyptian Myster-ies, the decline and burial of the star-wisdom, took place *before*. What once declined arose again as *esoteric Christendom*, as the *Christendom of the Holy Grail*. *Isis-Sophia*, the Ancient Egyptian star-wisdom, is the *pre-Christian revelation of the Holy Grail* (which, indeed, before it becomes the vessel of the Blood of the Redeemer at Golgotha, is car-ried down to Earth by hosts of angels from starry heights). With all that has been said on the early star-wisdom, we are ultimately looking at a *Mystery of the Holy Grail*, at a pre-Christian revelation of the Holy Grail. And in all the pictures during all the periods of Egyptian Mys-tery development, in various figures the Mystery of Isis is beheld, and these are somehow related to the great cosmic *Vessel-experience*, to the *Imagination of the Holy Grail Vessel*. Here *Isis* is always in some way the *soul* giving birth, or receiving. As the *Primal Feminine, lunar being of the world*, she takes up into herself, or gives birth to, the Primal Masculine, or solar being of the world, the *Spirit*, the *'I' Osiris*. The primal Mystery of the human being itself is beheld in the union of Isis and Osiris in pictures of extraordinary beauty and depth, which carry a different character depending on the period of development of the Mysteries in which it was experienced. It has already been stated that the whole revelation of this star-wisdom originally stems from Zarathustra. The difference between the Egyptian spirit and that of Zarathustra, which gradually comes forth, is connected to the whole varied development of human consciousness. The age of Zarathustra, of the *astral body*, goes over into the Egyptian age of the *sentient soul*. Consequently, with

Zarathustra there is everywhere the strong nuance of the primal male, in Egypt the deeply-felt meaning of the primal female element. Both revelations relate musically, one could say, like the *major* and *minor* moods; the strong *major* triad of Zarathustra becomes in Egypt in the sentient-soul the *minor* triad.

To the famous inscription of the goddess Neith-Isis of Sais, '*I am the Universe, I am all that was, that is and that will be. No mortal has lifted my veil*', there is a postscript: '*the fruit which I bore is the sun.*'[231] With these words, the Isis-Osiris Mystery is indicated, the great cosmic experience of love, the mystery of the cosmic human being, which the apocalyptist beholds anew in the tremendous picture of The Book of Revelation, Chapter 12, of the revelation given to Christ [Rev. 1:1]. The great vision of the apocalyptist is as if out of the spirit of the early star-clairvoyance, of the early fixed-star wisdom, which with him is newly 'Christened'. It can be a help for us, in order to transpose ourselves into that primal distant time of Egyptian Mystery wisdom, when still out of the spirit of the *wisdom of the fixed stars* the Mystery of *Isis and Osiris* was beheld as a picture. Here the clairvoyant view is directed towards a specific region of the dark night sky and experiences therein a mystery of the primal Motherhood of the world, the lap of the world, the cosmic womb, which bears in itself the seed of the light. The light was seen shining in *the bright star Sirius*. There it was felt radiating world-healing (cf. the above-mentioned hymn in the Avesta), world-renewing forces of love, a comforting, promising, warm breath of cosmic love, whereas it was felt, for example, out of the region of the Great Bear, something like coldness, an experience of the coldness of thinking. All this did not remain an undefined feeling, but it was really fashioned into the picture of the starry Queen and Virgin, as the apocalyptist also beheld. The sentient soul of the Egyptian looked quite differently into the realms of the stars, much more pictorially than the eye of somebody today. Then in this starry virgin and starry soul the picture was seen of the human soul, the *human soul* that still experienced itself in starry realms that saw in the star Sirius the soul of this soul, the *soul of Isis*. The experience of love for this soul was of the highest cosmic purity. In itself the soul received, or gave birth to the *spirit*.

The sexual side of marriage only appears in and through the earthly element. In the cosmic realm this remains virginal; in the cosmic realm all this is still virginal, here the cosmic Mother is still a virgin. Consequently, the relationship of Isis to Osiris cannot be compared to any earthly union; Isis is spouse and sister of Osiris at the same time, and at the same time she is the Mother who gives birth in eternity to the Son of the Sun.[232] When she gives birth to him *in time* he is called Horus. 'The fruit to which I gave birth is the Sun' (cf. the Sun, with which the apocalyptic Woman is clothed [Rev. 12:1]). And this cosmic Sun of Osiris is beheld where in the early fixed-star wisdom the gaze of the clairvoyant still reaches beyond the border of the solar system, to the *stellar constellation of Orion* of which it was felt that it stands inwardly related to *Sirius*. (This can still be felt today, as was always popularly in the picture of Hunter and Hound. In the pictures of the zodiacal creatures, the individual parts of the human being and of the human form were beheld; in the stellar constellation of Sirius-Orion—lying outside the zodiac—there was the *human picture* as such, the full human being that is expressed through the union of Male and Female.) In Sirius we behold the soul of Isis, the primal Feminine, the *Queen of the cosmic night* with her veil of colour; in Orion we see the soul of the Son of the Sun, of the Sun-bright Osiris, in whom is revealed the archetypal male element of the world and of the human being, the spirit, the 'I'. In the union of Isis and Osiris, the full divine union of the primal human being was experienced. Sirius becomes the chalice, the sublime starry chalice, for that which then becomes the revelation of the human mystery. In the Orion star-constellation this is magnificently built up in [the relationships of] number and picture.

***

From these exalted heights of the earliest Egyptian star-wisdom (fixed-star wisdom), we turn towards the later *planetary wisdom* (4242–2782 BCE). At that time the tremendous cosmic chalice-experience is no longer beheld in the distances of the fixed stars, but in the narrower realm of the solar system. Here it appears in the sky in the sickle form of the Moon-chalice that carries the matt-shining round disc in itself, reflecting the sunlight from the Earth, the *spiritual* sunlight (a picture, the cosmic origin of which can still be recognized in the cow-horns of the later portrayals of Isis). Here Isis becomes the Moon-virgin and the Moon-mother who receives into herself, or gives birth to, the Sun-spirit (Osiris). Here the great *Grail picture* appears in the Moon-chalice. The relationship of Osiris to the Sun also becomes clear. Osiris is not the physical Sun of the day. He has already a long time ago been removed from this realm, since Typhon, the dragon-power, robbed from Man the ancient Sun-clairvoyance, and Osiris was removed into the Underworld, into the actual lower human depths.[233] The Egyptians recognizes a fourfold activity of the Sun: the ascending Sun, in the morning and in spring, is venerated as the divinity *Ra*, the Sun at midday and the heights of summer (summer solstice) as *Horus*, the Sun in the evening and in the autumn *Atum*, the 'Sun at midnight', the winter solstice (our annual night of consecration) is venerated as *Osiris* (cf. Brugsch. *Religion und Mythologie der alten Ägypter*. Heinrich Karl Brugsch, Leipzig, 1887, 249ff.).

The Isis-experience of the *Moon-chalice* already lies in another sphere than that of the *star-chalice* Sirius-Orion. The experience of the fixed-star era connects the heights of the 'I' with the depths of earthly materiality, which is still perceived in an etheric-virginal condition, in an etheric seed-form (the mystery of the stars in its relationship to the mineral element of the Earth). In the age of the planets the connection of the *astral element* (Moon) with the *etheric element* (Sun) comes to the fore, the experience is moved more from the original sphere of the 'I' to the astral sphere. But as long as the Moon appears as the sickle-chalice, this experience still remains pure, the chalice modestly carries in itself the spiritual sunlight. Only the Moon progressing into the full-Moon phase extinguishes this spiritual sunlight, in the same way it takes away the clarity from the stars (cf. the poem by Albert Steffen in *Wegzehrung* [Basel, 1921], 'the Moon rises and loosens Earth-existence out of the structure of the cosmos. The shine *takes from the stars their necessity*, the 'I' in the fetters of fleeting ghostly clouds'), in the same way as an impure astral element in the human being extinguishes the 'I'. In this way the small sickle turned upwards, which decorates the starry heaven through its beauty without robbing it of its radiance, becomes the picture of the purified soul which takes into itself the spiritual element to become the Grail chalice.

The Indians call the Moon *Soma*, the wandering drop in the heavens, and for them Soma also means the *enlivening dew of the stars* of the cosmic element which finds in the milky juice of the Soma plant its earthly reflection. The Indian Soma is found with Zarathustra as *Haoma*; the Soma-mysticism here reaches its climax and echoes on in Egypt. In Greek *Soma* means the body, in so far as it is penetrated by the etheric body (for the concept of the pure physical lies *in sarx*, cf. Germ. *Sarg* 'coffin'). Here *Soma* is the host resting in the chalice, the *'wandelnde Wegzehrung'* the 'provisions for the way'.

***

In the union of *Isis* and *Osiris* there always lies the mystery of the cosmic Chalice, of the Holy Grail. Out of the sphere of Sun and Moon, which we still find in the time of the planetary wisdom, the picture descends into the (etheric) sphere of the Earth where we find it in the time of the wisdom of the elements (BCE 2782—1322). At that time it became the pure revelation of the etheric-astral element. Isis is revealed as the figure of a sylph in the chalice of the water-lily; the star-chalice has become a flower-chalice. The language still feels the connection of *star* and *flower*, when it speaks of 'flower, or blossom, stars'. Compare the Greek flower-name 'aster'. Star-mysteries are revealed in plants, in flowers.[234] And the *water-lily* becomes the picture of the pure etheric element, not yet touched by the physical. There is expressed therein a mystery of the eternal feminine in the higher kinds of ether, *sound-ether* and *life-ether* (the sound-ether becomes watery in the earthly element).[235] In the [Egyptian] *Book of the Dead* we find representations of the countenance of Isis raising itself out of the chalice of the water-lily.[236]

In the blossom, the etheric of the plant most closely touches the astral element of the higher world of life; this higher world of life approaches closest to the etheric nature of the plant in that appearance when we now ask, 'Where does Osiris join Isis, who is revealed in the flower's chalice?' At that point where the etheric life approaches the astral life of feeling the butterfly joins the blossom.[237] To each kind of flower a specific butterfly belongs according to historical, evolutionary development. A saying of Rudolf Steiner expresses this:

> Behold the plant: it is a butterfly fettered to the Earth.
> Behold the butterfly: it is the plant freed by the cosmos.[238]

In Egypt it is not the picture of the butterfly but rather the closely-related *winged beetle* (*cheper*) [cf. cockchafer] in which Osiris was seen. This winged beetle, *cheper*, for the Egyptians, as for us the butterfly, is the picture of life remaining in the metamorphosis of its form, the symbol of eternity and resurrection. When today we look at this picture out of a Christian consciousness, we feel how the *butterfly* has to take the place of the winged beetle of the early Egyptians. And the etheric-astral picture of Isis-Osiris, with a slight Christian metamorphosis, becomes the picture of *blossom* and *butterfly*. Already we can feel the word *Osiris* as an unfolding of the word *Isis*, in which the life freeing itself in light, whose symbol is the butterfly, is expressed.

***

The flower-revelation of Isis, too, disappears from the gaze of the initiate, when, in the crisis of the ancient clairvoyance of the elements, the transition into pure sense-perception takes place. Only the physical element of things remains for the one looking into the world. The physical element, behind which the spiritual is no longer visible, becomes the *grave* of spiritual perception. The end of all revelation that was once unfolded in the splendour of the early Mysteries becomes the *grave. And the flower, too, in which the eye that beholds the elements still saw the figure of Isis, sinks into this grave.* None of the great cultures of the Earth experienced the grave, all the mysteries and terrors of the grave, as deeply as did the Mysteries of Egypt. Here, not only does the Mystery-centre become the grave, but the grave becomes the Mystery-centre. The Pyramids, the Sphinx and the mummies tell of this cult of the grave of the early Egyptians. From the grave the early Egyptian takes a comprehensive knowledge, a deep knowledge of the physical [plane]. This was not outer knowledge as we understand it today, but an occultism especially connected with the nature of mummification, which might appear very faint today but at the time was relatively justified. In the clear air of Egypt the graves led a mysterious dialogue with the Moon and stars. What once was the mystery of the stars now becomes the mysteries of the grave; we can divine how the mystery of the stars is mirrored in the mineral element of the Earth, in the grave of the Earth. The development of his consciousness and his being as regards the Mysteries has led the Egyptian through all the levels and sheaths of the human being. What today anthroposophy names in concepts as the members of the human being when it speaks of the human 'I', of the astral body, etheric body and physical body, is revealed to the Egyptian initiate in great pictures in each of the great Sophis periods: the *star*, the *Moon*, the *flower* and the *grave* speak to him of the 'I', of the astral, etheric and physical nature of the human being.

***

But where are Isis and Osiris during this time of the cult of the grave and the wisdom of the grave? They themselves have descended into the grave of corporeality. Whoever is more deeply initiated beholds them there, and sees their influence in the organs of the human body. The beholding of these organs, which itself was once an experience of the stars mirrored in the body, then later an etheric experience, has progressively withdrawn into the mere physical, into the corpse, into the mummy. A science of the stars has become a science of the organs.

The others who do not possess the deep knowledge only speak of how Osiris is the fructifying River Nile and Isis the Egyptian earth fructified by him. They present Isis in the picture of the cow, the horns of which still recall the tremendous, ancient picture of the Moon-sickle. There still remains a deep wisdom behind all these pictures. They can be understood out of star-mysteries, which relating the cow to the Earth, allow the earth and the water to appear as transformations of the higher kinds of ether. But the early clairvoyance has increasingly withdrawn from the pictures. Consequently they have become dead pictures. And as such, everything of the Egyptian culture related by the scholars appears to us as dead pictures.

***

But 'where there are graves there are also resurrections'.[239] It was already mentioned that the splendour of the ancient Egyptian star-wisdom, which has sunk into the grave, arises again in esoteric Christianity with the Holy Grail at the beginning of the fifth post-Atlantean epoch. Deeper than any other Mystery-being of the Earth, the early Egyptian Mystery-being, precisely through the manner of its passage through the grave, aligns itself to the tremendous fact of Christ's Deed of Death-Resurrection. It leads us, as it were, right to where Christ Himself has descended into the depths of the Earth. Consequently, it helps us to experience the resurrection of Christ as a re-ascent of the early Mystery-knowledge and the early Mystery-splendour. Humanity on the path of its development shall one day awaken to this. That which in early Egypt descended from Sirius-period to Sirius-period will become in future an ascent for those members of humanity who take the Risen One into themselves. Humanity will arise again out of a mere knowledge of sensory experience towards a beholding of the living, etheric realm. Christ will also be beheld in his etheric body. Then a planetary wisdom—today already given us in its beginnings—will be present again. People today look up to the stars with narrow earthly-material ideas. In the far future, people will once again recognize spiritual beings and their own Christened human nature released from the fetters of matter, when they raise themselves to the Christened world of the stars. When they raise themselves again to a universally broad consciousness, a fixed-star wisdom will again be possible. This will be a new Christened star-wisdom, a new reading of the stellar-script. Mysteries will then be unveiled to the human being, not yet available today, that actually cannot yet be spoken.

But what remains reserved for the future can live already today in people as an inkling, especially in the season of Christmas and the New Year, when more brightly than usual the stars shine in the night sky—and amongst them that brightest star, about which some things have been said here. This can become for the soul an intuitive consciousness, can become the occasion for the soul to receive the Christmas and New Year thought, strong for the future. It can come strongly to consciousness for the soul how the year, that now passes over again to the New Year, is a reflection of the great cosmic year, the great renewal of all things. And we would like to close this contribution—written between Christmas and New Year—with the sentences with which Rudolf Steiner ended his New-Year lecture [Dornach, 31 December 1915, in GA 165]:

> The year is a picture of the aeons. The aeons are the reality for those symbols that meet us during the course of the year. When we understand this course of the year in the right way, the thought of the great cosmic mysteries penetrates us in this noble night, when a new course of the year begins. Let us try to tune our soul that it also can look over into the New Year with the consciousness: the course of the year is in itself a symbol for the great *cosmic* course that embraces all the mysteries which the divine beings move and weave through the world; we follow with our soul from aeon to aeon just as the lesser gods follow the mysterious becoming of the plants and the minerals during the course of a single year.

(Completed New Year's Eve, 1925).

The Name Isis

Amongst the many expressive names the early Egyptians gave to the goddess Isis—a collection can be found in Heinrich Karl Brugsch, *Religion und Mythologie der alten Ägypter* [Leipzig 1887; Nabu Press 2010/ Rarebooksclub.com 2012] in his chapter on Isis—we can find the main ones characterizing most immediately the being of Isis as the *lady* or *goddess of love*. The secret of Isis is none other than the *secret of love*. Love, seen more externally, is that power which *creatively fashions*, which magically fashions the substance of the world. More internally, it is the power that *awakens* the 'I' in human consciousness—in the highest sense that the word 'I' possesses. The Egyptian Isis is also the Mother of substance and the Awakener of the higher 'I' of Osiris.

As the *one giving birth to the 'I'* and *the fashioner of substance* she stands before us already in the sounds of her name. If we look at the sounds and the writing of the name, initially in its Egyptian form, already the Isis hieroglyph, the *seat (throne)* points towards that sublime region of that divine-spiritual world in which all those spiritual forces are active, revealed in all later fashioning of substance. We also find the throne-seat in the hieroglyph of *Osiris* (Egyptian: *wsjr, Usiri*), there still connected to the *eye (iri)* of the seeing consciousness, so that for *Usiri, Osiris*, in sound and pictorial image, the meaning arises: 'Eye of power, the Sun's power of seeing' (cf. Brugsch. 81).

With the throne-seat, built up out of squares and rectangles (for itself alone can mean Isis), we find from the sounds of the various words with the name Isis (Egyptian: *Isit*), connected to the t-hieroglyph, the half-moon ⌒, or the half-circle standing on the diameter as its basis and underneath an egg-shaped form indicating the feminine within Isis:

According to Dr Wachsmuth (*The Etheric Formative Forces in Cosmos, Earth and Man*) on the forming tendencies of the four kinds of ether (square with the life-ether, half-moonlike with the sound-ether) these Egyptian pictograms of the name of Isis are to remind us of the connection of the *life-ether* with the sound-ether that carries the force which fashions substance (cf. Wachsmuth, Germ. 1st ed. p. 164, Eng. tr. 143). With these two higher kinds of ether there lies the secret of the Tree of Life that has been lost to human beings in Paradise, and with this also the secret of the *Eternal Feminine* in its (today forgotten) higher spiritual meaning, that secret of the *Primal Feminine of the world*, which the early Egyptians expressed with the name of Isis.

The sounds of the name Isis have to be found from the Egyptian writing that does not picture the vowels. There we initially find 'H-S-T (with 'h the *spiritus lenis*, the 'silent breath', the sound standing at the border of the inaudible is indicated, corresponding to the Hebrew aleph). The still undifferentiated archetypal spiritual element (h) connects with the *principle fashioning matter* S-T. This connection of sounds works archetypally and expressively from the primal language right into modern languages, indicating the firm and rigid quality of the physical, mineral element (see the monograph, H. Beckh, *Etymologie und Lautbedeutung*, 24ff.)[240] The star-radiant (*Sterne-Strahlende*) element working *above* in the etheric element, *below* in the physical, mineral element becomes the firm, rigid, stony crystal (zum Festen und Starren des Steins, zum Kristal). To connect in the right way this *above* and *below* in the spirit, is to lead towards a veiled secret in Isis and the sounds in her name. The names of the gods are indeed above all others those in which there still communicates to us something of its divine archetypal meaning in each individual sound. Only out of this eurythmical, primal interpretation of the sounds, a name such as the Egyptian name Isis can be meaningfully read.

It is no mere whim that the vowels in the Egyptian as well as the Semitic scripts remain initially un-notated, but there are many reasons and spiritual contexts. The *pure spiritual* element uncoloured by the psychological, or soul-aspects of the being is presented in this writing without vowels. One may try slowly to speak the Egyptian name Isis 'H-S-T in this way purely consonantally and yet expressively; one will perceive something of the *sacred, primal keeping silence* of the '*voice of [thin] silence*' [cf. LXX I Kings 19:12] of that *divine, archetypal stillness* which the gnostic called *Sige* and revered as the female part, the archetypal consort of the World-Father.[241] This uncertain 'H-S-T (which in the trinity of its sounds keeps veiled the *secret of Christ*), the divine-spiritual, in which works the primal female force-fashioning substance, then becomes vocalized (though this involves much interpretation). The Egyptologists interpret *I-s-t, Iset Isit*, also as U-s-t (see Brugsch. 83). The archetypal sound *U* would still point towards the pure archetypal being, the archetypal darkness—Isis is truly also the Queen of the cosmic night. In the *I* there already lies the light shining in the darkness. The Egyptians thought of the star Sirius. In this light (*Lichte*) lies the German *Ich* ('I'), the vowel of light I, which at the same time is the vowel of the *Ich*.

This is no mere 'feeling of sounds', regarded with horror by our academic etymologists, but for the Egyptian language (as well as for the Assyrian and Hebrew languages, and then significantly for the Teutonic languages) a real fact of language that is expressed in the word *Ich*, or at least certain pronoun derivatives, for example, '*mein*, mine', etc. are expressed through the vowel I, or the I-suffix is grammatically expressed,[242] also the meaningful *Y* (yod) while in Hebrew the name of *Yahve*, or in the modern spelling *Yahweh* (Y-H-V-H), is to be recalled in this connection. [The Hebrew letter yod is used to represent both the consonantal Y and at times the vowel I.]

In this way the Egyptian name Isis *I–S–T, Iset, Isis* can appear to us truly like the archetypal word-connection of that which also in our language speaks to us out of the inscription to the goddess of Sais: '*Ich bin alles das … ist*—I am everything that … *is* ….'

***

In ancient languages as spoken, S and T frequently lie together, and so the name for the goddess became for the Greeks *Isis*. For academic etymologists, who only research the historical origins, this Greek form of the name as such has no significance. They take it as an aid to unlock the Egyptian form, especially the Egyptian vowels. But apart from this, that to all exploration of Egyptian word-forms something problematic and hypothetical always adheres, we can feel towards the Greek word Isis, as if a certain nuance of the archetypal word-content of the name of the Egyptian goddess is only then fully expressed therein. (The actual archetypal word lies indeed in eternity, outside time, not at all always in what historically went before.) There lives in the two equal syllables—only to be distinguished through the long and short vowels—a *rhythmic element* of repetition, corresponding to the nature of the *etheric*, and with it at the same time a secret of the *archetypal feminine*, ordered to the rhythm and the form-principle of the number two. In his book *Das Land der Inca in seiner Bedeutung für die Urgeschichte der Sprache und Schrift* ['The land of the Incas in its significance for the prehistory of language and writing'] (Leipzig 1883; Fourier 1989; Nabu Press 2010), Rudolf Falb shows with insight how in the various languages words relate on the one hand to the *rhythm of time*, and on the other hand to the rhythmic movements of the *maternal breast*. They connect amongst themselves and also with the Egyptian-Greek Isis.

Purely factually, Isis means in the most primeval sense, the *feminine aspect of the world*. This meaning already lies in the sounds, in the S as the sound of the earthly, feminine, material and sensory element. The ancient symbol for this was the snake. In this sense, in many of the old written signs (also in Egypt) the snake can be recognized in S and Z signs. In many primeval words, this S—and even more the sound combination ST—we recall the *snake of knowledge* that winds itself around the *Tree of Life*. And the double S of the Egyptian-Greek Isis causes us to think of the *two snakes* that wind around the staff of Hermes-Mercury. This Staff of Hermes with the two snakes is again a picture of the Egyptian Mystery-wisdom and star-wisdom. This, seen as a being, is Isis. Words, too, which mean the number six and the lily (the secret of the water-lily is connected to the secret of Isis and the number six)[243], possess in Hebrew and in Egyptian characteristically the double S (Hebrew *shushan* 'lily', Egyptian s-sh-n, Coptic *shoshen* 'water-lily, lotus').

In the name Isis we do not experience the physical content of matter, but the *etheric formative forces* that effect the fashioning of matter, and its connection with the 'I'. But where we behold the formative forces of the fashioning of matter in the *etheric element*, they are still shown as *related to the stars* (the Assyrian goddess *Istar*, who in her name is related to Isis, Isit, still clearly carries the *star* in her name, cf. in Avestan the primeval word *star*). All this is pictured and parabolic in outer nature, when we do not look at the fashioning of the physical, mineral element, where it takes its course here below on the earth, but in the higher regions of the atmosphere. Up there, where starry, cosmic activity still governs, there are formed out of the activity of the light-ether in the element of water in the atmosphere (see Wachsmuth, Germ. ed. 182, Eng. tr. 158) the ice-crystal forms of snowflakes with their expressive star-forms. And with the covering of snow formed by these ice-crystal snowflakes earthly matter still appears in its purest, *virginal* form, which is closest to the cosmos. In the *ice-crystal of the snowflake* we experience the *etheric-virginal quality of the cosmos*, which the Egyptians called *Isis*. As explained elsewhere[244] the relationship to the 'I' is indicated, the *force weaving in the etheric light of the snow-crystal enchants starry forms* (ibid. p. 110: 'As in the snow-crystals' feathery down of the ether a shining cosmic starry light condenses to a tender veil of earthly matter.') And if we have arrived at the stage of deeply

contemplating these spiritual contexts, it can be raised into meditation—for it is not only a superficial playing with speech sounds—then
we gain an inner right to point out how in the German word *Eis* (ice)
the same *etheric formative forces* out of the starry element of the cosmos
forming earthly matter are expressed right into the sounds themselves.
We are allowed, when we also call up before our souls the fairy-tale
figure of the *ice-maiden* with the ice and ice-crystal, to think of that
which is revealed in the sounds of the name *Isis*.[245]

That all this is truly more than a phonetic fairy-tale imagination
becomes clear from Rudolf Falb's interesting book, mentioned above.
The author points (57, 66, 69, 362, etc.) to the veil, or the 'weave' of
Isis, the veil of matter which in Egyptian would be called, as a reversal
of *Is-is*, *si-si*. Si-si-ra would then be the 'Sun-veil, veil of glory'. This
word *sisira* is meaningful for Falb, because he finds it again with a
similar meaning in the primal language and monuments of Peru,[246]
researched by him, pointing to primal Atlantean times. The same
word in the American primal language we find in Sanskrit in the form
shishira (emphasis on the first syllable); here it expresses the 'frozen
tears of the Sun', the hoarfrost, the ice, the coldness, and in this Indian
word we can find a true linguistic connection (based on metathesis)
with the German word *Eis* (in the older form *is*). The veil of maya of
Isis has here become the veil of the ice-maiden, which then especially
conjures up the shining red colour. One recalls the snowy mountains
glowing rosy pink in the crimson of the setting sun. (According to
Falb, this also relates to the Peruvian word—which has many other
meanings.) This meaning of 'the colour red' can also be found in the
Hebrew word based on the same consonants. We seem to be standing
here before one of the oldest and most universal, primal words.

Something quite meaningful arises when, to conclude, we direct our
gaze to the Peruvian hieroglyph of the word *sisira*, which can be found in
temples there as a sacred symbol (often mentioned by Falb). It consists of
two equal triangles, and underneath in the middle a *circle* in italics:

Δ Δ.
o

From Wachsmuth's book we know the *triangle* and the *circle* as the
forming tendencies of the two lower kinds of ether: *light-ether* and
warmth-ether.[247] If we place this facing what the *Egyptian* hieroglyph of
the name Isis has shown us, with its connections of the form-princi-

ples of the *life-ether* and *sound-ether* (forms of square and half-moon), then in the mystery of the two higher kinds of ether (life-ether and sound-ether), there appears to us the being of *Isis*, in the two lower kinds of ether (light-ether and warmth-ether), the *veil of Isis* (si-si-ra). Through the Fall of man, human consciousness has lost the immediate connection with the *Tree of Life*, with the two higher kinds of ether; the human being today only lives in that which reveals the lower kinds of ether. This revelation of light and warmth veil for man today the secret of the higher revelations of cosmic life and cosmic harmony (life-ether and sound-ether): the earthly and feminine veils to him the secret of the *higher*, the *Eternal Feminine*. Thus for him Isis is still the veiled goddess. One day human beings will lift her veil again when the power of the Risen Christ has become strong in them.

Rudolf Steiner movingly describes the decline and fall of the Egyptian Mysteries.[248] He describes when the soul of the initiate, having penetrated to the shores of cosmic existence, when it had become one with *Isis*, during the time of the glory of the ancient Mysteries, perceived the revelation of cosmic Music (music of the spheres) and the cosmic Word. In this the soul experienced how *Osiris* was born or spoken (*ausgesprochen*) out of *Isis*, how the soul then in later times, after the crisis of the year 1322, stood before the silent, the mute, muffled goddess of the 'mourning widow'. 'No Osiris could be born in the later time, no cosmic harmony could sound, no cosmic word explained that which fearfully showed itself now as cosmic-warmth and cosmic-light.' In *cosmic-warmth* and *cosmic-light* the higher revelation of *cosmic life* and *cosmic harmony* is veiled! In this way, we are impressively led by the spiritual researcher towards the same conclusion, from quite a different angle, arising from the sounds and hieroglyphic contemplation of the name Isis.

The Name Eve

and other connections of the wisdom of Moses with the wisdom
of the Egyptian Mysteries

[Note on the transcription of Hebrew: א (aleph) is represented by the
phonetic symbol /?/; ה (he) by 'h; and ח (heth) by 'h.]

In various lectures and lecture-cycles by Rudolf Steiner connections
are mentioned between the biblical wisdom of Moses and the wisdom
of the Egyptian Mysteries, of which Moses was an initiate. The connections are already referred to by Fabre d'Olivet (*La Langue Hebraïque*
appeared in Paris 1815);[249] as well as by Édouard Schuré.[250] These connections can be pursued right into the sound-structure of the Hebrew
language. Fabre d'Olivet goes so far as to insist on the direct ancient
Egyptian origin of the Hebrew language (new edition, p. xxivff, Redfield p.16). The similar sound of the name of the great primal initiate
of humanity, who after the Fall once more gained life for himself by
returning into the divine life, may be pointed out here (Genesis 5:24):
the name *Hanoch*, or *Enoch*, and the Egyptian word *ankh, anokh*, 'life',
the hieroglyph of which is the famous ankh-cross similar to the hieroglyph ♀ , the *sign of life*.[251]

Just as round, circular forms are mathematically inexpressible in
any straight-line system;[252] the mystery of life, of the etheric, cannot be
found through a thinking that is confined to physical, mineral, spatial
forms. What still lived for the Egyptian consciousness as the secret of
initiation in the *symbol of the picture*, for the wisdom of Moses—for reasons frequently mentioned in Steiner's lectures–this shies away from
creating outer pictures and mysteries for the Highest. It retreated into
the mere *word* and into the *mystery of the word*. Out of this comes that
writing which is no longer a pictorial script—yet it still carries the
mystery of the stellar script. The outer principle of form of the Egyptian *ankh*, the ankh-cross, can be found again in the Sanskrit word *anka*,
'hook'. A deeper meaning can be found as a *sign of life* in the Avestan *anghu*, 'life' (= Skr. *asu*), and in the Hebrew initiate-name *Hanoch,
Enoch*, 'the one who gains life'. As the sign of life, the ankh-cross *ankh*,
is held in the hand of gods and goddesses; it is also the *sign of initiation*
and in this sense besides the word *hanoch* it also recalls the other Heb.
word, differently vocalized, *hanich* 'the initiate'.[253] The word 'mystery'

of the Egyptian initiation itself has found the path into the Hebrew language of the wisdom of Moses.

***

To this connection of the Moses-wisdom to Egypt another is added, pointing towards *Zarathustra*. The Bible points towards him in its veiled manner in the story of the little casket in which the infant Moses, floating on the river, was found by Pharaoh's daughter. Rudolf Steiner speaks of this in his lecture-cycle on *The Gospel of St Matthew* [Berne 1910. GA 123]. In the article on the star-wisdom of Isis (pp. 151 above), it was mentioned with reference to this lecture-cycle how the astral body of Zarathustra, carrying the *wisdom of space* and wisdom of the stars passes over to the Egyptian Hermes, whereas the *ether-body* which carries the *wisdom of time* passes over to Moses, that is, at his birth. As Steiner points out, the picture of the casket given in the story also points to this (Exodus 2). In the lecture-cycle on *The Gospel of St Luke* [Basel 1909. GA 114] it is related how:

> the ether-body of Zarathustra passes over to Moses. The ether-body connects with everything that develops in *time*. And so, when he became conscious of the mysteries of his ether-body, Moses was able to awaken the processes in time in tremendous, magnificent pictures, which we encounter in Genesis.

Besides the Egyptian initiation, Moses has met with another great initiate whose being in the Bible is hidden behind *Jethro*, or *Reguel*[254] (Exodus 3). It is easy to imagine a connection between chapters 2 and 3 to a certain extent; if not with Zarathustra's being, yet Jethro was still connected to the wisdom of Zarathustra. Also the *earthiness* of the wisdom of Moses is connected to Zarathustra. 'Earthly wisdom' —says Steiner in Lecture 2 of the cycle on Matthew's Gospel—'is that which *Moses* had to bring, and *Sun-wisdom* is that which *Hermes* had to bring.'

To all these connections with earlier initiation, the ultimately decisive one comes with Moses. What was revealed in the eternal depths of his inner self, in the 'deepest, most sacred centre of the soul-life' (R. Steiner) was the mystery of the eternal 'I-AM'. The event of Meribah (Num. 20:10-13) shows that Moses himself was not yet able to penetrate to the final, full understanding of this *revelation of the 'I'* which was completed only in Christ. But it lies in the Voice that *spoke* to Moses out of the *Burning Bush* (Exodus 3:2ff., 14f.): 'I-AM the I-AM' (*Ehyeh asher ehyeh*), the most meaningful of all Christ-revelations of the Old Testament (cf. John 5:46, where Christ speaks: *'for he wrote of me'*. 'This is my eternal Name (*zeh shemi le'olam*)', the divine Voice proclaims to Moses.

***

Moses' experience of standing in the centre of everything, most connected with the eternal depths within, is also connected most significantly with the Egyptian Mysteries. In their origin they were also directed towards that central Mystery of the world and of the human being. The words themselves that Moses heard there, in their ultimate meaning, are none other than those which *Isis* once spoke to the initiates of the Mysteries. When Isis became mute, these words could still be read as the inscription before the *veiled picture* of the goddess of Sais: *'I am the All [Everything/ the Universe], I am everything that was, that is and that shall be.'* The postscript, *'No mortal has lifted my veil'*, speaks of that veil which in later Egypt increasingly covers the mystery of human consciousness, the veil of which Moses lifted a portion, but only a portion in an exalted inner experience. And another still more concrete connection with the Egyptian Mysteries exists with the experience of Moses. The decline of Egyptian Mystery-wisdom from Sothis period to Sothis period (see the Isis article), took place in such a way that an early period of fixed-star wisdom was succeeded by one of planetary wisdom, which at its ending still reached into the beginning of the third post-Atlantean (Egyptian-Chaldean) cultural epoch. Following this came a period of *wisdom of the elements*, which then finished when (in 1322 BCE) Moses led the Hebrews out of Egypt. (In the year mentioned one of the astronomical Sirius, or Sothis, periods ended.) *During this period of wisdom of the elements there occurs that which Moses still experienced with the Egyptian Mysteries,* that is, during that time when Isis still revealed herself out of the elemental realm of the Earth, out of the flower-chalice, out of the etheric, living element of the plant-world. Consequently, the divine *voice of the* 'I-AM' speaks to Moses—he hears it not only out of the depths of his own 'I'—but out of the etheric realm of the plant-world, out of the 'Burning Bush'. It is indeed no common earthly fire in which the Bush burns, for 'the bush was not consumed' (Exodus 3:2). It is a higher etheric fire, a fire as is also frequently meant with Zarathustra, in whose language the word for fire, *athar*, reminds us of the Gk. *aither*, 'ether' (cf. the article on Zarathustra).

Thus what ultimately was a revelation out of the eternal depths of his own inner being was connected for Moses with the Voice out of the

Burning Bush. That which was revealed to him of the Isis-Mysteries was connected with the revelation of the divine *I-AM*. What for him as a divine revelation of the inner being connected him with the Mysteries of Isis—disregarding all the imagery in which the revelation of the Egyptian Mysteries was still veiled—created for him an expression in the *word*, in the *highest Name*, in which at one time the divine Voice itself spoke to him (Ex. 6:2, 3). The name *I* without an image speaks in our inner being and sounds from us; the divine I-AM, too, spoke to Moses in the name Y-H-V-H. The name *I* is the one which can only be given each to himself (cf. Acts 19:12); the name Y-H-V-H, the divine I-AM, amongst all the divine names, given by man to the Divine, can only be given by the Divine itself. The consonantal inexpressible name is vocalized in the form Jehovah, Yahveh, or in a more correct vocalized form the H become E: *Yeve, Yewe*. This name is the shortened précis of what the Voice spoke out of the Burning Bush: *Eher asher eher*, 'I am the I am'.[255]

***

We shall not be concerned with everything that can been said from various viewpoints about the meaning of the divine name Y-H-V-H, but only its connection with the Isis-Osiris secret of the Egyptian Mysteries. The connection of the higher 'I', *Osiris*, with the cosmic primal power, the Eternal Feminine of the world, *Isis*, lies in a different form, looked at and expressed from a different point of view sounding also in the Hebrew name Y-H-V-H. H-V-H, or—when we proceed from the form Yewe – E-V-E, *Eve*, for the Hebrew initiate is the Hebrew cosmic primal power, which the Egyptian called *Isis* (*Iset, Isit, 'H-S-T*). But more than the original all-embracing Egyptian Isis-name is expressed by H-V-H, E-V-E, the *primal bride*, the female half of the archetypal divinity, that is, that which in Egypt became of Isis as the partner of Osiris. And then, too, it has to be understood that we are dealing here not simply with a simple equivalent, but that a difference of the names and sounds also contains a profound difference of viewpoints from which one can overview what is the same, or is similar.

***

We have to ask: what is H-V-H in Hebrew, and what lives in these sounds? How does it come to name the Eternal Feminine in the divine name Y-H-V-H? We can initially affirm that 'H-V-H, in that the first H is darkened from the pure sound of H [ה] towards the more earthly sound H [ח] (ch), it transforms into 'H-V-H [הוה], 'Havah, 'Heveh, into the Germ. name *'Eva'* (Eng. 'Eve'). (Havah is Heb. for *Eva*, Eve.) The Eternal Feminine becomes the earthy feminine; it becomes Eva. The Bible itself links this word etymologically with 'h-y-h [היה], to *live* (in the sense of physical, organic life): 'And Adam called his wife Eva, Eve (Havah), since she was the *mother of all living'* (em kol chay).

'H-V-H contains Eve *after the Fall*, and the earthly feminine lies in the H-V-H contained in the name Y-H-V-H, the mystery of the still divine primal Feminine and cosmic virginal [condition] (Eve before the Fall). 'H-V-H is the human mother, and H-V-H is still the divine, cosmic Virgin and Mother *Isis*. In the article on 'The name of Isis' it was shown how in Isis, Egyptian *Isit, Iset, H-S-T,* there is expressed a secret of the astral element, of the star-element, of the *wisdom of space*. Out of the undifferentiated primal spiritual element (/ʔ/ of the Heb. alphabet, [א] aleph, the Spiritus Lenis) the pure etheric being streams, which then below *condenses into the earthly veil of matter* (S-T). In the name Isis is expressed how the star-element of the cosmos is condensed into earthly matter out of the etheric element. The ice-crystal of the snowflake, formed as out of the starry substance of the cosmos, as we saw, is the outer picture, as it were, of this cosmic life condensing into virginal earthly matter of the covering of snow. The cosmic life and the cosmic light rigidify into the spatial nature, into spatial existence. Before the soul, in the name Isis the picture of the *ice-maiden* appeared for us beside the *star-maiden*. In this the whole starry-spatial wisdom of Hermes is expressed in concentrated form. The primal being embodied in Isis, appears—in the first instance at least—like a spatial being beheld in starry worlds. Thus Hermes as the bearer of the astral body of Zarathustra in which the spatial wisdom lived, has in the first instance put this *spatial wisdom* and *star-wisdom* into the name Isis.

Moses, the bearer of the etheric body of Zarathustra in which the *wisdom of time* lives, looks from the viewpoint of this time-wisdom towards the divine primal being and the Eternal Feminine of the world. 'H-S-T, *Isis* the *primal spatial word*, is H-V-H; E-V-E, *Eve* is the *primal time-word* of the world. *Primal being* is not as the starry spatial nature, but as the primal being of time as primal eternity resting in itself. And for us the sound of E-V-E, *Eve*, becomes for us meaningful in eternity in the light of the time-wisdom of Moses, whether explained by outer historical etymology or not. (The expression in the [re-worked Apostles] Creed [of The Christian Community], 'from the Father, born *in* eternity' receives thereby a new, uniquely profound meaning, which is emphasized even more through the subsequently stated relation to the Virgin Mary.) In the duality of the sounds (H-H, E-E) lives the great mystery of time, of the cosmic primal rhythm, which at the same time is the rhythm of the etheric-feminine (see the Isis article). And a word like the German *Ehe* [marriage] thereby receives an inner meaning, relating to the primal language, to the word Eva H-V-H, *Eve*, to that which is contracted *for eternity*, for that which is beyond time.

It is no 'speculation of speech sounds' when it is claimed here that H-V-H, E-V-E, *Eve*, would be the *primal time-word*—just as 'H-S-T, *Isis*, is in a certain sense the *primal word for space*. But, as Fabre d'Olivet describes in a significant section of his Hebrew grammar (new edition, Bk I, 96), H-V-H [הוה] *is really the primal time-word in Hebrew* [*hāvāh with vowels*]. He says that it would actually be the only time-word (verb) of the language, the *verb in and for itself*, and that all other words which are called verbs, or time-words, would actually only be nouns that receive their life as verbs *from this one primal time-word*. The use of the word h-v-h as the time-word 'to be' is not particularly frequent; according to the dictionary it means 'to become', 'to be', 'to remain'. The normal word for 'to become', 'to take place', 'to be', is actually *h-y-h* [היה] (it is related to 'h-y-h 'life' as is H-V-H to 'H-V-H, Eva [Eve]). h-y-h is indeed *revealed existence*—for y is the sound of revelation—h-v-h (with the primal sound v) the *primal existence*. (In Y-H-V-H the y of revelation connects with the h-v-h of primal existence, the cosmic primal power.) The original meaning of H-V-H is *primal being*, *primal events*, the *primal element of cosmic will*. It can also be expressed as the primal verbal element of the cosmos, that power of the will-element which makes the verb (time-word) a verb (in the time-word, or verb, the will-element always lies, immediately evident is the deed, as in the adjective the element of feeling is evident, and in the noun—Germ. *Hauptwort*, that is, 'head (= main) word'—the conceptually abstract (see the author's article 'Let there be light')).[256]

The cosmic Father Himself carries this primal element of the verb in the cosmos, this primal power of the word and active creative power of all the cosmic events, bound with his 'I' (y): Y-H-V-H. Already the Indians speak of this divine primal power of the word, *Vac*, regarded as the female part or feminine aspect of the primal godhead. In the word *Vac* there lies significantly the primal sound v (va) (see the later part of author's article 'Let there be light'), the same sound that we find in the Lat. *verbum*, and even in the Germ. and Eng. words for 'word', *Wort* and word (cf. also, Germ. *werden* [to become], *wachsen* [to grow], *sich wandeln* [to change yourself], *sich entwickeln* [to develop], and many other words). And we find the same sound in the primal word H-V-H, E-V-E, *Ewe*. We find it between the double H, the breath of air, the spiritual primal breath. This is what Gen. 2:7 says, 'Yahveh, Y-H-V-H, blew into the nostrils of man and thus created him as a living soul'.

Thanks to the primal word, in the words H-V-H, E-V-E, *Ewe* ['Eva']—which in Indian, as in the Heb. wisdom of Moses, means the *primal feminine of the world*, the primal spouse of the cosmic Father—there lies the primal cosmic power in the cosmic breath, which is the bearer of all the power of speech. In such a significant manner the word 'H-S-T, *Isis*, emerges as the *primal spatial-word* opposite H-V-H, E-V-E, *Ewe* ['Eva']—in its meaning closely related—as the *primal time-word* of the world.

***

When it can be shown, as in the Heb. H-V-H, E-V-E, *Eve* of the wisdom of Moses, that is rests on another viewpoint than in the similar-meaning Egyptian word 'H-S-T, *Isis* of the wisdom of Hermes, this is not to say that the sounds of the name H-V-H (Eva, *Eve*) can't be traced back to the Egyptian. Even in Egyptian there is H-H (Heh) of the primal breath, the original breath of air (see Brugsch, *Religion und Mythologie der alten Ägypter*. 132ff.), with the implied, secondary meaning of eternity, love and longing (cf. what is said on *va*, 'to waft', in relation to 'Eva, Eve' in 'Let there be Light', in *The Source of Speech*, pp.164f.). Something of cosmic life, cosmic love and creative longing also lies in the name H-V-H, in which the creative primal sound v joins the airy element of the Egyptian H-H. In contrast to /ʔ/ (aleph, *spiritus lenis*), to the pure, primal spiritual, there already lies in the h a certain luciferic element and in the ch an earthy-ahrimanic element. The extent, or range of the sound in the name Isis 'H-S-T is greater than that of the name Eva H-V-H, which in a one-sided way belongs to the upper element. More comprehensive, if still covered and veiled, the *Christ* lies more in the name Isis (H-S-T), than in the name Eva (H-V-H). Only when the yod is added to the name Eva H-V-H, does the name of God come about Y-H-V-H, which covers in itself the reflection of Christ's being. This name, when it becomes earthly (the S is the *earthly* counter-pole of the H), is changed to the name *Jesus* (*Jehoshuah, Jeshuah*, Joshua). In this form of the name, the Heb. name of God approaches again the Egyptian *Isis*. As in the Egyptian *Isis, Jesus* lies in *Jehoshuah, healing power*, the divine healing, saving power.

Like 'H-S-T, *Isit*, *Isis*, H-V-H, E-V-E, *Eve* is the upper, the higher, the divine element of life, the *eternal feminine* in this sense forgotten (through the Fall). In the essay 'On the name of Isis' it was shown how in the sense of the esoteric ether-research (cf. Dr Günther Wachsmuth. *The Etheric Formative Forces in Cosmos Earth and Man*) this higher life-element can be found in the *two upper kinds of ether* (life-ether and sound-ether), to which man has lost his immediate relationship through the Fall, in which he no longer works and lives consciously (today he can only do this with the two lower kinds of ether, light-ether and warmth-ether). Still within the light a division takes place which *separates the cold, upper light from the earthly-warm light.* Life-ether and sound-ether, cold light, are the upper life-element; light-ether and warmth-ether, warm light, are the lower life-element. And that upper life-element of life-ether and sound-ether, as we saw, is the *eternal feminine*, which mankind lost in Paradise, which has withdrawn from his consciousness. The Egyptians called it Isis (H-V-H). The lower life-element, light-ether and warmth-ether is—as we saw—that which for human consciousness today veils the higher element; it is the *veil of Isis*, the veil of maya [illusion]; the *earthly feminine*, the earthly Eve, veils for the human being today the *eternal feminine, the divine Eve.*

If we glimpse thus in H-V-H, E-V-E, *Eve*, also *Hevah, Heve*, the higher life-element of the life-ether and sound-ether, then the Heb. H-V-H, *Heve*, reminds us furthermore of the Gk. *Hebe*, to which it has a clear relationship as a primal word. H-V-H, *Heve*, is the Tree of Life lost in Paradise (the immortal life in the life-ether and sound-ether); *Hebe* in the Paradise of the gods offers the rejuvenating nectar of immortality from the Tree of Life (cf. Iduna in the Germanic). She was the spouse of Heracles—who, after passing through the flames of the earthly-feminine element, Deianira,[257] which burnt him—has himself wrestled through and raised himself to the higher element of life. Then *Hebe* receives him and gives him the rejuvenating drink of immortal life.[258] In the sense of the above-mentioned ether-research, Heracles wrests himself out of the element of the warmth-light, out of the sphere of the light-ether and the warmth-ether into the sphere of the higher light, of the sound-ether and life-ether. In ever-new light the name Eva H-V-H radiates to us, when we place it into such a context. And thereby an ever-new, deeper meaning also falls on to the name of God Y-H-V-H.

***

So H-V-H, as Eve in Paradise, the eternal-feminine before the Fall of Man, the pure, innocent primal nature, the cosmic-virginal element, is Isis. In the Christ-future of the redeemed, she is the *metamorphosed* Eve: *Ave*, Ave Maria, the new Isis, the human soul awoken in the Risen One. In her all the Mysteries are veiled, which the divine name Y-H-V-H veils from us. She becomes as the newly attained higher life-element that works again in the transformed, *renewed Earth*, which the Apocalypse calls the *New Jerusalem*. Only then will the name '*I*', whose ultimate depths even Moses himself did not yet recognize, become in *Christ* fully and completely achieved for human beings. And as already in the earlier name Y-H-V-H, there will be seen, also united with this new '*I*', the Mystery of the newly achieved eternal-feminine, the redeemed nature, the cosmic virginal element of the upper element of life. This is the physical element transformed by the '*I*', which the apocalyptist saw in the picture of the *City of God*, the *New Jerusalem*. This is the Mystery of Eve and the Mystery of Yahveh (Y-H-V-H) of Rev. 3:12: 'He who overcomes, him will I make a pillar in the temple of my God, ...'.

(This is always the name '*I*', the Y in the name Y-H-V-H.) In pointing to this deeply significant verse of the Book of Revelation, in another place (the author's meditative verse 'The New Jerusalem')[259] it could be said:

> In the heart the Foundation Stone has been laid
> upon which one day the city shall be founded,
> which shines in uncorrupted nature,
> a shining Temple of divine, eternal being.
> Within, as a living pillar there lives
> the human being who overcame the past,
> and who received the name '*I*' from God
> (around which *the eternal name Eve*
> is wound as a Mystery of the virgin bride).

Through the Fall of Man, the male and female [principles] of the world have landed in division. They are again united together in the divine, as they were in the distant Paradise and pre-paradisal age of the human race originally united in God. 'The Eternal Feminine leads us above' [Goethe. *Faust* II. Conclusion].

Buddha's Passing
with excerpts from the Pali canon

Too early, alas, the Holy One went from us,
too early, alas, is the Blessed One gone from us,
too early, alas, the eye, which was the Light of the World, has been
    extinguished for us.
Mahāparinibbānasutta

Unutterably rich and many-sided are the viewpoints from which the figure of Buddha is illuminated in the various writings, lectures and lecture-cycles of Rudolf Steiner. In contrast to those who present what has passed only philologically, or who want to present it in a one-sided preference as religion or world-view, it was Steiner's deed properly to place the *phenomenon of Buddha* like other meaningful appearances of the spirit, into the whole development of the consciousness of humanity. Meaningful connections with the central event of the history of the Earth, with *Christ*, come thereby to the light of day. One of the most meaningful takes place in Luke's Gospel, where it is shown how in the Nathan Jesus-child—already revealed in the angel's annunciation at Christmas—the Buddha's cosmic impulse of love manifests like a rejuvenated spring through contact with the Christ-impulse.

What has become old in the pre-Christian world, appears at the great turning point freshly rejuvenated through the power of Christ— Who later connects himself with the vessel of the Nathan-Jesus. In the same way as Zarathustra works into the story in Matthew's Gospel, Buddha works into Luke's Gospel. In a characteristic way, the gaze of the spiritual researcher sees Buddha's being continuing to work in world-events. In the light of Christ, wonderful new connections open up everywhere to the eye of the spirit, also when this eye turns to Buddha. Rudolf Steiner beheld Buddha, like all the other facts he spiritually researched, with the eye of a Christened vision.

To follow the spiritual researcher into such depths of vision would have been impossible for the early Buddhist. To *his* beholding Buddha departs into Nirvana. He would initially have no concept of a continuation of Buddha's being. And so it essentially remained through the five centuries after Buddha's departure, until the great turning point of time. This is exactly the time-span that, in conversation with his disciple

Ananda, Buddha prophesied that his teaching would remain pure.[260] And it is really highly interesting to see how, after this time, Buddhism becomes something else. In the phase of Mahayana Buddhism, which then over many countries in Asia becomes decisive, the teaching of *Nirmanakaya* appears. This looks towards a spiritual—indeed spiritual-physical—continuation of Buddha in higher worlds after his Nirvana. In place of the path of the merely individual self-redemption, another higher Path of the redemption of the Earth is given, of working for the redemption of all being, of the connection with the destiny of the Earth.

The development of the consciousness-soul in the Eastern soul is not attained in the same way as by the Western soul. Consequently, the taking up of the Christ-Impulse into the consciousness-soul, that is, a conscious looking at the Deed of Christ, is missing in Mahayana Buddhism. Mahayana Buddhism differs from the earlier Buddhism. In some souls, though not consciously to the souls themselves, the fact works *objectively* that Christ, through the Mystery of Golgotha (which also the Mahayana Buddhist himself does not recognize), has connected Himself with the Earth and with human souls. The clairvoyant gaze of this event has become different; it perceives facts and viewpoints for which previously no organ existed.

We shall not be concerned with this later phase of Buddhism. We choose to look entirely at the time that Buddha himself prophesied as the period during which his spiritual impulse would rightly last and the original teaching kept pure, that five-hundred-year period lying between Buddha's departure into Nirvana and the great Christian turning point of time. This age of the early pure and original Buddhism (the one and only age Steiner has in view in his lecture ['Buddha', Berlin, 2 March 1911. GA 60]) is the five centuries before the Mystery of Golgotha. We can really feel this as a final, tremendous blossoming of the early Indian spiritual life. We are clearly aware that the whole history of this early Indian spiritual life is in *decline*: the consciousness of the early Indian lives on the rich, splendid memories of a long past age. No documents have come down to us from this, the actual primal age of India. The spiritual researcher describes the heights of its spirituality—for the consciousness of humanity today unimaginable—a spirituality in which the consciousness itself still lived *as if* in *the memory of Paradise*. During the age of the Buddha, the Vedas and Upanishads, the great epics and puranas are but later memory-recollections of this time. And even the Vedas and their age had progressively become pale memories in the age of the Buddha. *Yoga*, which since the early ages in India maintained a lofty school of concentration and meditation, is the path upon which individuals repeatedly sought to link with the lost original consciousness. It gave the decisive stamp to all Indian spiritual life, also to Buddha's impulse. In this spiritual life, which seen as a whole is a descent from the primal age right to the great turning point of time, great individual personalities repeatedly arise, initiates who renew what remains of the early spirituality. This is also emphasized in Steiner's lecture.

And so, at the transition into the 'dark age', into *Kali Yuga* (the third post-Atlantean age), the figure of *Krishna* stands, who gives his pupil, the hero Arjuna (first syllable emphasized), the sacred teaching of the *Bhagavadgita*. Deep into Kali Yuga itself and approaching the great turning point of time—half a millennium does not count for very much for the great period that spans Indian spirituality—the figure of *Gotama Buddha* stands as the last of the great pre-Christian initiates, of the great pre-Christian initiates in *historical* times. (Zarathustra—that is, the first Zarathustra, about whom spiritual research speaks—belongs to prehistoric times.)

Indian spiritual history presents us with the picture of a descent out of bright heights of life into growing twilight, growing darkness, punctuated by brilliant individual lights, but which only in an ever decreasing measure were able to renew the light of the primal age—this is the picture of Indian spiritual history. And it is characteristic for Indian spiritual development (for the other great pre-Christian developments, too—to think only of Egypt—that there appears such a descent), that especially during the time of the last descent approaching the turning point of time, such a thoroughly bright appearance of light as that of Buddha could occur—radiantly bright in itself, although for the contemporaries it could only marginally renew the light of primal times.[261] A more beautiful, more suitable picture for this appearance of Buddha in the descent and the twilight of Indian spiritual life cannot be found than that of the *sunset*, as Rudolf Steiner once presented to us in a public lecture (Berlin, 2 March 1911. GA 60): As within the reddening sunset the daylight, before it wanes, lights up once more in the most splendid colours, the light of the early Indian spiritual life shone mightily once again also in its last great appearance, in *Buddha*. Out of his eyes there shone once again for his contemporaries the splendour of those primal times, the greatness of the ancient Yoga, the light of the old clairvoyance and worldwide consciousness, that increasingly tore itself away from humanity. Consequently, it is striking how with Buddha's passing, from human beings and supersensory beings, from the spirits of the air and of the Earth, the lament sounds:

> *Too early, alas, the Holy One went from us,*
> *too early, alas, is the Blessed One gone from us,*
> *too early, alas, the eye, which was the Light of the World, has been*
>   *extinguished for us.*

***

These words are taken from that text which more than any other enchants before us that mood of *sunset*, of the failing light, the most beautiful and most like the Gospels of all ancient Buddhist texts, which at the same time also presents most purely the being of early, original Buddhism, the *Mahāparinibbānasutta* in the Dīghanikāya of the Pali canon, the great narration of Buddha's passing from the Earth and of Nirvana.[262] In no other early text than this is the figure of Buddha himself and the time during which he lived so livingly portrayed. No other text of the early documents is so suited to illuminate more closely what has been said by Steiner in his lecture on the 'mood of farewell' of early Buddhism and the whole age of Buddha. As a spiritual impulse of the past shining in the evening twilight Buddha's impulse stands clearly before us. But in what we feel as something belonging to the past, such a *greatness of the purely human element* for us, is how we can experience this past element again as something close, indeed, almost as something of the present. It is the human, artistic, rhythmical, musical element of the presentation which today can still speak to us.[263]

When we allow it to speak to us, we will recognize in those farewell discourses in the Mahāparinibbānasutta a pearl of Indian literature, indeed of world literature, and beyond that one of the truly *sacred writings of humanity*.

***

Already over the beginning of the narration, where still worldly unrest and politics play in, lies the *mood of the first farewell*. Buddha's passing is not yet mentioned, but the word of the Master and the admonitions to his disciples are of such a kind that clearly point to this passing; the tremendous seriousness of the event can be felt in the background. The concern for the future and the spiritual impulse brought through him into the world must have moved Buddha at this time. The question must have been present for him: What can I still do to bring awareness to my disciples, that what has been achieved will not pass, that it may live on into the future? And as the peak of all his admonitions stands the solemn, urgent and persistent commandment to unite for the common goal. To the messenger of a sympathetic chief who planned to go to war against a neighbouring tribe, Buddha advised against war. He posed the question to his disciple Ananda, whether unity and other virtues that he mentions still reign under the representatives of the tribe who were threatened by the war-plan. With the disciple's confirmation, he then explained to the messenger, *as long* as chiefs remain amongst themselves *united and of one mind,* as long as they cherish the right common spirit, and so on, *so long will they prosper and not decline.*[264]

After the messenger had taken his leave, Buddha then directs the same admonitions to his disciples, thereby taking as a Leitmotif his previous words spoken to the messenger:[265] 'As *long as you disciples cherish the right common spirit, and take care to remain united and of one mind,* as long as you hold up the spiritual goods that have been entrusted to you preserve the right reverence, the right solemnity for the spiritual life, *so long will you prosper and not decline.'*

Where Buddha speaks to his disciples of the teaching—and still he travelled, as he did throughout his long, rich working life, teaching and preaching from place to place[266]—*one* sentence keeps returning, which expresses the quintessence of Buddha's impulse in a short rule, that he shows how the four main parts of the teaching and of the path—moral self-education, meditation, recognition, inner liberation—mutually carry and determine each other.

It is not these four main parts—although they contain several things in an esoteric context which not *only* concerns the Buddhist path—that interest us today in the first instance, but the rhythm of the sentences, the movement they bring about in the etheric body. These movements, Rudolf Steiner points out in *Knowledge of the Higher Worlds*[267]— 'are an image of certain cosmic rhythms which also at certain points repeat themselves and revert to former modes, the student listening to the wisdom of the Buddha unites his life with that of the cosmic mysteries'.[268] And here with *these* sentences we would like to think, as it were, on the rhythms of the cosmic ocean (with which Buddha himself compared his teaching in a famous parable),[269] on the pulse of the ocean waves pounding on the shore and streaming back again, which can become a meaningful picture of the rhythm of time and the rhythm of the etheric: 'Only when carried and purified by moral self-education can meditation bear fruit and blessing; only pervaded and purified by such knowledge can the spirit become free of all impurities of worldly illusion—as there exists the illusion of worldly passion, the illusion of worldly existence, the illusion of world view, the illusion of worldly error.'

***

Deeply impressive is the veneration that is still directed towards the Master from all sides. These farewell discourses in particular also witness to the geniality of this devotion. This is so far removed for the human being out there in the [bustling] world today. The world of women, too, took part in this general veneration of Buddha. Indeed, already in Buddha's time, it seems to have been that the female soul in a special way was inclined to venerate. This is shown in a living way with the episode of Bajadere Ambapali in Chapter two,[270] where Buddha accepts the invitation to a meal, whereas he declines the invitation from the Litshavi Princes who had approached him too late. After the meal Ambapali is elevated and rejoices through the spiritual teaching. In deep gratitude she bequeathes her extensive park to Buddha and his disciples as a present. Over the whole narration which in its simplicity speaks to the human heart and is also not without some humorous touches, lies the mood of deep veneration of the Master in all the social circles of India. Over Bajadere Ambapali herself there lies something like a gentle, distant similarity to Mary Magdalene.

***

Immediately after this cordial episode the seriousness of cosmic destiny knocks at the door, which until now one feels as in the far distant background: traces of a serious, painful mortal illness make their appearance.[271] According to what is said later about bleeding dysentery, and so on,[272] the seed of the illness must have been in the lower region, the digestive system. In order to speak once more to his friends, Buddha pushes back the illness through his willpower, retaining his life. A paralysing shock spreads amongst those surrounding him. Ananda speaks how the ground under his feet swayed, how dizziness and a lack of feeling for space takes hold of him. But then he is full of hope because the illness is held in check. He begs the Holy One to speak to the disciples. But Buddha replies he has nothing essential to communicate further. Old and feeble, he has reached the goal of his earthly life. Only with effort, like an old cart, he drags along his 80-year-old body; all his admonitions to the disciples culminate in standing firm on the ground of the sacred truth, to seek the goal and the light within themselves.

***

Buddha seeks to raise to consciousness the seriousness of the cosmic hour of destiny that has now tolled—this is the content of the next, the dramatic third chapter—in his favourite disciple Ananda during an intimate conversation. The tragedy of this chapter is that the seriousness of this chapter is not appreciated.[273] It was always emphasized, as also in this essay, that the path taught by Buddha is a path of individual self-redemption. (Only Mahayana Buddhism falling into the Christian era, as we have seen, moves towards this goal.) But it also has to be considered, that *Buddha himself* has trodden the 'greater path'; he was not satisfied to find salvation and redemption for himself—such a self-sufficiency stood like a temptation before him when he sat under the Bodhi tree and had found the redemptive knowledge.[274] But he *selflessly sacrificed himself in communicating his teaching to the world.* Rudolf Steiner once said, that the strange meal of pork with Chunda the smith[275] is a picture for the spiritual non-comprehension of the people, which brought his ruin.[276] Here it becomes suddenly clear why Buddha's body at the end fell into the weakness of old age 'like an old cart laboriously dragging himself along'. The yogi—and Buddha was Master of Yoga—if he had remained *in himself*, would also have remained master over the budding forces of the organism. But now—so Buddha in that destiny-laden dialogue teaches his disciple Ananda—the Sacred One, in a selfless way, could still call up the budding forces through the strength of Yoga for the salvation of beings, in order to connect himself with the destiny of the Earth, right to the end of the time, to work for humanity and all beings. To his favourite disciple Ananda, Buddha speaks of a certain possibility of an unheard of self-sacrifice surpassing all human imagination. Something lights up in ancient India of the world-encompassing breadth of the Christ-thought and of Christ's sacrificial Deed, that in actual fact took place quite differently. But 500 years before Golgotha, the world was not yet ripe to grasp the greatness of such a thought. Only because the nearest and dearest did not understand these indications—the others would anyway not have understood—Buddha now decides to let destiny (karma) hold sway, in order to take his leave of the Earth and to go alone into Nirvana. He allows the illness to take its course, which until now he had held back. The formative forces of life, which before he had held in himself, he now releases.

The fourth chapter reports on the outer reason given in that meal-time at the smith's, Chunda, which leads to the outbreak of the illness, or rather its intensified relapse.[277] We only understand rightly what is told there when we look at the inner connection of Chapter 3, with Ananda's failure in the test. If *one* person had understood the greatness of Buddha in the decisive moment the destiny of the Earth and humanity would have taken another course. A cosmic destiny lay in the balance. And the weighing pan in which Buddha's life and possibilities of further earthly activities lay sunk deep into the depths. Its sinking meant death, farewell to the Earth, Nirvana. The whole story of the illness, of Chapter 4, only reveals in outer events what was already decided in Chapter 3.

A scene is introduced at the end of this chapter[278] that has always been compared to the Transfiguration of Christ on the Mount, and we can really feel that here as well as in other places, already rays from Christ shine into Buddha's life. As Christ in his death shone on the cross, Buddha before his passing into Nirvana shone in a super-earthly glory. Both narrations clearly point towards the connection of this phenomenon with the event of death. And yet in the account of Buddha the worldwide connections are missing, to which in the gospel account the appearance of Moses and Elijah already point.[279] In the account of Buddha everything in the gospel story is missing that points towards the world-encompassing greatness of the Mystery of Golgotha and its meaning for the future. Over the *Transfiguration of Christ* there lies something of the light of a new *cosmic dawn*; over the Transfiguration of Buddha in full clarity and without any doubt, there lies the mood of the *departing light, of the great evening sunset*. Just as before its setting the day-star [the Sun] once more flames up in wonderful colours, so Buddha's body shines before his passing into Nirvana, once more in super-earthly glory. The glory rays beyond the yellow colour of two garments in gold brocade, which a member of the nobility had given to the Holy One in veneration.

> The Malla Prince had not gone long, when the venerable Ananda also put the second of the two garments, the shiny ones made out of gold brocade, on to the Holy One's body, and see, it shone clinging to the Holy One's body in radiant, bright glory as white as leprosy. Then the honourable Ananda spoke to the Holy One: 'A miracle, Master, it is a rare mystery, how here in transfiguration the skin-colour of the Holy One shines in clear white light. Here this pair of garments that shine, made out of gold brocade, I put them on to the body of the Sacred One and once they were on the body of the Sacred One, it shines in blinding bright glory, like white leprosy'.

'Yes, so it is, Ananda. There are two occasions when the Holy One's skin-colour shines in super-bright transfiguration, in bright pure white. Which two? First, during that night when the Perfected One, Ananda, awakes to his highest, complete Enlightenment, and during the other night when the Perfected One in Nirvana, free of the body wafts away in the sublime primal ground, dissolving all illusions of the world. With these two moments, O Ananda, the body of the Holy One shines over-bright in transfiguration, in bright, pure white. And now today, Ananda, in the last third of this night, at Kusinara, in the sala grove of Malla, in the "Garden of Homecoming", between two twin sala trees, the passing of the Perfected One into Nirvana will take place. Come now, Ananda, let us continue out pilgrimage to the River Kakuttha.'

'Yes, Master,' said the venerable Ananda to the words of the Holy One.

> The choicest pair of garments,
> shining like gold, that Pukkusa brought;
> when the Master was robed in it
> his colour shone white as snow.

At the end of the chapter,[280] we see the Holy One still lovingly concerned to avert everything that for the smith, Chunda could become a self-accusation because of his meal, which outwardly led to the death of Buddha, but which in the course of world-destiny has to be seen as the highest service.

***

Buddha's last earthly journey which led him, starting from Rājagaha, the capital of Magadha, south of the Ganges, then beyond the Ganges ever further to the north, comes to its end. Near to the Himalayas, at Kusinara, not far from the other town, where the great Holy One was born, his earthly pilgrimage found its goal. The mountains of eternal snow, which full of grace shone down on to the birth of the Bodhisattva in the blossoming garden, also look down on to the dying Holy One. Everything in this Chapter 5[281] becomes the poetic, rhythmical, musical climax of the whole narration, becomes the *great cosmic Imagination*. The *consciousness of the Indian primal age*, which itself was still like a pure *memory of Paradise* shines out mightily in these pictures. For it was the meaning of all Indian spiritual striving, of all Yoga, to lead back to this *primal human consciousness*, to re-find the path to Paradise, to the Tree of Life.

Buddha was the only one in later times able to renew the greatness and splendour of the early primal consciousness.[282] And now, when his etheric body begins to become completely loosened from the hemmed-in restriction of earthly physicality and to spread out into the ether-world, that consciousness spanning the paradisal heights becomes, as it were, free, as if poured out into the surrounding world. The whole of nature seems to participate, that which now in pictures of world-embracing greatness and splendour streams from the etheric body of the dying Holy One. All the paradisal pictures are present,

- the *north* itself with its mysterious relationship to the primal age of humanity,
- the picture of the *'cosmic fields of ice'* in the far *snowy Himalayan mountains*,
- the *Paradise garden* (here called 'Garden of Homecoming'),
- the *stream of Paradise*, which carries with it the mystery of gold,
- the *two trees* themselves, which, like the sublime cosmic pillars, the pillar of birth and the pillar of death, framing Buddha's death-bed,
- the heavenly blossoms,
- the sounding harmonies, and
- the etheric scents.

Buddha was the last of the great ones who still in pre-Christian times, was connected in full strength to the forces of the Tree of Life. And while the earthly eye sees how the two sala trees,[283] between which Ananda had made the last resting place for the Master, shower their blossoms on to the Holy One, the supersensory ether-eye beholds blossoms raining down from the blossoming *Tree of Life*. All the realms of the higher life-element that remained back in Paradise, of the *life-ether* and *sound-ether*, open up. The language itself becomes rhythm, becomes music, penetrated by the rhythm of the sound-ether:[284]

> Although not their flowering season then,
> the twin sala trees stood nonetheless in magnificent bloom,
> in over-abundance of newly opened buds,
> and let their blossom showers come
> pouring down, trickling down, flowing down,
> on the body of the Accomplished One,
> to honour the Earth's Accomplished One,
> and heavenly blossoms from the tree in Paradise Garden
> came floating and fluttering out of the air,
> pouring down, trickling down, flowing down,
> on the body of the Accomplished One,
> to honour the Earth's Accomplished One.
> heavenly scents of sandalwood filled with filigree dust the air
> and came pouring down, trickling down,
> flowing down on the body of the Accomplished One,
> to honour the Earth's Accomplished One,

and heavenly harps resounded in the air,
to honour the Earth's Accomplished One,
and heavenly harmonies filled softly the air,
to honour the Earth's Accomplished One.
Then the Holy One spoke to the venerable Ananda:
'Although it is not their flowering season now,
the twin sala trees stand nonetheless in magnificent bloom,
in over-abundance of newly opened buds,
and let their blossom showers come pouring down, trickling down,
flowing down on the body of the Accomplished One,
to honour the Earth's Accomplished One.'
And heavenly blossoms from the tree in Paradise Garden
come floating and fluttering out of the air,
pouring down, trickling down, flowing down,
on the body of the Accomplished One,
to honour the Earth's Accomplished One,
heavenly scents of sandalwood fill with filigree dust the air
and come pouring down, trickling down,
flowing down on the body of the Accomplished One,
to honour the Earth's Accomplished One,
and heavenly harps resound in the air,
to honour the Earth's Accomplished One,
and heavenly harmonies softly fill the air,
to honour the Earth's Accomplished One.
'Yet not by all this, Ananda, is the Accomplished One being honoured
    appropriately,
is he being celebrated, held up, truly revered
and true homage being done to him,
but it is the male disciple and the female disciple, Ananda,
the lay brother and also the lay sister
who in everything devote their hearts to Holy Truth
and lead their lives accordingly,
rightly treading the tried and tested path of truth,
it is they who honour the Accomplished One in the appropriate way,
celebrating him, holding him up,
venerating him in highest reverence.
And that is why, Ananda, you should try in this your schooling
to promise yourself steadfastly:
"We wish to lead our lives by devoting our hearts in all aspects to
    Holy Truth,
rightly treading the tried and tested path of truth."'

The following episode,[285] shows how the whole supersensory world participates in the events, how from all regions of the world spiritual beings approach in order for the last time to be near to the Holy One. Many of these are moved by the great suffering. 'Too early, alas will the

Holy One depart from us; too early, alas, the Blessed One will depart; too early, alas, the eye of the world will be extinguished.'

Completely *dipped into the mood of recollection* is also Buddha's pointing to the meaning of the sacred places of his life as places of devoted memory:[286]

> Four, Ananda, are the holy sites a son of noble birth will come to visit, and where his heart will be moved. Which four?
>
> 'Here the Holy One was born!'—The place where he can say that to himself, is the first site a devout son of noble birth will come to visit, and where his heart will be moved.
>
> 'Here the Holy One awoke to the highest perfect enlightenment!'—This, O Ananda, is the second site a devout son of noble birth will come to visit and where his heart will be moved.
>
> 'Here he has, the Earth's Accomplished One, turned the Wheel of Truth for the very first time.'—This, O Ananda, is the third site a devout son of noble birth will come to visit, and where his heart will be moved.
>
> 'Here at his end the Accomplished One entered the heights of Nirvana, the body-free sublime primordial ground of world dispersal!'—This, O Ananda, is the fourth site a devout son of noble birth will come to visit, and where his heart will be moved.—These are the four holy sites, Ananda, which a devout son of noble birth will come to visit, and where his heart will be moved.
>
> And likewise the male disciples and the female disciples, the lay brothers and the lay sisters, when they come as pilgrims, they too will come and say to themselves in devout veneration:
>
> 'Here the Holy One was born.'
>
> 'Here the Holy One awoke to the highest perfect enlightenment.'
>
> 'Here the Earth's Accomplished One moved the holy Wheel of Truth for the very first time.'
>
> 'Here the Accomplished One finally entered the heights of Nirvana, the body-free sublime primordial foundation of world dispersal.'
>
> And all those who then in devout pilgrimage come in search of the holy sites, finding the tranquility of their hearts while reaching the goal of their time, they will in death, after the dissolution of their physical bodies, reach the bliss of the heavenly world.

> 'How shall we behave towards the female half of mankind, Master?'
> Look away, Ananda!
> 'But if our eye should somehow see them, what shall we do then?'
> Be silent, Ananda.
> 'But if we should nevertheless get into conversation with them?'
> Then, Ananda, wakeful self-reflection must be the strong refuge of your inner world.

> 'What shall we do, Master, with the corpse of the Accomplished One?'

Be not worried, Ananda, with regard to the funeral celebrations for the Accomplished One. Just strive for true salvation, always clearly strive for true salvation, live in steady striving towards your aim, with all the forces of your soul towards true salvation.

There are clever noblemen, Ananda, priests and citizens who are devoted devoutly to the Accomplished One, and who will surely deal with the funeral celebrations for the Accomplished One.

'What is supposed to be done with the corpse of the Holy One?'

Treat it like the corpse of a great king, of a 'ruler of the earth circumference'.

'But what do you do with the corpse of a ruler of the earth circumference?'

To begin with, Ananda, you wrap it in new, pure linen, then in combed cotton cloth, then again in new, pure linen. If you have wrapped the corpse of the ruler of the earth circumference five-hundred times this way with a two-fold layer, you put it into an iron container with oil, which you cover with another iron container. Then you build the pyre with all sorts of fragrant substances and fragrant wood, and let the corpse of the ruler of the earth circumference be devoured by the heat of the flames, and then, near a major crossroads you erect a holy shrine for the relics of the ruler of the earth circumference.—This is what you do, Ananda, with the corpse of a ruler of the earth circumference.

And the corpse of the Accomplished One, Ananda, you just treat the same, and erect for him at a major crossroads a shrine for relics. And all who deposit a garland there, all who put down sacrifices with fragrant smells or colourful dyed cloths, or who simply express their reverence in silence there and find the devout tranquility of their heart by it, it will bring them salvation and blessing for a long time.

After speaking about the more earthly, practical things of cremating the body and respect for the body, Ananda is overcome by grief. He is painfully aware of the whole measure of his failures and omissions in the great testing. With absolute clarity the Buddha (in Chapter 3) has revealed to him the measure of his omissions—he had accused him how already earlier, on various occasions and various places, he had repeatedly given him those indications, and *every time* he was not aware of the meaning of the words. The Buddha now comforts him with immeasurable love, that love which out of the whole narration with its down-to-earth simplicity speaks of such pure and beautiful humanity and which is revealed everywhere as a trait of the Buddha.[287]

Enough, Ananda, mourn not and lament not, have I not already told you this clearly before again and again: of all that we love, all that our heart gets attached to, from all this we will one day have to separate ourselves, will have to let it go and avoid it, will have to experience that the path of our existence separates us from it.

For how, Ananda, could it be achieved in any possible way in this world that what was born, what has become, what has been moulded by the forming forces of existence and is subject to the law of decay, that this also would not perish in reality, this would be impossible.

You, Ananda, have loyally served the Accomplished One for a long time, have been near to him in pure, genuine, selfless-immutable, limitless love, and this pure, genuine, selfless-immutable, limitless love was in all your deeds, in all your words, was in all your thinking. In your deeds lived sheer goodness, so, Ananda, only engage the whole force of your spiritual striving, and you will soon be free of any stains of earthly tarnishing.

Buddha's last conversation that he still permits with a pupil of another spiritual school who wishes to speak with the Holy One at all costs is historically highly interesting. The passage shows us how many sought a conversation with the Buddha and how those around him had to guard the Master from too many approaches from other people. In this case, the one who requests is three times deflected by Ananda.

Enough, brother Subhadda, do not bother the Holy One, let go of questioning the Accomplished One, the Holy One is tired and exhausted.[288]

But Buddha, who had heard that conversation, himself allows Subhadda to approach. Subhadda, who carries esoteric questions in his heart, recognizes that he now is speaking to him, the true esotericist and that his path is the true, the *one* path, the primal, sacred path of knowledge. He is overcome by the Buddha's spiritual greatness, He is the last personal pupil of the Holy One.

Before his passing into Nirvana, Buddha arranges with love and care all the necessary personal arrangements for the continuation of things. 'The essence of the formative forces of existence are transitory. Always remain firm in [your] attempts to strive,'[289] is his final admonition to his disciples. Then his spirit ascends and descends all the steps of the ladder of consciousness that was traversed in the yogic meditation (p. 187). For several of the levels of consciousness mentioned here—'Facing nothing' ('sphere of nothing is'), sphere of the infinity of the cosmic ether, and others—a still hardly noticed key can be found in the first lecture of Rudolf Steiner's lecture-course *The Mysteries of the East and Christianity* [Berlin, 3 Feb. 1913. GA 144]. After Buddha had descended once more onto the first level of immersion, from the fourth level he enters the great Nirvana, the Parinirvana.

And when the Holy One had gone over into the great cosmic-dispersal, simultaneously with his entering Nirvana there was a great earthquake on this Earth, which made all the world shiver in fearful awe, and darkly rolled heavenly thunder.[290]

And when the Holy One had gone over into the great cosmic-dispersal, simultaneously with his entering Nirvana, Brahman spoke, the Lord of the Vault of Heaven, the following words:

> One day all beings in the world will cast off their bodily fabric,
> just as here now the great Master, without comparison in all the world,
> who thus has walked the Buddha-way, the Master of Power,
> the fully Awoken One, has entered Nirvana.

And when the Holy One had gone over into the great cosmic-dispersal, simultaneously with his entry into Nirvana, the 'Archangel of Power', the Dragon-Slayer of the heavenly hosts,[291] spoke these words:

> Of non-eternal nature are the forming forces of existence.
> The law of becoming and decaying holds them together.
> The way they came into being, the same way they will fade.
> Their fading is the highest bliss.

And when the Holy One had gone over into the great cosmic-dispersal, simultaneously with his entry into Nirvana, the venerable Anuruddha spoke this stanza:

> Not heavily his breath went in and out,
> he who in silent thought was strong and firm.
> Without a stir he entered his rest,
> the Lord of Silence, when he went from us.
> With a spirit free from anything earthly,
> he bore with patience any pain of death.
> Like the extinguishing of a lamplight
> was the loosening of his spirit to behold.

And when the Holy One had gone over into the great cosmic-dispersal, simultaneously with his entry into Nirvana, the venerable Ananda spoke these words:

> It was a holy dread,
> a trembling shiver went through the world,
> when the Awoken One entered Nirvana,
> who was for us the epitome of all things noble and beautiful.[292]

The funeral festivities lasted seven days, which are arranged with great splendour by the noble dukes of the realm where the Buddha died.

The atmosphere is still filled with supersensory scent from all that streams etherically from the dying of the great Holy One. Right to the edge of the Path (as it says, p. 135), everything is still covered with blossoms from the Tree of Paradise. And a fine scent of higher reality wafts through the seemingly fairytale-like narration, with which we would like to end here. Here as it happens Kashyapa, or, Maha-Kassapa as he is called in Pali, Buddha's great disciple[293] (Maha means 'great'), has just arrived, who was not present at Buddha's Nirvana—he was on his was to Kusinara. The narration says that, according to the decision of the gods, the Buddha's death pyre should not go up in flames before the great Kashyapa with his disciples has paid his respects. On his way, Kashyapa encounters a holy beggar, who had just come from the place. For this 'beggar for the spirit' whose supersensory, etheric eyes had been opened, the higher organs of his soul are fully opened up for all the inexpressible, mysterious element, which like an etheric [emanation] from the Tree of Life in Paradise [still] fills the whole aura of the place of dying with its fine scent, with soft musical sounds, with light-filled pictures. In its language, the narration tells that the beggar has kept 'a heavenly blossom from the Tree of Paradise'. The passage runs as follows:[294]

> In Kusinara at just that time, a 'beggar for the spirit' had picked up a heavenly blossom from the Tree of Paradise to keep for himself, and was on the road to Pava with it. Then the venerable Mahakássapa saw the 'beggar for the spirit' approach in the distance and asked him:
>
> 'Do you, brother, know our Master?'
>
> 'Yes, brother, I know him; it is seven days today that the spiritual disciple Gótama entered the cosmic dispersal. That is why this heavenly blossom from the Tree of Paradise came to me.'
>
> There were among those disciples some who were not free yet from earthly passions and stirrings of emotions who fell down on the ground then, with arms outstretched, as if swept into a sudden abyss, writhing to and fro, weeping and wailing:
>
> 'Too soon, alas, has the Holy One gone from us! Too soon, alas, has the Blessed One gone from us! Too soon, alas, has the eye that was the light of the world, been extinguished for us! alas, has the Holy One gone from us, too soon, alas, has the Blessed One gone from us, too soon, alas has the eye that was the light of the world, been extinguished for us.'[295]

In the whole narration of Buddha's passing a great farewell to humanity, a leave-taking of old spiritual forces of humanity, is movingly expressed. This farewell led us into a blossoming Garden, into a Garden that once more blossoms at a late time. The solemn farewell is followed by the great reunion of humanity in that great cosmic moment—again in the blossoming Garden of the Resurrection miracle that is kept in the heights of the ether like a seed not yet descended to the Earth—when Mary Magdalene meets the 'heavenly Gardener'.

The Tree of Life

1.

Like a great Imagination shining over the Earth's past and the Earth's future, the New Testament shows us Christ-Jesus on the Mount of Transfiguration between Moses and Elijah as the two powers carrying the evolution of the Earth. We feel how the destiny of the Earth and the destiny of mankind receive a new meaning, now that Christ, the Sun of Love of Christ, has appeared between the two figures.

The two powers, whose main bearers in the Transfiguration stand before us in Moses and Elijah, are the same that are shown us in the story of Paradise as the *Tree of Knowledge* and the *Tree of Life.* They appeared in the age when the human being still did not possess a self-conscious 'I'. In the early Lemurian age of earthly evolution man still lived in the 'Garden of Paradise' in a plant-like innocence. He still organically bore the 'two Trees' in his own being. And today, because of the Fall of Man as described by Rudolf Steiner in the lecture-cycle held in The Hague [March 1913. GA 145. *The Effects of Occult Development*], the once para-disal splendour of the 'Garden' has become the 'shrivelled product' of today's hard and constricting corporeality. The human being carries the essence of the 'two Trees' in a certain way organically in himself. In him they have become the 'Tree of Blood'; the arterial blood has become the 'Tree of Life' and the blue venous blood has become the 'Tree of Death'. The transformation of the blue blood into the red blood of life, still takes place today through the oxygen exhaled by the plant-world. The human being will one day be able to manage in his own consciousness through the power of transformed breathing (see the lecture by Rudolf Steiner of 15 May 1905 on the *Golden Legend*).[296] Then the 'Tree of Life', which in Paradise was lost, will be newly achieved for human beings in Christ. The apocalyptic picture of the Christened human future in the 'New Jerusalem' shows amongst other things the new, transformed 'Tree of Life' (Rev. 22:2).

The once plant-world innocence of human nature corresponds to the paradisal picture of the 'two Trees'. Through the Fall of Man this innocence, and with it the true human nature itself, was also increasingly lost. Solomon's Temple stands as symbol for this lost true human nature to be regained in the future. It was built out of the dead materials of the Earth. In this Temple what were once Trees have become pillars, the 'Pillar of Wisdom' and the 'Pillar of Strength' (I Kings 7:21).[297] The one pillar (Jachin) corresponding to the Tree of Life stands for the great Mystery of Birth. These are the forces which place the human being through birth into earthly life, the waxing forces of growth of the organism. What is wrested from them will become in the evolution of human life those forces that become thinking consciousness in the human being. What earthly wisdom exists that has passed through the Fall of Man has allowed the Tree of Knowledge to become the Tree of Death. And higher wisdom, *spiritual knowledge*, has first to be wrested again from this death. Consequently, the other pillar (Boaz) earnestly stands for the Mystery of Death.

In the deeply moving picture of fratricide, the story of Cain and Abel in the Bible shows how the two human forces still united in Paradise, are torn apart through the Fall of Man. Abel (Hebel)—the word in Hebrew means 'breath of air'—draws back to the super-earthly realm, to the upper life-element, which we also encounter as the 'Elijah element'. Cain, the bearer of the element of knowledge, which is earthly knowledge gained through killing, remains bound to the forces of the Earth.[298] The harmony and higher unity of the human being has been lost. Only in Christ—announced in the initiation of Lazarus-John carried out by Christ—do we find again both of these human forces that have been torn apart.

From here light also falls on the Mystery of the 'two Jesus children'.[299] In the 'Nathan' Jesus-child of Luke's Gospel live the pure forces of childhood. There lives that substance of humanity which as the 'Tree of Life' in Paradise remained behind, withdrawn from the prevailing consciousness of human nature that had fallen into sin. In the 'Solomon' Jesus-child of Matthew's Gospel, of the re-embodied Zarathustra, lives the 'Tree of Knowledge'—which as the higher wisdom, as spiritual knowledge, is wrested again from death. For this reason the early maturing child dies of that death of wisdom; with his wisdom he offers himself, as it were, bodily into the other Jesus, who is the blossoming force of the Tree of Life. These 'two Jesus children' bear the sustaining forces of all development. We behold them in the picture of the Trees in Paradise, and in the Temple in the dead picture of both pillars. They become human again in the adult vessel of Jesus of Nazareth, resulting from the unifying of both powers of humanity; this vessel receives Christ at the Baptism of John in the Jordan. In Christ the Temple once again becomes a human body. In Him wisdom and strength, the Tree of Knowledge and the Tree of Life, are re-united through love.

As shown at the beginning, the two powers of humanity are already there as Moses and Elijah. But they are there still as one-sided, incomplete and torn apart. With Moses wisdom comes completely to the Earth; it becomes earthly thinking in which the thoughts of the gods in the early Mysteries have to allow themselves to be crucified. The Mystery of Christ that is revealed in the Burning Bush is consequently not able to be understood in its ultimate depths (Num. 20:12).[300] Steiner's public lecture on Elijah (Berlin, 14 Dec. 1911 [GA61]) helps us to see how Elijah is but loosely bound to the earthly element, is not at all able to be laid hold of, how something of maya [illusion] is attached to this whole earthly appearance. (Already in the Bible it is remarkable how the stories of Elijah are only recorded in the Books of the Kings and not in the parallel account in both Books of Chronicles, apart from the somewhat obscure passage, 2 Chron. 21:12 where Elijah does not appear at all in person.) Elijah's actual being lives and works in the upper life-element, in the 'fire of the higher world'. He calls down this fire in the verdict upon the priests of Baal, [and] upon other adversaries of Yahveh (2 Kings 1:10). Finally, he disappears in this heavenly fire and ultimately, like Christ in the 'Ascension' who disappears from the vision of the disciples, disappears from the clairvoyant vision of his initiated pupil, who alone is able to behold him in his true nature. 'My father, my father, the chariot of Israel and the horses thereof' [2 Kings 2:12]—in these words, which Elisha calls after Elijah disappearing in the fire of heaven, there is the tremendous poetic expression of that life-element of Elijah, of the 'power from above'. We feel how this higher life-element cannot yet live in the earthly sphere.

The secret of the whole story of Elijah is intimately woven with the secret of the Tree of Life, lost in Paradise and in Abel disappearing into the cosmic heights. With the 'Expulsion from Paradise' the higher life-element, the 'Tree of Life', withdrew from human consciousness (Gen. 3:22). A veil of Isis covers the secret of Life. Is it not pretentious to want to bring the essence of the Tree of Life into human thinking? Does this not mean to drag it down into the sphere of the Tree of Knowledge, of the dead Tree of Death? Does not the mystery of life have to remain inexpressible; can it not be explored alone from life itself? In what is said here concerning Christ and His relationship to the 'two Trees', it has already been expressed that this actually is not the situation. In that Christ hangs on it, the dry wood of the cross of human knowledge—for the Tree of Knowledge *dries up* through the Fall of Man, as the Tree of Life was lost through it—begins again to send forth shoots. The Tree of Knowledge unites again with the other Tree. The Tree of Death can become again the Tree of Life. In *'christened' Anthroposophy* we receive insight, as a gift, insight that *is allowed* again to glimpse the Tree of Life, because it rests on a living, pictorial thinking, on the forces carried by this Tree. In that the great facts of the suffering, death-resurrection of Christ begin, as it were, of themselves to think in us, and the tremendous pictures of Paradise come alive in us, in whose middle-point stands the Tree of Life—here these pictures of Paradise may and do become for us a new form of recognition and expression of cosmic Mysteries.

***

In the Paradise experience of primal human times the 'two Trees' were not actually separated. There they were still as *one* Tree, inclining their tops to each other. The human being still lived, cared for and nurtured by the forces of the Tree of Life; he did not need to pick the fruit. When he did pick it prematurely, it became the fruit of death-bringing knowledge. He lives with the etheric part of his being in the upper life-element of the heights of Paradise, in the *cold light of the cosmic fields of ice* (cf. the articles on Isis and Eve), in the sounding cosmic harmonies, in the flowery scent of life. The cosmic Tree was still the *singing Tree of Life*; the essence of the life-ether is connected with the sound-ether and the pure (cold) light. The eternal masculine and the eternal feminine element are still bound together in the spiritual human being of the archetypal beginning (Gen. 1:27); in the human being's etheric body light-ether is still bound together with the 'upper kinds of ether'—the sound-ether and life-ether. An original binding together of the two Trees in this sense also means the *archetypal binding together* of the masculine and feminine elements with the essence of the total human being.

Only in the light that in the 'Fall of Man' it connects with the earthly fire, with the *warmth-light* (light-ether connected with warm-ether) does 'earthly knowledge' as the *eternal masculine* part of his being become separated (*sondert sich*)—in German the words *Sünde*, 'sin' and *sondern* 'to separate' are related. The higher, the *Eternal Feminine* part of his being lives in the upper element of the sound-ether and life-ether, and it also remains there after the Fall. The *Eternal Masculine* belongs to the *Tree of Knowledge*; the Eternal Feminine belongs to the *Tree of Life*. This is simply a cosmic fact. Today this has become difficult to recognize, because through the Fall, the feminine element of humanity has become estranged from the Eternal Feminine; it is drawn towards the Eternal Masculine. The veil of Isis is spread over the Mystery of the Eternal Feminine until the awakening soul of humanity, which in Christ can see again, lifts it...

This paradisal life in the sounding, living harmonies, in the sound-ether and life-ether is clearly expressed by Rudolf Steiner in lecture four of the course *Building Stones for an Understanding of the Mystery of Golgotha* (Berlin, 12 April 1917. GA 175). There he says how originally every human being:

> was so constituted for his own musical sound. In the whole Harmony of the Spheres, he lived with his own musical sound and with his own primal vitality, so that the ether-body would always have been able to preserve the immortality of the physical body *if* this ether-body had retained its original life.

Also the first beginnings of the division of the sexes in the picture in Genesis of *Adam's sleep* and the *creation of Eve out of Adam's rib* in early Lemuria allows for the retaining of the innocent binding together of life between the female and the male in Paradise. Only through the *Fall of Man*, which we should imagine as pictorially as possible as a real fall, a sinking through gravity into the depths occurs, the actual *division of the sexes, the division of wisdom of the two Trees*. The lower element sinks with the human being into the depths, the upper element, the life-ether, sound-ether, the cold light, remains back in its pure etheric nature in the heights (below in the earthly element, life-ether and sound-ether are enchanted into the firm and liquid forms). It was not given to man to drag down the higher life-element with his Fall (Gen. 3:22).

In lecture four of the cycle *Christ and the Human Soul* (Norköpping, 16 July 1914. GA 155) Steiner mentions how through the Fall, the light-ether is killed for the eye of man which has become estranged from clairvoyance; in the same way for man, as long as he does not accomplish the higher transformation of breathing, the air that he takes in by breathing transforms into the air of death. This influence of the human being who has become sinful has its limits with the light-ether. Divine love hindered, as it were, the human being from also tearing away the higher part of his being from the Eternal realm. (Consequently, the Eternal Feminine, whose counterpart caused him to sink, can draw him up again.) This is the true sense of the commandment of the Father not to eat of the Tree of Life and the overcoming of this in Christ. In the above-mentioned lecture-cycle, it was said that that commandment, if in the sense of the ether-teaching it received its exact expression encompassing both life-ether and sound-ether, would say: 'The human being shall not eat of the Tree of Life and *he shall not hear the spirit of matter.'* Rudolf Steiner adds, how only through a certain procedure in the early Mysteries, the candidates, when allowed to see [the pre-existing] Christ in an out-of-the-body preview, also perceived the sounds of the Music of the Spheres and the cosmic Life pulsing through the world.

The upper region of the life-ether and the sound-ether, the world of the Tree of Life, is also that out of which Christ descended in the Jordan-baptism into the [human vessel, the prepared] sheaths of Jesus.

***

The whole esoteric prehistory and history of the Mysteries of humanity show how the Tree of Life was not lost at one moment; its forces diminished only slowly and gradually. Even geographical differences played a role—as was shown in a lecture held by Dr Günter Wachsmuth in Dornach.[301] And so did certain clairvoyant powers, which according to their nature are indeed the forces of the Tree of Life. They were preserved the longest with the northern Germanic peoples—right into the time of the Mystery of Golgotha and here and there still longer. To the southern Latin and other peoples [e.g. the Middle Eastern cultures—*Tr. note*], who are more *thinking people*, it was lost much earlier. Consequently, as a world necessity Christ had to incarnate precisely with a people of the Tree of Knowledge.

As in the primal Mystery centres, initiates through processes of purification of the soul know how to purify themselves from the consequences of the Fall and how to re-connect with the forces of the Tree of Life. This is mysteriously indicated in the Bible (Gen. 3:24) in the name *Enoch* (cf. the article on Eve), of whom it is said that 'And Enoch walked with God: and he was not; for God took him' [Gen. 5:24]. The Tree of Life has become unapproachable from the earthly level, it is now in the etheric high *above the Earth*. (Novalis expresses this in his *Hymns to the Night*: 'The miraculous homeland vanished into the ether.')[302] Consequently, Enoch was transported to the supersensory hidden place of the primal Mysteries, where humanity can no longer see him. Perhaps the name *Enoch* in a summary manner indicates the [culture of] Initiation of Atlantis, and the name *Jared* who precedes him points to the Initiation culture of Lemuria.

The decline and disappearance of the forces of the Tree of Life in humanity should also not be imagined as an even, steady decline. When the decline of the old forces has brought the Earth into a catastrophe, there always occurs, as it were, a rejuvenation of humanity, a new quickening of the Tree of Life, yet in such a way that it can also be felt how it is removed ever further from the Earth. After the destructive fire-catastrophes in which the karma of sin in Lemuria was fulfilled, humanity experiences a new childhood during early Atlantis, especially with the two first races. Once more humanity lives in the 'Garden'—or is it only a dream-memory of the 'Garden'? Once more a picture of this quickening, blossoming, ether-substance is conjured before our eyes, the picture of the *Tree of Life*. Yet the Tree of Life is already removed from the day-consciousness, from the day-side of human life. This day-side of life has become invisible for human beings, as if filled with fog. Only during the night does the blinding, bright light of the heights of Paradise open up for him. Then Atlantean man lives again in cosmic harmonies, feels again surrounded by the sounds of the primal waters, of the etheric sea of life. This Atlantean *connection of the Tree of Life with the night* is of deep significance to understand the nature of later Mysteries of humanity.

The *Tree of Knowledge* and the *Tree of Life* behave from then on like *day and night*. Indeed, still today it is the night in which sleep, which through kindly beings was given us from the Tree of Life, builds up again that which has been used up in our organism through the forces of the Tree of Knowledge or of death, that which has become tired and withered. And in the night of the Mysteries, in the *sacred Christmas night*, that which in normal sleep is withdrawn from the consciousness of humanity becomes higher conscious experience. In this sacred night of consecration the Tree of Life becomes the great *cosmic Tree of Lights*, the *cosmic starry Tree of Life*. That poet, who in recent Christian times has in particular deepened himself with the *Elijah-forces of the Tree of Life*, has consequently also looked especially deeply into those *Mysteries of the night* and in this beholding has given to his *Hymns to the Night* a sublime poetic expression. These, in quite clear and pictorial memories of earlier Atlantis, are woven into the *Hymns*. In his prose poem, *The Novices of Sais*, Novalis has a passage where the experience of sleep and the night is meaningfully connected with experiences of the Tree of Life of Atlantis, where the 'stirrings of the primal waters' within us are mentioned:[303]

Even sleep is nothing other than the high tide of that invisible ocean, and awakening but the commencement of its ebb. How many a human being stands on the brink of the heady flow and does not hear the lullaby of these maternal waters; and does not enjoy the enchanting play of their infinite undulations! In the golden age, we lived like these waves; in brightly coloured clouds, in those swimming oceans and primordial wellsprings of all life on earth, in perpetual frolic, the races of man loved and begot one another, and were visited by the children of heaven; until finally, in that event that sacred tradition terms the Great Flood, this flourishing world perished; the earth was laid low by an inimical being, leaving behind a few human stragglers marooned on the craggy mountaintops of a strange new world.

The disorder and black-magical degeneration of the forces of the Tree of Life in the third and fourth Atlantean races—compared to which in the fifth race the development of the *force of thinking* out of the forces of the Tree of Knowledge meant once more a progress and a balance—finally led towards the fall of Atlantis in the great catastrophe of the Flood. After the Atlantean catastrophe, of which the narrative of the Flood in the Bible contains a memory, humanity once more experiences a childhood, a rejuvenation in the two first (prehistoric) post-Atlantean epochs, the original Indian and original Persian—which we should not imagine too geographically limited to the India and Persia of today. In particular the first of these two cultures, the primal Indian culture, is still completely carried by the forces of the Tree of Life, although this Tree itself is removed ever further from humanity—consequently, the strange element of Indian spiritual life hovering over the Earth. The inner connection with the Tree of Life is still so strong that the objectively existent falling away of the physical corporeality is still not fully consciously experienced as death in our sense today. The legends from the golden age, as far as they do not relate to Atlantis, contain a memory of this time. All this still works into the later Indian spiritual life and its literature. A tragic experience of death as we find, for example, in the *Epic of Gilgamesh*, is still completely wholly distant from the Indian *Upanishads*.

In the Mysteries—Steiner emphatically points this out—thinking power as an impulse for the future is already quite consciously developed, but in such a way that all this still derives from the forces of the Tree of Life that are still available to humanity, which at the same time continue to live like a primal memory in the Mysteries. In what follows, this side of the early Mysteries, the continuing influence of the Tree of Life in the Mysteries, will be discussed.

***

2.

Just because the true prehistoric, primal Indian culture (BCE 8000—6000) was still carried by the pure forces of the Tree of Life—as if raised into the air—nothing outwardly visible of it and its Mystery-being has remained for us. It can only be reached on paths of pure spiritual research. Whatever has been documented of Indian wisdom belonging to a very much later time has all been carried down to the sphere of the Tree of Knowledge. With full recognition of everything that is great and sublime which in this wisdom has been contained for us, therein we recognize especially clearly the ever-stronger drying-up of the Tree of Knowledge. This is the profound reason why with Buddha this wisdom of the Indian Brahmins, although rich but old and dried up, retreats, and why he so little revealed the intellectual side. He intended to lead humanity out of the 'bushy jungle of theory'[304] towards a living knowledge, on a path on which the forces of the Tree of Life germinate again within human beings. He himself describes this path to his disciples with a picture of the Tree of Life that starts to sprout again, leading to blossoming. He does not only compare the unfolding and development of the inner organs of the pupil in meditation with the growth of the Tree of Life, with the unfolding and development of its leaves, the buds of its flowers and then the fully opened blossoms. He speaks, moreover, how in higher worlds, for beings of the higher hierarchies, the process presents quite directly such a growth and unfolding of the Tree of Life. [305]

In Buddha himself the early forces of the Tree of Life were alive once more in the strongest manner. The early Paradise-consciousness paled ever more for humanity, the retrospective memory of which still lived in the primal Indian age. All early Initiation-culture, all Indian Yoga, aimed to seek again the connection with the lost primal consciousness. Yoga, the training in concentration and meditation, practised since the early days in India, was a systematic working with the forces of the Tree of Life. But in the course of time it became progressively less possible to re-enliven these ancient human forces. In Buddha they were once more present in their archetypal cosmic greatness; Paradise-consciousness shone out once more in a mighty way. In Buddha's etheric body the Tree of Life lived with all the other pictures of Paradise. In that moment when the life-streams of the earthly bodily sheath of the dying Holy One begin to stream away, we see how with them, such pictures of Paradise are poured out into the surrounding world (cf. the author's translation *Buddha's Passing*,[306] and the article on

'Buddha's Passing', above). The sacred narration tells how *the Tree of Life in Indra's Paradise* unites its heavenly flowers with the abundance of blossoms that the two Sala trees, between which Buddha's last resting place had been, caused to rain down on the one dying.[307]

This narration belongs to a time which only lies a few centuries before the turning point of time, and yet we feel the *Tree of Life* nowhere in the whole Indian literature so strongly and immediately than here in this narration of Buddha's passing. In the whole early Brahman culture and its writings there is nothing that could be compared with the impressive grandeur of this episode. Nowhere, we feel, do we reach in those writings the true early Indian primal consciousness—everywhere there are only echoes. But here, where the dying Buddha lies under the Sala trees, we are closest to that primal consciousness; there it shines in such a way when the Sala trees blossom once more, in that late time of Indian development, once more in the great Holy One. The Tree of Life is once again present; its heavenly blossoms, heavenly harmonies and heavenly scents are poured out into the surrounding world. Here they work right into the language of those who proclaimed the sacred experience to the subsequent world. Sound-ether and life-ether, which in themselves contain and present the being of the Tree of Life, are revealed in the language of the early Pali text.

***

When we look from this already late Buddhist account to the much earlier Brahman literature, at first to the earliest document of Aryan humanity, the Rig-Veda, here especially we can find the vitality of the picture is fading. Especially the great 'riddle song', Rig-Veda I, 164,[308] contains a memory of the Tree of Life. As in the life of Paradise, of the primal time of humanity, before the Fall of Man, both Trees were actually not separated; they still turned their crowns to each other. So too that Mystery-culture that most strongly retained its retrospective character in the early consciousness of the Paradise of humanity, in the early Indian culture—in which all consciousness was strongly tuned towards 'unity'—looked at the 'two Trees' as the 'one Tree'. Initially it was still seen as the 'Tree of Life', as the Tree that carries the golden, heavenly fruit hidden in its crown.

The cosmic polarity that as a seed was already present in this primal existence is not seen in the picture of two Trees, but in the picture of *two Eagles* nesting in one and the same Tree. Thus it is described in the above-mentioned song, v. 20:

> Two beautifully winged Eagles, as firm friends,
> embrace the one and the same tree;
> one of them eats the sweet fig,
> the other one only looks down, does not eat.

The 'sweet fig' is the fruit of immortality, as another verse sings:

> Where on the tree, the ones looking for sweetness:
> the *two Eagles* nest and lead their lives,
> there in the crown, one says, lies the sweet fig,
> which nobody eats who does not know the *Father*.

With the world ash Yggdrasil of the early Norse Edda—which contains the memory of the Tree of Life in such a way as corresponds to the nature of the Teutonic peoples—the Eagle nests in the heights, whereas the Snake—the dragon Nidhöggr—gnaws at the root. Eagle and Snake are the cosmic polar opposites, which amongst other things are also expressed in the two corner signs (*Eckzeichen*) of the Egyptian hieroglyphic alphabet. If we transform the *two* Eagles of the Rig-Veda tree into snakes, there stands before us the well-known symbol of the *staff of Mercury*. It symbolizes the *wisdom* wrested from Death, the Tree of Knowledge, and the *healing force*, the Tree of Life. We recognize how, following the changing human consciousness, the pictures and symbols themselves change.

More clearly than in the Rig-Veda, we find the Tree of Life in that other Veda that still contains the *magical* element, which most strongly contains in itself the magical element that otherwise in India where it existed abundantly in the primal Mysteries, comes increasingly into discredit. Against the one-sided (mystical) element, it retreats into the *Atharvaveda Veda*. But *magical forces*, magical healing forces in particular, according to their nature and origin, are indeed forces of the Tree of Life. Consequently, it is inwardly founded in the nature of the magical Atharvaveda, when the world fig tree—which with Buddha has become the Tree of Knowledge—is honoured as the Tree of Life (Atharvaveda 5, 4; 6, 95; 19, 39).[309] In the second of these songs, it first sings of the all-healing herb kushtha and then this is connected to the Tree of Life:

> The sacred fig tree, the home of the gods, is found from here in the third heaven,
> there is the revelation of deathless[310] life, there the gods found the herb of life.
> A golden ship on a golden rope swam on the heavenly lake.

> There the gods found the healing herb, the flower of immortal life.
> You are offspring of the plant, the offspring of the snowy mountains,
> you are the offspring of the whole world, O free me from sickness!

The picture of the golden ship, the 'Moon barque'[311], swimming on the heavenly lake, the *etheric ocean*,[312] is especially meaningful for it is a primal form of the Grail Imagination. The Moon, which is also called *soma* in the Indian language, is connected with the Imagination of the 'transforming provisions for the way',[313] the cosmic Grail essence, the heavenly drop of soma. According to the teaching of the ether, the Moon is cosmogonically connected with the essence of the sound-ether, which with the life-ether, belongs to the Tree of Life. Where the Tree of Life grows has to be the home of the heavenly soma—about which more has to be said in what follows. In this sense we also meet the soma in the Atharvaveda. In the first of the three above-mentioned songs (5, 4), it is mentioned how it is found with the sacred herb kushtha, the 'mightiest of all plants', which grows in the mountains, 'in the Himalayas where the eagles nest':

> You are born of the gods, *you are the close companion of soma*,
> bless my breathing, my life-stream, my eyes, ….

The third song (19, 39) also speaks of this connection of the herb of life with the soma:

> Kushtha, the all-healing herb,
> grows everywhere where the soma grows.
> Drive away from me the sickness of fever, drive away all demonic hauntings.

After the verse on the sacred fig tree and the golden barque, which follows again as above, there comes a recollection of the Atlantean Flood and the story of Manu (who corresponds to Noah in the Bible):

> Where the ship [of Manu] sailed down, on to the Himalayas' highest
>   mountain peak,[314]
> there is the revelation of deathless life, there the healing herb of life grew.
> Kushtha the healing herb grows there together with the Soma.

The word *soma* for the early Indian embraced a sacred mystery. The soma-sacrifice, the soma-cult and soma-mysticism stand, beside the sacred sacrificial fire (agni, Avestan *athar*) itself, in the centre of the Indian Mysteries, as well as of those of Zarathustra and, if we look more deeply into them, also of the Egyptian Mysteries. From here there exists a connection to the Christian Mystery of bread and wine, body and blood (in Gr. *soma* means 'the body').

In Indian the word *soma* initially indicates a certain plant, the milky juice of which is pressed out between wooden sticks and when enjoyed mixed with cow's milk awakens higher consciousness, the divine enthusiasm, the heavenly ecstasy. Then soma is this higher, cosmic consciousness itself, the consciousness of immortal life. One is not yet separated from the cosmos as is the case today; it was still felt how from the stars, the Moon, out of all the cosmic spaces and from the great cosmic starry Tree of Life, healing, enlivening forces are received, nourishing the higher heavenly consciousness in the human being. Soma as the earthly plant becomes the picture of a higher, heavenly soma, which the gods drink and in enjoying gain their immortal life. Thus it is expressed in the Rig-Veda (10, 85):

> Many take the plant, the juice of which they drink as the soma,
> of the soma, which the gods know who are wise in knowledge,
> no other will drink.

Whoever has drunk *this* soma sings (Rig-Veda 8, 48, 3):

> We have drunk the soma,
> we have become immortal,
> we have penetrated towards the light,
> we have found the gods.
> What of mortality, you immortal one,[315]
> of all jealousy and all adversity
> can do us harm?

For the Indians the connection of the Moon with the soma plant arose— we saw that the Indian word *soma* had both meanings; already for this reason, the Moon as such was seen as the 'lord of the plants'. It had to do with everything concerning the circulating life-juices in the plant and in the human being. All primal wisdom and all primal knowledge of cosmic facts lives in such meanings of words, lives in those places common in Sanskrit where various meanings of a word frequently seem conceptually to lie so far apart. On the *Ancient Moon*, the sound-ether appeared for the first time (cf. G. Wachsmuth. *Etheric Formative Forces*, pp. 44-7), and so not only the external milky juice is [the subject] for a deeper esoteric account of the soma as a plant, but the sound-ether and sounding life-ether playing around the flower-chalices.

***

Zarathustra and the Avesta know the soma as *Haoma*, which according to the phonetic laws is the same word as the Indian *soma*. The soma (Haoma) 'that keeps death at bay and carries the sacred cosmic rhythm' appears to Zarathustra during the enactment of the cult as an essential entity. Vivanhvat the Sun-initiate and Manu of the Avesta, and his son Yima with the Sun-eye, the King of the Golden Age, are called the first pressers of the soma; with it at the same time they are the inaugurators of the primal Mysteries (cf. the Zarathustra essay, where it was shown that the Egyptian word *Osiris* has the same meaning). The Tree of Life itself appears with Zarathustra as the tree Hvapi, as the etheric archetypal plant, out of which 'all plants and all kinds of plants increase to hundreds and thousands of myriads', which recalls Genesis 1:11, 12: then, under another name Vispobish in a picture very much recalling the world ash Yggdrasil and some details of the Atharvaveda picture as 'the Tree of the Eagle. This stands in the midst of the etheric ocean, bringing beneficial, strong remedies; in this Tree all the plant seeds are contained.'[316]

***

These day-bright pictures receive another nuance in Egyptian tradition. Here the memory awakens of the Earth-Moon time [the period that recapitulated the Ancient Moon incarnation of the Earth], of that time when the Tree of Life is increasingly connected with the night. With the sentient soul, which precisely then opens up in wonderful depths, the early Egyptian looks out into the starry realms and experiences there the Tree of Life as the great *cosmic starry Tree*, which was already mentioned in this article. And this looking out in the early Egyptian Mysteries, was no mere gazing, but like a breathing-in, a sucking-in of enlivening forces, like a drinking of the heavenly soma, of the starry soma. Something healing, making whole, enlivening—as has been shown in the essay on Isis—was then felt by the early Egyptian, like a direct effect of the Tree of Life when he looked out into certain realms of the starry heavens. And all these enlivening, healing, health-bringing effects of the Tree of Life and cosmic starry Tree were then essentially embodied for him in the being Isis whose countenance still shone to him like the countenance of the soul of humanity out of the stars. Isis and Osiris appear here like the two still intimately connected entities, the 'two Trees', the Tree of Life and the Tree of Knowledge, of the Eternal Feminine and the Eternal Masculine, of the upper and lower kinds of ether. The Egyptian *temple sleep* meant putting humanity, who has fallen into the sickness of sin and thereby also into bodily illness, under the Isis-forces of the Tree of Life.

> (i) During the earliest time of the fixed-star wisdom that enlivening 'draught of health' [a phrase from the Offertory of The Act of Consecration of Man of The Christian Community] was still the soma of the stars.
>
> (ii) During the ensuing time of the planetary wisdom when Isis was perceived in the Moon-sickle chalice, it appeared as the soma of the Moon. This helps us better to understand why Soma in Indian means 'Moon'.
>
> (iii) During the wisdom of the elements, when Isis was revealed in the chalice of the blossom, it became the soma of the plants; the weaving of the sound-ether and the life-ether around the flower-chalice. We always see the mystery of the sound-ether and the life-ether as connected with the Tree of Life, and in this way connected with the Eternal Feminine, which the Egyptians called Isis.
>
> (iv) And when around the great crisis of the year 1322 BCE, the wisdom of the elements also subsided, when the great period of the tombs of the Egyptian Mysteries began and the Tree of Life outwardly disappeared, then the Tree was as if magicked into the mineral element of the Earth (which in reality is the transformed life-ether), and the *pyramid* (whose origins reach much further back to earlier times) can be seen as the picture of this mineralized Tree of Life, of that Tree 'whose roots are in heaven, and whose branches reach down to the Earth', as the Indian Upanishads express it.[317] This really is deeply significant, when we recall that the pyramid, elongated [imagined reflected, that is, doubled] below, is nothing other than the crystal form of that mineral which as coal is at the same time the basic material [carbon] of everything living, of all organic compounds, the form of the octahedron of the *diamond*. The mysteries of life of higher alchemy rest in the diamond; they similarly rest in the pyramid. And so the *Tree of Life* mysteriously speaks in early Egypt even where it is seemingly magicked into the deepest, dead earthly matter.

***

The gradual disappearing of the Tree of Life in the developing consciousness of humanity, as well as the development of the Mysteries, can be noticed in particular in Assyria. Here death was experienced for the first time in a tragic, deeply moving fashion. Gilgamesh, the heroic king and superman, who was two-thirds a god and only one-third a human being, is so deeply moved by the death of his very close friend that he seeks high paths of initiation to find the answer to the riddle of death. Passing terrible scorpion-powers, through the gruesome darkness of a long abyss lasting twelve double-hours, he fights his way towards the exit, the Gate of the Sun; before him lies the garden of the gods with the Tree of Life. But the goddess of the

Tree of Life[318]—she also appears in the *Egyptian Book of the Dead*, dispensing bread and wine to the one wandering through the Underworld—the divine hostess Siduri addresses him:[319]

> Gilgamesh, whither do you run? The life that you seek you will not find. When the gods created man, they appointed death as man's destiny and kept life for themselves. So, Gilgamesh, turn back to Uruk, to your city, as the acclaimed king and hero!

Then Gilgamesh, amongst many difficulties and dangers, still accomplishes the crossing of the waters of death until he meets the island of Anherrn [Utnapishtim—*Tr.*], who saving himself from the waters of death like Manu and Noah, once more gained for himself the immortal life of the gods. But what was possible for Utnapishtim is no longer possible for his follower, the great Gilgamesh, although he still had the strength to find the place of life, but did not possess the strength to keep himself in it. He is no longer able to achieve the test to remain awake for six or seven days. Bread is being baked, which is supposed to help him to stay awake, but before the bread is ready Gilgamesh is fast asleep. The time has already arrived when the soul lacks the *bread of life*. And the One who calls Himself the Bread of Life has not yet appeared. The power of the great I-AM in the human being is still too weak in this pre-Christian age, even in the superman Gilgamesh; during the test he was not able to stay awake. Thus Gilgamesh fails also with a final attempt once more to lay hold of the ancient life-forces: the herb of life already gained from the bottom of the sea—we are reminded by the Atharvaveda—becomes the plunder of the Snake, which also in Paradise cheats the human being of the fruit of the Tree of Life. Gilgamesh, in the height of life, did not find it; he finally turns down to the shadow and sinks in the darkness of death into 'mud and earth'. The whole thing is a tragic picture of an initiate who did not attain his height, a deeply affecting document of the whole situation of the human soul of the later pre-Christian age, of the human being who can no longer find access to the forces of the Tree of Life.

***

As in the founding of all the early Mysteries, the after-effects of the Tree of Life are revealed in the Greek Eleusinian Mysteries. These Mysteries link to the name of the initiate Orpheus, who was called a 'Son of Apollo'. As Rudolf Steiner once elaborated,[320] as a soul he carried in himself that *Eternal Feminine*, which the Greek myth meant with the name *Eurydice*. And it is the tragedy of Orpheus and his time, that he could not lay hold of this Eternal Feminine, which also means the Tree of Life, so that Eurydice is torn from him into Hades. From here, when we look towards the Eternal Feminine as the connection of sound-ether and life-ether, we also understand why the Mystery-culture of Orpheus was a musical one, touching on an *enlivening of the Mystery of the sound-ether*. Still in the Underworld, where Orpheus seeks the lost Eurydice, Orpheus has the power to move beings through his music. Even the name of the immediate inaugurator of the Greek Mysteries, he who set up the consecration at Eleusis,[321] *Eumolpos* ['beautiful singer or chanter'] points linguistically to the connection with this musical, sound-ether culture. And when we recall what resulted from the considerations on the Mystery of Isis (see the articles above, pp. 174–180) on the connection in the Mysteries of Isis between the sound-ether and the life-ether (or of the life-ether, sound-ether and the cold light) with the fairy-tale picture of the *Ice Maiden* (which we encountered purely in the sounds of the Egyptian *Isis*, *Isit*, as in the Celtic-Nordic Isolde, Is-hild, and Isot), it can appear significant to us when we read that Eumolpos was a son of *Chione*[322] (the word means 'snow maiden' or 'ice maiden' [from *chiōn* (feminine) 'snow']), herself a daughter of Boreas. And when Rudolf Steiner in the above-mentioned lecture speaks of how it was felt that the music of this Mystery-culture *comes out of the realm of the light*, with this 'realm of the light' we shall have again to think on the *cold light of the cosmic fields of ice*.

***

Of the Hebrew Mysteries of Moses—from which we are indebted for the picture in Genesis of the Tree of Life forming the basis of this whole investigation—there would still be but this to say. Moses is precisely the one who, as already mentioned, reveals the essence of the other Tree, the Tree of Knowledge. Only in the picture of his magically powerful rod is something expressed that also relates to the forces of the Tree of Life. According to the 'Golden Legend' this rod, and similarly the pillars in the Temple of Solomon, which were placed into the Pool of Bethesda, lending it healing forces, and most especially the Cross of Golgotha were all taken from the wood of the Tree that grew out of the seeds of the Tree of Life, which after the Expulsion from Paradise Seth planted in Adam's grave.[323] Everything in this study that has to be told about the after-effects of the Tree of Life in the history of mankind finds in this legend the most beautiful and profound pictorial expression.

3

These seeds are woven into the whole history of the Earth and the history of mankind; everywhere they contain the indication to that which in the turning point of time brings again the dry wood of the Cross of the Tree of Death to send shoots again, by planting the Tree of Love and watering it with his Blood, by combining through His love the Tree of Knowledge with the Tree of Life. The physical appearance of Christ on the Earth was preceded by *the eloquent figure of the prophet Elijah*. It will be shown in this study, how he revealed the essence of the forces of the Tree of Life. Likewise, preceding the appearance of Christ in his etheric body, comes the eloquent figure of the young poet with the seeing eye. Spiritual science shows us how the Mystery of his personality is linked to that of Elijah: *Novalis*.[324] And even were we to know nothing of these Elijah Mysteries, we could immediately feel how deeply he, Novalis, was rooted with his whole being in the being of the Tree of Life. The Tree of Life newly flourishing out of death becomes in Novalis the revelation of humanity and the revelation of Christ.[325]

We saw how in the *Hymns to the Night* the being of the Tree of Life is expressed. From whichever side we view the Tree of Life, we can find it again in the whole being and poetic creations of Novalis. If we look at the appearance of the Tree of Life in the life-ether and sound-ether, in *cosmic life* and *cosmic harmony*, then we can feel, how deeply this cosmic life and this cosmic harmony is revealed in Novalis, whose life taken outwardly was so poor in harmony, was a sad wrestling with death. Just by reading the first pages of the prose-poem *The Novices of Sais*, we feel we are surrounded by cosmic life and are carried by cosmic harmonies. The words characterize Novalis himself: 'Whoever speaks truly is imbued with eternal life, and his scripture appears to us to be miraculously affiliated with authentic mysteries, for it is in accord with the symphony of the cosmos.'[326] In Dornach, 9 April 1921, Rudolf Steiner spoke how actually the whole being and the work of Novalis is to be understood as proceeding out of cosmic music. With Goethe the sculptural element of the light is decisive—that of the lower kinds of ether; with Novalis it is the musical element, the upper kinds of ether: the sound-ether and life-ether. Amongst the sounds of musical harmonies—he had begged his brother still to play something on the piano[327]—Novalis passed over into the spiritual world. 'He sought,' Rudolf Steiner said then, 'for that *musical homeland*, which he had left in the full meaning of the word with his birth, in order to draw from it the musical element of poetry.'[328] Into the sounding paradisal harmonies, in which Novalis lived during his life, he went into sleep, passing over *consciously*.

To him who led such a profound dialogue with cosmic life and cosmic harmony, *the night* became a revealer of wonderful mysteries of the Tree of Life, of the Eternal Feminine, of the cosmic virginal element. These Mysteries were shown in the essay 'On the name of Isis', how in early Egypt they were revealed in the name *Isis* (Iset, Isit) and in another Mystery tradition, the Celtic Mysteries, in the name *Isolde* (Is-hilde, Eis-holde, Isot) as the most profound musical secret of the world. Sound-ether revelation and life-ether revelation, *frozen cosmic music, in connection with cold light* lies in the picture of the *ice-maiden*, who again is so mysteriously connected to the *virgin of the stars. The Eternal Feminine of the world* was once revealed to the Apocalyptist John, and she was also revealed to the young poet Novalis in the cosmic power of the sounding starry Tree of Life. She is the Queen of cosmic power, *Isis* with the starry diadem, who then becomes 'Christened' for him, the Virgin-Mother. To her, many of his most beautiful *Hymns* are dedicated. In these *Hymns* a secret comes to life that again connects him to Raphael. He mentions the name Isis itself where, looking back in his prose poem *The Novices of Sais* and in *The Fairytale of Rose-blossom and Hyacinth* contained in it, where at the end Isis merges gracefully with Little Rose-Blossom—the Lily with the Rose. In Novalis, we can feel, that *Christening of the Egyptian Mysteries* takes place, which is in actual fact the meaning of the development of the immediate future. Rudolf Steiner spoke in Dornach [24 Dec. 1920. GA 202. Eng. tr. as Appendix 3 in the author's study *Mark's Gospel: The Cosmic Rhythm*] on the *new Isis*—the human soul who has awoken in the Risen One; this we encounter in the poetry of Novalis, sometimes more revealed, at other times more veiled (the latter, for example, where in *Christianity or Europe*, the name 'Schleiermacher', Eng. 'Veilmaker', alludes to the veil of Isis). Novalis is the first, who as a great guide of humanity, a guide towards the approaching Christ, formed this thought of the *new Isis*. Out of the highest heights of the Eternal Feminine of the world, of the cosmic virginal element, which lived so magically in Novalis, that super-earthly resurrection-conversation is created ending with the name Maria in the concluding part of *Heinrich von Ofterdingen*. Here the words occur:[329]

> 'Have you died once before?'
> 'How could I live otherwise?'

A passage can be found in the section 'The Expectation' of the same work, which like a recollection of the Mystery of Elijah, of the entelechy of Novalis, can speak to our consciousness:

> Who knows whether our love will not one day become flaming wings bearing us upwards and carrying us to our heavenly homeland, ere old age and death reach us?[330]

The inwardly profound relationship to Isis, to the *Eternal Feminine*— and with it, as we always emphasize, to the being of the Tree of *Life*— was decreed through the life of Novalis, through his destiny, in that Sophie von Kuhn, the love of his youth, was taken from him by death when she was still a child. Into the four years between Sophie's death and his own during his twenty-ninth year, the whole abundance of his poetic creations poured. Because Sophie died still as a child, that love remained in the pure sphere of the Tree of Life before the arrival of puberty and the passing over to the other Tree. It is not a contradiction when it is said that at the same time a wonderful consecration of death ennobled this love. For with Novalis in a deep Michaelic sense, the Tree of Life grew out of what is seen from the earthly side as death. Light and warmth, which flowed to him from thence, were mysteriously combined for him with cosmic life and cosmic harmony, with the forces of the Tree of Paradise that has been lost to humanity. In the way that Novalis connects himself with the essence of the interior of the Earth in the chapter [5] on the miner in *Heinrich von Ofterdingen*, one can find mysteries of the life-ether enchanted into the earthly mineral element. Mysteries of Isis, of the life of the stars, and the essence of matter are contained in the words [*The Novices of Sais*, 'Nature']: 'I know not whether anyone ever truly understood the rocks and stones, but any such needs must have been a sublime being.'[331]

The Christian-Johannine Mystery of the connection of the Tree of Life with the Tree of Death through Love lives as destiny in the love of Novalis for Sophie; it lives in his whole poetic works, also in his Fragments, insofar as here the strongest inner life is expressed again in the form of pure thought. It lives especially clearly in the symbolic picture of the connection of *Lily* and *Rose*, the flower of life with the flower of death, as we find them in the passage in the miner's chapter in *Heinrich von Ofterdingen* [Chap. 11]. Only for this reason was Novalis able, in his sickly body, to be so strongly connected with the forces of the Tree of Life, because he took up death so consciously and transformed it into love. Out of that region of death and the Eternal Life there grew for him the transfigured view of love for everything earthly. And so there lived in him as well as in John the Christ-Sun of Love, connecting the Death-Tree of Knowledge with the Tree of Life, the Christ-Sun that helps us to see like a *'Tree of Love'*[332] the *one Tree*, in which the human being experiences his resurrection.

The Christ-Secret of the Early Mysteries

In his book *Christianity as Mystical Fact* [GA 8], Rudolf Steiner shows first how the revelation of Christ lived in the primal Indian Mysteries, how what later became earthly history in the Mystery of Golgotha was seen prophetically in the supersensory sphere. It will depend on how this truth is perceived, to a theological thinking of today a repugnant truth, whether a cognition of Christ bearing an enhancement of consciousness of humanity could exist in the future.

In the primal Indian Mysteries, the revelation of Christ is the most difficult to conceive. Here everything is present still as a recollection of the lost Paradise. After the Fall of Man, Paradise has remained in the upper etheric regions, in the region of the higher ethers. The homeland of the primal Indian consciousness was still completely 'in the wonderland volatilized into the ether', of which Novalis speaks in his *Hymns to the Night* [5]. The cosmic revelation of Christ lives in this consciousness. But the other [revelation] would be difficult for the Indian consciousness, whereby for us today, our consciousness of Christ first receives its full, true content. That is, to look not only for the Christ in the supersensory, to the pre-natal revelation of the Christ, but for that which Christ signifies for the Earth and humanity, to look to Him as to the Spirit, Who—to use Steiner's words—'went through the Mystery of Golgotha for the salvation of the Earth, and for humanity's freedom and progress'.[333] Such looking towards that Event as the midpoint of human history, as to something prophetic would, though, have been thoroughly inconceivable within the early Indian Mysteries. It actually did take place in the Mysteries of Zarathustra. In the Indian Mysteries there were no such centres, the traces of which we could somehow discover. The eye for that which resulted from the effects of the Fall of Man through Ahriman, though, is simply lacking with the Indian— but consequently also for the whole earthly revelation of Christ. Only where He is glimpsed in the midst between Lucifer and Ahriman does the Christ appear in full reality.

How Christ as the world-Creator lived in the primal Indian consciousness is preserved, as Rudolf Steiner emphasizes,[334] as an echo by the Rig-Veda in the hymns to *Vishvakarman*, the 'Creator of all' (Rig-Veda 10, 81 and 82). There we feel we approach more closely to the old, primal wisdom than in the whole later Brahman philosophy.

The Rig-Veda directly presents the tremendous picture of the *cosmic Sacrifice*, like that other important picture of the *cosmic Carpenter*, who is drawn in detail with the wood, the trees, the timber, and so on. This cosmic carpenter Vishvakarman is also called Tvashtar. His helpers are elemental beings, the *Ribhus* (linguistically = Germ. *elbisches*, 'like an elf'). Today we experience this whole picture of the cosmic carpenter as a softly distant, cosmic resounding of Christ's earthly life in the Middle East (on this, see Rudolf Steiner's lectures in Christiania (Oslo) [*The Fifth Gospel*. 1-6 October 1913. GA 148–*Tr. note*]. In the Vedic hymns, Vishvakarman is called, as Christ is in the Gospels, 'Lord and Master', with *suri*, a word related to the Greek *kyrios* ['Lord'], and at the same time this contains an echo of *surya* 'Sun' (which says nothing much to philologists), that is, 'the Lord of the Sun-I'. And, as Rudolf Steiner always points out, in Rig-Veda (10, 82, 2) Vishvakarman is beheld as that commanding being in the upper heights, above the seven Rishis, like an undivided divine light, that with the Rishis divides as into seven single colours.

Furthermore, as in other Mysteries, we feel in early India the *thought of humanity*, and moreover, Christ as the *Representative of Humanity*. The human being still merges into the general wholeness of all being. All the deeper is the impression made by the song of the Rig-Veda (10, 90), addressed to the primal human being, Purusha; here indeed in early India the human being appears as the beginning of all things. Through a tremendous cosmic sacrifice of himself, he objectifies, expels out of himself, all the lower realms of beings—a thought which, as Rudolf Steiner shows in *Riddles of Philosophy*,[335] appears again in modern thought. With all the ritual and cultic details this great cosmic sacrifice of the human being is pictorially presented. We can feel this song like a last echo in the memory lost to later Indian wisdom; in the earliest primal Mysteries it was once indeed present in the thought of humanity. The cosmic intuition of Christ would be complete and overwhelming, unless this cosmic self-sacrifice of the creation of the world were linked to the counter-pole of the sacrificial deed of Golgotha, as *for us today* it is always linked with this song of Purusha in the Indian Rig-Veda. In the cosmic heights this sacrificial Deed remains, to which we today look as to the Event in the midpoint of the Earth and of human history.

***

Vishnu, the Nathan-Jesus and Krishna

How today, in the anthroposophical sense, do we have to designate the being who initially revealed himself to the consciousness of the early Indian in the etheric heights, when he looked in the direction of Christ? Who is the being, who, though not Christ Himself, lived like a soul-revelation of Christ in the time before Golgotha, precisely in those regions which were lost to the human being after the Fall of Man with the 'expulsion from Paradise'? Who is that being who, as it were, carried in himself the substance of humanity, who did not take part in the Fall into sin, did not enter into human incarnations on the Earth, that being who remained in the pre-natal realms?[336] Anthroposophy calls this being the *Nathan-Jesus*, or more correctly expressed, it points to the connection that this being had with Jesus of Nazareth, with the Nathan-Jesus of Luke's Gospel, in whom he was incarnated on the Earth. In his lecture-cycle, *Christ and the Spiritual World* [GA 149, Leipzig, 28 Dec.—2 Jan. 1914], Rudolf Steiner shows how the pre-existing Christ before Golgotha during Lemurian and Atlantean prehistory penetrated this being three times, who then later on the Earth incarnated as the 'Nathan-Jesus', who, as it were, 'ensouled' him, and how it brought harmonizing effects on what, through the consequences of the Fall repeatedly brought disorder and disharmony to man's inner being. Thus, throughout the pre-Christian age the revelation of Christ and the sacrificial deed of Christ, there shimmers in a certain way through the spheres another, angelic-like being, remaining a stage above that of the human. This same being, on the Earth as the 'Nathan-Jesus', could give up his bodily vessel for the earthly Incarnation of Christ. The pre-earthly sphere of this being is the same in which the Indian primal consciousness still lived, the same out of which the Indian Mystery culture of primal times received its actual inspirations and revelations.

We also could designate this sphere as the Tree of Life remaining behind in the etheric heights, of the Eternal Feminine and pre-natal [realm] (cf. the previous article). Out of this sphere the great Indian initiate *Krishna* descended, in order to give Indian spiritual life its decisive direction with the descent into the dark ages (Kali-Yuga), in the third post-Atlantean culture-period. This earthly appearance of Krishna is presented to Indian consciousness as what is called the 'descent' (Indian: an *Avatara* of Vishnu) precisely that godhead, in whose image later Indian consciousness perceived the cosmic Christ, even if in subdued rays. The entire Indian teaching of Avatara is such a subdued, but for that reason a no less significant recognition of His cosmic sacrificial work. Indian consciousness beheld a whole series of Avataras of Vishnu [e.g. in the widely known *Dashavatara*]. Initially, the incarnations are in lower stages of being. One of these, for example, is the fish-incarnation, the Matsya-Avatara of Vishnu. Translated into the language of modern spiritual science, it means that the Indian primal consciousness looks back to the earlier ages of the evolution of the Earth, when the Earth and the Sun were still united, or had just divided. At that time the Sun and human beings stood in the *sign of the Fishes*, that is, the human being initially touched the earthly fire with those parts of his still etheric being that correspond with the zodiacal signs, in order to embody himself in those parts. The form of the fish corresponded to the stage of evolution of that time. The Indian said: the divine has sacrificed Himself at that time to the being of the fish, *Vishnu incorporated himself as a fish.*

Through the series of stages of animal forms the physical human being gradually develops the human form of today. Thus Rama also follows the pre-human Vishnu-Avataras, the kingly initiate of Indian primal times, and Krishna, the initiate of later times, who are the most eminent of these human precursors of Vishnu. Buddha, too, was seen by the Brahmans as such an Avatara of Vishnu.

Even though it has to be seen how close Krishna is to Nathan-Jesus, with Krishna's descent out of the sphere of Nathan-Jesus, it is not to be understood as though Krishna would be an actual incarnation of the being of Nathan-Jesus. When we are told that in the 'Nathan-Jesus' that being lived, who hitherto had never gone through an earthly incarnation, who after the Fall of Man belonged completely and utterly to the substance of humanity kept back in higher worlds, this being could not already have been there as Krishna. Rudolf Steiner also emphasizes that Krishna was a kind of maya-embodiment, not a real earthly incarnation of this being [see GA 142 and 146].[337] This is a fact that receives its full confirmation through an independent inspection of the Indian documents. We see this personality of Krishna only once, as described above all in the Mahabharata epic, in the narration of the great wars. There he frequently stands before us as the cunning politician, who plays such a difficult role to appreciate in the whole story of the great war. We only receive the key by telling ourselves: for this being himself, the role he played on earth, as everything earthly, was actually completely meaningless. It was maya; he lived completely in his super-earthly sphere. He placed himself into all the earthly events and into humanity, so as to reveal to the human soul how non-essential they are. The whole war, we feel, has to happen in order to show, in the destruction of everything earthly, the invincible nature of the higher life.

Something of this mood also weaves in the *Bhagavadgita,* in the teaching that the divine Krishna, as the charioteer, gives to the hero Arjuna, in sight of the warriors aligned for battle: 'Fight on, do your warrior duty, but in all of this be indifferent to victory and defeat, life and death, be only given up to the divine in yourself, so you will come to me, to unite with me, your divine self.'[338] One might be tempted here, concerning the manner as to how, from the divine perspective, the accomplishment of earthly tasks are demanded, to link this with the *Christian impulse.* But that would be to overlook the decisive viewpoint. This fulfilment of earthly duties, the duties of war in the Bhagavadgita are not demanded in order to plant the divine, creative love for the Earth. It is there in order, through tireless managing to fulfil the destined tasks with the earth, that one's own emptiness of being is abandoned. In the background of all Krishna's admonishments is the attitude of a release from the earthly, rather than uniting with the earthly in the sense of the Christ-Impulse. A being speaks in them, who himself is released from the earthly, whose whole earthly incarnation is but maya.

In the Indian presentation of the young Krishna, it is quite clear how far the region of the higher ether, to which Krishna actually belongs, is that of the Eternal Feminine, the Isis formative forces (sound-ether and life-ether). A breath of the cosmic-virgin enwraps the Indian Krishna, as it does the figure of the Nathan-Jesus. We encounter part of the narration in delicate, fragrant pictures, where the playfulness and pranks of the young Krishna with the shepherdesses are told.[339] We feel we enter a sphere similar to that of the Song of Solomon [in the Tanakh, the Old Testament], that also must have originated out of the mysteries of the higher Eternal Feminine. The figure of the young Krishna stands much closer to that of the Nathan Jesus than the figure of Krishna in the Mahabharata. But what here, with the Nathan-Jesus, is a real earthly incarnation, still remains as maya with Krishna, as indeed in general in the Indian Mysteries the whole relationship to the earthly element is still tuned to maya. Characteristically, the name *Maya*—although not a woman's name in India—also appears as the name of the mother of the Buddha, who recalls so much, yet not everything of the Christian *Maria,* Mary. And again we feel how a mystery, that became in Mary full earthly reality and earthly revelation, in the Indian story of Buddha is still covered as in a veil of maya.

***

The Mystical side of Yoga

The word Yoga, in which all the admonitions and teachings of Krishna reach the highest point in the Bhagavadgita, contains the central impulse of the Indian Mysteries and of Indian spiritual life. Indeed, the more the early primal consciousness declines in the course of time, 'volatiles into the ether', it was all the more important for Indian initiates and spiritual teachers to unite themselves with this primal consciousness through Yoga, through the methodical practice of concentration, meditation, contemplation, which, different from today's spiritual schooling, in India was built more upon the rhythmic system.

In a double manner the *Christ-Mystery of the early Mysteries* is revealed in this Indian Yoga. Here there is that side we could call the *mystical side* of this Indian Yoga; Yoga appears as the way of mystical internalizing, the *path within* that is taken in order to find the human higher self , the 'I'. *Peace in the 'I' (Kaivalyam)* is the *mystical aim* of Yoga. This peace in the 'I' remains, as the name Kaivalyam (seclude oneself) says, likewise the Buddhist Nirvana, to the Indian something negative, a secluding oneself from the world. The positive content of this 'I' is not yet found in the full, awake consciousness; the early Vedic Brahman experienced it more in a dreaming consciousness. Only in Christ is this positive content of the 'I' found. In this sense *Christ* is the One who completes the *mystical side of Yoga*, is that One who takes away the one-sided mystical side of Indian Yoga.

Characteristic in all this is how in Indian Yoga the divine Self is seen as the *Lord in the 'I', Ishvara* (spoken Ish-vara, first syllable emphasized)—the word comes from *ish*, 'to be special/ characteristic; to govern', and is related to Old German *aigan*, and thereby once again with 'Ich'. Where, namely in the Yoga sutras, the being of this Ishvara is characterized more closely, he appears as the part of humanity (Purusha) that has not entered incarnation, that has remained untouched by the Fall of Man and karma, in other words not yet as the Christ in the comprehensive sense, but as the *Jesus-Krishna being*, standing everywhere in the background of the Indian Mysteries. This is the being of the *Nathan-Jesus,* whose relationship to India was mentioned above.

In the Bhagavadgita, too, Krishna is frequently termed Ishvara. Whether the linguistic connection between *Ishvara* and *Jehoshuah, Jesus,* that people often want to find, really exists, remains undecided. It can be found, if the *cosmic healing power* (this meaning lies initially in Jehoshuah) is experienced with the 'I', if one learns to see the divine power, which 'heals the Self in the depths of the soul' (Easter Epistle of

The Act of Consecration of Man). That is, Christ is the real fulfilment of Ishvara, the 'I'-side (or mystical side) of Indian Yoga.

The Magical Side of Yoga

Alongside this mystical side, Yoga has another, the *magical* side. We speak everywhere of *magical* forces where spirit-power lives not only in itself, but where it is evident creating and transforming matter, the earthly element. The area of magical activity was rich in early India, as this earthly element in the primal time itself was still nearer to the etheric realm. Magical forces were still at work in the word, in the mantras; through magical forces the teacher still directly influenced the pupil. The Atharvaveda in particular—no longer appreciated by the Brahmins—retains a memory of this magical epoch, also of Indian spiritual life (cf. the article on 'The Tree of Life', above.). Here the discussion is much concerned with magical healing, transforming, exorcizing, conjuring forces. According to its being, magic is *effective on the Earth*; it transforms the Earth. So with inner consistency in this important Hymn Atharvaveda XII. 1, too, the *Earth*—in India otherwise rather insignificant—is celebrated in its divinity. Right at the beginning, with a certain Christ-depth the *Earth* is presented as the cosmic altar of sacrifice (v. 8), where it is said (v. 11):

> For my healing be thy snow-clad mountains and forests, O Earth,
> On the brown, the black, the ruddy, the multi-coloured firm Earth,
> Unconquered, uninjured, unwounded, I set foot upon this Earth.

But this element of the Earth in the other, the actual canonic Vedas, increasingly steps into the background in Indian spiritual life. And so it is also with the *magical element in Indian Yoga*. It lies in the essence of Yoga that this magical element enjoys a certain position. Still in the relatively late Yoga sutras of Patañjali (third syllable emphasized) the magical forces (*Siddhi*) are mentioned, which through spiritual concentration on specific points can be achieved: taming of wild animals through thoughts of love, overcoming the gravity of the Earth, penetrating the thoughts of others, and many other things we find there, besides wonderful stages of controlling and perfecting the body—the physical, medicinal element did originally play the greatest role in Yoga. But these magical forces, only appearing as accompaniments on the way, have to be relinquished when the actual aim of Yoga is to be achieved, the self-contained 'I' (*Kaivalyam*). In the earthly realm, it is said, the [lesser] perfections are hindrances for the highest aim, lower forces that have to be relinquished for the sake of the higher [goal].

Consequently, in Indian Yoga, too, the *magical* side retreats before the *mystical* side. Indian spiritual life increasingly strives towards one-sided mystical contemplation; magic comes increasingly into discredit, with which the Indian legends, as well as the Indian primal consciousness are filled. The exercising of forces, which were once sacred to the Indian, was felt as a lower sensation. In this sense, Buddha—who out of the spirit of the ancient Yoga built up his teaching and the Path—also warns his pupils to put aside such arts, which were felt as a contradiction to the dignity of the higher spiritual striving. Buddha himself certainly knew the higher side of magical workings. Once in a world-significant moment he spoke of this to his favourite disciple Ananda, of the connection with the earthly realm and the transformation of the earthly body through such forces *for the sake of healing the Earth and humanity* (cf. the writer's article on 'Buddha', above). But his words were not understood. The Earth and humanity were not yet mature enough to receive their meaning. In the sublime and sacred sense Buddha meant, magical forces in those days were as yet unable to be placed into the service of earthly activity. That which was not possible in Buddha's time, five hundred years before Golgotha, becomes *earthly fact in Christ*. In another way than the one indicated by Buddha, that is, *not through remaining in the earthly body* but precisely *by going right through death* we find the fact of the Resurrection.

All true love, also in its lower forms, works magically, contains an element of magic in itself. Likewise the *Mystery of Golgotha* as the *highest Deed of Love of the gods,* and with this at the same time there is *the highest Earth-transforming Deed of white magic, the greatest magical event of the entire history of the Earth*. Here, though, the exercising of magical forces, which once in Indian Yoga, where it was especially at home, was felt as an abbreviation of true spiritual aims, led towards its true fulfilment. *Christ*—when the word is rightly understood—is the Fulfiller also of the other, the *magical side of Yoga*. Transformation of the Earth through the power of Christ is now the high *magical* goal of all Christened earthly activity, according to its inner being. From now on, in Christ the negating of the earthly activities for the sake of the mystical contemplation of the 'I is no longer justified. Rather, the human 'I', as the Christ-earthly-'I', is to that degree fulfilled as it has become conscious also in its magical capability of working from the spirit to transform and re-fashion earthly nature.

***

In contrast to Indian spiritual life and its Mysteries where the magical impulse increasingly retreats towards the one-sided *mystical* one, the Mysteries of Zarathustra (second post-Atlantean cultural epoch) are strongly carried by *magical* impulses. Zarathustra stands before the spiritual gaze as the true *primal magician*. Quite differently from the Indian Mysteries, *earthly activity* and the *transformation of the Earth through spiritual forces*—but this, according to its nature, is magic—steps into the foreground with Zarathustra. This can be the case here, because Zarathustra also directs his gaze towards that being who through the Fall has become the ruler in the realm of death of earthly matter that has become estranged from the spirit—*Ahriman* (*Angromainyush*; see the writer's essay on Zarathustra). Through this looking on Ahriman that is still strange to the Indian, the *beholding of Christ* also gains a heightened reality with Zarathustra. From the Indian world of the state of being that rests in being, we have now stepped into that world of *revelation*, possible through the fact that darkness is opposed, is contrasted to, the light. In the overcoming and transformation of the ahrimanic being, in the transformation of darkness into light, earthly activity is clearly given its task. Here *magical forces* in their whole application are something other than in Indian Yoga. When, through the forces of love of the holy one, of the yogi, wild animals are tamed, then this for him is a mere confirmation of the reality of spiritual forces; everything remains here in a sphere reminding us of Francis of Assisi. Only with Zarathustra, there comes also into this realm the possibility to bring it to a positive outcome. Here wild animals are tamed through magical forces, but not in order to reveal the power of the truth of Yoga, but that with the tamed animal species a companion and helper for man may grow in his work of cultivating the earth.

This *taming of wild animals* becomes the picture for taming and purifying the astral body of the human passions. Yet besides this it has a quite down-to-earth meaning, also with Zarathustra. Obvious earthly activities like agriculture and cattle-breeding were first called into being in the Zarathustra Mysteries of primal times through the employment of magical forces. In the article on Zarathustra it was pointed out that we cannot ever imagine from Buddha, or some other

Indian wise person and leader, words spoken as we find in the Avesta. Here Zarathustra is called the first priest, the first warrior, and *the first cattle-breeder*.[340]

A strong *Christ-element* lies in this emphasis with Zarathustra on earthly activity and the earthly personality. We feel in India there is not yet the fully human individuality at all. Even great beings like the seven Rishis still manifest themselves like the seven rays of colour from the *one* primal light. Only in Zarathustra is the primal picture and ideal of the strong individuality and earthly personality present. And in this Zarathustra, as the first who points to the great *representative of humanity, Christ* himself appears. In the article on Isis, it was shown how, in one of the sacrificial deeds preparing for Christ and Christ's earthly Deed, Zarathustra gradually pours out his spiritual being into the great Mystery-impulses of pre-Christian humanity. This sacrificial deed finds its conclusion in his incarnation as the Jesus-boy of Solomon's line, of which Matthew's Gospel speaks. This boy sacrifices himself, as it were bodily, into the being of the Nathan-Jesus (this is the spiritual background of the event told in Luke 3:41ff., cf. the present writer's essay on 'The Tree of Life', above). This is in order, after he had carried over his 'I', the great Zarathustra 'I' of humanity, into this other Jesus-boy, later also to sacrifice this 'I' at the Baptism in the Jordan, to the cosmic Sun-'I', the Christ, Who then enters the bodily sheaths of Jesus of Nazareth.

In the background of the primal Indian Mysteries, the being of the *Nathan-Jesus* appears; in the background of the Zarathustra-Mysteries the being of the *Solomon-Jesus*. Only in this way, that behind this [Solomon-Jesus] the *Christ* Himself is seen much more clearly than as is the case in India. In the great Christ-prophecy of the Avesta, proclaimed at the end of the essay on Zarathustra, there appears powerfully and impressively the way the Christ-Sun-aura is distinguished from the personality of the Redeemer (in the same way as *Jehoschuah, Jesus*, the word *Saoshyant* also means, *the Saviour, Redeemer*), to whom this Being should be conveyed. Equally impressive is the way how 'the apostles' are mentioned in this connection, how *'bringing the world forwards, advancing the world'* (an impulse which in this way cannot be found in early India), of *'the re-enlivening of the dying Earth-existence'*,[341] the *overcoming of death* and the *resurrection of the dead* are mentioned; finally especially the *impulses of freedom* of that which we call *The Philosophy of Freedom* (which helps the world to eternal life, to eternal growth, *towards free will*). The Indian does not yet actually know of the will; he hardly has a word for it. The meaning of Zarathustra for the world is that, as the proclaimer of the earthly personality and of earthly activities, he is the *inaugurator of the will*. 'When through the will the world is brought forwards' the great Christ-prophecy ends. And the words given for one of the glass windows [of the Goetheanum] in Dornach (*'Es gebiert sich der Wille*—The will is being born')[342] truly characterize the impulse of Zarathustra. With this impulse Zarathustra becomes the preparer of the Christian *initiation of the will*.

***

Wisdom of the fixed-stars

In the background of the primal Indian Mysteries appears the being of the Nathan-Jesus; in the background of the Zarathustrian Mysteries appears the being of the Solomon-Jesus (and behind him the Christ); in the background of the Egyptian Mysteries the *being of Christ* Himself appears, the *Representative of Humanity* in His whole comprehensive, universal-earthly meaning. What is experienced here through all four Sothis periods, or Sothic cycles (cf. the Isis article, above) on various levels and in various pictures, is simply *the human being* himself in all the parts of his spiritual-physical being. In ancient times the wisdom of the fixed stars of this human being was still experienced in a *universally wide consciousness*. The 'I' shines towards the initiate out of the widths of the fixed stars. And Zarathustra, the greatest initiate, the great inspirer of all post-Indian Mysteries—even the star-wisdom of the Egyptian Hermes, for Hermes carried the astral body of Zarathustra—knew as his 'I' the comprehensive, divine soul of humanity itself. This human soul, Isis, had her likeness in the brightest fixed star in the heavens, the shining *Sirius*. She was the starry Grail-vessel for the 'I' of humanity (the Indian called it Purusha): Osiris—Orion. In the Mysteries of the sound-ether and light-ether, [or] cosmic life and cosmic harmony, Isis was experienced uttering the eternal Cosmic Word.

Meeting the upper gods in the sphere of the Thrones was still the Christ-experience of the old fixed-star wisdom for humanity. And in the union of Isis and Osiris, Sirius-Orion, the divine unity of the human being was presented, in its original union of the Eternal Masculine and the Eternal Feminine. This union, though, is the *Christ*. The sacred name Isis itself, 'H-S-T, carries in itself as a veiled Mystery that of the Christ, of the Representative of Humanity. The same Mystery is indicated in the three figures of the Christ-group [the wooden sculpture] in the Goetheanum, Dornach, Switzerland. Yet they appear in those three sounds [of the name Isis], all three as in their divine nature, on their Saturn level. In one of his last lectures, Rudolf Steiner himself spoke about how the soul of humanity, the new Isis, can be seen as if sleeping behind this Christ-group in Dornach.[343]

This Christ-experience in the cosmic, starry Tree of Life was like a great Christmas-experience of humanity's childhood. Here the maternal principle of the world, Isis, the starry-virgin, as the bearer of all healing, health-giving forces of the cosmos, was beheld. And the experience was like drinking-in an enlivening, health-giving drink of the starry soma (cf. the article 'The Tree of Life'). The Indian Rig-Veda still contains an echo of this soma mysticism, which in a certain way belongs to *all* pre-Christian Mysteries, even that of Zarathustra. In the midst of all the Mystery-beings *agni*, the sacrificial fire, and the soma stand there as two linked divine beings. *Agni* had a double side. It was the outer fire and the inner fire in the human being; the fire in the blood, in the digestion, in the enthusiasm and elevation of the soul. The *Mystery of the Blood* is hidden in *agni*—the cosmic fire of sacrifice in the primal beginning, the *warmth of [Ancient] Saturn* lives on in the blood; that is, the *Mystery of the Body* (soma in Gk. means 'body'), for on the *Ancient Moon* this human body was still a fluid being that only on the Earth solidified into the bony system.

Wisdom of the Planets

From the oldest fixed-star wisdom, let us proceed to the next Sothis period, to the time of the wisdom of the planets. Here we still meet the third of the great Mystery-experiences, the *beholding the Sun at midnight*.[344] And *Osiris*—as the Egyptologists know[345]—is this spiritual Sun of midnight. Now it is the Moon-sickle of Isis, who, experienced as the cosmic Grail-vessel, carries in herself the Sun-host.[346] (Yet Isis is actually not a Moon-goddess; her planet is Venus, and her fixed-star Sirius.) The Christ-experience has jumped over from the star-stage to that of the planets, to the *Sun-stage*. And the cosmic *draught of health* has now become the Moon-soma (in Indian soma means 'Moon'); at the same time it is the human *astral wisdom*, now experienced in the Moon.

On the next stage, that of the wisdom of the elements, the human being Isis-Osiris is experienced in the elemental kingdom of the Earth, in the etheric world of the plants; the soma is now the plant-soma, has now become the etheric soma. In the fourth and final Sothic-cycle, or period, so decisive for the Christ-experience, this aroma of the etheric also sinks into the grave of the physical, of the earthly body. The cosmic time approaches when the 'I', that at one time was experienced in the universally wide consciousness out of fixed-star widths, begins itself to speak within human beings themselves. But this final and decisive experience takes place no longer in ancient Egypt. In the story of Moses, the miraculous and disturbing pictures of the *Egyptian plagues* shows how this experience was not taken in by ancient Egypt and its Mysteries. The whole Egyptian Mysteries are concerned with this decisive experience of humanity. But 'what shall come to pass' was not to take place on Egyptian soil.

Egypt retains from everything that now takes place in this decisive fourth Sothic cycle-period only the outer sheath, the *grave*, the Egyptian Mysteries have entered the period of the graves. The completely external spiritual culture of Egypt has become a culture of graves and mummies. The mouth of Isis has become mute. *The approach to the portal of death* alone, behind which a light-filled view no longer lights up, remains a Mystery experience. It is the darkness and loneliness of death and of the grave that the candidate for initiation still experiences at the sacred Mystery centre. At no period of human history have the grave and death been experienced with such concern. And this experience of the grave and of death, this *laying in the grave* of old Mystery wisdom, had to precede its resurrection in Christ. Christ Himself, Who in the Solomon-Jesus was significantly connected with Zarathustra, the inspirer also of the Egyptian Mysteries—the journey of the child Jesus to Egypt is meaningful in this regard—arrives for his earthly incarnation and earthly revelation in the country neighbouring Egypt, [the earlier] Palestine.

Thither Moses, the initiate of the Egyptian Mysteries and its wisdom of the elements wanted to lead the Hebrews, but into which he did not set foot. Ancient thinking of the gods had to be crucified in earthly thinking. Moses' mission was to bring this thinking to humanity, and the end of this crucifixion was the physical crucifixion of Christ-Jesus on Golgotha. In the countries of the early Mysteries, India, Persian and Egypt, it would never have come—Rudolf Steiner once said this—to the crucifixion of the Christ. In reverence, Persians, Indians, Egyptians would have sacrificed to Him the gold of their wisdom, the incense and the myrrh of their devotion. But only through earthly death could the meaning of earthly events be fulfilled, could the great experience of freedom in the 'I' be found towards which Zarathustra had already in prophecy pointed. Soma, which at one time in the countries of the ancient Mysteries was drunk as starry soma, as Moon-soma, and soma of the elements, became in the earthly body of the Christ-Jesus, which now has become the divine Grail-vessel, that which soma means in the Greek language: a human body. This body unites in itself the essence of the divine forces of the universe.

If we look in such a way on to the great connections with the pre-Christian developments, then it can be felt how the decisive element of the fourth Sothis period no longer takes place in Egypt but in Palestine, in the Mystery of Golgotha. The Mystery of Golgotha itself, which was already prepared in the exodus[347] of the Hebrews out of Egypt, can be felt as the fourth and concluding epoch of the ancient Egyptian Mysteries, which are the actual Christ-Mysteries in the pre-Christian age. Through this Mystery of Golgotha, to the outer culture of graves in Egypt, which was deserted by the soul of its Mysteries, the living content is added. Christ strides right through the grave of the Earth, towards the Resurrection, which will be fulfilled in the Earth's future. In Him the sunken treasures of the ancient Mysteries also find their resurrection. Early star-wisdom, the pre-Christian Grail-revelation arises again as esoteric Christianity of the Holy Grail. And awoken in the Resurrected One, the human soul, the new Isis, becomes to humanity a new revealer of the secret of the starry script.

IV.

APPENDICES

The Rainbow's Revelation

(*Die Christengemeinschaft*, 5. Jg. Nr. 9. Dez. 1928. 260-64)

Many people recall the joy they felt already as children with the rainbow and its colours, perhaps in seeing the real rainbow in the sky, or perhaps some glass prism or thermometer hanging in the window threw the rainbow colours into the room. Something is revealed in this joy. The rainbow colours also appear in crystals, which is the archetypal picture or mirror of the cosmic-forming capacity in the world of sensory revelation. Children still experience in the rainbow the 'archetypal phenomenon' of all sensory appearance. It appears when the heavenly light shines through the murky veil of matter, perhaps this 'turbid veil' like the actual rainbow is formed through a wall or rain-clouds (when the beholder has the Sun behind him) or through the veil of drops of a waterfall—here the appearance of the rainbow is especially poetic—or it is formed through a crystal surface or a glass prism. In his tremendous Faustian creation *Manfred*, the poet Byron sings of the tender appearance of the colourful veil of colours at the Staubbach [literally, 'dust brook'] in the valley Lauterbrunnental in the highlands around Bern, that strange waterfall whose stream of drops in falling from the perpendicular 300 metres-high rock-wall disappears into air, like dust dispersing into thin air. It is the same Staubbach where Goethe received his inspiration for the 'Song of the Spirit over the Waters', the picture of which he may have had before him when, concluding the opening scene of *Faust* II, he composed words about the rainbow:

> Faust:
> *Allein wie herrlich diesem Sturm entsprießend,*
> *Wölbt sich des bunten Bogens Wechseldauer,*
> *Bald rein gezeichnet, bald in Luft zerfließend,*
> *Umher verbreitend duftig kühle Schauer.*
> *Der spiegelt ab das menschliche Bestreben.*
> *Ihm sinne nach und du begreifst genauer:*
> *Am farbigen Abglanz haben wir das Leben.*
>
> Lifted on high in many a flying plume,
> Above the spray-drenched air. And then how splendid
> To see the rainbow rising from this rage,
> Now clear, now dimmed, in cool sweet vapour blended.

So strive the figures on our mortal stage.
This ponder well, the mystery closer seeing;
In mirrored hues we have our life and being.
[Tr. Philip Wayne]

The whole of Goethe's doctrine on colour, the *Theory of Colours*, is built up on this 'phenomenon'. The phenomena are the 'deeds and sufferings of the light'. Three elements, *light, turbidity/cloudiness,* and *darkness*—here Goethe approaches a primal Mystery knowledge of humanity that is also contained in the Indian Sankta philosophy and its teaching of *sattva, rajas* and *tamas*—create the conditions for the appearance of colour.[348] If the light shines through the turbidity, then yellow appears, which with increased turbidity becomes red—as sunrise or sunset often make this visible. Darkness behind the lit-up turbidity allows blue to appear: the darkness of space seen through the lit-up atmosphere (as the 'element of turbidity') appears as the 'blue sky'. Especially with increased turbidity light blue comes about, with less turbidity dark blue: the clear air of the south allows the sky to appear deep blue; the turbid atmosphere of the north lets it appear pale blue; in the clear air of the Alps at great heights, the sky shows deepest dark blue.

As a transition colour between red and yellow, orange appears; as a transition colour between the upper yellow and lower blue, as 'colour of the middle' and as balance of the scale of colour, green appears, whereas like a transition between the lower blue towards red, violet appears on the further side of indigo-blue. We can divine, that the bow of colours somehow beyond the sensory visible, as in a 'higher level', closes the circle—what is above and what is below meet in what is beyond. In this direction also lies the mystery of the etheric 'peach blossom', which Goethe points out in his *Theory of Colours*.

Thus the colours of the rainbow rise: red, orange, yellow, green, blue, indigo and violet.[349] The human eye is originally attuned to see these colours. Forms and figures first arise for the eye as colours come about from other colours. Colour is the primary fact of the sensory world—or, the visual world—form is secondary. It is understandable that the Indian word *rupa* not only means 'form' (with which it is frequently one-sidedly translated), but also 'colour'.

Joy in the 'primal phenomena' of the rainbow is found not only as an individual experience of people's own childhood, but as an experience of the childhood of humanity. The Greek word *iris*—which can also mean a part of the human eye, the 'rainbow skin' of the pupil—means at the same time 'rainbow'. The eye that sees and the primal phenomenon of seeing itself coincide in this word. With its vibrating, raying *r* and the 'vowel of light' *i*, this word *iris* appears to us like a primal experience of humanity. In a language that especially approaches the primal experience of mankind's childhood, old Egyptian, *iri* means 'the eye'. This word *iri* 'the eye' is contained in the divine name *Us-iri* (actually 'eye of strength', 'eye of the power of seership of the Sun'), which then in Greek became *Osiris*. One of the profound myths recorded by the Greek writer Plutarch[350] tells of the Sun-bright Osiris, the representative of the ancient power of the seer, who once as the wise king, ruled as the Lord of Peace and benefactor of humanity on Earth, was killed by his dark brother Seth (Gk. Typhon) and mourned by his wife Isis. He was removed to the Underworld, became there the Lord and Judge in the land of the dead. From then on only through the 'portal of death' and the path of spiritual trials and purification connected to it could the soul find the entrance into the bright realm of the Sun of Osiris. In the Egyptian *Book of the Dead* these things are referred to in attractive pictures. Primal memories of the human race of the childhood of humanity, of lost powers of a more spiritual epoch of humanity, live in these sagas. They also live already in the names, in the name Osiris as well as in the name Isis.

Something like a connection between the two names Isis and Osiris shines towards us (in the Egyptian pictograms both share the same basic hieroglyph; with Osiris it is connected with the picture of a seeing eye, with Isis with another, a form expressing the primal feminine of the world). The vibrating rays of light and rays of the Sun of the R in the name Osiris (*rā* in Egyptian means 'Sun', in Hebrew 'to see') leads to S in Isis, into the earthly material, as it were into that veil of cloud necessary for the visible appearance of the rainbow, *Iris* is the physical condition. In Egyptian *Isis* originally meant 'H-S-T (one recalls the 'voice of thin silence'), which then become vocalized to I-S-T, to that I-S-T which so significantly is contained in the word *Kristall* ('crystal') and in the name Christ. We mentioned how the crystal magics forth the bright appearance of the rainbow colours. We stand before the oldest primal word for the phenomena in which the mystery of becoming of all earthly material is revealed out of the spirit, its 'origin in the light'.

*

The manner how the heavenly light, the light of the Sun, shines through the 'cloudiness' of the earthly element—with the veil of rain of the bank of cloud, with the veil of drops of the waterfall, with the crystal or glass prism—reveals the appearance of the rainbow, which can be seen as the picture for the whole relationship of the earthly-material world, the sensory world, to the world of the spirit in whose power it fundamentally stands. Like a shining bridge the rainbow spans the heavens, like a bridge from the sensory to the spiritual world from which it descended—this is how children experience it unconsciously and how the ancient peoples of the childhood of the race experienced it half-consciously. *Osiris* and *Isis* become here the expression of the early experience of humanity in which the 'origin in the light' shone through the veils of the earthly element becoming ever-denser.

The rainbow appears most significantly at the beginning of the Bible in the story of Noah after the Flood (Genesis 9:13-17). In this story there lives not only a primal memory of the early human races of the early age after the subsidence of the waters of the Deluge, of which not only in the Bible, but a memory has been retained in the myths and sagas of nearly all the people of the Earth. With the clearing of the atmosphere of thick fog and watery clouds, the outer phenomenon of the rainbow for the first time became physically possible. And in it there also appears something like a picture of the whole transition that took place at that time in the becoming of the Earth and humanity, of the transition from an earlier more supersensory, spiritual-etheric condition into the later earthly-physical condition. The spiritual primal light also shines through the turbid veil of the becoming earthly matter. And so there arises—before the spiritual eye of the seer—the picture of the rainbow (cf. the author's book *Our Origin in the Light*, Chapter 7 on the rainbow).

Spiritual creative power still shines through the veil of what has been created. The spiritual creative power is called in the beginning of the Bible 'Elohim'. Luther [and the AV/KJV] translate, 'In the beginning GOD created the heavens and the earth.' Actually, or rather in the original text, the word 'Elohim' is a plural, of creative beings. Many people object when in anthroposophical texts the Elohim are mentioned as a plural, when they are mentioned as a Godhead of seven creative members. They feel disturbed in their veneration of the one Father-God, although they do not object to the thought of the Trinity, the Triune unity of Father, Son and Spirit. In particular the rainbow and the way the *one* sunlight breaks up into a seven colours, could teach people how the primal Unity can coincide with the fact of a plurality of creative divine Beings working out of the primal depths of the

Fatherly Ground of the World (cf. Doldinger's poem: 'They are seven … seven / They are … and They are all but the One,' etc.).[351] Goethe looks deeply into the revelation of the rainbow in [final] § 919 of his teaching on colour, or *Theory of Colours*, where the 'initiate' in Goethe who otherwise holds himself back, for once gently lifts the veil of sublime mysteries:

> When the distinction of yellow and blue is duly comprehended, and especially the augmentation [intensification] into red, by means of which the opposite qualities tend towards each other and become united in a third; then, certainly, an especially mysterious interpretation will suggest itself, since a spiritual meaning may be connected with these facts; and when we find the two separate principles producing green on the one hand and red in their more intense state, we can hardly refrain from thinking in the first case on the earthly, in the last on the heavenly, generation of the Elohim.

And in Rev. 4:3 the rainbow appears like a primal revelation of creation.

*

Like a bridge to the spiritual world the rainbow appears in Teutonic mythology where it divides the light-filled home of the gods from the earthly, human world of the world ash, Yggdrasil, whose root is gnawed at by the powers of death. In Wagner's *The Rhinegold* we see the gods, after their world has already been overcast by the Fall, but Thor's [= Wotan's] hammer of thunder has once more cleansed the atmosphere of the turbid vapours, returning over the rainbow bridge to their sublime, divine stronghold Valhalla. This episode is composed in Wagner's music in that key on the circle of fifths that marks the transition from the upper to the lower side, from the day side to the night side, from the earthly to the spiritual, in the 'key of the threshold', Gb-major.[352]

And so the rainbow stands as in the primal becoming of creation, where what has been created of the earthly element returns again to the spiritual realm whence it originated. In this way the rainbow appears in the Bible, we also behold the future light of humanity when, at the end of the Advent Epistle of The Act of Consecration of Man, the picture of the bow of colours, comforting and prophesying, stands before the spiritual eye. That which is prophetically carried in the womb of worlds is greeted, in the raying of the chariot of the Sun, and in the shining of the bow of colours, spanning the heavens.

The Dream of Eden in the Light of Christmas

(*Tatchristentum*. 1. Jg. Nr. 9. 1923. 96-7.)

A wisdom of earlier times flowing from unconscious depths of the folk-soul has given the day before Christmas, the day before the sacred night of birth, the name 'Adam and Eve's' day. Not only the Fall of the first humanity and the birth of redemption are to face each other in an abstract theological sense, but it is as if alive in tangible pictures, memories and lost visions would light up again in the soul-light of Christmas, meaningfully pictured in the candle-light of the Christmas tree itself.

In the Christmas light, in beholding the Child lying in the crib, human beings look up towards the forgotten origin of their own being in the light. Memories become alive in the soul lying like dream-pictures over the childhood of the human race, sounding across to us like early sacred legends which we heard in our own childhood. What remains childlike in us feels the childhood of humanity in the cosmic Christmas-Child. Paradisal light rays out of the crib of the Christmas-Child; memories of Paradise, memories of the lost Tree of Life, are awoken by the radiating Tree of Light. At Easter there stands the picture of a distant, spiritualized human future; at Christmas there stands before us the picture of our own primal past, the paradisal childhood of man. Out of those heights lost to humanity, in the light of the Christmas night, we feel the soul of the child descends, lying before us in the crib. That which the human being once had when Adam and Eve were in God's presence, living together in innocence in Paradise, and what was then lost in the Fall, is there again in this Child. In him the dream of Eden that gradually became darkened for fallen humanity, has become a higher reality.

In the shimmer of the Christmas candles we allow our inner gaze to look back to a time of human development, which for the meeting of old and new soul-light was especially important in the thirteenth century. That which can become conscious to the soul as the new radiating light of Paradise, as the re-enlivener of the dream of Eden in the light of the world-Christmas, was fashioned at that time into a wondrously significant picture. What could be consciously beheld in the bodily sheaths of the Jesus-child, can shine again in heavenly innocence; what has become the vessel of cosmic light, appeared before the soul in radiant light; in the middle of the night it shines brighter than the Sun of day, the picture of the sacred vessel that is carried on the mount Montsalvage by the virginal queen, *the Grail*. Thus it was beheld in his poetic work *Parzifal* by Wolfram von Eschenbach (Bk. 5, 345-60). We can feel how here the Grail, the stone of light that has been carried down by choirs of angels from starry heights (9, 651-55), is, as it were, seen in the Christmas light, whereas those who venerate it more as the vessel in which the blood of the Redeemer was collected, see it in the Easter light of Golgotha, on Good Friday.

In this Christmas light we seek intuitively to understand why Eschenbach calls the Grail carried by the virginal queen the 'wish for Paradise' (5, 351). Sunlike, the picture of Eden rays before the inner gaze, of the cosmically comprehensive primordial homeland of paradisal Man still living in the light of his spiritual origin. The homeland of light disappeared to the earthly darkened consciousness of man fallen into sin. From paradisal heights, the human being sank down to the Earth. For a long time Eden still lived in his memory. The paradisal light that he had lost in his waking condition still inhabited his dreaming. An inner experience of light goes through the sleep of humanity in which sometimes more clearly, sometimes but vaguely, the dream of Eden lights up. It still stood ceremoniously before the soul-eye of the early Chaldean when he read in the starry-embroidered night-sky the shining script of the universe, in that bright primeval homeland of the Patriarchs from which Abraham migrated towards the land of Canaan. And it dimly continued to live in the soul of the Patriarchs. So it lived again under the sparkling starry heavens, when once more in a destiny night uniting with future prophecy, the light of Jacob's soul-eye was kindled.[353] In clearest light the dream was beheld by the spirit to whom we are indebted for the Book of Genesis. In Moses the early experience of the light united with that earthly light of the 'I' in which the heavenly light was slowly extinguished. Once again there arises out of the darkness of time the inner light-experience overviewing world-contexts and human contexts in Solomon's wondrous dream-wisdom.[354] In it the dream of Eden became the concept of the building, the Temple, which is built in earthly materials by Hiram's hand, the skilful builder. In the mysterious pictures of the Temple, humanity's past and future are united.

And so it continued for long ages, until even the dream of Eden dissolved from the consciousness of earthly man. The world of light of Eden became ever dimmer and without its essence, comparable to a retreating star. The Earth would have been estranged forever from the cosmic heights had not those heights lovingly inclined towards it. Into the deep night of the Earth rays the highest cosmic light, descends the revelation of the highest cosmic love. In the cosmic Christmas-Child the building-concept of the Temple, the dream of Eden itself, becomes Man. All this lives in the Christmas story of Luke's Gospel. And it lives in the picture of the Grail carried down by hosts of angels from the starry heights to the Earth. As the budding life of the plant is contracted in the narrow space of the seed out of which the new plant will grow, so all the rays of the one-time primordial light are gathered in that stone of light, the Grail. In the Holy Grail descends again what has remained of the world of light, of Eden, out of the starry heights to the Earth. In the Holy Grail there lives the seed of light of Eden, which can grow in the Earth as a seed of new heavenly light. Past and future of the plant are in the seed; past and future meet in the Holy Grail.

The meaning of the pictures is only revealed to him who does not take all this literally, but knows in the soul-light how to read the light of Christmas. And only in freedom can the soul open itself to this light. The pictures are to speak for themselves in such a way that at their warmth the heart can be kindled and the soul open up.

Queen Māyā: the Christmas-Mystery in the Indian Flower-Garden

(*Die Christengemeinschaft*, 1. Jg. No. 9. Dez. 1924. 254-58.)

The Mysteries of Birth and of Death

In human life, birth and death are two tremendous Mystery portals when the Sun of Christ shines over them. 'We come from the Mother and go to the Father'—a cosmic Mystery is contained in these words, when we know how to take them in the sense of Christ. A new connection between the story of birth and the story of the death is then revealed in the Gospels.

Facing everything pre-Christian, the revelation of death through Christ is new. It was the Mystery that the disciples at first could not grasp, as it was linked with the words, 'I go to the Father' (John 14:28). In earthly death, in earthly depths revealing the Mystery of the cosmic Father, Christ could say, 'No one comes to the Father, but through me.' Consequently, we do not find in any pre-Christian religion that which was revealed only through Golgotha. Indian legends movingly tell the story of Buddha's death, his dissolving into the great *nirvāna*, the primal foundations of the world. Buddha's *nirvāna* is no passing through the depths of the earthly element as in the death on Golgotha; it does not lead, like Golgotha, to resurrection and transformation, but to the dissolution of the earthly element. Buddha disappeared from the Earth into *nirvāna* returning forever back into the realm out of which his mother received him into earthly life. In Christ's deed on Golgotha the doors of death were opened; in Buddha's *nirvāna* the portal of birth was closed. Thus in the story of death the Christian and the Indian story of salvation separate. The gospel of death and resurrection has nothing corresponding to it with Buddha.[355]

It is different with the birth story. It leads us into the Mysteries of pre-birth which already in the pre-Christian times was present. These are the Mysteries concerning which, already before Golgotha, Christ-Jesus discussed with Nicodemus at midnight (John 3:3-7), and which He presumed he knew. Through these Mysteries the initiate glimpsed into the human paradisal, primordial past, into the light-filled heights of his spiritual origins. The revelation of death opened the gaze into a distant human future, of a new and transformed Earth, as it opened to the spiritual eye of the Apocalyptist. In the Mystery of

Easter the transformed Earth formed the resurrection body of Christ; in the Mystery of Christmas we behold the radiant Earth still in the light of Paradise that condensed into the body of the divine Child, the pure virginal element of the cosmos, unclouded by the Fall of Man.

Mother and Child

In death the cosmic Father is revealed; in birth the great Mother speaks to us. In cosmic sublimity and cosmic glory they stand; before Raphael there stands the Mystery of the Virgin veiled since eternity, when he bequeathed to us the Sistine Madonna. And poetically the cloudy veil of the divine Virgin weaves in the songs of Mary in Novalis, as also in a more hidden manner in his other creations.

Not only in the Christian era were such pictures beheld as the cosmic Imagination of the Virgin with Child. As the expression of deep cosmic Mysteries it lived in early Egypt, in those pictorial depictions of the goddess Isis, who carries the child Horus in her arms. At a Christianized stage, the connection with Michael's combat with the dragon arises afresh in the Apocalypse, in beholding the woman clothed with the Sun. She is giving birth to the infant boy and has the Moon under her feet (Chapter 12). The Apocalypse, which in other sections uncovers further Mysteries of Easter, has here its Christmas episode.

Thus the pre-Christian era already knew the great Christmas-Mystery, the Mystery of the Virgin and of the Christmas-Child. Not only was a picture beheld for the mystical experience of the spiritual re-birth, the 'birth of the child in the lap of the soul'. In the early Mystery-centres, the endeavour was to guide the birth of the one being initiated, of the spiritual leader and teacher called to announce the cosmic Mysteries. [The candidate] himself experienced this second birth in himself, in such a way that he beheld the Light of the World as the Christmas-Child in an unsoiled, undarkened conception not sullied by the elements of earthly passion.

At the beginning of the [Grimms'] fairy tale of 'Snow White' we feel echoing something of these Mysteries of Christmas and of birth of the early Mysteries.[356] The Christian story of the Holy Night is so to speak but a closing and crowning earthly-physical revelation of that which as content of the early Mysteries already lived in pre-Christian Mystery-centres. As the last and highest, not the only earthly revelation of the great Holy-Night revelation of mankind, we recognize the birth of Jesus of Nazareth. In what is told in the Indian legends of the *birth story of the Buddha* lies the highest of its pre-Christian revelations.[357]

The Christian and Indian stories of death are different; with the birth stories the similarity is inwardly founded.

The outer circumstances of the two birth-stories are different. Jesus is born in a place of poverty, in a stable. The Indian prince, who in later life became the Enlightened One, the Buddha, was born in a flowering garden during the tropical splendour of spring. And this difference of the outer historical circumstances is at the same time a *picture* for the difference of the human and earthly situations into which the Indian Holy One and Christ-Jesus were born. But beyond this as a decisive similarity we find in both birth-stories the great Christmas Mystery of conception through the Holy Spirit. The Christmas story of the Mysteries helps us see the virginal-maternal element of the cosmos, the Mysteries of pre-birth, in the paradisal primordial human past in the heights of light. This virginal-motherly element of the cosmos, the feminine, cosmic primordial power, the ancient Indian called Māyā.

The immaculate power

Māyā, miraculous power, cosmic magic power, creator-power of the Imaginative power of the spirit, was for the Indian the feminine element, out of whose lap the cosmic master-builder makes the cosmic forms to arise. Only in later Indian philosophy is Māyā merely the illusion of the world, in contrast to which Brahman, the paternal substance of the world, is seen as the only real entity. But originally Māyā is the virginal, maternal entity of the world. This same word Māyā, otherwise not used in India as a female name, becomes the name for the mother of the last and greatest Indian initiate in pre-Christian times, of the Buddha.

Already the name Māyā reminds one of the Christian name *Maria*, Mary. And the key to many secrets that the name Mary contains in itself lies in the Indian Māyā. The Mystery of conception by the Holy Spirit that was misunderstood becomes completely clear in the birth legend of the Buddha. There it is quite apparent that the Mystery of this conception does not mean there is no father—if it were meant to go against nature, what meaning would the genealogies of Luke and Matthew have that so clearly point towards the *father*? But the element of earthly passion, the sickness of sin, is eliminated with this ['immaculate'] conception. The consciousness of the mother does not consist of the feelings that arise here on Earth, but only that which out of heavenly heights descends by grace on to her; she feels herself as the pure receiving vessel.

From here it is only one step to that great Imagination, with which in later Christian times this Mystery was clothed, to the picture of the *Holy Grail*. In the Holy Grail lives the pure virginal, earthly element, which could receive the rays of the cosmic, primordial light. That which during the plunge into the abyss fell as a precious stone out of Lucifer's crown, so the legend relates,[358] was carried by hosts of angels on the sacred, consecrated night on to the Earth and hidden in a secret, consecrated place. Only the pure virgin can become the bearer of the Grail. In the highest sense, the bodily sheath of the divine child, woven out of the noblest substances of the cosmos, is itself the Holy Grail. And the one in whom the virginal force of the cosmos lives in the purest way becomes the Mother of that Child.

Queen Māyā

Out of paradisal heights, out of what mankind was before the Fall of Man, out of the supersensory realms of light, the Child of the cosmic Holy Night came down to Earth, to the vessel of the virginal, unsullied Earth. In a dream, so the Indian legend relates, Queen Māyā was transported to those paradisal heights. In the picture of the highest snowy mountains of the Earth, the icy climes of the Himalayas she beheld the heights of light, out of which the being of the future Buddha descended to the Earth. She was received there by goddesses, led to a lake she was bathed clean of all earthly dust. Then she was anointed by them and dressed in heavenly raiment adorned with flowers. In dream she was taken to ever-higher regions, finally arriving on a silver mountain where, coming from a golden mountain, the future Buddha approached in the form of a young, white elephant—symbol of the highest initiate. Bowing full of devotion before the mother-to-be, the Bodhisattva entered on her right side the womb of the Queen Māyā. In super-earthly bliss, the Queen awoke out of her dream.[359]

In this fragrant, etheric picture the Indian legend relates the 'conception by the holy spirit'. It is the holy spirit of the Bodhisattva himself, descending to earthly incarnation, who in the earthly realm leads and guides all the events. He himself from the higher worlds decided the time and place of the earthly birth and sought the suitable parents for this earthly incarnation. The ray of the divine eye fell on Māyā, the young Shakya princess, who is pure, without guile, full of divine grace, the epitome of sweet maidenly virtue. The legend praises her smiling countenance, her beautiful brow, her lovely voice, her immaculate stature, her kindliness and gentleness. She is presented in Indian culture as 'free of the weaknesses of her sex'.[360]

The Indian, who is otherwise ever inclined to see in everything feminine only the effects of the Fall of Man and the forces of temptation, beholds in the picture of the young Queen Māyā, the Mother of the Buddha, the virginal virtue of the cosmos itself that is not darkened through the Fall of Man. The glorification of Māyā in the Indian legend can be felt as a premonition of that which only through Christ can be brought as a reinstating of the feminine element towards the spirit. In the virgin, in the purified feminine element returned to its height, the Indian already intuited the divine Mystery, the esoteric side of the world.

The effective grace of the holy spirit rayed around Queen Māyā already before the heavenly-earthly conception. The legend tells, in the house where she dwelt everything was bare and pure, harmful animals avoided the place, wild birds came from the Himalayas and sang on the gables, trees blossomed out of season, ponds covered themselves with lotus flowers, stocks remained inexhaustible, musical instruments sounded by themselves, vessels shimmered in enhanced brilliance, and a wonderful, glorious shining light of Sun and Moon rayed over the whole house.[361]

Thus the rays of light of the spiritual world reach the mother-to-be. Maidenly seclusion fills her whole being—that 'seclusion' that Meister Eckhart[362] speaks of so finely, that was also in the Virgin Mary. Smiling, she appears before her husband asking him to be allowed to take on herself a vow of modesty. No demands of love should the king demand of her at this time. Resting on a bed of flowers, where no noise of the outer world reached her, no word of anger or argument was audible, she passes the hours, giving herself to lovely pictures, listening to gentle sounds, breathing sweet scents. Goddesses strewed her with heavenly flowers and heavenly maidens glide around her as she rested on her bed of flowers. A tremendous dazzling light filled all the worlds when the Bodhisattva descended out of heavenly heights. Sun and Moon paled before this light, which penetrated into the Underworld, there easing the sufferings of the damned. All lower feelings were silenced in people, and a warming ray of love reached into every heart.

The Holy Grail

Something of the paradisal light and shimmer of the Grail certainly also lies upon this Indian narration. Is not the picture of the Holy Grail that appeared before us in the cosmic Mystery of the Holy Night, of Christmas, somehow already particularly to be found in India? That this meaning of the Grail, whereby it becomes the vessel in which Joseph of Arimathea received the blood out of the wounds of the Redeemer cannot apply in India is obvious. This meaning cannot, of course, already exist before Golgotha. But before it became the vessel for the blood, the Grail was the heavenly precious gemstone, the focal point, the raying power of the primordial light of the cosmos. In the form of this gemstone, it slipped with the Fall of Lucifer out of the crown of the Angel of Light at the primordial beginning of the world. We can seek *this* aspect of the Grail in pre-Christian times.

A legend[363] tells that amongst the treasures which the Queen of Sheba presented to King Solomon, the Holy Grail was found as a wonderful chalice, or bowl, made from a bright green gemstone, beryl or emerald.[364] After what arose out of the connection of the Grail with the Mystery of the Holy Night, we can feel it as something deeply meaningful when we encounter this bowl of beryl in the Buddha legend,[365] too, where the Mystery of the immaculate conception and birth become the object of study.

As long as she bore the future Buddha in her womb, Queen Māyā lived in bright divine dwellings—so the legend tells—in 'higher worlds' as we would say. In a wonderful manner, she is seen at the same time in all the dwellings of the gods. (Compare here what Goethe says in *Wilhelm Meister's Journeyman Years* concerning Makaria's sojourn in spiritual, planetary spheres.) The Bodhisattva himself rests in the meditation position in the womb of his mother. So that no earthly impurity may soil him, he is surrounded by a housing of radiant beryl, which after his birth is taken up by the gods (angels) into Brahman's heaven and is kept there as a sacred relic. (In the Christian Holy Night of Christmas, in the holy night of Titurel [the Grail king], we could add, in the sense of the Grail legend, that jewel which was kept until then in the higher world by angels, is brought to the Earth.)

During the night in which the future Buddha enters the body of the mother, a lotus grows out of the Earth that reaches to Brahman's heaven. But only Brahman himself can see it with supersensible eye. The essence of strength of the whole universe is collected in this lotus as a drop of honey. Brahman himself gives the child in his mother's body this drop of honey in a *chalice made of beryl*. The legend says, no being would have been capable of taking up this cosmic nourishment. Only the Bodhisattva standing in his final incarnation is able, because in numerous earthly lives he has accomplished deeds of love, and did not tire of giving comfort and relief to suffering beings. A host of angels surround mother and child constantly; from all regions of the world high beings approach to honour the child.[366]

With the beryl housing which encloses the becoming earthly sheaths of the child as well as the chalice made out of beryl, which the god Brahman offers to the child in his mother's body, we feel we are quite close to the Grail Imagination, as far as this Imagination can exist at all before Golgotha. The cosmic Mystery of the heavenly Virgin, of the sacred conception, speaks to us in these pictures; the cosmic history of the mother, which otherwise on Earth, because it is darkened there by the Fall of Man, cannot be revealed in its purity.

Because this super-earthly purity, this virginal aspect of the cosmos is revealed in her, Māyā cannot live more than seven days after the birth of her child. In graceful pictures this birth, too, is described for us. It is the time of the first spring, and the grove of Lumbini (the place where still today an ancient memorial stone recalls the birth of the Indian saviour). The grove of Lumbini is completely filled with the scent of blossoms, all the trees flower and supersensible flowers of the gods mix between the earthly flowers. Queen Māyā enters the garden and walks from tree to tree. A fig tree that she approaches bends to the Earth through the spiritual power of the Bodhisattva. Māyā stretches out her right hand and lays hold of a branch (we recall the tree, which according the Christian legend, on the Flight into Egypt, bends towards Mary).

As Māyā thus in graceful stance looks smiling up to heaven, the Bodhisattva steps out of her body on the right side. Heavenly virgins minister to the Queen with their service. Gods shower flowers and fragrant scents. They receive the child and give him his first bath. And again the great glory of light fills the whole world and a ray of divine love penetrates all hearts. In the Christmas story of Luke's Gospel, the shepherds in the field experience something similar.

Queen Māyā herself suffers no pain. Her body shows no sign of birth. During the seven days when she still remains on Earth, heavenly beings attend her. Then she dies and is raised into Indra's heaven. The meaning of her life, to become the mother of the future Buddha, is now fulfilled. The virginal part in her is too sublime to be touched further by the earthly element. The mother of *each* Buddha, the legend say, dies this early death. The soul has sacrificed itself for the becoming of the spirit-child in her womb. In this too lies a deep trait of the ancient Mysteries, which in the fairy tale of Snow White still softly echoes with the death of her mother.

Etheric Formative Forces and Hieroglyphs

(Gäa-Sophia: Jahrbuch der Naturwissenschaftlichen Sektion.
Bd. 1. Dornach 1926. 383-393)

The riddle of the Egyptian and other hieroglyphs will be brought nearer to a true solution when it is recognized how these hiero-glyphs do not only picture outer sensory objects, but how an early imaginative consciousness of mankind still lives in them. At that point where Egyptology today has reached the border of its inter-pretation, the question concerning Egyptian and other hieroglyphs only begins to become interesting for someone who has the cour-age to go beyond that border with anthroposophical methods of research. Significant views open up where the Egyptologist of today does not even see the questions, or allow them to exist, let alone dares to solve them. One may be allowed to express the hope that, fructified by the method of anthroposophical research, Egyptology will one day move on to a future of which it does not dream.

Today the opinion in the realm of scholarly research still goes against such progress with the belief that human consciousness remains the same for all times. One first has to reach the point of applying the insight also to Egypt and the riddle of the hieroglyphs, that human consciousness changes and develops over the course of time.

In the light of anthroposophical research, the essence of the primal Indian consciousness appears as a perceiving of the physical from the ether-body; the *essence of the Egyptian consciousness appears as the per-ceiving of the etheric from the astral body.* If this corresponds to the facts, it seems appropriate to seek such a view on to the world of the etheric also in the Egyptian hieroglyphs. One will then not be satisfied with establishing pictures of outer sensory objects with them (within cer-tain limits that do, of course, exist). Rather, it will be appropriate to pose the question whether what anthroposophical research can say about the *form tendencies of the etheric formative forces*[367] is somehow reflected in the Egyptian hieroglyphs, in the pictorial writing of early peoples in general.

Light-ether

Let us proceed from the form-tendency of the *light-ether*. Concerning this, we find with Dr Wachsmuth, 41f.:

The light-ether to which we refer, which calls forth for the human eye the phenomenon of light (in a manner to be explained later), does in fact induce, among other things, a transverse oscillation; but in addition to what has been said above we must add that this occurrence describes the figure of a triangle (see fig.), so that light-ether, as we shall see when it can exert its effect unhindered in nature, also produces there *triangular forms* there, whereas warmth-ether produces spherical forms ... We may say, then, that an oscillation, a form which is caused by light-ether in a substance-medium, takes the shape of a triangle.

If we compare with this the hieroglyph for 'light, to shine, sunlight' it is usually given in this form:

To this we find with Brugsch[368] the remark, that with this pictogram in larger hieroglyphs each of the rays poured out from the Sun-disc appear as if made up of a series of pyramidal triangles.

Brugsch points out that this form derives from early concepts of how light is thrown and that with both, *benben, belbel,* accompanied by the picture of:

Fig.1. ⌂   Fig.2. △

the obelisk (fig. 1) or the pyramid (fig. 2) presents the *light-source* in the original sense of the word.

In this connection it should also be pointed out that the elongated triangle is the hieroglyph of Sirius.

***

Sun disc

What has been found about the light-ether opens up the question whether the form-tendencies of the other etheric formative forces could not be found in such a way in the hieroglyphs. The circular

Sun-disc connected with the light-beam hieroglyph—the common picture still known as the astronomical symbol for the Sun—we take simply as a picture of the Sun-disc, without at first seeking in it a relationship to the spherical form-tendency of the warmth-ether. However, *objective* connections do exist. That connection of the Sun-disc with the light-triangles, when the etheric formative forces and their form-tendencies live in us, allow us to sense 'warmth-light' as objectively real, as a connection between the light-ether with the warmth-ether.

The obelisk figure of the inscriptions in the private graves in Memphis from the fifth and sixth dynasties (see Brugsch, 256) also show this connection.

That sphere to which this hieroglyph initially relates, is indeed the earthly sphere of the 'warmth-light'.

Half-moon form

What is the situation with the half-moon form-tendency of the sound-ether ⌒ (Wachsmuth, 42f.)? In the 24 Egyptian hieroglyphs for the letters, this forms the *t*-hieroglyph, the Egyptian Tau. The Egyptologist believes everything has been said about this hieroglyph in the picture of the loaf of bread that has been found in it. One could, of course, just as well call this Egyptian form, even if one initially only keeps in view the physical symbol, the horizontal *half-moon form*. And where we too seek the physical similitude for this *t*-hieroglyph—though we look for it not in the physical but in the etheric world—its form corresponds with that which Wachsmuth gives for the form-tendency of the sound-ether. And this agreement appears to be more than merely a coincidence, when we consider that the *t*-sound indeed expresses that which *forms*, that which *fashions* (whereas the *s*-sound initially expresses only the streaming of substance), exactly like what is said of the sound-ether, that its forces are those *which fashion matter*, cf. Wachsmuth, 42:

The third ether is *chemical ether,* or *sound-ether*. Its forces, that is, cause the chemical processes, differentiations, dissolutions, and unions of substances; but also—though, as it were, through activities in another field—its forces transmit to us sensory-perceptible sound. The inner kinship of these two spheres of action will be clear to us from the phenomenon of Chladni's sound-forms. For it is musical sound which causes the uniting together, the orders and forms, of substance and bodies of substance.

We shall now return to this connection of the Egyptian *t*-hieroglyph with the essence of the sound-ether in looking at the Egyptian name for Isis and the hieroglyph for Isis.

***

With all this it is important to keep in view that Egyptian hieroglyphs not only concern the 24 hieroglyphic sounds for the written signs of the 24 speech-sounds of the alphabet, but the much greater number of purely *pictorial hieroglyphs*. These either present linguistic meanings directly and on their own merits, or suggest a supplement to a hieroglyph of the sound of speech. It can even be that a pictorial hieroglyph, which could express a word on its own merits, just presents single sounds of this word—in no way all of them—in hieroglyphs of speech-sounds. This should be said right at the beginning so the current view can come about through the choice and grouping of the hieroglyphs, suggesting connections which lie beyond what is clear from the mere script. It could be that we are led to the deeper meaning of several Egyptian hieroglyphs precisely at this point.

For such contemplations, the Mystery names of the divinities in particular are most revealing.[369] According to their nature, these names are also most revealing for the spiritual primal significance of the speech-sounds, for the 'divine essence of the speech-sounds'. From this viewpoint we will look at the sacred name of *Isis*, along with Osiris the central divinity of the Egyptian Mysteries. Amongst the many names expressing the nature of the goddess Isis (see Brugsch, 646f.), such as 'the one from the primal beginning', 'the primal picture of all pictures', 'the queen of goddesses and women', 'the mistress of the year's beginning' (relationship to the star Sirius), 'the brightest amongst the shining ones', 'queen of the Earth', 'mistress of warmth', 'mother of god', 'lady of the birth-chamber', 'giver of life', 'leading mistress of magic', 'mistress of love'; the last-mentioned in particular expresses most directly the being of Isis. Everything lying in the realm of the forces of love belongs to the being of Isis; the veil of Isis is none other than that which is spread over the Mystery of love. (In Goethe's *Fairy tale*, the Green Snake speaks to the Old Man with the Lamp, whispering into his ear; concerning the same mystery Fabel and Sphinx hold a dialogue in the fairy tale which Klingsor tells [in Novalis, *Heinrich von Ofterdingen*, Chapter VIII]:

> 'What is the eternal mystery?'
> 'Love.'
> 'With whom does it rest?'
> 'With Sophia.'

Sophia, however, is Isis, the Christened Isis, Isis-Sophia. The mystery of love, that in Isis is ever more deeply veiled, is revealed in Christ. Inwardly love is the *'I'-awakener*; outwardly, she is the being *forming* creatively the Earth-element; both lie in the nature and in the name of Isis. And certainly, if we look to the sound-qualities of the name Isis [we find] the forming of material more in the consonants of the name, the 'I'-awakener in the vowels.

Of the three consonants of the Egyptian name of Isis 'H-S-T',[370] the first aspirate, still standing on the boundary of the inaudible (Hebrew aleph), in Egyptian delineated through the hieroglyph of the *eagle*— and in the sibilant speech-sound marking the counter-pole, through the hieroglyph of the *snake*—expresses the still undifferentiated, unrevealed divine-spiritual element. S is then the streaming of substance, T the fulfilment in form. It is now indicative and significant that the name Isis, which in Egyptian alone through the picture of the bull or of the throne can be delineated:

is also so expressed that this hieroglyph-meaning inserted as a speech-sound hieroglyph becomes one—only one—of the sounds of the name. It is precisely that sound whose hieroglyphic form reminds us of the form-tendency of the material-fashioning sound-ether, the *t*. Beneath the *t*-hieroglyph an egg-shape is placed, which expresses that Isis is a female being, a goddess. Thus there arises the pictorial script:

The name Isis

This hieroglyphic pictogram of the name of Isis becomes extremely eloquent when we think of the following. Let us look first from the aspect of the ether-teaching on the fact of the Earth's development, which in *Esoteric/Occult Science* is described as 'the splitting-off of the Sun'. The higher kinds of ether, life-ether and sound-ether, remain above with the Sun, light-ether and warmth-ether remain with the Earth. Especially in that fact of the development of the Earth described in the Bible as the Fall of Man, the separation of the upper and lower ethers becomes complete. The *Tree of Life*, which from then on was denied to man remains connected to the upper kinds of ether, life-ether and sound-ether (cf. the lecture-cycles by Rudolf Steiner, *Genesis* [GA 122] and *Christ and the Human Soul* [GA 155], and others). The human being succumbing to the forces of death of the Tree of Knowledge unfolds on the Earth in *light-ether* and *warmth-ether*. All human thinking and consciousness bound to the Tree of Knowledge lies in the sphere of the light-ether and warmth-ether.

The separation of the upper and lower ethers in the separation of the Sun and the Earth is mirrored on Earth again in the separation of the sexes. In the paradisal time and pre-paradisal age of man, the Tree of Life and the Tree of Knowledge, as well as the feminine and masculine principles of the complete human being were united. With the separation, the Eternal Feminine remains in the sphere of the Sun in the higher ethers, the Eternal Feminine and the Eternal Masculine remain from then on like the Tree of Life and the Tree of Knowledge. The earthly feminine principle of today is not the Eternal Feminine, but it is the feminine principle placed into the sphere of the Eternal Masculine. The veil of the Mystery, the veil of Isis, is still spread over the Eternal Feminine today. The Mystery of Isis is none other than the mystery of love and the Eternal Feminine. The Egyptians called this Eternal Feminine Isis. In the sense of the ether-teaching, the sphere of this *Eternal Feminine* belonging to the Tree of Life and the Sun is that sphere of the *life-ether and sound-ether.*

Seen from this vantage point, the above pictogram of the name of Isis appears doubly meaningful. We have the equation Isis = Eternal Feminine + life-ether and sound-ether. We found the sound-ether in the *t*-hieroglyph ⌒, the life-ether we can find in the preceding part of the Isis-hieroglyph, in the image of the throne ⌐┐, which on its own can also mean Isis.

The ⌐⌐ , initially means 'seat' or 'throne', yet this means as little as does the 'loaf-of-bread'-form of the ⌒, as an interpretation of the form in the sense of the etheric formative forces, quite apart from the fact that 'throne' does also point to a specific exalted region of the divine-spiritual world in which the material-forming forces are at home. In the realm of the etheric formative forces alone we find the true being of Isis (also where she becomes the 'fashioner, the former of material'). We have to look to the etheric formative forces if we want to establish the deeper meaning of the Isis hieroglyph.

What initially concerns the form-tendency of the life-ether is presented (Wachsmuth, 42f.) as approaching the square form. Not only the narrow sense of the square, or cubic form, but it is shown in all the related formations, for example, in the salt-crystal, also cited by Wachsmuth. They also ingeniously interplay, so that sometimes small temple-buildings arise. Forms like those of the Isis-throne hieroglyph are not infrequent. The form duly belongs in the realm of form-tendencies of the life-ether. (Here, too, the complicated formations given by Wachsmuth, 214, should be mentioned.)

After what the previous results show, the relationship of Isis as the Eternal Feminine to the essence of the life-ether and sound-ether in the sense of the etheric formative forces, it must appear to us as really significant when we find linked in the written images of the name of Isis the hieroglyph that expresses the feminine as such (the egg form) with two other hieroglyphs. The one recalls the form-tendency of the life-ether, the other the form-tendency of the sound-ether.

***

Isis and Nephthys

Isis has a sister Nephthys (Egyptian *nebthat, nebthit*, the 'mistress of the house'), who presents her [Isis'] more sub-earthly, chthonic counterpart. To Isis belongs the upper life-element, the visible earthly element, to Nephthys the sub-earthly element (Brugsch 735). Especially from the viewpoint of the ether-teaching, this is understandable when we remind ourselves that in the firm earthly element, the transformed, as it were enchanted, life-ether, and in the liquid element, the transformed sound-ether is contained. The being of Nephthys presents the reverse and completion of the being of Isis, according to the earthly element. To Isis birth and life is allotted, to Nephthys dying.

The Festival of Isis is celebrated in the autumn, that of Nephthys in the spring, which makes sense particularly from the anthroposophical perspective.

From here, it appears remarkable to see how the Nephthys hieroglyph is a reversal of the Isis hieroglyph: the square construction of the life-ether form, which with the Isis hieroglyph turns to the outside, with the Nephthys hieroglyph is turned to the inside. The half-moon form of the sound-ether with Isis is turned downwards, with Nephthys it turns upwards:

This relationship appears the more remarkable through the fact that the Nephthys hieroglyph has to do with a union of pictorial hieroglyphs (the sound-ether form has nothing to do with the *t*-hieroglyph here, but ⌣ *neb* means 'mistress', *het* (see fig.) 'the house'.

Here in particular it can be seen how a hieroglyph in certain circumstances can stand not only as the representative of the value of its sounds, but for quite different reasons and contexts.

***

How the union of sound-ether and life-ether speaking to us out of the Isis-hieroglyph helps us to look into depths of the Egyptian primal Mysteries becomes clear in an exceptional manner in Lecture 3 of Rudolf Steiner's lecture-cycle *Mysteries of the East and Christianity* [GA 144. Berlin, 5 Feb. 1913]. It is mentioned there how Isis is experienced in the primordial, flowering time of the Egyptian Mysteries as giving birth to, or speaking, the eternal cosmic word: Osiris. In cosmic life and cosmic harmonies, it is said there—but this means in the sense of the ether-teachings, in life-ether and sound-ether—the being of Isis and Osiris is revealed. The Osiris hieroglyph arises when the eye of the seeing-consciousness is added to the Isis-throne hieroglyph.

In this, however, consists the tragedy of the Egyptian as well as all pre-Christian Mysteries, that the archetypal revelation became increasingly veiled during the course of time. In the above-mentioned lecture, Steiner stresses that the year 1322 [BCE][371] meant the decisive crisis for the Egyptian Mysteries. It is the year in which Moses led the Hebrews out of Egypt, taking with him the essential secrets of the Egyptian Mysteries. From then on, for the initiate who approaches the 'shores of the wide expanses of the cosmos', Isis is the mute, the silent, the veiled goddess. From then on a veil of Mystery covers her originally revealed being. Out of which element this veil and that being are woven, is beautifully and clearly expressed in the lecture:

> No Osiris could be born in the later time, no cosmic harmony could sound, no cosmic word explained that which was now revealed as cosmic warmth and cosmic light.[372]

In the lecture-cycle *The Gospel of St John*[373] the connection of the cosmic word with the light-ether was already explained; cosmic harmony is the revelation of the sound-ether. Cosmic warmth and cosmic light are the revelation of warmth-ether and light-ether. In other words: out of warmth-ether and light-ether the veil is woven which covers the being of the mysterious goddess: light-ether and sound-ether. This is still today the situation of human consciousness, as long as the soul, through the power of Christ, has not begun to lift once again a part of the veil.

***

The veil of Isis

Here the question arises for this 'veil of Isis', woven out of warmth-ether and light-ether, whether perhaps we likewise find a clear hieroglyphic expression for the 'being of Isis', woven out of life-ether and sound-ether. In the Egyptian [documents] this does not in actual fact appear to be the case. However, as is shown above, the triangular form can be found in a hieroglyph pointing towards the essence of the light-ether. Consequently, it was of interest to note a discovery of the seismographer Rudolf Falb [1838-1903], in his remarkable book *The land of the Incas in its significance for the prehistory of language and writing,*[374] concerning ancient primal cultures of humanity, possibly pointing back to Atlantis. He mentions an inscription discovered on an ancient Peruvian temple-monument, the prehistoric Sun-gate monument of Tiahuanaco on Lake Titicaca. Two triangles are linked to a circle (67f.); this, in the sense of the ether-teaching, connects the form-sign of the light-ether with the warmth-ether, with the *veil of Isis*. As the linguistic interpretation of that pictorial hiero-glyph, Falb finds the word *sisira*, in which he believes he recog-nizes one of the primal words of humanity, a true 'bridge from the New World to the Ancient World'. Somehow this word glim-mering in many nuances of meaning always has something to do with 'veil', 'woven fabric'. And regarding the Egyptian language (which I could not yet check myself) Falb suggests the meaning of *sisi* 'woven fabric', thence *sisira* would mean 'Sun-veil', 'weav-ing of the whole'. With Falb we also frequently find the meaning of this word as 'veil of mist', the watery veil of the light, the 'tear pearls of the Sun'. And on the other hand, the rosy sunrise and red sunset is also associated with the veil of mist, or veil of duskiness, especially in the mountains when this appearance that today is called *Alpenglühen*, 'alpine glow' appears, which for the early people was something thoroughly sacred, revealed in the red of the mountains (Falb 433).[375] From this Peruvian meaning of the word *sisira* 'red of the mountain', there easily arises for Falb the meaning 'red colour' that is the same word in Hebrew (only with other vowels): s*hasher* [Jer. 22:14, usually translated as 'vermilion']. We recall that red is also the colour-tendency of the warmth-ether, as well as the sphere is its form-tendency, in the same way as in the mountains the Sun-veil is revealed as red in colour, so the 'tear-pearls of the Sun' become there 'frozen Sun-tears' icicles and hoar-frost. From here we can understand the meaning of the word *śiśira* (spoken, 'shishira', in Skr. (Pali *sisira*), frost, hoar-frost, ice, cold time of the year. When her veil of light becomes a veil of ice, Isis, the virgin of the stars, appears as the 'ice maiden'. Mysteries of the 'cold light' (Wachsmuth, 126, 130f.) are connected with those of the sound-ether of the frozen cos-mic harmonies, enchanted into the liquid element of the Earth. Falb connects the archetypal meaning of this word *sisira* 'veil', or 'sheath/ covering', also with that of the Gk. *sisyra*, meaning 'smutty covering [a cloak of goat-hair]'.

From the etheric, the Gk. meaning of the word leads us more into the physical realm. If we want to rid ourselves of the pictures and comparisons of the sensory world and concern ourselves purely with the etheric and cosmic essence of *sisira*, then with Falb we find in it the 'veil of Isis', which covers over the higher essence of the things for us, covers the higher element of life. In the sense of the ether-teaching, this higher element of life is given as life-ether and sound-ether, the veil covering the higher element is composed of light-ether and warmth-ether, and the Egyptian hieroglyph of Isis:

speaking to us of the Eternal Feminine in life-ether and sound-ether, finds its beautiful counterpart in that Peruvian hieroglyph indicating the 'veil of Isis'.

This hieroglyph clearly brings before our eyes the connection of the light-ether with the warmth-ether and shows us how these forms, brought near to us today again through anthroposophical teaching, lived meaningfully in a primal time of human consciousness.

***

The inscription, always mentioned by Rudolf Falb, on the monument of the temple-gate of Tiahuanaco, when viewed more closely, can show us the connection of all the four etheric formative forces. On the chest of the depicted Sun-divinity, a plate is found, according to Falb the belly of a ship, which on its front part runs out into an upwards-turned head of a whale, or head of a sea-monster (cf. Falb 54).

We are concerned less with the whale's head than with the fact that the *anchor sign* contained in it can be seen as the connection of a sound-ether form with the *t*-form. (In the Egyptian language we found the form of the sound-ether itself as a *t*-hieroglyph; in the forming-fashioning quality of the '*t*' there always lies the connection to the sound-ether.) In the rear part of the assumed ship we find a little square and a larger rectangle, that is, the forms of the life-ether in full clarity, so that the whole can indeed appear as a uniting of the four etheric formative forces. On this breast-plate of the Sun-divinity we can consequently find presented:

above the formative forces of life-ether and sound-ether,
below the forces of the light-ether and warmth-ether;

a true symbol of the supersensory-etheric nature of man.

Egypt in the Light of the Grave and Resurrection

(*Die Christengemeinschaft*. 3. Jg. April 1926. 8-12.)

Closer than any other of the great pre-Christian Mysteries, the Egyptian Mysteries approach Christ, the great fact of Christ, death–resurrection. The Indian knows in a certain way the cosmic, creating Christ (which he calls by the name of Vishvakarman, or Twashtar, 'the cosmic carpenter', and other names). But he has no relationship to that which Christ means for the *Earth*, because he himself has no real relationship yet to the Earth as it has become through the Fall of Man. Consequently, he misses seeing the event of Golgotha, the great Christ-event of earthly history. The Iranian Mystery-culture of Zarathustra completely inspired out of the Sun-Mystery, reflecting the age of the Sun, looks in a magnificent manner on this Christ-event, on the turning point of the Earth. In December we published one of the great Christ-prophecies of the Avesta [see p. 146f. above]—yet everything still sounds as an indication of a very far-distant future. The immediate link with what takes place on the Earth through Christ is still missing.

In contrast to this, the great thing about the *Egyptian Mysteries* is that it contains this direct link. In these Mysteries, seen as a whole in their development stretching through long periods of time, everything seems focused towards the great Christ-event of death–resurrection. Thereby, it is certainly significant that Egypt outwardly, geographically, borders on that country in which the historic earthly events of Christ have taken place, that land whose people were called to offer the Christ his bodily instrument. The story of Moses shows what connection of destiny this folk had with Egypt already in pre-Christian times. Moses was an initiate of the Egyptian Mysteries. When in these Mysteries the early powers of vision dimmed and this darkening became a crisis for the spiritual life in Egypt, and soon after also for the political life, he took the Egyptian temple Mysteries with him to Palestine and connected them with what was revealed to him in the 'Burning Bush', in the voice of the divine 'I'. The Christ-Mystery of the Burning Bush itself goes back to a Christ-Mystery of the Egyptian Mysteries. And it is no chance, but of quite deep, inner significance that as a boy the Jesus of Matthew's Gospel, the same person in whom spiritual research finds connections to Zarathustra's being, in early childhood goes to Egypt, to the land which with its own Zarathustra past and Christ-future is so mysteriously connected. In their origin the Egyptian Mysteries, too, were inspired out of the star-wisdom of Zarathustra.

The primal Indian Mysteries took place in the ether-heights more over the Earth than on the Earth. Even today, when after millennia they have fallen into decadence, they still lie there always mysteriously invisible, as if in the air, in the spiritual atmosphere of India. An English protestant millionaire, whom I met years ago in Berlin, told me how strongly he always felt this in India. What he perceived there he called the 'eternal India'. In early Egypt the progress of the Mysteries was different. The Mysteries united ever more deeply and finally completely with the Earth. They were as if lowered into the grave of the Earth. Even today they still rest as if in their grave. All the sphinxes and pyramids, all the monuments of the world of Egyptian tombs hold mysterious dialogue with the stars in the wonderful clear air of Egypt.

What appears so dead to us today, was once in the distant primal times blossoming life. Like a jewel of unique beauty the primal Mysteries of Egypt shine in the spiritual heaven of mankind. Egypt can appear to us as the most beautiful blossom of the entire pre-Christian Mysteries. For a long age – since about the middle of the second millennium BCE—this blossom has sunk into the grave.

Already in the third millennium, when a sublime star-wisdom (planetary wisdom) was living in the Egyptian Mysteries but already facing its end, the tremendous pyramids were built, which still today astonish the visitor to Egypt. Already then Egypt received its image of graves and tombs, still belonging to it today, set up by the prophetic gaze of the great initiates. It was indeed the tragedy of all pre-Christian Mysteries, that they signified precisely a spiritual life finding itself *in decline*. And in Egypt, so it appears, the fact was looked into quite consciously. Isis, who at one time in the far distant past spoke with the initiates of cosmic Mysteries, became silent and veiled her countenance. The veil of mystery, the veil of Isis, the black covering of death increasingly spread over the Egyptian Mysteries. When in later ages the initiate still remained at the sacred Mystery-centre, he beheld Isis as the silent, masked goddess, out of whose mouth no longer sounded the cosmic word, no longer could Osiris be born. Increasingly the horror of graves and tombs was experienced by the initiate at the sacred Mystery-centre, the darkness and loneliness and anxiety of death. And the number ever decreased of those who had the courage to meet this darkness of the grave and the loneliness of death.

If we place ourselves with the eye of spiritual vision into that far-off primal time, which was also the time before the first pyramids were built, still long before there were any pyramids and mummies in Egypt, everything was still in spiritual, blossoming life. That time is described as the fixed-star wisdom (preceding the time of planetary wisdom). The nocturnal experience of the Mysteries was not yet the night of the grave and of death. It was still the sacred, consecrated night. In that sacred, consecrated night the initiated still experienced the cosmic Tree of Light, the cosmic star-spangled Tree of Life. Even if he was not looking into the outer starry heavens, he experienced his own human existence in a universal, expanded consciousness, behold-ing this great cosmic starry Tree. And when he looked up to the outer starry heaven, this starry heaven showed him not only the little points of light which the human eye of today sees in it. A rich and mysteri-ous pictorial script of the heavens was revealed to his clairvoyant eye and feeling-soul. Human faces beheld him out of this pictorial script; in the human picture and human countenance his own soul, the soul of humanity, was revealed out of the starry heavens. He called this shining, virginal, starry picture, this starry countenance of the soul of humanity that shone to him out of the starry heavens, *Isis*. When he beheld this he felt a wonderfully warm, enlivening and health-giv-ing breath of cosmic love from the stars. Illuminated by [the cosmic] Christ's light, millennia later, after the great turning point, the disciple of love was able again to perceive the vision of the early fixed-star wisdom, and described it for us in Revelation 12.

In the space available it is not possible to show how the pictures in the decline of the Egyptian Mysteries slowly pale. They took on different forms in various periods of the development of the Myster-ies, in order finally to sink completely into the grave. It was Christ's revelation which in the wonderful Isis star-pictures of primordial time radiated from cosmic widths to the open eye of the seer. The human 'I' at that time did not dwell so deeply in the earthly human sheaths as it does today. It still shone as from cosmic widths towards man; it was itself still the star shining in cosmic distances. In order that man would find earthly freedom in the earthly 'I', the early pictures had to become dim and pale for him. From cosmic widths, Christ entered into the mortal sheaths of earthly man, in order to give Himself to crucifixion. We can find: not only the physical nailing, the piercing of the hands and feet on Golgotha is this crucifixion, but it already begins when Moses leads the Hebrews out of Egypt. Already then the ancient thinking of the gods and the Mystery-vision had to become increasingly crucified, so that in the earthly thinking that Moses taught his people, the human being could awaken to earthly freedom, and to the earthly 'I'. This was the deeper reason why with Moses' exodus, the Egyptian Mystery-being went into an unstoppable decline, or perhaps more correctly: why the exodus had to fall during the time of the decline of the Egyptian Mysteries.

The divine thinking of the early Egyptian Mysteries did not possess the possibility in itself to enter that epoch of humanity of earthly thinking that had now arisen. This epoch could not take place at the consecrated Egyptian Mystery-centre. Rudolf Steiner once said that if the Christ had incarnated during the time of the Indian, Zarathustrian, or Egyptian Mysteries, with the ancient Indians, Persians or Egyptians—according to cosmic laws this is not possible, but assuming it were possible—then in those countries it would never have led to a crucifixion of Christ. Instead, in an unending deep reverence, these Mystery-peoples would have revered Christ. Their initiates would have brought the gold of their wisdom to him, would have sacrificed the incense and myrrh of their reverence. In order to go towards His crucifixion, Christ had to go to that folk into which he actually did incarnate. And so the 'exodus from Egypt' was a necessity.

We can feel: what had happened up to then continued in Palestine. The wisdom of the fixed stars, the wisdom of the planets, and beholding the elemental world, followed each other in the history of development of the Egyptian Mysteries. What now followed, the crucifixion of the thinking of the gods, for the sake of developing thinking on earth could no longer take place on the ground of the early Egyptian Mysteries, it had to seek its venue in that country so historically meaningful for the world, bordering the N.E. of Egypt. It was like a last Christ-phase of the Egyptian Mysteries, what took place in Palestine.[376]

For this reason, from this moment on Egypt lay as if fossilized, as if a splendidly beautiful human body and human corpse had been abandoned by the soul. Since then Egypt has become a great burial ground. And still in the death of the old spiritual life we are astonished at the wonderful beauty of this burial ground; we feel the warm breath of love wafting from the Egyptian burial grounds and burial monuments. Indeed, the ancient Egyptian knew love. How inimitably it speaks out of those gestures where on so many graves the picture of the 'beloved spouse' lays her hand on the shoulder of the husband. And, as Nietzsche reminds us, 'only where there are graves are there resurrections'.[377]

For this reason Christ died for mankind, for this reason ancient divine thinking had to allow itself to be crucified in human earthly thinking, that out of earthly thinking earthy freedom and the earthly 'I' may come about, which then, once again, in freedom is to become the chalice for a new divine thinking of the future. Not for this reason was the splendour of the old Mysteries sunk, that it be buried in eternity, but that in Christ—which also means in the freedom of the human 'I'—it may experience a new resurrection.

It would be mean thinking concerning Christianity and Christ if we wanted to convince ourselves that we had brought our Christianity so splendidly far, and out of this proud feeling of having brought it so splendidly far, to want to patronize the old 'heathen' Mysteries, or only with a certain condescension recognize their relative greatness. But that signifies for these Mysteries that what the death and the resurrection of Christ over a long period of time gradually dims down, can one day in a distant future of mankind be there again. Only when we look with humility at what today we have already achieved, can we properly experience this future of mankind. On a freer, higher stage of the human 'I' what at one time sank down will be able to be there again.

When we look thus at the Mysteries in the light of Christ, the world of the Egyptian graves also speak of resurrection. No other Mystery-entity was led so deeply into the grave, but no other approached so closely the world of Christ as the Egyptian Mysteries did. In the grave the early Egyptian, Egypt itself, encountered Christ. As a prophecy the early Egyptian experienced there the Christ and the resurrection in Osiris and Horus. As a symbol Osiris speaks of the meaning of resurrection in the light, for us today recalling the butterfly, but which in Egypt was the 'winged beetle' (*cheper*). This for the Egyptian was the symbol of the eternal, in the change of form (as for us it is the metamorphosis of [larvae into] the butterfly). *Cheper*, Germ. *Käfer*, 'beetle', as a verb means 'to become, change oneself, develop oneself'.[378]

With all this an Easter-Mystery is expressed. The Mystery of Easter is especially deeply experienced in Egypt. For this Easter-Mystery is not only simply that of spiritual resurrection. Spiritual resurrection in the death of the natural life we celebrate at Michaelmas. In the time of the resurrected natural life, in the spring, there falls initially the death of the spirit, its sacrifice of itself into the earthly realm: Good Friday and Easter Saturday. Only when we regard this memorial day of Christ's death with complete earnestness and complete devotion, are we able intimately to experience the meaning of the Easter festival. Here we find something like death, like the air of the grave pouring out in brilliant sunshine, in the breathing of the Earth. We feel our very selves dying into this death of Christ, but then we also feel how in this death with Christ something like a breath of health, a breath of recovery streams. By allowing this breath of Christ to be carried into our soul and into our body, we look out in such a way on to the bright spring landscape, so that everything that blooms outside and soon again grows beyond [this stage], may become for us a *picture* of that other, higher spiritual resurrection.

Something of *this* feeling concerning death, that yet already carries in itself the seed of resurrection, also lies over early Egypt. Still on yonder side of the grave, in the kingdom of the dead, the soul of the early Egyptian encounters the sublime Christ-Sun-being, *Osiris*. Through the death of Christ this being comes to us on the Earth. Here we can find this being today in the awake consciousness of our earthly life. And if we find the Christ, by descending quite deeply into our inner world, there is revealed to us, too, pouring out over the Egyptian kingdom of graves, death breathed through with new mysterious life. The kingdom of graves of early Egypt begins to speak to us of the resurrection of early Mystery splendour in the future of mankind.

Notes

1. The German edition was published by Michael Verlag, Munich 1924—Tr.
2. In the light of what follows in Professor Beckh's account, we should perhaps note that Philo of Alexandria (20 BCE – c. 50 CE) perceived that Eve in Genesis represented 'external sensation' (*On the Creation*, Book 3). Whereas Philo is more usually known as an Alexandrian who adopted an allegorising approach to the Scriptures, Beckh's 'Gnostic' is not entirely inappropriate: Philo also outlined a system of emanations from God which are reminiscent of the more directly Gnostic traditions. Jakob Böhme (1575-1624) explicitly founded his own, unique insights into Genesis on the prayerful meditations on speech-sounds. In his extensive treatise on Genesis, *Mysterium Magnum* (1622), Böhme observes (Chap. 30) that the 'v' in Eva (Eve) conveys that the Holy Voice descends into manifestation. Louis-Claude de Saint-Martin (1743-1803) studied theosophical literature and was the first French translator of Jakob Böhme. Antoine Fabre d'Olivet (1767-1825) published the original French version of *The Hebraic Tongue Restored* in 1815—*Ed. note.*
3. Rudolf Steiner, *Man as Symphony of the Creative Word*. Lecture-cycle, Dornach, Oct. 19-Nov. 11, 1923 (GA 230)—*Tr.*
4. The website rsarchive.org is useful—*Tr.*
5. In Böhme's study of Genesis, *Mysterium Magnum*, Chapter 30, it is pointed out that the speech-sounds of *Kenan* represent 'an outgoing refashioning of the Divine contemplation of Divine Love'—*Ed. note.*
6. Such turns of phrase are circumstantial evidence of Beckh's connection to Freemasonry.
7. The Grail can be regarded in the light of Christmas or in that of Easter. The former is reflected in the image of the gem carried by hosts of angels down from the starry heights, the latter in the image of the holy vessel into which the blood of the Redeemer is collected. The Christmas image we find especially in Wolfram von Eschenbach's (*Parzifal IX*, 654f.):

ein schar in uf der erden liez:	A host [of angels] left him on the Earth
diu fuor uf über die sternen hoch…	which rose up high across the stars…

   Wolfram felt the inner connection between Paradise imagination and Grail imagination, and so he called the Grail the *'Wunsch von Pardies'*—the 'wish for Paradise' (*Parzifal IX*, 350ff.):

uf einem grüenen achmardi	On a green cushion
truoc sie den wunsch von pardis	she carried the wish for Paradise
bede wurzeln unde ris	both roots and stem
daz was ein dinc, daz hiez der Grâl	it was a thing that was called the Grail

erden wunsch überwal	the wish for the Earth it overcame
Repanse de schoye sie hiez	*Repanse de schoye* she was called
die sich der grâl tragen liez.	by whom the Grail allowed itself
	to be carried.

8. This primordial creation, the purely spiritual creation of heavenly man by the Elohim, is the subject of Genesis, Chapter 1. Chapter 2 tells of the creation of earthly man by Yahveh. Accordingly, the first word *bere'shit* 'in the primordial beginning' which is related to Hebrew *rosh* 'head', has a secondary meaning 'first in the spirit', which is juxtaposed in Chapter 2 by 'afterwards in earthly matter'.

9. Prof. Beckh takes his place within an established tradition. *The Zohar*, late thirteenth century, explains through the speech of Rabbi Shim'on (1.11b) that the Hebrew for 'In the beginning'—*b'reshith*—can mean 'to introduce awe'. Rabbi Shim'on explains that 'Awe of God' is the quality on which the entire world is founded. This is the ultimate cause of Creation—*Ed. note.*

10. All of Böhme's major works are founded on his personal illumination: the Godhead has manifested Himself through seven Qualities. What we encounter here as seven Elohim is found in Böhme as the seven 'fountain-spirits' (*Quelle-geister*)—*Ed. note.*

11. When William Blake engraved *The (First) Book of Urizen* in 1794 and attempted to expand the vision into *ValA, or The Four Zoas,* c. 1797-1800, he was able to draw upon Jakob Böhme's spiritual illumination of the Divine Mind to re-express the Genesis Creation in terms of a changing consciousness—*Ed. note.*

12. Hebrew: *bara* 'to create': This word is only ever used for the creation of the Elohim, a creation that takes place still entirely in the spiritual sphere; neither for the creation of Yahveh, nor ever for human creation. Its root *br'h* reminds us of the root √*brh* of Skr. '*brahman*', the creative cosmic word and creative cosmic force.

13. Hebrew *elohim,* plural of *eloah* 'God', often appears with the meaning 'gods, spirits, angel beings' as plural word (for example, in the story about the witch of Endor (1 Sam. 28:13), often it also takes, as here at the beginning of the creation story, the verb *bara* in the singular. The original plurality is experienced as a unity there. In the passage of Genesis 1:26, *na'haseh adam* 'Let us make man', the verbal construction characteristically shifts back into plurality. Hence the word 'Elohim' is neither purely singular, nor purely plural, but singularity mysteriously interwoven into plurality, plurality into singularity. We can only render it approximately, translating something like: 'First in the spirit wove the gods' creative being the heavenly above, the earthly below.'

14. This 'brooding and hovering', 'hovering-spreading-of-wings' lies in the Hebrew *merachepheth*, participle of r-ch-ph. The only time it appears elsewhere in the Bible (in Deut. 32:11) it similarly signifies an 'eagle hovering

protectively over his young'. For a spiritual contemplation, the spreading of wings is already indicated in the sound *ph* (see note 57, below).

Note how [both] the German [and the English] language use the word '*brüten*', 'to brood', in the literary sense of the word, 'the physical activity of sitting on a bird egg warming it', as well as for deep 'thought activity'. We find something similar with regard to the Sanskrit word '*tapas*' with which the Indian hymn of cosmic creation, Rig-Veda (X, 129), describes the creator activity. Tapas literally means 'heating up', 'warmth created by brooding', then also 'the flexing of spirit and will muscles' in Yoga. In The Creation Song of the Vedas, these two nuances of meaning flow together, so that we can experience '*tapas*' as 'the creative brooding of the primordial spirit which kindles the cosmic warmth'. In the creation narrative of Manu and elsewhere, the divine spiritual creative act is presented as Yoga meditation, *dhyana*.

15. In the image of the water, the supernatural primordial substantiality is seen. Note the similar sounding of Hebrew *may* 'water', plural *mayyim* with Sanskrit *maya* 'the primordial female', 'the world enchantress' who weaves the 'illusion' of the material world.

16. It is this rhythmic movement of the cosmic pulse, and not merely the idea of chaos, which underlies the word *tohu-va-bohu*. Rudolf Steiner explains the sound pattern in *Genesis*, Lecture 3.

17. We have to feel how also in the German [and English] language this '*und*, and' is more than a mere conjunction. Something 'working', 'effecting', 'carrying out' underlies it, allowing the will to become deed. To a heightened degree this is the case for Hebrew ו [Editor's Note: Hermann Beckh, having learned O.T. Hebrew, is perfectly justified here. The conjunction most often represents 'and', but is also translated in other contexts as 'consequently' and 'hence'], cf. the essay 'Let there be light', in *The Source of Speech*, Temple Lodge 2019.

18. Clearly explained by Rudolf Steiner in *Genesis*, Lecture 8, with regard to the words in Genesis: 'And the Elohim saw that the light was beautiful.'

19. Hebrew '*h-m-r*, Infinitive *amor* 'to speak'. The first sound aleph (here shown as '*h*) expresses the not yet manifest, *m* is the cusp between silence and speaking, the resting in the depth of our hearts, *r* radiates outward, revealing itself. It can be experienced as more than just a sheer coincidence that the same sound complex '*amor*' means 'love' in Latin and 'speaking' in Hebrew. The connection between sound forces and love forces is a physiological and spiritual reality. Dante calls the divine entity and quality expressing itself in the speaking of the primordial creative word '*il primo amore*' — 'the very first love'.

20. A word like Hebrew *yōm* 'day' — The writer of Genesis himself experiences it as a primordial word. Activity *y* of the divine centre *om* stands before us, when we think of the primordial meaning of the sounds. Steiner puts together with Hebrew *yōm* the Greek word *aion* (*Genesis*, Lecture 5), which

like Hebrew *layláh* 'night' reminds us of Skr. '*laya*', '*pralaya*'. Of course, here also 'day' and 'night' are images through which we can glimpse vast cosmic expanses of time, which the Indian calls 'the days and nights of *brahman*' ('*manvantara*' and '*pralaya*').

21. Cf. Rudolf Steiner, *Genesis* (GA 122) Lecture 9. The picture of a spiritual primordial man who contains the beings of the lower realms within himself and only later puts them outside, is very old. We find it in the Nordic-Germanic ice-giant Ymir, and above all in the Indian *purusha* (Rig-Veda X, 90) whose sacrifice at the creation of the world brought about all the kingdoms of nature and all beings.

22. The root meaning of Hebrew 'kadmon' is 'from the East', hence 'the original Adam'. The term 'Adam Kadmon' entered the *Christian* kabbalah from Jewish traditions during the Renaissance—*Ed.*

23. The sounding of Hebrew *raqia'h* reminds us of Indian *rajas*, *rajah* which signifies the realm of air, the realm of atmospheric vapours between light (*sattva*) and darkness (*tamas*) as the opaque between the two, so that we can discover in those three Indian principles an equivalent to those found in Goethe's *Theory of Colours*. [See Beckh's essay 'Sankhya Philosophy' in *Hermann Beckh and the Spirit-Word*, Anastasi 2015, pp. 67-71.]

24. In his *Occult/Esoteric Science* [GA 13], Rudolf Steiner calls this first stage of pre-earthly evolution, which is repeated in the earthly one, the 'Ancient Saturn stage'. It is followed by the 'Ancient Sun stage', in which life develops, and the 'Moon stage', in which the feeling realm evolves. The fourth stage would then be the current 'Earth stage' proper.

25. Jakob Böhme from the beginning in *Aurora* (1612) especially used this term for the creation of divine nature—*Ed.*

26. These mysteries, together with other references to the primordial creation in Genesis, have been worked into an old Latin verse for baptism which we find in Éliphas Lévi, an excerpt of which reads:

'*In yonder salt lies wisdom, and may it preserve our souls and our bodies from all decay, through the spirit of divine wisdom and the power of divine wisdom; may all the deceiving pictures of materiality yield before it, so that the salt of the Earth and the salt's Earth can become a heavenly salt. [...] May the ash return to the source of living water to become fertile earth and let the tree of life grow, through the three names of heavenly splendour. [...] In the salt of eternal wisdom, in the water of renewal and in the ash which lets the new earth grow, may all be done, through the Elohim, through Gabriel, Raphael, Uriel, throughout all circles of time. May an in-between space come about between the waters and divide water from waters, above from below, and below from above, to work the miracles of the One. The Sun is its Father, and the Moon its Mother, and the wind carried it in its motherly womb. It rises from Earth to Heaven, and returns from Heaven to Earth. I implore you, Being of the Waters, to be a reflection of the Living God in his works, a source of life, and a washing-away of sins.*'

The trinity of elements, discussed here in the language of the early Rosicrucians, can be found woven in mystery within the whole biblical creation myth. [Professor Beckh probably had in mind the flowering of the broadly Rosicrucian movement in the first half of the C17th as well as the principal publication, *The Chymical Wedding* of 1616. The authors were able to take up Paracelsus' (1493-1541) philosophical alchemy with regard to Salt, Mercury, and Sulphur as the three fundamental Qualities of the process of the Genesis creation—*Ed. addition.*]

27. Most Christian liturgies, including the Lutheran and Roman Catholic which were most familiar to Hermann Beckh, include 'Do this in memory of me' from Luke's Gospel after the words of the Institution of the Bread and Wine. Here the Anamnesis (remembering) can be also understood as to mean 'in memory of myself': the 'I' re-collects itself. It was so considered, for example, by James Pike, Episcopalian Bishop of California 1948-56—*Ed.*

28. Rudolf Steiner, *Knowledge of the Higher Worlds*, Chap. 2. To understand properly the relationship between this seed meditation and the Genesis image of the Third Day of Creation, we need to consider how in the Genesis passage the Hebrew words 'seed' and 'insemination' repeatedly recur (six times altogether).

29. Cf. Steiner's lecture mentioning the butterfly (Dornach, 26 and 27 October 1923. GA 230).

30. Hebrew *hoph* which well-known translations render as 'bird', signifies any 'winged animal', including the insects, especially butterflies. Hebrew *scheres*, the other word used in a related context, means 'slithering animal', the primordial form of worm or caterpillar.

31. Hebrew *tanin* does not actually signify the 'whale', but a 'dragon being', cf. Isaiah 51:9 and other biblical verses.

32. The fertility blessing Genesis 1:22, if rightly understood, does not yet refer to physical procreation, but rather to that which nowadays the scientific community would call the 'evolution of species'.

33. Prof. Beckh alludes here to the zodiacal 'sequence', or rhythm, which sums up the human form pure and simple. This 'rhythm', as he said, is 'my theme'. It features in his monumental gospel studies as well as a complete survey of the art of music. Today, research into the self-awareness of *musica* herself in the consciousness of its creators reveals sustained attempts to work with the divine creative principles. Two initiators linking to sacred traditions are J.S. Bach, effectively the father of tonality, and Chopin, the first major composer to celebrate the circle of fifths. In Bach's cycle WTC Bk. 2 (Bk. 1 appears to have begun as a collection rather than a cycle), and Chopin's cycle *24 Preludes*, op. 28, the major keys are researched respectively as the spiritual, 'divine' archetypes, and the minor keys as portraying the human condition—in the terminology of Genesis, drawing on the Elohim and Yahveh creative heritage. Chopin even composed op. 28 as a homage

to Bach, shown in his creative use of the notes B-A-C-H (= B♭, A, C, B; the definitive triple citing comes in Prelude 19 in E♭-major, bb. 29-312. See foot note 61 below; the Introduction by Alan Stott to H. Beckh, *The Language of Tonality*, Anastasi 2015; and article 'Celebrating the Musical System' in *Festschrift: Essays in Honour of Hermann Beckh*, Anastasi 2016, pp. 165-81— *Tr. note.*

34. Gen. 1:27. In a characteristic way, here too in the Hebrew the singular is mysteriously inwoven with the plural, the plural with the singular. It reads first: '...as the image of the divine he created *him*', then 'he created *them* (a) female (a) male'. It is also expressed here grammatically, how the duality of the opposite sexes is still contained within the unity of primordial human-ity. The Hebrew words *zakhar neqebah* do not just mean 'man and woman', but 'male-female being' in a much broader than merely human sense, and they express the opposite of male and female even in the sounds.

35. Rudolf Steiner speaks here in *Genesis*, Lecture 10, from a deeply anthropos-ophical insight of 'moonlike earthly dust'. The Hebrew expression in Gen-esis 2:7 is *haphar min ha adamah* 'dust of the earth', yet it needs to be taken into consideration that for 'earth' a completely different word is used com-pared to the Earth of the first creation, i.e. the word *adamah*, which is related to *adam* 'Man'. *adamah* is used only once (Gen. 1:25, in the expression *remes ha adamah* 'worms of Earth'), whereas otherwise in Gen. 1, the word is *erets* 'Earth'. *adamah* expresses the connection with Man; *erets*, however, is the opposite of *shamayim* 'Heaven'.

36. In Genesis 2:4, the Creation chapter, for the race of Man to come, the Hebrew word *toledoth* 'descendants' is used, a fact which in Luther's Ger-man translation was completely lost. Rudolf Steiner points out that this should be taken quite literally, that the earthly human being of Genesis 2, Yahveh-Man, is the *descendant* of the heavenly-earthly Man, the Elo-him-Man (cf. *Genesis*, Lecture 11).

37. Compare Rudolf Steiner, *Genesis* (GA 122), Lecture 11.

38. It is one of the subtle nuances of the German word '*Ich*' that it gives us a feeling of the connection (which is also present in YHVH) between the pri-mordial 'I'-sound and the essence of the breath.

39. To the Indian this female primordial force is known as *shakti* or *svadhá* ('inner force'). Each Indian deity is attributed with such a *shakti* or female aspect. The Creation Song of the Ríg-Veda (X, 129) says about the Divine One, the Primordial Deity, that already prior to the actual creation of the world He was breathing spirit without any outward breath through his female primordial force (*svadhá*).

40. We revisit this motif again in the myths and mystical traditions of other peoples, especially those of India. So there is, for example, a Buddhist '*Sutra of Primordial Myths*' (The *Aggañña Sutta in the Dighanikaya*) which tells a similar story of Paradise and the Fall. There too it says that in the

distant past, humans still used to live off light and joy as Beings of Light in the airy circumference of the Earth. Only by developing cravings (one of the Beings of Light tries the 'sweet cream of earth'), do instincts for nourishment grow slowly coarser, and so the Beings of Light become entangled with the earthly realm which at the same time is becoming denser, until the squalid sin and social squalor of today are reached. This interesting text seems to be a decadent remnant of ancient clairvoyant memories of the human race. This decadence is contrasted in Rudolf Steiner's *Occult/Esoteric Science* with a new clairvoyance which undertakes now in a living way to explore our origins in the light.

41. Cf. Rudolf Steiner, *The Effects of Occult Development*, Lecture 6 [GA 145]. Towards the end of this lecture, Paradise and Grail Imagination are described as the greatest Imaginations one can experience during the time on Earth.

42. Mentioned by Rudolf Steiner in a Christmas lecture, Berlin, Dec. 21, 1909, 'The Christmas Tree as Symbol', in the compilation *The Festivals and their Meaning*, London: RSP 2002.

43. The legend first explicitly appeared in The Golden Legend (*Aurea Legenda*) by Jacobus de Voragine in 1275. It reappears also in the Cornish Mystery Play 'The Origin of the World' (*Ordinale de Origine Mundi*) in the late fourteeth century. The legend is addressed by Rudolf Steiner in Lecture 13 of *The Temple Legend* (GA 93)—Ed.

44. Cf. the Introduction, and Rudolf Steiner, *The Effect of Occult Development*, Lecture 6 [GA 145].

45. Rudolf Steiner (ibid.): We quote excerpts from an interesting passage, wherein Steiner describes what would be experienced if the human being in deep sleep could clairvoyantly become aware of his vacated physical and etheric body:

'And so with the feeling we are left with, we look back on what lies there embedded in the mist formation, in that always dynamic mist formation of our etheric body, as our physical organ... An incredible sadness, a deep misery overcomes us, when we now look up at the cosmic thoughts streaming into us. These thoughts illuminate this formation which is our physical body, and tell us: All you can see here is the final product of decay of a once existing glory... Like a final memory—hardened into physicality—of a distant glory in the past appears to us what is embedded there in our etheric body.

'Then we become aware of our different physical organs... We behold them clairvoyantly from outside, and behold, they appear to us in such a way that we realize: all we are left with here in the physical body are the shrunken withered products of once existing living beings... which used to live in splendid surroundings and which have now shrunk and decayed... And to clairvoyant vision, these organs slowly form into that which they once used to be...

'The lungs grow... into the imagination of the Eagle... And if we turn in retrospection towards our heart, then we feel... how we are led back into ancient times, into primordial distant pasts to a being which the occultist describes as the "Lion". And then the lower, intestinal organs appear before us as a memory of what in occultism is called the "Bull". The whole nervous system dissolves and differentiates into a sum of primordial plant entities, so that for us really something is depicted like a vastly expanding plant entity, in which those animal beings we just mentioned live...

'That is why the physical body at first sight makes such a sad impression, because we recognize it as something which came about as the final cosmic result of a former glory which now lights up before the eye of the clairvoyant... And now the question arrives: Well, who is responsible for this shrinking process? Who turned this form you see before you with clairvoyant eyes, this wonderful plant being with the perfect animal forms... into today's shrunken result, the physical body? Now like an inner inspiration it sounds out of yourself: that was you yourself who did this, you yourself! ... Your own being seeping like poison into this old glory caused it to shrink to its current state...

'And man in his astral body increasingly wants to know how that came about. At this moment there appears to him among the primordial animal beings of his vision, so-to-speak at the back wall of the garden, in a slithering motion... in a most beautiful form, Lucifer himself! Here man's clairvoyant vision first encounters Lucifer...

'Man connected himself to Lucifer, and as a result... the Beings of the higher hierarchies came pushing through, ... pushing man out in front... Man was pushed out through the openings that today have become our physical senses. So today he lives in the world of the senses, whereas the world he once used to live in has shrunk now and become his inner world... The human being is aware of the things outside him now... In the past he knew what was *inside*, but this inside was tremendous, it was Paradise.'

46. How important the inner devotion to the processes of blossoming and wilting, of growth and decay are for the higher development of the student of the Spirit, is explained in Rudolf Steiner, *Knowledge of the Higher Worlds*, in Chapter 2 concerned with preparation. What is said there can also be viewed in the light of the pictures in Genesis.

47. The rite of the Catholic Church brings the four rivers of Paradise into a meaningful relationship to that new river of life taking its origin from the cross on Golgotha. But all this can still be deepened from an anthroposophical point of view, which shows us how on Golgotha in actual fact the seed for a new Earth and for a future Sun of the dying Earth was planted. Just as the life of the new Earth originates from the river of blood on Golgotha, so the life of the dying Earth, as it has become, originates from the four rivers of life of Paradise.

With regard to the above-mentioned Catholic rite of the blessing of water for baptism, in Anselm Schott, *Messbuch der heiligen Kirche* [Mass Book of the Holy Church] (22nd edition, p. 362) the following interpretation is found: 'The priest divides the water in four parts in form of a crucifix to show that from the four-armed cross the flood of mercy of the precious blood streams into the four world directions of the new Paradise.'

The following prayer is added, addressing the water: 'He who made you stream forth from the source of Paradise and bade you make the Earth fruitful through four rivers; who transformed your bitterness in the desert into sweetness and made you fit for drinking; who coaxed you out of the rock for the quickening of the thirsting people: I bless you too through Jesus Christ, his only son, our Lord, who in Canaan in Galilee by a miraculous sign of his omnipotence turned you into wine; who with his feet walked upon you; who was baptised with you in the River Jordan by St John; who let you pour forth from his side together with his blood; who bade his disciples baptise the believers with you in saying: "Go forth and teach all nations, and baptise them in the name of the Father and the Son and the Holy Spirit".'

48. Professor Beckh discusses gold, Bedolah and Soham in greater detail in *Alchemy: The Mystery of the Material World*, Temple Lodge 2019—*Ed.*

49. Cf. for example, Rudolf Steiner, *At the Gates of Spiritual Science*. Lecture-course, Stuttgart, 22 Aug.-4 Sept. 1906 [GA 95]. London: Rudolf Steiner Press 1976.

50. The period primarily in focus is 1550-1650 for central Europe. One can observe the classical tradition of Prima Materia becoming Paracelsus' 'Alkahest', the corner-stone of Christ in Böhme, and then 'The Water-stone of the Wise' for Ambrosius Siebmacher in Frankfurt, 1619. Again, Hermann Beckh goes into considerably more detail in *Alchymy—The Mystery of the Material World—Ed.*

51. *Christianity or Europe* [more correctly *Christianity in Europe*], written in 1799, but first published in 1826, from Paragraph 17.

52. The story is found in the Old Norse *Sigrdrifumal*: the valkyrie is Sigrdrifa and the earthly hero is Sigurd—*Ed.*

53. Only a sketch is given here, not an exhaustive explanation of this mysterious picture in Genesis. The picture of Adam's sleep and his rib refers to the prehistoric events which Steiner describes as the transition from Hyperborean times (where the human being still contained both sexes, undifferentiated as male-female) into early Lemurian times, where the division into sexes was prepared. Undivided Man slowly separated into male and female.

It is as though we are regarding an exalted height of consciousness followed by a decrease in consciousness. The zodiacal sign relating to such a turning point of consciousness is the Crab, 'Cancer'. Within the great Cosmic Year, the Sun then stands in the Crab, just as it does annually at midsummer. The days are longest and start getting shorter; in the sky the Sun has reached its northernmost point and returns towards the south. [*Professor Beckh extensively considers the signs of the zodiac in relationship to the Gospels of Mark and John in two major publications:* Mark's Gospel: The Cosmic Rhythm *and* John's Gospel: The Cosmic Rhythm—Stars and Stones. *These two expositions, together forming a unity, are profoundly connected with Beckh's later study of the zodiac and the circle of musical keys in* The Language of Tonality; *all three pub. Leominster: Anastasi 2015; Temple Lodge, forthcoming—Ed.*] Within the human bodily organization, 'Cancer—the Crab' is represented by the two halves of the chest that are also present in the symbol of the star-sign. On a soul-level, that inner human member is called in anthroposophy the 'sentient soul', that is, that element of our inner life through which the human being connects in soul with the surrounding world. This is one of the aspects leading us back to Genesis 2:22, for when Man begins to open himself for the outer world represented by Woman; it awakens his sentient soul. Hence this awakening stands in direct connection with the creation of Eve out of Adam's rib. The New Testament parallel to 'Adam's rib' is the wound in Christ's side, John 10:34.

54. The radiant light of the etheric, in which the physical body of Man is embedded, is portrayed in church services by the white garment of the priest at the altar, while the black garment he wears hidden underneath is a symbol for the earthly-physical part of his being, which Paradise Man still carries unconsciously within him in the form of the seed of Earth planted into him by Yahveh.

55. Cf. Rudolf Steiner's profound explanations in *Evolution from the Viewpoint of Reality*, 5 lectures, Berlin, Oct.-Dec. 1911, Lecture 5 [GA 132]. In the previous Lecture 4, Steiner points out how the New Testament provides a reflection of the cosmic renunciation of the gods that allowed evil to become part of cosmic evolution: at the Last Supper, Christ Jesus dips the bread in his bowl and gives it to the traitor.

56. Hermann Beckh has in mind the battle between Indra, Lord of the Devas, and the Asuras. The story also appears in the Mahabharata and the Rig-Veda—*Ed.*

57. Heb. *pheri* 'fruit'; *'hes-pheri* 'fruit tree', which apparently is related to Gk. 'Hesperides'. *P*, *ph*, variations of the same blowing sound, express in image-form the twofold opening lips, and anything else that opens similarly in a twofold, wing-like and diverging way. Especially in the Hebrew this primordial meaning of the sound seems obvious. We feel the Hebrew sounds and their meaning still in Latin *fructūs* 'fruit', which stands in close inner proximity to *fractūs* 'fracture'.

58. The linguistic connection between Germ. *Sünde* 'sin' and *absondern* 'to separate'. Hence Eng. 'sunder'.

59. Mereschkowski in his historical novel *Leonardo da Vinci*. Germ. tr. *532*. [Editor's Note: Originally published in 1900, it became Book Two of 'The Christ and Antichrist trilogy' with the publication of Book Three 'Peter and Alexis'.]

60. One might perhaps mention here Hamerling's remark in *Aphorismen und ästhetische Notizen*, ['Aphorisms and Aesthetic Notes'] Vol. 16, 250 of the Rabenlechner ed. Hamerling calls the idea of the apple, with which Eve tempts Adam, standing for sexual intercourse, ridiculous and philistine. It seemed absurd to him to regard as something inherently sinful the union for which the Creator had organized Man and Woman. The 'Tree of Knowledge' could not have such a trivial meaning. Hamerling's ideas certainly have some truth in them. Already in the chapter on the primordial creation, we find procreation associated with the divine and traced back to Divine Will. But what Hamerling does not take into consideration enough is the distinction between love and its demonic-earthly antagonist, sexuality. That sensual desire could enter into an area of originally unconscious-innocent events and pure divine forces, can nevertheless be inherently attributed to the biblical Fall, but it is one of its *effects*, not its cause or characteristic. [Robert Hamerling (1830-89) was one of the personalities considered at length by Rudolf Steiner in *Karmic Relationships*, Vol. 2, Lecture 4, given at Dornach, 26 April, 1924—*Ed. addition.*]

61. That Bach did this in his musical pilgrimage through all the major and minor keys, portraying the *Heilsgeschichte*, the 'story of salvation', was discovered by Hans Nissen ('Der Sinn des *Wohltemperieren Klaviers* II. Teil', *Bachjahrbuch* 1951-52, 54-80), confirmed by further detailed study of the score by Hertha Kluge-Kahn, *Johann Sebastian Bach: Die verschlüsselten theologischen Aussage in seinem Spätwerk*, Wolfenbüttel & Zürich: Mösler Verlag 1985. Eng. tr. forthcoming—*Tr. note.*

62. Paul could be referring to the lost Shekinah (the divine indwelling glory, or life), e.g. 2 Cor. 4:6 and Romans 3:23. 'All have sinned and gone short (ὑστεροῦνται) of the glory of God.' See Margaret Barker's contributions to Temple theology, e.g., *The Great Angel: A Study of Israel's Second God* (1992) and *The Risen Lord* (1996)—*Tr.*

63. Beautifully expressed by Rudolf Meyer in *Tatchristentum*, No. 6. 62 ('When Adam dares make the first excuse before God's judging question, the illuminating Power of the Word is shrouded in mist for the very first time...') [Rudolf Meyer (1896-1985) was a founding priests of The Christian Community which issued a monthly, *Tatchristentum*, ed. Friedrich Rittelmeyer (soon to be re-named *Die Christengemeinschaft*). The first issue was for Easter 1924—*Ed.*]

64. Compare Rudolf Steiner, *Knowledge of the Higher Worlds*, in the chapter on 'The Second Guardian of the Threshold'. This light-form of the 'Greater Guardian' has as much to do with the future of Man as another figure, that

of the first or what is called 'lesser Guardian' with his past. The encounter with the lesser Guardian is needed for the experience of the second one. Cf. Rudolf Steiner's *The Threshold of the Spiritual World*, and *Secrets of the Threshold* [GA 147].

65. The idea of Eva/Ave which took hold of The Roman Catholic imagination in countless hymns found an early classical expression in the Latin hymn ascribed to Venantius Fortunatus (c.530-c.609): *Sumens illud Ave / Gabrielis ore / Funda nos in pace / Mutans nomen Evae*—*Ed.*

66. Translated in AV/KJV as 'I have gotten a man from the LORD'. While early Jewish commentaries, such as that by Rashi on Genesis, do indeed agree that Cain's conception was before the Fall, the argument here suppresses the first part of Gen. 4:1 'And Adam knew Eve his wife; and she conceived, and bare Cain…'—*Ed.*

67. Even if the passage were translated, 'I have won a man with Yahveh' (in which case the 'man' would be the male child), the meaning would remain the same. It always concerns Cain's direct descent from a union between Eve and the divine. A certain tradition which one cannot go into now is profoundly connected with this biblical passage (see also H.P. Blavatsky, *Secret Doctrine* II, 135 (in a distorted way regarding the same problem, 406).

68. Professor Beckh's approach, here and above, is more fully demonstrated in his contributions to etymology translated and presented in the collection of essays, *The Source of Speech*, Temple Lodge 2019—*Ed.*

69. Rudolf Steiner speaks about this very serious issue in the already-mentioned lecture-cycle, *The Effect of Occult Development upon the Self and Sheaths of Man*, The Hague, 1913, GA 145, Lecture 8. In the human being, he explains, seen from a spiritual perspective, a certain outer nature can experience itself as guardian of an inner one. Through the Fall of Man this relationship is reversed. The same being when confronted on Earth with the other, the better and more selfless one, begins to complain: I do not want to be your keeper, where even in the deepest, most secret soul the decision is made to kill the other whom one feels to be superior (even though under current conditions the deed is not carried out on the physical plane). Just as in The Act of Consecration of Man [of The Christian Community church], so also in this esoteric imagination, the sacrificial smoke is a picture for human soul-life. Steiner emphasizes in another place that the story of Cain and Abel is nothing but the description of an esoteric experience and the reflection of a tremendous sacrifice.

70. That the 'Sons of Cain' was a title applicable to Freemasons is demonstrated in T.H. Meyer, *The New Cain*, Temple Lodge 2017. See also the lecture 'The Contrast between Cain and Abel' in R. Steiner, *The Temple Legend*, RSP 1997—*Ed.*

71. The German text has '*aus dem Lande der Not*' meaning 'out of the land of need', but there is a play on words with the biblical 'land of Nod', Gen. 4:16.

The O.T. Hebrew נוד (Nōd) means 'the wandering of an aimless fugitive' from the verb n-u-d—Ed.

72. The AV/KJV reads: 'then began men to call upon the name of the LORD'—Ed.

73. With regard to the whole problem of the 'primordial waters' which have accompanied us from the beginning of 'primordial creation', a passage from Novalis' in *The Novices of Sais* may be offered:

'Not without reason did the sages of yore seek in water the origin of all things, and verily did they speak of a higher water than sea or spring water... How few have yet deeply delved into the mysteries of the fluid element, and this intimation of the highest form of enjoyment and of life itself has probably never dawned on many a drunken soul. In thirst the world-soul is revealed... and ultimately, all pleasant sensations in us are manifold streams, stirrings of those primordial water. Even sleep is nothing but the high tide of that invisible cosmic ocean, and waking up the setting in of low tide. How many people stand by the shores of intoxicating rivers but cannot hear the lullaby of these motherly waters nor enjoy the sweet play of their endless waves! Like those waves we were in the Golden Age; in colourful clouds—those swimming oceans and primordial springs of earthly life—generations of mankind loved and procreated, endlessly playing; we were visited by the children of heaven; and only in that mighty event, which sacred legends call the Deluge [*Sündflut*, the Fall of Man, literally, 'Flood of Sin'] did this blossoming world go under. A hostile being smote the Earth down; some were scattered by the waves onto the cliffs of the new mountains, left behind in the strange world.'

Concerning the question of the Ark, this much can be added, that it is a symbol, as Louis Claude de Saint-Martin already pointed out in *Tableau naturel des rapports qui existent entre Dieu, l'Homme et l'Univers* (1782), [Chap. 14] which like the tabernacle and the later Temple represents a certain stage of human evolution. In the end, all these symbols are connected with the human physical body.

74. The story is presented in the Satapatha Brahmana, the Mahabharata, and a number of *puranas*—Ed.

75. See H. Beckh, 'Contribution to Sankhya Philosophy: *sattva, rajas, tamas* and their Relationship to Goethe's *Theory of Colours* in the Light of Linguistics.' In *The Source of Speech*, Temple Lodge 2019, pp. 64-71.

76. Here there is also a passage in Goethe's *Theory of Colours* [the pub. title; it is rather a treatise, strictly speaking not at all a 'theory'—Tr.] which shows how closely the great poet's inner life was connected with the spiritual problems we are dealing with. § 919 (the final para. freshly translated here) of the *Theory of Colours* states: 'When one first observes how yellow and blue separate, especially however when you observe thoroughly enough the intensification into red, through which opposites lean towards one another

and unite themselves to form a third, then one will certainly come to an especially mysterious realization, that to these two separate beings which stand in opposition to one another, one may attribute spiritual significance, and one will hardly refrain, when one sees them form green below and red above, to be reminded of the earthly and heavenly offspring of the Elohim.'

77. Various mentions. See GA 201 (1987), Hinweise.

78. Various mentions, e.g. GA 60, *Turning Points in Spiritual History*, 16 Feb.1911.

79. GA 62, 10 April 1913.

80. GA 236, Lecture 3, 8 Jan. 1922.

81. GA 60, op. cit.

82. Lecture 7 of 'Theosophy and the Gospel of St John' in GA 94, 5 Nov. 1906.

83. English translation from GA 265, *Freemasonry and Ritual Work*, Steiner Books, 2007, p. 184.

84. See N.V.P. Franklin, *Rudolf Steiner and Freemasonry*, Temple Lodge, 2020, Chap. 5.

85. Friedrich Nietzsche. *Thus Spoke Zarathustra* (1883). Tr. Graham Parkes. Oxford World's Classics, OUP 2005 (Parkes' introduction and notes are useful); and Tr. R.J. Hollingdale, Penguin Books, London 1961. Page numbers here refer to the former's 2005 edition. (Several versions are readily available online.)

86. The greater part of the Avesta is supposed to have been burnt by Alexander the Great. 'Avesta' means the work, 'Avestan' the language in which it was written. 'Zend' actually means 'commentary, explanation'.

87. Plutarch on Isis and Osiris, Book 3, 46. (http://penelope.uchicago.edu/Thayer/E/Roman/Texts/Plutarch/Moralia/Isis_and_Osiris*/C.html):

46. The great majority and the wisest of men hold this opinion: they believe that there are two gods, rivals as it were, the one the Artificer of good and the other of evil. There are also those who call the better one a god and the other a daemon, as, for example, Zoroaster the sage, who, they record, lived five thousand years before the time of the Trojan War. He called the one Oromazes and the other Areimanius; and he further declared that among all the things perceptible to the senses, Oromazes may best be compared to light, and Areimanius, conversely, to darkness and ignorance, and midway between the two is Mithras: for this reason the Persians give to Mithras the name of 'Mediator'. Zoroaster has also taught that men should make votive offerings and thank-offerings to Oromazes, and averting and mourning offerings to Areimanius. They pound up in a mortar a certain plant called omomi at the same time invoking Hades and Darkness; then they mix it with the blood of a wolf that has been sacrificed, and carry it out and cast it into a place where the sun never shines. In fact, they believe that some of the plants belong to the good god and others to the evil daemon; so also of the animals they think that dogs, fowls, and hedgehogs, for example, belong to the good god, but that water-rats belong to the evil

one; therefore the man who has killed the most of these they hold to be fortunate.

Further details on the question of Zarathustra, see two articles in *Aus der Welt der Mysterien*, Basel 1927, 7-36, Eng. tr. *From the World of the Mysteries*, below. Also *John's Gospel: The Cosmic Rhythm—Stars and Stones*, Leominster: Anastasi, 2015, 229ff.)

88. Cf. H. Beckh, *From Buddha to Christ*. Temple Lodge, 2019, p.4.

89. The German translation first published in *Die Christengemeinschaft*, winter 1925. For the Eng. tr., see p. 115 below.

90. Zarathustra, Part 2, 11 'The Grave-Song'. Parkes 97f.

91. Zarathustra, Part 2, 2 'Upon the Isles of the Blest'. Parkes, 75.

92. Part 2, 2, 'Upon the Isles of the Blest'. Parkes, 74.

93. Part 1, 1, 'On the Three Transformations'. Parkes, 24.

94. Part 3, 12: 3, 'On Old and New Tablets'. Parkes 171f.

95. Part 3, 13, 'The Convalescent'. Parkes, 192.

96. Part 13, 'The Convalescent', 2. Parkes, 193.

97. Part 1, 8. Parkes, 39.

98. E.g. Part 1, 22, 'On the Bestowing Virtue', 3. Parkes, 68.

99. Part 3, 5, 'On the Virtue that makes Smaller', 3. Parkes, 149.

100. This passage, too, is understood rightly if we do not think about lower selfishness, but think about the 'search for the Higher Self'.

101. Part 3, 10. 'On the Three Evils.' Parkes, 166.

102. Part 4, 13, 'On the Superior Human', 15. Parkes, 256.

103. Part 4, 16. 'The Seven Seals', 1. Parkes, 200.

104. Part 3, 12. 'On Old and New Tablets', 28. Parkes, 186.

105. Part 2, 18, 'On Great Events'. Parkes, 115.

106. Cf. H. B., *Our Origin in the Light*, Germ. ed. 140. See above.

107. Part 1, 22. 'On the Bestowing Virtue'. Parkes, 65.

108. Rudolf Steiner, *The Inner Realities of Evolution*, Berlin 1909 [GA 132], 1969, p. 30. Eng. tr. RSP, 1953, p. 27.

109. Part 3, 12 'On Old and New Tablets', 3. Parkes, 172.

110. Part 3, 2, 3. Parkes, 134.

111. Part 3, 12, 'On Old and New Tablets', 19. Parkes, 181.

112. Part 3, 9: 'The Homecoming'. Parkes, 161.

113. In this form it is found significantly in the *name of Christ*—or the name of the future saviour—*Astvatöröta*, which means, literally: 'the great cosmic rhythm incorporated right into the bony skeleton.'

114. Cf. H. B. 'Rhythmical Events in the Gospel', in *John's Gospel: The Cosmic Rhythm—Stars and Stones*, 439-446; also, H. B. 'The Cosmic Cultic Experience in Humanity's Past and Future', in *Collected Articles and Essays* (forthcoming), and elsewhere—*Tr. note.*

115. Part 3, 16, 3. Parkes, 201.

116. Part 2, 11, 'The Grave-Song.' Parkes, 97.

117. Part 3, 4 'The Seven Seas', 4. Parkes, 202.

118. Cf. H. B. 'The Sacred Primal Word of Zarathustra with excerpts from the Avesta', in *From the Mysteries* below—*Tr. note.*

119. Cf. Rudolf Steiner, especially the lecture-cycle *The Mysteries of the East and Christianity*, Berlin 1913 [GA 144].

120. Zarathustra's Prologue, 1. Parkes, 9.

121. Part 3, 4. 'Before the Sunrise'. Parkes 141.

122. Part 4, 19 'The Drunken Song', 2 & 3. Parkes, 279f.

123. Part 4, 'The Drunken Song' 5. Parkes, 281.

124. Part 4, 19, 'The Drunken Song' 6. Parkes, 281.

125. Ibid. 10. 283.

126. Ibid. 7. 281.

127. Ibid. 12. 284.

128. With 'Mysteries' we always understand here schools of a higher spirituality in which an intercourse with the spiritual worlds and the leading spiritual powers is maintained, in such a way that that which certain moments of the Earth's evolution no longer accessible to the common understanding of humanity are preserved for the future by those who through certain inner schooling and purification have prepared themselves for this knowledge.

129. We find an echo of this in Nietzsche's *Zarathustra* with the sentence, 'Thoughts that come on doves' feet direct the world' (Part 2, 22, 'The Stillest Hour'. Parkes, 127).

130. Zarathustra's appearance entered into the prolonged battles of *Iran* and *Turan*, between Iranianism and Turanianism. The struggle lasted for centuries and was significant in the development of history. Rudolf Steiner points this out, wherein (as is also known to academic research) the contrast of the two peoples has its deep cause. With the Turanian peoples in the north of Asia (as far as Siberia), a dreamlike soul-condition of a confused lower clairvoyance lived, contributing to all sorts of wild magic, adverse to a genuine work in a culture of the Earth. With the more southerly Iranian peoples the forces of clear thinking were awakening also enabling them to found a culture by mastering the earthly forces, working on and ennobling earthly material. These forces of clear thinking were inspired through the shining Sun-spirit, which Zarathustra called the Sun-ether-aura, Ahura Mazda. Viewed spiritually, the outer historical battle stretching through long periods of time between Iran and Turan, is the battle of the bright spirit, the cosmic Spirit of the Sun, with the power of darkness, with Ahriman.

131. See R. Steiner *The Spiritual Foundations of Morality*, Lecture 2, Nörrkoping, 29 April 1912, included in GA 155.

132. The differentiation given here of the Mystery-stream of Zarathustra from the Mystery-stream of Buddha does not quite mean the same as that other important differentiation characterizing the essence of the pre-Christian Mysteries. This latter involves two different paths of initiation.

[1] The one is always shown as penetrating through the veil of the sensory world, where one reaches into the cosmos. And out there in the cosmos the pupil encounters his higher Self. 'Thou art that!' (*tat tvam asi*) says the Indian Mystery-saying. This path of initiation, not completely unknown in early India, was taken over by the followers of the more northern (*e.g.* the Teutonic) folk.

[2] The other, the more southern path of initiation, is the counter-pole to the first path, it is not a path penetrating into the cosmos, to the other side of the veil of the sensory world, but the descent into the depths of the soul, into the depths of the unconscious. Here not the veil of the sensory world, but the veil of the soul-world within oneself is penetrated. Here the 'I' is found within the soul. 'I am Brahman' (*aham brahmasmi*) is what the early Indian Mystery-saying says.

Where both paths of initiation are travelled—and only thereby is the initiation completed—it will be found that both lead to the same goal, 'Atman is Brahman', as the early Indian Mystery-saying puts it.

The Indian pathway—and in time gradually more so, with Buddha exclusively so—the second pathway is predominantly followed, whereas *originally* the path of Zarathustra was followed penetrating through the world of sensory appearances. But, as will be shown, all the later Mysteries that rely on Zarathustra meet and adjust again their viewpoints: the Egyptian initiation resting completely on Zarathustrian star-wisdom became increasingly a path to the inner realm (especially, too, a way of penetrating through the human physical element), whereas the Chaldean initiation, which increasingly transforms that star-wisdom of Zarathustra to the sense of *outer* star-wisdom that takes the path to the outside, towards the cosmos. The importance of the *Christian initiation* consists in uniting both paths. Here too, as in everything else, Christ is the higher synthesis. In the lecture-cycle on Matthew's Gospel, Steiner shows how Christ-Jesus Himself lives the two sides of initiation: the descent into the inner realm (the physical and etheric bodies) is shown by the *story of the Temptation* of the Gospels, the storming into the cosmic element—so that the physical body left by the soul then shows its condition of fear—is shown in the scene of Gethsemane.

133. From this the connections of space and time, of the astral body and the etheric body, also with the *Mysteries* of *body* and *blood*, are expressed liturgically again in the Mystery of bread and wine. The little book 'Isis' will offer the possibility of presenting this central Mystery with the detail it deserves [apparently not published under this title but see the Isis articles in H. Beckh, *Collected Essays and Articles*, Temple Lodge, forthcoming—Tr.].

134. When here and in the following *reincarnation* and other details of an anthroposophical world-view are mentioned, it has to be emphasized no 'dogma' is meant, binding for any group of people, and least of all a 'dogma of The Christian Community'. Such dogmas do not exist. But these things

are offered as *results of anthroposophical spiritual research* in such a way that *examination of these results of research* remains for the freedom of the individual. These results are addressed not to any dogmatic belief, but only to the unbiased thinking and bona fide search for truth. One can take the position neither to accept nor dismiss, but take them as a key to see whether and what it unlocks. Thus the *anthroposophical knowledge of repeated earthly lives* can be a *key* with which out of our thinking today we approach the *Zarathustrian thought of 'eternal return'*. That this thought calls for the use of such a key to knowledge does not lie in the personal 'opinions' of the writer, but the objectives of the Zarathustrian thought. Those who want to look beyond what is suggested here may seek the anthroposophical path of knowledge. What is meant here as 'examination of the results of research with unbiased thinking' is a walking on this path; it is not a requisite.

135. Included in Emil Bock's *The Childhood of Jesus: The Unknown Years*, Edinburgh: Floris Books, 2007, the 'Gospel of Pseudo-Matthew', pp. 225-277; also the 'Arabian Gospel of the Childhood', pp. 279-305. The translation in the *Ante-Nicene Fathers*, Vol. 8, 1886. Ed. Alexander Roberts, Sir James Donaldson, Arthur Cleveland Coxe, is available from several websites, e.g.: http://www.gnosis.org/library/psudomat.htm/ and http://biblehub.com/library/unknown/the_gospel_of_pseudo-matthew/

The tradition of the two Jesus boys was known to the School of Chartres in the Middle Ages. Researchers since Beckh's day have identified a significant number of representations not only in the cathedrals and churches of Medieval Europe, but also those of several renowned painters of Renaissance Italy. In particular, the critical meeting of the two 12-year-old youths in the Temple is pictured. Other overt examples (Raphael, Leonardo da Vinci, *et al.*) include three infants: John (the future Baptist) with the two Jesus-boys. In addition to Bock (see above), see also: Hella Krause-Zimmer, *Die Zwei Jesusknaben in der bildenden Kunst*, Stuttgart: Freies Geistesleben 1997; David Ovason, *The Two Children: A Study of the Two Jesus Children in Literature and Art*, London: Century 2001; also a shorter introduction: Bernard Nesfield-Cookson, *The Mystery of the Two Jesus Children: and the Descent of the Spirit of the Sun*. London: Temple Lodge 2005. The first theological study on the subject: Christoph Rau, *The Two Jesus Boys*, Temple Lodge 2019—*Tr. note.*

136. Rudolf Steiner, *The Gospel of St Matthew* [GA 123]. Lecture 2. Berne, 2 Sept. 1910. Tr. Catherine E. Creeger, *According to Matthew*. Great Barrington: Anthroposophic Press 2003.

137. The exact dates can be found in the essay 'Isis' in *From the World of the Mysteries*, p. 156 below. (Germ. ed. *Aus der Welt der Mysterien*, Basel: Rudolf Geering, 1927. 43).

138. See *Our Origin in the Light*, Germ. ed., p. 20 and p. 18f. above.

139. An interpretation of Gen. 22:17. The Hebrews, a recognized 'twelve-tribe nation', attempted to arrange earthly life according to the heavenly order

(see John Michell and Christine Rhone, *Twelve-Tribe Nations*. London: Thames & Hudson 1991)—*Tr. note.*

140. A beautiful passages occurs in Ecclesiasticus, 43:9: 'The beauty of heaven, the glory of the stars, an ornament giving light in the highest places of the Lord' (KJV). 'The stars in their brilliance adorn the heavens, a glittering array in the heights of the Lord' (REB).

141. As He was shown to be the fulfiller of the Buddha, cf. in particular Chapter 4 of Hermann Beckh, *From Buddha to Christ*. Temple Lodge, 2019.

142. Rudolf Steiner, *The Gospel of St Matthew*. GA 123. Lecture 2. Berne, 2 Sept. 1910. Tr. Catherine E. Creeger, *According to Matthew*. Great Barrington: Anthroposophic Press 2003.

143. From this viewpoint a connection is shown of the mystery of space and time, of the astral body and the etheric body, also with the *mysteries* of *body* and *blood*, which are again expressed sacramentally in the mystery of bread and wine. The booklet 'Isis' will offer the opportunity of presenting this central mystery within the space it deserves. [Apparently this booklet did not materialize, but much can be found on this theme, for example, in Beckh's expositions on Mark's Gospel and John's Gospel and in *The Collected Essays and Articles*, forthcoming—*Tr. addition*].

144. Novalis. *The Novices of Sais*, from Chapter 4.

145. The consciousness summarized here Beckh recognized as 'his theme', expounded in detail in his studies on music and of the gospels. The musical system offers a tangible, experiential access to the comprehensive experience discussed in this passage. Chopin was the first major composer to celebrate the 'circle of fifths' of the musicians' tonal system, in his cycle of *24 Préludes*, op. 28. See A. S., 'Celebrating the Musical System: Bach and Chopin', in *Festschrift: Essays in Honour of Hermann Beckh*, Leominster: Anastasi 2016, pp. 165-81—*Tr. note.*

146. Rudolf Steiner, lecture, Dornach, 31 Dec. 1915. GA 165.

147. See Friedrich Creuzer, *Symbolik und Mythologie der alten Völker*, Bd. I, p. 106.

148. At the time of writing, almost 90 years on, the number of followers of this ethnic religion is drastically reduced, something like tenfold, due to migration and the falling birth-rate—*Tr. note.*

149. Extracts are given in a transliteration of the original language with an accompanying translation in the article 'The Original Sacred Texts of Zarathustra with excerpts from the Avesta' (in Hermann Beckh, *From the World of the Mysteries*, below), from which some things are taken in what follows.

150. Novalis *Religiöse Fragmente*, Das Christentum, in the section headed *Negativität des Christentums*. On the terms and insights shared here with Fr. Schlegel, see also the article on Novalis by John M. Baker in Angela Esterhammer (Ed.) *Romantic Poetry* Volume 7, John Benjamins Publishing, 2002—*Ed.*

151. Farvardîn Yasht 1. Full Avestan transliterated text in Beckh's 1926 article on Zarathustra in *Die Drei*. Henceforth as Z 1926. The 'spirits' here are *fravashi* (Eng. tr. in *From the Mysteries*, below).

152. Günther Wachsmuth. *The Etheric Formative Forces in Cosmos, Earth and Man*,Vol. 1 [Germ. ed. 1924], London & New York, 1932 (download available from: https://www.scribd.com/).

153. Both quotations here are from Fravardin Yasht 57, with Avestan text in Z 1926—*Ed.*

154. Tishtar Yasht—*Ed.*

155. The name means 'Star of the Master / Leader / Chieftain'—*Ed.*

156. Tishtar Yasht 2—*Ed.*

157. We recall here once more the 'dancer' Zarathustra in Nietzsche (see Chapter 1, above).

158. Yasht 19.89 (Samyad Yasht)—*Ed.*

159. 'In the Zoroastrian religion, *saoshyant* refers to one who will 'make existence brilliant'. 'Since He is [the One] to be chosen by the world therefore the judgment emanating from truth itself [to be passed] on the deeds of good thought of the world, as well as the power, is committed to Mazda Ahura whom [people] assign as a shepherd to the poor.'—Yasna 27:13, the Ahuna Vairya prayer.

160. A painting (1512-16) by Matthias Grünewald (c. 1470-1528), part of the Isenheim altarpiece in the Unterlinden Museum, Colmar, Alsace-Lorraine, N.E. France. During the ravages following the Reformation in Europe the whole thing survived, apparently hidden in a barn under mounds of straw—*Tr. note.*

161. Rashn Yasht 17 (X)—*Ed. note.*

162. Goethe's discovery arising during his visit to Italy, 1786-88. See his *Metamorphosis of Plants* (1790), ed. Gordon L. Miller. MT Press, 2009—*Tr. note.*

163. Vendidad, Furgard (XX) 4 / 15—*Ed. note.*

164. Zamyad Yasht, 88-96, especially v. 92—*Tr. note.*

165. The following explanation is based on Rudolf Steiner's spiritual research reported in *The Gospel of St Matthew* [GA 123], lecture-course Berne, Sept. 1910; *The Gospel of St Mark* [GA 139], Lecture 8. Basel, 22 Sept. 1912—*Tr. note.*

166. That is, the Zarathas or Nazarathos as discussed in Rudolf Steiner, *The Gospel of St Matthew* [GA 123], lecture Berne, Sept. 2, 1910. Tr. Catherine E. Creeger, *According to Matthew*. Great Barrington: Anthroposophic Press 2003—*Ed. note.*

167. The word *hvaröno* delineates in a certain way the phenomena of the aura, the divine being Ahura Mazda who stands behind the phenomena.

168. Samyad Yasht, especially vv. 34, 51, 56-64, where the adverse Turanian is named as Frangrasyan—*Ed. note.*

169. See Rudolf Steiner, *Occult/Esoteric Science* [GA 13], Chapter 4 [Tr. Creeger, p. 262; tr. Monges, p. 237; Tr. Adams, p. 207].

170. To lay hold of the Zarathustra-concept quite tangibly, observe those phenomena where the sculptural activity of the etheric 'formative forces' (the great divine 'aura' in the sense of the Avesta) are physically most directly revealed—for example, the flowers appearing on frozen window-panes, crystal snow-flakes, rock crystals and other crystals, the forms of the plant world—and contemplatively observe the artistic element that is revealed.

171. Yasht 44.5 (Ushtavaiti Gatha). Full transliterated text in Z 1926—*Ed. note.*

172. In such places in the Avesta we strongly feel the thought of the first Zarathustra. Here we recall once more what was said in Chapter 1 concerning Nietzsche, how in *Thus Spoke Zarathustra* morning, midday and midnight are experienced and come into play. In particular all Nietzsche's saying concerning the 'great midday' as the turning point of time, of destiny, of the cosmos, of life, bear in themselves an authentic spirit of Zarathustra.

173. Yasht 44.3 (Ushtavaiti Gatha)—*Ed. note.*

174. Goethe, *Faust*, Pt. 1, Scene 1, Prologue in Heaven, tr. P.B. Shelley—*Tr. note.*

175. From Yasht 43. Full text in Z 1926—*Ed. note.*

176. From Yasht 36. Full text in Z 1926—*Ed. note.*

177. Yasht 65.14—*Ed. note.*

178. Yasht 45. 2 (Ushtavaiti Gatha). Spoken by Rudolf Steiner towards the end of the public lecture in Berlin, 19 Jan. 1911 [GA 60.9], p. 283, and also presented by Beckh in Z 1926—*Ed. note.*

179. Yasht 45.2 (Ushtavaiti Gatha). A very similar idea is also found in Yasht 19.15—*Ed. note.*

180. From Yasht 49. Full text in Z 1926—*Ed. note.*

181. The names of these nine hierarchies are already to be found in the early Christian esotericism of Dionysius the Areopagite. It may be useful to list and compare the names in the Avesta, regarding:

- angel (angeloi), archangel (archangeloi), primal powers (archai);
- powers (exusiai), mights (dynameis), rulers (kyriotetes);
- thrones, cherubim and seraphim.

The last three mentioned are summarized as the beings of the First (highest) Hierarchy, the three first mentioned as the Third (lowest) Hierarchy, the three in the middle as the Second (middle) Hierarchy. The exusiai we also call the 'Spirits of Form', dynameis 'Spirits of Movement', kyriotetes 'Spirits of Wisdom'. The Avesta does not name all nine categories. Ahura Mazda in this sense would be the 'Sun-Spirit of Wisdom'. If we imagine

- the Third (lowest) Hierarchy are particularly related to *thinking*, to the spirit in the human being,
- the Second Hierarchy to the *feelings*, to the human rhythmic system,
- the First Hierarchy to the physical and to the human will-nature,

then we can well understand why Ahura Mazda, who as the 'Sun-Spirit of Wisdom' is the leading being of the Second Hierarchy, in the Avesta he always appears as the *bearer of the sacred cosmic rhythm*.

182. In the sense of the above order, they would correspond to the 'Spirits of Form' (Exusiai).

183. Both quotations from Yasht 13.81. Full text in Z 1926—*Ed. note.*

184. Yasht 16 (Zamyad Yasht III). Full text in Z 1926—*Ed. note.*

185. In the collection *Erda-Maria*, p. 85.

186. In this sense he would then be the 'Sun-Spirit of Form'.

187. Mihr Yasht 13 (IV)—*Ed. note.*

188. Mihr Yasht 52 (XII)—*Ed. note.*

189. Translated into German by H. Beckh, *Der Hymnus an die Erde*, Urachhaus 1934, 2nd edition 1960. English translation, Temple Lodge, forthcoming. Online text at www.ancient-buddhist-texts.net/Buddhist-Texts/S1-Udana-varga/index.htm

190. Yasht 13.9. Full text in Z 1926—*Ed. note.*

191. Thus right into the linguistics something of the authentic Zarathus-tra-spirit—or Zoroaster-spirit—something of the meaning of the name Zarathustra itself in Nietzsche's Zarathustra-saying: 'If I myself am a grain of that redemptive salt which ensures that all things in the mixing-jug are well mixed...' [Z III, 16. 'The Seven Seals', 4. Parkes 201].

192. Further details in Rudolf Steiner, *The Spiritual Hierarchies* [GA 110], Lecture 2, Düsseldorf, 12 April p.m., 1909.

193. The expression is widespread in Böhme's works after 1618, probably reflecting his increasing familiarity with Paracelsan language. See e.g. *The Three Principles* 5.10 (1618-19), *The Threefold Life of Man* 7.80 (1620), and *On the Incarnation of Christ* 9.8 (1620)—*Ed. note.*

194. From Yasht 36. Full text in Z 1926.

195. Hom Yasht 9.2. Full text in Z 1926.

196. From Yasht 43. Full text in Z 1926.

197. Hom Yasht 10.8.

198. Begotten of the Father in eternity.

199. The translation of this verse from Yasht 19 also appeared in *Die Christenge-meinschaft*, Dec. 1925, 281, with a note. 'One can read in such prophecies, as Apocryphal gospels relate, that the Wise Men from the East came to the child Jesus, motivated through Zarathustra's star. Also purely linguisti-cally the Avesta word for 'saviour' *saoshyant*, 'the saviour, the healing one', corresponds to the Hebrew *Jehoshuah, Joshua, Jesus.'*

[Another translation:

'That will cleave unto the victorious Saoshyant and his helpers, when he shall restore the world, which will [thenceforth] never grow old and never die, never decaying and never rotting, ever living and ever increasing, and master of its wish, when the dead will rise, when life and immortality will come, and the world will be restored at its wish...' [Tr. L.H. Mills & James Darmesteter, *Sacred Books of the East*, 1898.]

200. Heinrich Kerler Verlags-Konto, Ulm, 1912. English 'authorized' translation by Erich Hofacker and George Bennet Hatfield, *Behold the Man*, Macmillan, N.Y., 1930.

201. *Rudolf Steiner Enters My Life*, tr. D.S. Osmond, Christian Community Press, London 1954, p. 27f.

202. Verlag Urachhaus, Stuttgart, 1936.

203. Ibid., p. 5; Eng. tr. by A. Stott.

204. *Christus*, pp. 7-8.

205. Günther Wachsmuth. *The Etheric Formative Forces*, Vol. 1, London & New York, 1932 (download available: https://www.scribd.com/). See also Ernst Marti, *The Four Ethers*, Schaumburg Pubs. Inc. Roselle, 1984. Marti claims Wachsmuth fails to differentiate the ethers from the formative forces. Download from several internet sites, e.g. at the time of writing: www.reddit.com/r/FringePhysics/.../ernst_marti_the_four_ethers_pdf/
https://keychests.com/item.php?v=bvdhrswofno—*Tr. note*.

206. The time of the Babylonian captivity of the Jews falls in the sixth and fifth century BC, the time of the initiate Nazarathos. Many things point to the fact that the earlier (second) Zarathustra lived 800–1000 years earlier, perhaps in the time of Moses.

207. *De Iside et Osiride*, Book 3.46. Beckh's '*Magier*' here reflects the Greek *magos* as attributed to Zoroaster. The latter is often translated as 'sage' although Mathew's Gospel has Greek plural *magoi*, and the Latin Vulgate *magi*. Martin Luther, avoiding the long classical tradition of associating '*magoi*' with ancient Persia, diluted the N.T. Greek to 'die Weisen'.

208. Principally Franz Cumont, 1868-1947. The identity of the Avestan Lake Kansaoya where the saoshyant is supposed to be begotten is known. It is commonly known as Hamun-e Hirmand, or Lake Hamun in Sistan. The River Hirmand (the current form of its name is derived from the Avestan Haetumant) flows into it. Ruins of the Zoroastrian temple of Mount Kwajeh (known as Mount Ushidarena in the Avesta) are next to it. The temple was built for Zoroastrian priests to be ever present here to possibly witness a sign of the expected miracle. It was also an important place of pilgrimage for the ancient Zoroastrians. Some of the temple decorations and paintings partially survived, including the depiction of the advent of the expected saoshyant.

209. The passage from Goethe's alchemical *Fairy tale* runs: 'No sooner had the Snake beheld this reverend figure, than the [Gold] King began to speak, and asked: "Whence comest thou?" "From the chasms where the gold dwells," said the Snake. "What is grander than gold?" inquired the King. "Light," replied the Snake. "What is more refreshing than light?" said he. "Conversation [*das Gespräch*]," answered she.'

210. The following should help pronunciation. In transcribing the sounds (the original is written in Middle Persian Pehlevi letters) the attempt does not rely

on philological tradition (which transcribes differently), but the greatest possible general understanding has been striven for. Certain subtle differentiations with individual sounds (e.g. sibilants and aspirates) are consequently exposed. In contrast to our language, in order to reproduce the much richer treasure of the sounds at least approximately—the Avestan alphabet contains 48 letters—some special signs could not be avoided. *ao* means a broad, open, a lying towards the *o*, similarly as the Scandinavian *å*, *a'* nasal a (like the French *an*). *ö* is to be spoken like the Fr. *e* as in '*le'*, *kh* like Swiss *ch*; *gh* is the corresponding soft sound; th corresponds to the hard Eng. th; *dh* corresponds to the soft Eng. th, *y* is Germ. j; *sh* (differentiated into 3 different sounds in the Avesta) is the Germ. *sch*, *z* is not the Germ. *z* ('ts') but like a sounding soft s (like the *z* in Fr. and Eng.); *zh*, the corresponding soft sch (Fr. *j*); *v* like the Eng. & Fr. v; *w* is the actual Germ. *w* [Eng. v] (the existence of this primal sound is especially characteristic for the Avesta and a sign of great antiquity.) The vowels in italics are *long* and emphasized / *ae* is not ä but a diphthong, similar to *ai*. *ao* is a diphthong similar to *au*, that is, it differs from ao.

The right emphasis is important and essential in order to achieve the mantric rhythm. One approaches this most closely by clearly distinguishing the long from the short [syllables], partly indicated through the italicized vowels and partly through the grouping of vowels which dictate the lengths. This means, to speak the lengths as *very drawn out*, and the shorts very short.

211. Always to be spoken as the wide, long, open *ö* [similar to the vowel in 'birth'], as opposed to aö.

212. Tr. W.H. van der Smissen. On the aural experience of the Sun with Zarathustra, cf. Rudolf Steiner's remarks in the lecture-cycle, *The Gospel of St Matthew* [Berne, 1-12 Sept., 1910. GA 103, especially Lecture 12].

213. This word is more appropriately correct than the one in the dictionary, 'creation', which here does not fit. The biblical creation is also a 'development' stretching over long earthly periods; ultimately creation and world-development are one and the same.

214. *Köhrp* = *corpus*, Germ. *Körper*, 'body'.

215. According to Steiner's lecture, the seven Ameshaspents mentioned in the Avesta are related to the seven bright zodiacal signs, the five others to the dark signs. Because the planets have their 'houses' in the zodiac, it will be possible to find a relationship to the planets. Ahura Mazda belongs to the Sun, Vohu Mano, possibly to the Moon, Amereta to Venus, Armaiti (related to 'harmony') to Jupiter, Haurvatat (cf. the Gk. *plutos* in Rev. 5:10) to Saturn, Kshathra to Mars, Asha to Mercury.

216. Beckh uses the exact words of Novalis 'erhabenen Dom des Steinreiches' from *Heinrich von Ofterdingen*, Chap. 25—Ed.

217. The article which led to the 'Zarathustra' issue of *Die Drei*, Jan. 1926 for which Beckh was invited to contribute—Ed.

218. This alludes to the tradition of two Jesus-children, known to the School of Chartres in the late Middle Ages and evident in much subsequent European art (scenes in stained glass, murals, paintings, and so on). The tradition is confirmed from independent research by Rudolf Steiner. In Matthew's and Luke's Gospels the two different infancy narratives, including the genealogies, are accounted for. Matthew describes the Solomon-child, Luke the Nathan-child (see GA 123 and GA 114). See also David Ovason, *The Two Children*. London: Century 2001; Bernard Nesfield-Cookson. *The Mystery of the Two Jesus Children: and the Descent of the Spirit of the Sun*. London: Temple Lodge Publishing, 2005; Christoph Rau, *The Two Jesus Boys and the Messianic Expectations of the Essenes*. Forest Row: Temple Lodge, 2019 (the first theological study)—*Tr. note*.

219. Begotten of the Father in eternity.

220. The translation of this verse from Yasht 19 also appeared in *Die Christengemeinschaft*, Dec. 1925, 281, with a note: 'One can read in such prophecies, as Apocryphal gospels relate, that the Wise Men from the East came to the child Jesus, motivated through Zarathustra's star. Also purely linguistically the Avesta word for "saviour" *saoshyant*, "the saviour, the healing one", corresponds to the Hebrew *Jehoshuah, Joshua, Jesus*.'

221. *Die Drei*, V. Jg. 10. Heft, Jan. 1926. 783f. Tr. A S. 2015.

222. GA 60, Lecture 9.

223. The publication of Beckh's 'Isis' here coincided almost exactly with the publication of Alan Gardner's monumental *Egyptian Grammar*, Clarendon Press 1927, where some correspondence between 'Thoth' *ḏḥwty* and 'hand' *ḏrt* is noticed with the latter being influenced by old Semitic yād, 'hand', p. 447.

224. Leipzig: Weber 1883; Fourier 1989; Nabu Press 2010.

225. Common reference books often present Thoth as the ancient Egyptian god of wisdom, and the inventor of art, science, letters, etc., ibis-headed, with a tau-cross **T** in his hand as the symbol of death.

226. This appears to concern a double meaning that lies in the word *kyon* (the word for Sirius in Greek). On the one hand *kyon* means the 'dog', but then it is also the participle of *kyo* 'to swell', and this then leads to certain names of the goddess Isis venerated by the Egyptians, to names which are related to the swelling fruitful forces of the feminine nature and the swelling of the River Nile. On the other hand in Egypt the shining divinity Anubis, which is also brought into connection with Sirius and often merged with Hermes, is frequently presented with a dog's head.

227. For a highly relevant discussion in modern scholarship of Beckh's topic here, see David Ulansey, *The Origins of the Mithraic Mysteries*. Oxford: OUP 1989—*Ed*.

228. The ritual of *Sagdid* is explained in Fargard 8 of the Vendidad—*Ed.*.

229. W.B. Yeats came to a comparable distortion of such traditions connected with the Great Year in the poem 'The Second Coming', published in 1921—*Ed*.

230. Recorded by Plutarch in *Isis and Osiris*, Chap. 9—*Ed.*

231. The 'postscript' was added more than 300 years after Plutarch by the Neo-platonist philosopher Proclus who wrote of the same statue in Book I of his *Commentaries on Plato's Timaeus*. In this version, 'no mortal' is replaced by 'no one' and a third statement is added 'The fruit of my womb was the Sun'—*Ed.*

232. This precise point regarding the Mother—Daughter—Spouse is also made explicit in the early Kabbalistic text *Sepher Ha-Bahir*, no. 63 in the bilingual edition by E. and H. Collé, 2014—*Ed.*

233. Only from this moment onwards of the 'murdering' and 'dismember-ing' of Osiris did the path of the Egyptian Mysteries become a mystical path within. In the primal times the Mysteries opened up experience of the stars, still led into cosmic widths. The Egyptian wisdom of the stars became progressively an experience of the human organs, an experience of the reflected nature of the stars mirrored in the human body.

234. See, for example, Keith Critchlow. *The Hidden Geometry of Flowers*. Edin-burgh: Floris Books 2011—*Tr. note.*

235. See, for example, G. Wachsmuth, *The Etheric Formative Forces...*, Vol. I, Chap. 2, A.P., London and NY, 1932. First German edition 1924.

236. The water-lily here is to be understood as the lotus flower—*Ed.*

237. Victor Hugo's (1802-85) poem *'La pauvre fleur disait au papillon céleste'*, in the form of a dialogue between a 'poor flower' and a 'heavenly butterfly', plays with the idea of the butterfly as a disembodied flower: *'Fleurs tous deux!'*—*Tr. note.*

238. R. Steiner,*Wahrsprucheworte*, GA 40, p. 151. Eng in *Truth Wrought Words*, trans. E.M. Ege, Anthroposophic Press, 1979 with the title 'Ein Geheimnisse der Natur'.

239. The last line of 'The Grave Song' in *Thus Spake Zarathustra*—*Ed.*

240. Pub. separately Edition Geheimes Wissen 2013, also incl. in *Neue Wege zur Ursprache*. Stuttgart: Urachhaus 1954, Eng. tr. 'Etymology and the meaning of speech-sounds' in *The Source of Speech*, Temple Lodge 2019, pp. 112-34.

241. Thus, for example, in Valentinian Gnosticism the first syzygy, the most exalted 'pair' before any divine manifestation is Bythos (Abyss / Profun-dity) and the feminine Sige (silence)—*Ed.*

242. Hebrew verbs use the suffix -i (yod) to indicate the first person singular. The possessive pronoun 'my' + noun is also represented by adding the same suffix to the noun—*Ed.*

243. Hebrew *shesh* 'six', *shishshah*, 'sixth'—*Ed.*

244. H. Beckh, *'Das neue Jerusalem'*, a work in verse; Eng. tr. 'The New Jerusa-lem' in *John's Gospel: The Cosmic Rhythm*, Anastasi 2015, pp. 459-77; also in *Alchymy: The Mystery of the Material World*, Temple Lodge 2019, pp. 100-13.

245. If we turn from Egypt and its Mysteries to the group of legends of Old French and Middle High German which is inspired by the Christianized

echoes of the Celtic Mysteries, to which also belong the Grail legend and the Parsifal saga, then we find there the cosmic-virginal element of the ice in the likewise significant *secrets of the higher Eternal Feminine* veiled in the name *Isolde*, if the exploration of this name with the Nordic *Ishild* (= Eis-Hilde, Eis-Holde) given by linguistic research is correct. The Old French form of the name *Isôt* (also used in the Middle High German poetry) appears quite close to the Egyptian *Iset, Isit*. The more we penetrate into the esoteric connections of these names, the more *this* echo [to Isis] is lifted out of the realm of the mere arbitrary into an inwardly meaningful realm.

246. I.e. Primarily Quechua languages and culture—*Ed.*

247. Etheric Formative Forces, op. cit., Chap. 2—*Ed.*

248. Rudolf Steiner, *The Mysteries of the East and of Christianity*. GA 144. Berlin, 4 lectures, 3-7 Feb. 1913. London: Rudolf Steiner Press 1972. Lecture 3: http://wn.rsarchive.org/GA/GA0144/19130205p01.html).

[Synopsis: *Lecture 3*: Ascent into the spiritual worlds is accompanied by certain unavoidable experiences. Possibility of a retrospect into the far past, a reading of the Akashic Record. In the higher worlds a seer is able to discern the activities of beings associated with the Sun and the Moon in engendering the physical and etheric bodies of men. How the astral body and ego are brought into being is veiled in secrecy. The Zarathustrian Initiation. The Hermes Initiation. Two phases of the Isis Initiation, separated by the point of time when Moses lived. When Moses led his people out of Egypt he took with him the part of the Egyptian Initiation which added the Osiris Initiation to that of the mourning Isis. 'Sons of the Widow.' In the later Egyptian Initiation the candidate experienced the dying of a God in the Heavens in order that he may descend into another world. *5 February, 1913*]

249. English translation, *The Hebrew Tongue Restored*, tr. N.L. Redfield, Putnam's, 1921; Kissenger (reprint); Samuel Weiser 1991; Nabu Press 2010.

250. Édouard Schuré (1841–1929) *The Great Initiates*. Fr. ed. 1889. Eng. tr. Harper Collins 1980. SteinerBooks 1992. Internet: uncletaz.com/great_initiates/allen.html/.

251. This observation was repeated by Emil Bock, *Genesis*, 1934, Chapter 4—*Ed.*

252. E.g. computers, in whose binary system 'curves' consist of numerous tiny tangents—*Tr. note.*

253. Cf. the Hebrew noun 'hanukah, dedication or consecration. In Islamic traditions Enoch is often equated with Idris, the 'interpreter', especially of divine mysteries—*Ed.*

254. 'Reguel' is the form adopted by Luther; A.V. and RSV prefer 'Reuel' which is closer to current Hebrew texts; the R.C. tradition from the Vulgate opts for 'Raguel'—*Ed.*

255. Also rendered 'He who causes to be', or, in William Propp's trans. of Ex. 3:14 in *Exodus* for The Anchor Bible Series:'I will be who I will be'—*Ed.*

256. English translation in H. Beckh, *The Source of Speech*, Temple Lodge 2019, pp. 154-80.

257. The classical sources for the account of Herakles and his spouse Deianira 'man-slayer' include Hesiod, *Catalogue of Women*, 2.5; Ovid, *Heroides 9*; Ovid, *Metamorphoses* 9:238. The subject was reviewed by Robert Graves, *The Greek Myths*, 1955, p.142f.—*Ed.*

258. Both Ganymede and Hebe were bearers of ambrosia to the Greek pantheon on Olympus—*Ed.*

259. In Band 16 of Christus aller Erde, *Gegenwartsrätsel im Offenbarungslicht*, Verlag der Christengemeinschaft, Stuttgart, 1925, pp. 105-21. English translation in H. Beckh, *John's Gospel: The Cosmic Rhythm*, Anastasi 2015, pp. 459-77; also in *Alchymy: The Mystery of the Material World*, Temple Lodge 2019, pp. 100-13.

260. As spoken to Ananda, Vinaya-Pitaka 2. 253f.—*Ed.*

261. None of the great initiates revealed so little as the Buddha; none as the Buddha has pointed human beings so much towards 'keeping pure' the inner life. The Indian in earlier times had eaten from the over-abundant table of spirituality. Over this the purity, the inner discipline of spirituality, has been increasingly lost. The prerequisite for everything else lay in its re-establishment. Buddha saw his task in this direction, which he fulfilled with unique, unrestrained consequence. He was able to renew the purity of the earlier vision, not its richness. He can frequently appear to us like the physician who prescribes for his patient the strictest diet after the all-too-rich spiritual meal of the past. Today, we would starve with this diet; the spiritual life would dry up unless new content were to be offered to the vision.

262. Freshly translated into German by the author of this essay, under the title *Der Hingang des Vollendeten*. Eng. tr. 'The Passing of the Perfected One' (Temple Lodge, forthcoming).

263. The translation mentioned above attempts to give an impression of the rhythmical, musical element, as far as this is possible in the German language. [The same comment is relevant to the Eng. tr. (forthcoming)—*Tr. addition*].

264. *Hingang*. p. 24.

265. *Hingang*, 27ff. Here the extensive text appears, which is shortened above.

266. In *Hingang* (Intro. p. 14f.) it is pointed out how the Mahaparinibbanasutta allows us to follow the geographical overview of Buddha's last journey.

267. Rudolf Steiner. *Knowledge of the Higher Worlds and its Attainment*. Tr. George Metaxa, rev. Henry B. and Lisa D. Monges. New York: Anthroposophic Press 1947. P. 117.

268. *Hingang*, 20f.

269. The extended sea-parable forms most of the Uposathasutta in the Udana (5.5)—*Ed.*

270. *Hingang*, 52f.

271. *Hingang*, 57.

272. *Hingang*, 94.

273. *Hingang*, 60ff. This chapter was already mentioned in the essay 'Ein entscheidungsvoller Augenblick im Leben des Buddha' (*Die Drei*, April/ June 1924). Linguistically, the translated passages given in *Hingang…* are partly superseded. Notice the earthquake rhythms, p. 68f. and other things.

274. Cf. *Buddha und seine Lehre*. Sammlung Göschen, I. 64. English translation, *Buddha's Life and Teaching*, Temple Lodge, 2019, pp. 62f.

275. The various problems of these mealtimes cannot be elaborated further here, but can be found discussed in the author's *Buddha und seine Lehre*, I, 73. *Hingang*, note 56, p. 153.

276. This place can be found in the lecture-cycle, *Universe, Earth and Man* [GA 105] Lecture 11 [Stuttgart, 16 August 1908]; literally: the seemingly trivial matter of that mealtime 'is a picture for how Buddha stood to his contemporaries… He was ruined through having given out to the world a surfeit of occultism [of "what was hidden"].'

277. *Hingang*, 93ff.

278. *Hingang*, 101f.

279. Ex. 34:29; Matt. 17:3; Mark 9:4—*Ed.*

280. *Hingang*, 104.

281. Ibid., p. 105ff.

282. Consequently, in the text the *untimely* blossoms of the sala trees are also significant. Like a late untimely blossom there once more flourished mightily in Buddha the early paradisal consciousness of the primal time, which for a long time had faded in humanity.

283. These are high, majestic trees (*Shorea robusta*) with strong resin and oil content. Oil, too, is a sacred symbol of the circulating, all-penetrating etheric life.

284. Mahāparin. 5.2-3.

285. *Hingang*, p. 108f.

286. Ibid., p. 110f. Mahāp. 5.8—11.

287. Ibid., p.114. Mahāp. 5.14.

288. Mahāp. 5.24.

289. Mahāp. 6.7.

290. Mahāp. 6.10. The following extracts continue from the same section.

291. Buddha's life and activities fall into the previous age of Michael's regency.

292. *Hingang*, p. 129.

293. Interesting things about him can be found in Steiner's Easter lectures in Köln, 10/11 April 1909. GA 109.

294. Mahāp. 6.19 ff.

295. *Hingang*. p. 137f.

296. In GA 93; English translation by John M. Wood, *The Temple Legend*, RSP 1985, 1997, 2002—*Ed.*

297. Note, however, that the terms Pillar of Wisdom and Pillar of Strength do not occur in the biblical text—*Ed.*

298. For a more detailed inquiry into Cain and Abel, see H. Beckh, *Genesis*, Temple Lodge, 2020.

299. See Notes 135 & 218 above.

300. Numbers 20.12 only states: 'And the Lord said to Moses and Aaron, "Because you did not believe in me..."'—*Ed.*

301. Shortly afterwards published as *Gäa-Sophia*, G. Wachsmuth, Erden Antlitz und Menschheits-Schicksal, Bd 1, 1926—*Ed.*

302. *Hymns to the Night*, section 5, in prose—*Ed.*

303. *The Novices of Sais*, Chap. 5, para. 3—*Ed.*

304. The phrase is from *Majjhimanikāyā*, 1, p. 485 in the original text which Beckh refers to in *Buddha's Life and Teaching*, Temple Lodge, 2019, p. 110.

305. The very significant passage can be found in the author's *Buddha's Life and Teaching*, p. 169f., as also in the book *From Buddha to Christ*, p. 69f.

306. *Die Hingang des Vollendeten*, Verlag der Christengemeinschaft, Stuttgart, 1925; reissued with an introduction by Diether Lauenstein, Urachhaus, 1960; English translation, Temple Lodge, forthcoming.

307. *Mahāparinibbānasutta* 5.2. English translation by Maurice Walshe in *The Long Discourses of the Buddha. A Translation of the Dīgha Nikāya*, Wisdom Publications, Massachusetts, 1987, 1995—*Ed.*

308. The 'Dirgatamas Hymn'.

309. This is not to be taken as a contradiction against what has been said above about the *Tree of Life* with Buddha. The Tree of Life, which rains its blossoms onto Buddha is in the heavenly heights; the sacred fig tree on the Earth has become the Tree of Knowledge (Bodhi), but it still flourishes with an abundance of leaves; knowledge is still connected to life. This then lasts for 500 years, exactly as long as Buddha prophesied his teaching would be valid. Then the great Christian Imagination of the cursing of the fig tree through Jesus Christ, which is followed by its dying, marks the cosmic moment in time when the old forces of knowledge have finally died.

310. This word, which also appears in one of our ritual texts today [the Burial Service of The Christian Community], is the most literal translation of the Skr. word *amrta*, otherwise mostly translated 'immortal'.

311. Engraved by William Blake for Bryant's *Mythology*, 1774; thence in *Jerusalem* Plate 44—*Ed.*

312. With Zarathustra, too, the word usually translated 'sea' (*Vourukasha*), means the etheric ocean.

313. Beckh refers to Albert Steffen's poems *Wegzehrung*, 1921.

314. At this place in the biblical story there stands Mount Ararat.

315. The soma is meant.

316. For an extended consideration of the points briefly mentioned in this paragraph, see H. Beckh, *Zarathustra*. The English translation (above) includes the relevant references to the Avestan texts—*Ed.*

317. Most notably as the Ashwatha Tree in the Katha Upanishad, 2.3—*Ed.*

318. Hermann Beckh may be recalling Iusaaset 'the great one who comes forth' or Iusaas, the name of a primal goddess in Ancient Egyptian religion. She is described as 'the grandmother of all of the deities'. Iusaaset was associated with the acacia tree considered the tree of life, and thus with the oldest one known situated just north of Heliopolis, which thereby became identified as the birthplace of the deities. Iusaaset was said to own this tree—*Ed.*

319. Gilgamesh, Tablet X.

320. In the lecture 'The sphere of the Bodhisattva', 25 Oct. 1909, in the cycle *The Christ-Impulse and the Development of the Ego-Consciousness* (GA 116).

321. Cf. Friedrich Creuzer. *Symbolic und Mythologie der alten Völker*. Vol. IV, p. 339f.

322. Ibid., p. 340.

323. The legend first explicitly appeared in *The Golden Legend* (*Aurea Legenda*) by Jacobus de Voragine in 1275. It reappears in the Cornish Mystery Play 'The Origin of the World' (*Ordinale de Origine Mundi*) in the late fourteeth century. The legend is addressed by Rudolf Steiner in Lecture 13 of *The Temple Legend* (GA 93)—*Ed.*

324. Rudolf Steiner spoke several times of the entelechy who incarnated in Elijah, John the Baptist, Raphael and Novalis. Beckh first heard Rudolf Steiner speaking on Elijah (Berlin, 14 Dec. 1911); he was present at the 'Last Address' (Dornach, Michaelmas Eve, 28 Sept. 1924), and clearly responded to the appeal to continue research in a Michaelic spirit. In his studies on Mark's Gospel and John's Gospel, Beckh develops what could be unique insights into the 'two Johns'. See also Sergei O. Prokofieff, *Eternal Individuality: towards a Karmic Biography of Novalis*, London: Temple Lodge 1992—*Tr. note.*

325. Cf. with what follows, the author's article 'Death and Novalis' (*DieChristengemeinschaft*, Nov. 1925); English translation in *Collected Esssays and Articles*, forthcoming. See also Rudolf Steiner's lectures mention of the musical element, the prose-poem of Novalis and Isis: 'Die Kunst des Mündlichen Vortrages', Dornach, 6 April 1921, as well as 9 April 1921, 'Die Psychologie der Künste', are available in German <anthroposophie.byu.edu>—*Tr. note.*

326. *The Novices of Sais*, Chap. 1, para 3.

327. His brother Karl played, Novalis fell asleep and did not waken, March 25, 1801—*Ed.*

328. Both the quotation and the reference to the brother being asked to play the piano occur in the lecture 'Die Psychologie der Kunst', Dornach, 9 April, 1921 (GA 271). Hermann Beckh was present during the various talks and events which took place at this time, the 2nd Hochschule. Two days before

Steiner's lecture recalled here, Beckh had himself given one of his earliest great lectures on language: 'Etymology and the Meaning of Speech in the Light of Spiritual Science', in *The Source of Speech*, Temple Lodge 2019, pp. 112-34.

329. *Novalis Werke*, ed. G. Schultz, Verlag C.H. Beck, 2001, p. 267.

330. *Novalis Werke*, ed. W. Schultz, Hädecke, Stuttgart, 1922, p. 204.

331. *Die Lehrlinge zu Sais*, ed. K.-M. Guth, Sammlung Hoffenberg, Berlin, 2016, p. 26.

332. The expression is formed by Albert Steffen in his poem '*Warum hat nicht Kraft*' in *Wegzehrung* that ends with the words, rendered into English: 'Tree of Love, you shine, I behold in you the light of the Redeemer, for I die *in Christo* and am born again in the Holy Spirit.'

333. The concluding words of 'The Golden Legend and a German Christmas Play', Berlin, 19 Dec. 1915 (GA 157a). The lecture has a particular focus on the Tree of Life and the Tree of Death—*Ed.*

334. *The East in the Light of the West*, Lect. 9, Munich, 31 Aug. 1909 (GA113).

335. Rudolf Steiner, *Riddles of Philosophy* (GA 18), Steiner Books, Inc., 2009.

336. Both Rudolf Steiner and Hermann Beckh also addressed this archetype of the human being as Adam Kadmon, using the term from Jewish tradition—*Ed.*

337. Beckh's biographer Gundhild Kačer-Bock provides the information that the author attended the first of these lecture cycles, in Köln at the end of 1912, and that Steiner particularly spoke with Hermann Beckh in mind—*Ed.*

338. A presentation of Chap. 2, v. 38—*Ed.*

339. Notably in the Bhagavata Purana, Ch. 10—*Ed.*

340. Reminiscent of Genesis 31—*Ed.*

341. This phrase appears in the Creed of The Christian Community church—*Tr.*

342. The Green Window in the North. This picture appears as the frontispiece in the January 1926 issue of the journal *Die Drei* in which the essay on Zarathustra first appeared, also reproduced here—*Tr.*

343. The conception of a new Isis lying invisibly behind the statue was clearly explained as early as 6 January, 1918 in Lect. 10 of *Alte Mythen und ihre Bedeutung*, Dornach (GA 180). For a full discussion, see S.O. Prokefieff, *Rudolf Steiner's Sculptural Group*, Temple Lodge, London, 2013, Chap. 14—*Ed.*

344. Cf. Rudolf Steiner's lecture-cycle held in Berlin, *The Mysteries of the East and Christianity* [3-7 Feb. 1913. GA 144].

345. Cf. Brugsch, *Religion und Mythologie der alten Ägypter.* 249.

346. 'The host' refers to sacramental bread, in circular form as the Sun-disc—*Tr.*

347. Cf. The Transfiguration of Christ, where Moses and Elijah 'spoke of his departure [Gk. *exodus*] which he was about to bring to fulfilment in Jerusalem' (Luke 9:31 NIV)—*Tr.*

348. Prof. Beckh develops these ideas in his third Hochschule lecture, 'Contribution to Samkhya Philosophy: sattva, rajas, tamas and their relationship

to Goethe's Theory of Colours in the light of linguistics', printed in *Kultur und Erziehung*, Vol. 3, Der Kommende Tag A.G. Verlag, Stuttgart 1923. Eng. Translation in *The Source of Speech*, pp. 56-71.

349. In all fairness, it should be noted that Goethe's 'colour circle' or 'wheel' consists of six colours, rather than the seven that Newton proposed out of sympathy for some mystical ideas—*Tr. note.*

350. De Iside et Osiride in *Moralia*.

351. In the poetry collection *Erda-Maria*, ed. Fr. Doldinger, Verlag der Christengemeinschaft, Stuttgart, 1926.

352. See H. Beckh, *The Essence of Tonality* (1925), trans. A. Stott, Anastasi 2001, p. 24.

353. The story of Jacob's Ladder, Genesis 28: 10-17.

354. E.g. I Kings 3:15.

355. See H. Beckh, *From Buddha to Christ*, Temple Lodge, 2019.

356. Beckh's insights were presented in 'Schneewittchen', *Die Christengemeinschaft,* Aug. 1924; Jg. 1, pp. 138-46. Eng. Tr. appended to H. Beckh, *Alchymy*, Temple Lodge, 2019.

357. Especially in the *Lalitavistara*, presented by Beckh in *Buddha's Life and Teaching*, Temple Lodge, 2019.

358. The 'legend' was first expressed by 'San Marte' (pseudonym for Albert Schulz) in *Parcival, Rittergedicht von Wolframvon Eschenbach. Im Auszuge mitgetheilt von San Marte*, Magdeburg, 1832.

359. Many significant details are provided in H. Beckh, *Buddha's Life and Teaching*, Part 1, Temple Lodge, 2019.

360. See for example the Eng. tr. of *Lalitavistara* by Bijoya Goswami, Bibliotheca Indica Series No. 320, Kolkata, 2001, Chap. 3.

361. Ibid., Chap. 5.

362. The inner separation (*Abgeschiedenheit*) from everything casual, sensual, and earthly, and the yielding to the work of God in the heart, is the seclusion or tranquility of which Eckhart repeatedly speaks—*Ed.*

363. The story became widespread in medieval western Christianity, and is typically portrayed in a window of the Church of St. Urban, Strasburg—*Ed.*The inner separation (*Abgeschiedenheit*) from everything casual, sensual, and earthly, and the yielding to the work of God in the heart, is the seclusion or tranquility of which Eckhart repeatedly speaks—*Ed.*

364. See H. Beckh, *Buddha's Life and Teaching*, op. cit., 'Entering the Mother's Womb'.

365. This largely belongs to the 'Medicine Buddha' Bhaiṣajyaguru of Tibetan tradition, where the bowl is fashioned from blue beryl—*Ed.*

366. Hermann Beckh first surveyed the traditional stories of the Buddha's conception and birth as told in the Lalitavistara Sutra in Vol. 1 of *Buddha und seine Lehre*, 1916. Eng. tr. *Buddha's Life and Teaching*, Temple Lodge 2019.

367. See Note 205.

368. Karl Brugsch, *Religion und Mythologie der alten Ägypter*. op cit., p. 255.

369. See H. Beckh, *The Source of Speech*, Temple Lodge, 2019, pp. 102f.

370. See the article in *Die Drei*, Feb. 1926, [Zum Namen der Isis, 861-67, also 'Isis: die Sternenweisheit des Hermes und der altägyptischen Mysterien und ihre Zusammenhänge mit Zarathustra', 827-49, both reprinted in *Aus der Welt der Mysterien*, Basel: Geering 1927, 66-74; 33-65. Eng. translations above. 'The Name Isis' is also pub. as Appendix V in Hermann Beckh, *Mark's Gospel: The Cosmic Rhythm*, Leominster: Anastasi, 2015. 465-72].

371. Current scholarship also includes views dating the Exodus towards the end of the eighteenth Dynasty, c. 1350-1295 BCE, while others have opted for a more recent period.

372. R. Steiner, *The Mysteries of the East and of Christianity*, trans. C. Davy, RSP, 1972, p. 51.

373. Rather than the cycles on John's Gospel, Prof. Beckh may have been recalling Lecture 4 of *Genesis*, GA 122, Munich, 20th August—*Ed.*

374. *Das Land der Inca in seiner Bedeutungfür die Urgeschichte der Sprache und Schrift* ['The land of the Incas in its significance for the prehistory of language and writing'] Leipzig 1883, Fourier 1989; Nabu Press 2010.

375. The well-known phenomenon in the high mountains arises when the Sun, seen from the valleys, has disappeared from view. The snow of the peaks and the rocky walls dramatically catch the colour—*Tr. note.*

376. With Imaginative insight regarding the decline of vision (clairvoyance) along with the ruling Jewish opposition to the traditions of the Divine Feminine (the latter presented conclusively by Margaret Barker in *Temple Wisdom*, SPCK 2011), Beckh's observations lead to the otherwise difficult story in the O.T. where Jael ('God is Jahve') slays Sisera by driving a tent-peg 'into his temple' (Judges 4:21*)—Ed. note.*

377. Friedrich Nietzsche, *Thus Spoke Zarathustra*, Part 2, 11, The Funeral Song, tr. Hollingdale (Penguin Books) 138; The Grave Song, tr. Parkes (Oxford Classics) 98.

378. Harold Bayley, *The Lost Language of Symbolism*, The Book Tree, San Diego, 2007, further explains: 'The Egyptian for scarabæus was chepera, and the word chepera signified also *being*…At the time the morning Sun was worshipped under the name *Khepera*, and *Chefura* was a name among the Egyptians for their kings or "Sons of the Sun"', p. 327 of the first edition, Barnes and Noble, New York, 1912—*Ed. note.*

Bibliography

'An abundance of books came into existence whose significance perhaps will only be properly appreciated in the future.'

(Lic. Emil Bock, 'Hermann Beckh' in *Zeitgenossen Weggenossen Wegbereiter*, Stuttgart: Urachhaus 1959. 132)

Die Beweislast nach dem Bürgerlichen Gesetzbuch

'The burden of proof according to the Code of Civil Law'

Prize essay, awarded distinction from the Law Faculty the University of Munich

München und Berlin 1899. Download: http://dlib-pr.mpier.mpg.de/m/kle-ioc/0010/exec/books/%22103926%22/

Ein Beitrag zur Textkritik an Kālidāsas Meghadūta

'A contribution for the text criticism of Kālidāsa's Meghadūta'

Doctorate dissertation approved by the Department of Philosophy of the University of Berlin 1907.

Die tibetische Übersetzung von Kalidāsas Meghaduta

'The Tibetan translation of Kalidāsa's Meghaduta'

Edited and with a German translation, Berlin 1907/2011.

Beiträge zur tibetischen Grammatik, Lexikogaphie, Stilistik und Metrik

Habilitationsschrift. Berlin 1908.

'Contributions to Tibetan grammar, lexicography, style and meter'

Inaugural dissertation.

Udānavarga

A collection of Buddhist sayings in the Tibetan language.

Berlin 1911 (also reprinted by Walter de Gruyter, 2013).

Verzeichnis der tibetischen Handschriften

'Catalogue of Tibetan MSS in the Royal Library in Berlin' (Vol. 24 of the Manuscript Catalogue). First division: Kanjur (Bhak-Khgur).

Berlin 1914/2011/14.

Buddha und seine Lehre

'Buddha and his Teaching.' Vol. 1: The Life. Vol. 2: The Teaching.

Sammlung Göschen. Berlin & Leipzig 1916. Third edition 1928.

Later one-volume editions, Stuttgart: Urachhaus 1958/98/2012. Tr. into Dutch and Japanese.

Eng. tr. *Buddha's Life and Teaching*, Temple Lodge 2019.

'Rudolf Steiner und das Morgenland'

in *Vom Lebenswerk Rudolf Steiners*

Ed. Friedrich Rittelmeyer, München: Chr. Kaiser 1921

Reprint by HP, Univ. of Michigan (www.lib.umich.edu) (download: www.archive.org).
Eng. tr. in *Hermann Beckh and the Spirit-Word*, Leominster: Anastasi 2015. 33-65; also in *The Source of Speech*, 16-71.

—*Der physische und der geistige Ursprung der Sprache*

The physical and the spiritual origin of language. Stuttgart 1921.

—'*Es werde Licht!*'

'Let there be light!'

The primal biblical words of creation and the primal significance of the sounds in the light of spiritual science. Stuttgart 1921.

—*Etymologie und Lautbedeutung*

Etymology and the significance of speech-sounds in the light of spiritual science. Stuttgart 1922/2013.

All three essays on language (above) reprinted in

Neue Wege zur Ursprache, Stuttgart 1954.

Eng. tr. *The Source of Speech*, with all relevant essays and articles. Temple Lodge, 2019.

Anthroposophie und Universitätswissenschaft

'Anthroposophy and University Knowledge'

Breslau 1922. Eng. tr. in *Hermann Beckh and the Spirit-Word*, Leominster: Anastasi 2015. 71-101; also in *The Source of Speech*. 181-207.

Vom geistigen Wesen der Tonarten

The Essence of Tonality: An Attempt to view musical Problems in the Light of Spiritual Science. With diagrams. Breslau 1922. Third edition 1932. Eng. tr. Leominster: Anastasi 2008.

Der Ursprung im Lichte. Bilder der Genesis

Our Origin in the Light: Pictures from Genesis. Stuttgart 1924. Eng. tr. with *From the Mysteries*, Temple Lodge, 2020.

Von Buddha zu Christus

From Buddha to Christ

Stuttgart 1925 (tr. in Norwegian, Oslo 1926); Eng. tr. of short digest Floris Books 1978.

New Eng. tr. of full text, with additions, Temple Lodge, 2019.

Das neue Jerusalem

'The New Jerusalem'

A poetic work, in the collaborative work *Gegenwartsrätsel im Offenbarungslicht* ('Problems of the present in the light of revelation'), Stuttgart 1925. Eng. tr. incl. in *John's Gospel: The Cosmic Rhythm—Stars and Stones*.

Leominster: Anastasi 2015. 459-77; also in *Alchymy*. 100-13.

Der Hingang des Vollendeten

'The Passing of the Accomplished One and His Nirvāṇa (Mahāparinibbāna Sutta of the Pali canon').

Translated and with an introduction. Stuttgart 1925/60. Eng. tr. *Buddha's Passing*, forthcoming.

Zarathustra

Stuttgart 1927

Eng. tr. with additional articles, pub. with *From the Mysteries*, Temple Lodge, 2020.

Aus der Welt der Mysterien

From the Mysteries

Seven articles (reprinted). Basel 1927. Eng. tr. as triple book, Temple Lodge, 2020.

Der kosmische Rhythmus im Markus-Evangelium

Mark's Gospel: The Cosmic Rhythm

Basel 1928/60/97. Eng. tr. Leominster: Anastasi 2015.

Der kosmische Rhythmus, das Sternengeheimnis und Erdengeheimnis im Johannes-Evangelium

John's Gospel: The Cosmic Rhythm—Stars and Stones

Basel 1930. Eng. tr. Leominster: Anastasi 2015.

Das Christus-Erlebnis in Dramatisch-Musikalischen von Richard Wagners 'Parsifal'

The Parsifal=Christ=Experience in Wagner's Music Drama

Stuttgart 1930. Eng. tr. with 'Richard Wagner and Christianity' (1933) and essays by Emil Bock (1928) and Rudolf Frieling (1956), Leominster: Anastasi, 2015.

Vom Geheimnis der Stoffeswelt (Alchymie)
Alchymy: The Mystery of the Material World
Basel 1931/37/42/2007/13. Eng. tr. with appendices, Temple Lodge, 2019.

Der Hymnus an die Erde
The Hymn to the Earth: From the Old Indian Atharvaveda: A memorial to the oldest poem and to the early Aryans. Stuttgart 1934/60. Eng. tr. forthcoming.

Psalm 23 aus der Heilige Schrift
Psalm 23: Newly translated from the original text and set to music, op. 7. Stuttgart 1935.

Die Rosen von Damaskus
The Roses of Damascus. 'Thibaut von Champagne'. The ballad by Conrad Ferdinand Meyer. For solo high voice with piano accompaniment set to music, op. 8. Stuttgart 1937.

Die Sprache der Tonart
The Language of Tonality in the Music from Bach to Bruckner with special reference to Wagner's Music Dramas
Stuttgart 1937/87/99. Eng. tr. Leominster: Anastasi, 2015.

Richard Wagner und das Christentum
Richard Wagner and Christianity
Stuttgart 1933. Eng. tr. incl. in *The Parsifal=Christ=Experience in Wagner's Music Drama*. Leominster: Anastasi, 2015.

Indische Weisheit und Christendom
Indian Wisdom and Christianity
Articles: 10 reprinted and 9 from the literary estate.
Stuttgart 1938. Eng. tr. forthcoming.

Der Mensch und die Musik
The Human Being and Music
A recently discovered history of music in Ms:
Five chapters pub. in three articles in *Der Europäer*, Basel 09.2005/09.2006/02.2007-08.

http://www.perseus.ch/archive/category/europaer/europaer-archiv

Full restored text translated into English, Temple Lodge, 2019.

Collected Articles and Essays translated into English, two volumes, forthcoming.

Biography:

Hermann Beckh: Leben und Werk

Hermann Beckh: Life and Work

by Gundhild Kačer-Bock (d. 2008)

Stuttgart 1997. Eng. tr. Leominster: Anastasi, 2016.

Hermann Beckh and the Spirit-Word:

Orientalist, Christian Priest and Independent Scholar

- A. Stott, 'Hermann Beckh and the Twenty-First Century'
- H. B., 'Rudolf Steiner and the East'
- H. B., 'Anthroposophy and University Knowledge'
- H. B., 'Meeting Rudolf Steiner'
- Numerous appreciations by Beckh's colleagues and his biographer;

introducing the *Collected Works of Hermann Beckh.*

Festschrift in Honour of Hermann Beckh

on the Centenary of *Buddha und seine Lehre*

and the publication of the English translation

Buddha's Life and Teaching

also

the first publication of Beckh's

The Mystery of Human Creativity: The Human Being and Music

and

the English translation of

Gundhild Kačer-Bock's biography

Hermann Beckh: Life and Work.

includes:

- Prof. Hermann Beckh: 'Steiner und Buddha' (1931; previously unpublished)
- Prof. Hermann Beckh: 'Buddhism and its significance for humanity'
- 'Buddhism and its Significance for Humanity' (1928)

- Prof. Hermann Beckh, 'The Little Squirrel, the Moonlight Princess and the Little Rose', illustrated by Tatjana Schellhase
- 'Prof. Hermann Beckh' by Johannes Lenz (Berlin)
- 'Daniel Simeon and Asita the Sage' by Manfred Krüger (Nuremberg)
- Oliver Heinl: 'Prof. Dr. Hermann Beckh—Pioneer linguistic work in the light of Christ'
- Susana Ulrich-Alvarez Ulloa (Öschelbronn): 'The Search for the Lost Word'
- Katrin Binder (Nottingham): '*Buddha's Life and Work* one hundred years on'
- Alan Stott (Stourbridge): 'Hermann Beckh: Musician' (a lecture, Dornach, April 2016)
- Rosemaria Bock (Stuttgart): 'Recollections' (with photos)
- Gundhild Kačer-Bock (1924–2008) Memories & Appreciations.

A note from the publisher

For more than a quarter of a century, **Temple Lodge Publishing** has made available new thought, ideas and research in the field of spiritual science.

Anthroposophy, as founded by Rudolf Steiner (1861-1925), is commonly known today through its practical applications, principally in education (Steiner-Waldorf schools) and agriculture (biodynamic food and wine). But behind this outer activity stands the core discipline of spiritual science, which continues to be developed and updated. True science can never be static and anthroposophy is living knowledge.

Our list features some of the best contemporary spiritual-scientific work available today, as well as introductory titles. So, visit us online at **www.templelodge.com** and join our emailing list for news on new titles.

If you feel like supporting our work, you can do so by buying our books or making a direct donation (we are a non-profit/charitable organisation).

office@templelodge.com

TEMPLE LODGE

For the finest books of Science and Spirit